I0210164

ELEANOR SMITH'S *HULL HOUSE SONGS*

Studies in Critical Social Sciences Book Series

Haymarket Books is proud to be working with Brill Academic Publishers (www.brill.nl) to republish the *Studies in Critical Social Sciences* book series in paperback editions. This peer-reviewed book series offers insights into our current reality by exploring the content and consequences of power relationships under capitalism, and by considering the spaces of opposition and resistance to these changes that have been defining our new age. Our full catalog of *SCSS* volumes can be viewed at https://www.haymarketbooks .org/series_collections/4-studies-in-critical-social-sciences.

Series Editor
David Fasenfest (SOAS University of London)

Editorial Board
Eduardo Bonilla-Silva (Duke University)
Chris Chase-Dunn (University of California–Riverside)
William Carroll (University of Victoria)
Raewyn Connell (University of Sydney)
Kimberlé W. Crenshaw (University of California–LA and Columbia University)
Heidi Gottfried (Wayne State University)
Karin Gottschall (University of Bremen)
Alfredo Saad Filho (King's College London)
Chizuko Ueno (University of Tokyo)
Sylvia Walby (Lancaster University)
Raju Das (York University)

ELEANOR SMITH'S
HULL HOUSE SONGS

The Music of Protest and Hope
in Jane Addams's Chicago

GRAHAM CASSANO
RIMA LUNIN SCHULTZ
JESSICA PAYETTE

Haymarket Books
Chicago, IL

First published in 2018 by Brill Academic Publishers, The Netherlands.
© 2018 Koninklijke Brill NV, Leiden, The Netherlands

Published in paperback in 2020 by
Haymarket Books
P.O. Box 180165
Chicago, IL 60618
773-583-7884
www.haymarketbooks.org

ISBN: 978-1-64259-073-9

Distributed to the trade in the US through Consortium Book Sales and
Distribution (www.cbsd.com) and internationally through Ingram Publisher
Services International (www.ingramcontent.com).

This book was published with the generous support of Lannan Foundation and
Wallace Action Fund.

Special discounts are available for bulk purchases by organizations and
institutions. Please call 773-583-7884 or email info@haymarketbooks.org for
more information.

Cover design by Jamie Kerry and Ragina Johnson.

Printed in United States.

10 9 8 7 6 5 4 3 2 1

Library of Congress Cataloging-in-Publication Data is available.

Contents

Acknowledgements

This project began in the summer of 2014, when one member of our team found the manuscript *Hull House Songs* in the special collection archives of the University of Illinois, Chicago. Since then, numerous scholars, musicians, administrators, friends, and family, have made possible the transformation of an idea into a book. Both time's passage and imperfect memories make it impossible to name all those who have contributed along the way. But we owe a special debt to Lisa Junkin Lopez, Executive Director of the Juliette Gordon Low Birthplace in Savannah, Georgia, and previous Director of the Jane Addams Hull-House Museum, at the University of Illinois at Chicago. While at the Jane Addams Museum, Lisa Junkin Lopez inspired and mediated the intellectual connections that eventually evolved into this project. Jackie Wiggins, the former Director of the Oakland University School of Music, Theatre and Dance, was also instrumental in making this book possible. She introduced two of the authors, and was a constant source of support, both material and spiritual.

We owe an important debt to the Special Collections archive at the University of Illinois, Chicago, for giving us permission to publish *Hull House Songs* and the related materials. Associate Professor Valerie Harris, the Special Collections Librarian at the University of Illinois, Chicago, has been an invaluable resource, guiding us with her knowledge of the collection, and making the process of securing permissions easy and efficient. Cathy Moran Hajo, Assistant Professor of History and Director, Jane Addams Papers Project, College of Ramapo, New Jersey, provided access to materials associated with the Jane Addams Papers.

Jocelyn Zelasko (soprano) and Amanda Sabelhaus (piano) brought these songs to life through their live performances and through their recordings (found at the *Hull House Songs* website, hullhousesongs.org). Terry Herald engineered, mixed, and mastered Zelasko's and Sabelhaus's *Hull House Songs*. Ros Hartigan designed and built the *Hull House Songs* website.

We are also indebted to Jennifer A. Scott, Director, the Jane Addams Hull-House Museum, University of Illinois, Chicago, to Kevin Corcoran, Dean of the College of Arts and Sciences, Oakland University, to Anne Hitt, Interim Associate Provost, Oakland University, and to Dorothy Nelson, former Chair of the Department of Sociology, Anthropology, Social Work, and Criminal Justice, at Oakland University, for supporting this project and helping fund public performances of *Hull House Songs*. Professor Jo Reger, of Oakland University, encouraged us to publish the manuscript in its present form. In addition, input from a number of scholars helped us refine our ideas and arguments. These include

Ann Durkin Keating, Professor of History, North Central College, Naperville, Illinois, Ellen Skerrett, Historian and Chicago Researcher, Jane Addams Papers Project, Victoria Bissell Brown, Emerita Professor of History, Grinnell College, Grinnell, Iowa, Dr. Barbara Dobschuetz, Independent Scholar, Contributing Editor, *Urban Experience in Chicago: Hull-House and Its Neighborhoods, 1889–1963*, Suellen Hoy, Guest Professor and Independent Scholar, University of Notre Dame, South Bend, Indiana, and Fran Shor, History Professor Emeritus, Wayne State University. Bia Cassano assisted with editorial work, helped find citations, and participated in the fastidious process of manuscript correction. This project would never have been completed were it not for the support of our editor, David Fasenfest, Associate Professor of Sociology, Wayne State University.

Finally, we would like to thank our partners, Ros Hartigan, Richard M. Schultz, and Michael Gurevich, for bearing with us during the necessarily obsessive process of creating a new kind of intellectual engagement with the past, the present, and the future. Because of their support, we have had the time and energy to build new disciplinary and intellectual bridges. This book is the result.

Illustrations

ILLUSTRATION I.1   Portrait of Eleanor Smith, circa 1910
SOURCE: JANE ADDAMS MEMORIAL COLLECTION (JAMC), SPECIAL
COLLECTIONS, DALEY LIBRARY, UNIVERSITY OF ILLINOIS AT CHICAGO.

Introductory Note

Jessica Payette, Graham Cassano and Rima Lunin Schultz

Eleanor Smith's Hull House Songs: *The Music of Protest and Hope in Jane Addams's Chicago* is unique both in structure and content. As authors, our goal is two-fold. We hope to bring attention to little known, but important, work by a talented early-twentieth century American composer; and we attempt to provide the context necessary for understanding that work. In order to do so, we have developed three separate, but inter-related, lines of inquiry: sociological, musicological, and historical. Eleanor Smith's songs emerged from her experience at the intersection of economic disenfranchisement and gender oppression; and any useful understanding of Eleanor Smith's work must emerge from the intersection of complimentary disciplines. Too often, disciplinary specialization can limit our understanding of an object, and expertise becomes what Kenneth Burke, following Thorstein Veblen, called a "trained incapacity" (Burke, 1984: 7). Our very ability to gain insight through theoretically structured methodical observations blinds us to other ways of seeing. In this book, we are attempting to break through disciplinary barriers, to supplement each other's specializations, to illuminate blind spots, and so get closer to the object at hand: the work, and its meanings. We want to understand *Hull House Songs* musically *and* politically; we hope to situate that work within musical traditions *and* within socio-historical contexts; and we want to understand Smith as she understood herself, a collaborator in a project that was larger than the individuality of any single woman at Hull-House. Thus, as Smith did in her compositions, we use each other's disciplinary lens as counter-point, to emphasize and underscore a fundamental melody and to enrich our shared perspective. Specialists in musicology and social history may benefit from this work, but, for the most part, we composed our arguments using language oriented toward non-specialists. Through this book we hope to introduce Eleanor Smith's *Hull House Songs* to academics and specialists, but also to working musicians, to childhood educators, and to any reader interested in the history of feminism and other social justice movements in the United States.

Chapter 1, "*Hull House Songs* and the 'Public,'" offers a discussion of Smith's songbook itself, and a study of its context and sources. In this "Introductory Note," however, we provide a short historical prelude to Smith's work at Hull-House, followed by a narrative concerning the origin of our collective endeavor, and an explanation of the text's overall structure. The three authors approach Smith's work, and the work of the women at Hull-House, from different positions, but, like Jane Addams, Florence Kelley, and Eleanor Smith, we share an interest in social justice and cultural transformation. Thus, while we identify the external, and too often internalized, forces of domination (class position, racial identity, patriarchal disenfranchisement) that limited the work of the Hull-House women, we also attempt to recover the sometimes hidden emancipatory possibilities of their legacy. And we hope that by interweaving three disciplinary imaginations, we come closer to producing a dialectical understanding of Eleanor Smith and, perhaps, of Hull-House itself.

The Hull-House Music School was the first settlement music school established in the United States and Eleanor Smith (1858–1942) served as its director from its inception in 1893 until 1936. While not widely known today, Eleanor Smith's *Hull House Songs*, a collection of five songs, was released in 1915 as a folio to celebrate the twenty-fifth anniversary of the Hull-House settlement. As this book will demonstrate, the score is the first American song cycle that captures the perspectives of the working class and serves as a compact keepsake for posterity that commemorates the settlement's early initiatives. These projects are enumerated in Jane Addams's preface to the score: "the protection of sweat-shop workers, the abolition of child labor, the relief of the anthracite coal miners during a great strike, and the movement for granting votes to women."

A short notice in *The Survey* ("Songs for the Hull-House Quarter Century," 6 March 1915: 597) elaborates on the events surrounding the publication of the score and the work's premiere at Hull-House on 14 February 1915. The article's introductory paragraph reveals that Addams and the Hull-House community was too emotionally consumed with impending global and personal tragedies to organize and host a joyous celebration.

> On September 18, 1914, twenty-five years had elapsed since Jane Addams and Ellen Gates Starr had moved into the "fine old house" at the corner of Polk and Halsted, which has now become the widely known and well-beloved Hull-House. In the autumn, there was, however, in the minds of Miss Addams, the trustees, and residents of Hull-House little desire for anything in the nature of a celebration. Bowed by the sense of the war tragedy and under the shadow of the illness of her close friend, Mrs. Louise de Koven [Bowen], no thought of a jubilation could be entertained.
>
> In memory, however, of the years' labor and effort, it was decided to record the ending of this quarter-centennial by publishing five *Hull House Songs* composed by one of the earliest residents.

As this volume documents, the settlement's recurrent practice of heightening public awareness of critical political and social issues and helping its constituency to combat socio-economic and educational adversity took place through the creation and presentation of original artworks, which generally fuse American subject matter with European aesthetic archetypes. This practice was fundamental to Hull-House's impact and legacy.

Smith's identity as a musician was first solidified as a composer, and she composed music to support her mission of providing serious music instruction to immigrant children at Hull-House. In 1883, when Smith was twenty-five, her precociousness and promise as a composer was already noted by the *Chicago Tribune* on the occasion of the premiere of her cantata entitled *The Golden Asp*, which occurred prior to her embarkation to Germany to obtain advanced musical training. Smith's aptitude as a composer made the Hull-House Music School different from other music schools that sprouted up in settlements on the East Coast. The directors of these schools—such as Melzar Chaffee, head of The Third Street Music Settlement in New York, and Johan Grolle, director of the Settlement Music School of Philadelphia (Cords, 1970: 108)—were not acting in the capacity of composer-in-residence as Smith was. In addition to *Hull House Songs*, Smith composed an extensive graded music curriculum for the School, which displays her keen understanding of children's voices, and three full-length dramatic works (two operettas and one cantata).

Hull House Songs was not Smith's first published score in the art song genre. In 1885, W.H. Willis and Company published a collection of five of Smith's songs, denoted as opus 7 on the frontispiece. These songs, with titles like "The Quest" and "She Kisses with Her Eyes," are set to conventional romantic poetry. This is further indication that, after working at Hull-House for nearly a decade, Smith felt compelled to use music as a vehicle through which to respond to what Hull-House deemed as current societal crises, especially labor exploitation and other struggles that weighed heavy on the minds of residents of the neighborhood and the country. As will be discussed later in the volume, "The Sweatshop," composed and performed in 1901, is the first surviving example of a Smith composition that uses musical performance as a platform for social activism.

The Survey article concludes with a discussion of the dissemination and premiere of *Hull-House Songs*, providing evidence that Hull-House Music School students, as opposed to professional musicians, premiered the work.

> Copies of the songs have been widely distributed, but it seemed also fitting for old residents and friends to hear them together. Consequently, on Sunday evening, February 14, there gathered at Hull-House many who had lived and worked there during these wonder years of service and revelation to hear students from the Music School sing the compositions of their brilliant teacher.

Examining the involvement and collaboration of student musicians and actors, skilled amateur practitioners, and professional female artists at Hull-House is an important achievement of this book. Jane Addams and the women that she entrusted with the arts programs at Hull-House were among the first in the United States to adamantly declare that arts pedagogy and performance could raise the self-esteem of disadvantaged immigrant children, ultimately making them feel invested in the future of their new country, as well as furnish adults who worked long hours in factories with therapeutic benefits and an outlet for self-expression.

In August 2015, this book project was informally launched by Jocelyn Zelasko's and Amanda Sabelhaus's centenary performance of *Hull House Songs* at the Jane Addams Hull-House Museum in Chicago. On that occasion soprano Jocelyn Zelasko spoke to the audience about how she approached the performance of an early twentieth-century song cycle by a female composer whose music has disappeared from the vocal repertoire. At the end of this volume, Zelasko expands upon her comments to address her portrayal of the cast of characters that Smith includes in *Hull House Songs* and to highlight the interpretive nuances that she brings out in her vocal performance of each of the five songs, which can be heard on the companion website (hullhousesongs. org). Prior to Ms. Zelasko's performance, sociologist Graham Cassano and musicologist Jessica Payette presented a condensed version of Chapter 1, entitled "*Hull House Songs* and the 'Public.'" This chapter explores the background and significance of the poets whose words Smith chose to set to music, details how Smith uses music to impart the emotional outlook of the people affected by the contemporaneous events that Addams mentions in her preface, and provides analysis of the musical structure, influences, and stylistic features of each song.

The post-concert discussion at Hull-House raised many questions that we hadn't yet considered. What other types of pieces did Eleanor Smith compose? How did the Hull-House Music School engage with the other equally prosperous Hull-House arts programs, including the art school and drama clubs? How did arts pedagogy end up playing a pivotal role in the entire enterprise of Progressive Era educational reform? Why was Jane Addams so critical of popular culture? The myriad of questions that arose after introducing a twenty-first century audience to Smith's long-forgotten song cycle stretched outward to encompass broader societal issues, like feminism and racial segregation. The book truly necessitated a multidisciplinary collaboration of scholars to begin to answer those questions. At this point it was clear that the book would not reach completion without inviting a historian of Hull-House and Chicago to join the team. Rima Lunin Schultz joined the *Hull House Songs* project, generously shared her expertise with the other authors, and contributed extensively to this volume. Our collective work uncovers the goals of cultural production at Hull-House through the compilation and study of a large collection of primary source texts, ranging from essays by Jane Addams to manuscript scores by Eleanor Smith.

The artistic activities at Hull-House would not have thrived to the extent that they did without Jane Addams's vision for making the arts a priority. In "*Hull House Songs* and Jane Addams's Political Aesthetic," Graham Cassano turns to Addams's *The Spirit of Youth and the City Streets* (1972 [1909]) and *The Long Road of Woman's Memory* (1916) to unpack her aesthetic values, lending insight into the types of ideas that she may have conveyed to Eleanor Smith and the other women who led arts programs at Hull-House. In these texts Addams expresses concerns about the susceptibility of the working classes to the rise of popular culture, especially cinema and "street music," which rely on erotic images and new social dances to trigger sensual, as opposed to intellectual, responses. Cassano demonstrates that Addams's critique of the culture industry's valorization of capitalism anticipates that of Adorno and Horkheimer. At the same time, Cassano finds in Addams's attack on mass culture symptoms of her ambivalent relationship to working class agency. While she looked to the working class as agents of social changes, she distrusted and feared the working class culture that was emerging because of its basis in shared forms of popular commercial entertainments. For Addams, popular culture was disabling and a threat to social solidarity. Cassano then examines *The Long Road of Woman's Memory*, a text that presents a different aesthetic perspective through its discussion of collective memory, and he illustrates Addams's perpetual vacillation between the valorization of traditional forms of working class culture and the distrust of working class youth. While Addams was able to envisage agency among young women strikers, she remained blind to the ways in which those workers were empowered by mass culture and new forms of entertainment, and so remained largely insensitive to the aesthetic revolution happening around her. Cassano ends his discussion with a coda that finds a parallel blindness in Addams's relationship to Black cultural production. Addams was in Chicago for the birth of jazz, but she was probably unable to understand the meaning of that moment. At the height of the jazz age, when she reaches for an example of the pinnacle of jazz artistry, Addams cites *Porgy and Bess*. This repression of African American cultural production beneath George Gershwin's white mask reveals the color-line that regulated Addams's artistic imagination, and, Cassano argues, her sociological vision.

After discussing the theoretical sources for Smith's work, we turn to a close examination of some of her lesser known projects. Surprisingly, Eleanor Smith's large-scale dramatic works, a sizable portion of her output, have not been published. Smith's operettas—*The Trolls' Holiday* (1905), *A Fable in*

Flowers (1918)—and the cantata entitled *The Merman's Bride* (1925–28) were composed for her Hull-House pupils and reviewed in the *Chicago Tribune* and specialized journals. Unfortunately, Smith's scores for the dramatic works have not been preserved in their entirety. Several musical numbers from each work—piano reductions handwritten on loose-leaf music paper—are contained in folders in the Hull House Collection and the Eleanor Smith Papers at the University of Illinois–Chicago. Although many numbers appear to be clean manuscripts, it is difficult to determine with certainty whether these are sketches or the final versions, especially since no parts for individual instruments are extant and it is clear from the press reviews that the instrumentation for each work extended beyond solo piano. In "Eleanor Smith's Operetta's for Children," Jessica Payette assesses Smith's manuscript scores, the original libretti (scripts), and the reception history, to propose that the works were created to socialize the community's children through the staging of allegories of real-world scenarios that depicted neighborhood social dynamics and feminist pragmatism.

From this close reading of Smith's work, we turn to the social and historical context of that work. Rima Lunin Schultz's four chapters on Hull-House's cultural programs and politics represent a veritable book-within-a-book. While they serve to contextualize Smith's work, they also take up broader issues and debates in the history of Hull-House and Chicago progressive politics. Few historians have made the connection between Hull-House's innovative cultural pedagogy and its reform politics and, instead, have focused on the latter, overlooking the settlement's residents who were cultural leaders. Lunin Schultz suggests that we rethink progressive reform as a project of cultural production. This starts with Addams's own assertion that she was unable to reach working people and engage them as political actors and, instead, turned to drama and the arts as a variant on instigating neighbors' agency in self-government. Thus, Lunin Schultz explores the circle of cultural workers who surrounded Addams and Eleanor Smith. Then she establishes how Addams conceived of culture as a way to redefine social roles and yet guide the formation of a working class equipped to participate, without resort to class conflict, in the life of the democracy. Finally, Lunin Schultz raises the issue of race in Addams's cultural project, identifying a relatively unexplored area of scholarship. What accounts for the failure of Hull-House to incorporate Black people and their cultural work? These chapters identify the roots of the failure to deal with race in the conception of culture at the core of Addams's progressivism.

In comparison to some of her peers, Eleanor Smith was much more highly accomplished as a musician and pedagogue, but an extensive network of professional creative women populated Hull-House and the city. Some were married and esteemed members of salons or women's clubs, and some, like Smith and many of her colleagues, were not. In "Eleanor Smith and Her Circle," Lunin Schultz investigates Eleanor Smith's circle of women associates to evaluate how her professional relationships and intimate friendships impacted her creative philosophy and teaching. In addition to documenting the close-knit nature of the women's personal ties to each other, the chapter reveals how this circle designed pedagogical approaches based on the theories of influential European educational reformers, like Friedrich Froebel and Johann Pestalozzi, and captured the attention of John Dewey and the University of Chicago Laboratory School.

Chapter 5, "Cultural Pedagogy at Hull-House," and Chapter 6, "Democratizing Culture and Mediating Class," explore issues surrounding the cultural upbringing and worldview of Jane Addams and the upper-middle class women who oversaw the arts programs at Hull-House. Although Addams is now credited as the founder of social work, she and her colleagues were raised in well-to-do families and received a comprehensive religious and humanistic education, supplemented by frequent travels to Europe. This informed their belief that the formation of strong civic and individual identity was influenced by participation in cultural production, whether that be acting in a play or making pottery. Lunin Schultz argues that Hull-House's most pressing objective for participant recruitment parallels that of arts outreach today: to convince the neighborhood's constituents that art can inspire life-changing experiences. She writes that "music, drama, and art pedagogy at Hull-House sought formats that embraced the classical Western tradition—highbrow—but incorporated the narrativity of the neighborhood." This was manifested in several impressive pursuits involving both the performing and utilitarian arts. In addition to the ongoing performances presented by the music and drama schools, the Labor Museum and the Industrial Shops offered working people the space and equipment to further develop their craftsmanship and teach their skills to others.

Finally, our examination of Hull-House's arts programs often revealed the names and nationalities of the immigrant participants, and uncovered events geared toward specific immigrant groups, such as the performances of Greek tragedies by Greek immigrants. Hull-House never reached out to African-Americans to the extent that it did to national groups. In "Hull-House and 'Jim Crow,'" Lunin Schultz reflects on racial segregation in early twentieth-century Chicago and the nineteenth ward's attitudes toward race. A century later, the United States as a nation continues to ignore high-poverty urban neighborhoods and make sharp distinctions between citizens and immigrants. Thus we felt it imperative to reignite conversation on the historical roots of this issue and we express gratitude to the many artists who are currently creating work that interrogates the etiology and ramifications of economic and social injustice.

Hull House Songs

by

Eleanor Smith

∵

Reproduction of 1915 Folio published by Clayton F. Summy Co.
Source: Hull House Collection, Special Collections, Daley Library,
University of Illinois at Chicago.

Hull House Songs

by *Eleanor Smith*

The Sweat Shop
The Shadow Child
The Land of the Noonday Night
Suffrage Song † †
Prayer † † † †

Chicago
Clayton F. Summy Co.   64 E. Van Buren Street
Weekes & Co.   London.

On its twenty-fifth anniversary, Hull-House publishes this group of songs composed by Miss Eleanor Smith, for many years the director of its Music School, considering it a legitimate function of the settlement to phrase in music the wide spread social compunctions of our day.

Four of the songs were written at various times in response to public efforts in which the residents of Hull-House were much absorbed—the protection of sweat-shop workers, the abolition of child labor, the relief of the anthracite coal miners during a great strike, and the movement for granting votes to women. We believe that all of the songs in this collection fulfil the highest mission of music, first in giving expression to the type of emotional experience which quickly tends to get beyond words, and second in affording an escape from the unnecessary disorder of actual life into the wider region of the spirit which, under the laws of a great art, may be filled with an austere beauty and peace.

The last song, a prayer to be saved from the eternal question as to whether in any real sense the world is governed in the interest of righteousness, voices the doubt which so inevitably dogs the footsteps of all those who venture into the jungle of social wretchedness. Because old-fashioned songs, with the exception of those of religion and patriotism, chiefly expressed the essentially individualistic emotions of love, hope or melancholy, it is perhaps all the more imperative that socialized emotions should also find musical expression, if the manifold movements of our contemporaries are to have the inspiration and solace they so obviously need.

Jane Addams.

THE SWEAT-SHOP

MORRIS ROSENFELD.
Translated by
James Weber Linn.

ELEANOR SMITH

Con moto.

The roar-ing of the wheels has filled my ears, The clash-ing and the clam-or shut me in, My self, my soul in cha-os dis-ap-pears; I can-not think or feel a-mid the

Copyright 1914 by Clayton F. Summy Co.
International Copyright Secured.

C.F.S. Co. 1584-5

din. Toil - ing and toil - ing and toil - ing,—end-less toil, For
whom? for what? Why should the work be done? I do not ask or know, I on - ly
toil, I work un - til the day and night are one;
work un - til the day and night are one.
The clock a-bove me ticks a-way the

day, Its hands are spin-ning, spinning like the wheels; It

can-not sleep nor for a mo-ment stay, It is a thing like me and does not

feel. It throbs as though my heart were beat-ing there. A

heart? my heart? I know not what it means. The clock ticks and below I strive and

stare, And so we lose the hours. We are machines!

Noon calls a truce and end-ing to the sound,

As if a bat-tle had one mo-ment stayed. A blood-y field,— the

dead lie all a-round, Their wounds cry out un-til I grow a-fraid.

comes, the sig-nal,—see the dead men rise,

They fight a-gain, a-mid the roar they

fight,

Blind-ly, and know-ing not for whom or why They

fight, they fight, they fall, They sink in-to the night, They fall, they sink in-to the

night.

THE SHADOW CHILD

HARRIET MONROE

ELEANOR SMITH

Why do the wheels go whir-ring round, Moth - er,

Moth - er? Oh! Moth-er are they gi - ants bound, And will they growl for-

ev - er? Yes fi - ery gi - ants un - der-ground,

Poem used by kind permission of the author, The Century Company and The Mac Millan Company.

Copyright 1915 by Clayton F. Summy Co.
International Copyright.

C. F. S. Co. 1585 - 4

p
f
poco rit.
Daugh-ter, lit-tle daugh - ter, For ev - er turn the
a tempo
poco rit.
wheels a-round, And rum-ble, grum-ble ev - er.
a tempo
Why do I pick the threads all day, Moth - er,
Moth - er, While sun-shine chil - dren laugh and play, And

must I work for - ev - er? Yes, shadow child, The live-long day

Daugh - ter, lit - tle daugh - ter Your hands must pick the

threads a - way And feel the sun - shine nev - er.

And is the white thread nev-er spun, Moth - er, Moth - er?

C. F. S. Co. 1585 - 4

And is the white cloth nev - er done, For you and me done nev - er? Oh! yes our thread will all be spun Daughter lit - tle daugh - ter When we lie down out in the sun, And work no more for - ev - er, And work no more for - ev - er.

THE LAND OF THE NOONDAY NIGHT

ERNEST HOWARD CROSBY.

ELEANOR SMITH.

Somewhat Slowly.

1. We have
2. But our

eyes to see like you, In the heart of the deep, deep mine, But there's
home is not like yours; 'Tis a bare, un - paint - ed shack, Where the

Copyright, 1902, by Charles H. Kerr & Co.
Copyright assigned 1915 to Clayton F. Summy Co.

C.F.S.Co. 1586. 2.

nothing to mark but the dreadful dark, Where the sun can   nev-er shine. On the
rain - drops pour on the shak-y floor, And the coal-dust stains it black. Not a

banks of clam- my coal   Our   lamps cast a flick-'ring light,   At the
flow'r or blade of   grass   Can   es-cape the   grim-y blight,   For the

bot-tom drear of the moist black hole   In the land   of the noon-day night.
face of   our yard is seared and scarred In the land   of the noon-day night.

3. And we labor with straining arms
   For the pittance they deign to give,
   And our boys must quit the school for the pit
   To drudge that we all may live.
   And our teeth feel the grit of the mine
   In the very bread we bite,
   And our inmost soul is defiled with coal
   In the land of the noonday night.

4. Who was it that made the coal?
   Our God as well as theirs!
   If he gave it free to you and me,
   Then keep us out who dares!
   Let the people have their mines
   Their own by immortal right,
   And the good prevail under hill and dale
   In the land of the noonday night.

C. F. S. Co. 1586. 2.

PRAYER

Words from *Stagirius*.
By MATTHEW ARNOLD.

ELEANOR SMITH.

Thou, who dost dwell a - lone— Thou who dost know thine own— Thou to whom all are known From the cra - dle to the grave— Save, oh! save. From the world's temp - ta - tions, From tri - bu - la - tions, From that fierce an - guish Where-in we

Copyright 1914 by Clayton F. Summy Co.

International Copyright.

C.F.S Co. 1577-4.

lan-guish,   From that tor-por   deep   Where-in we lie a - sleep,

Hea - vy as death, Cold as the grave, Save,   oh! save.   Save,   oh!

save.   Where sor-row treads on joy,   Where sweet things

soon-est cloy,   Where faiths are built on dust, Where love is half mis-trust,

C. F. S. Co. 1577 - 4.

C. F. S. Co. 1077-4.

Hun - gry and bar - ren and sharp as the sea, Oh! set us free,

O let the false dream fly,_____ Where our sick souls do lie_____

Toss - ing con - tin - ual - ly.

O where thy voice doth come Let all doubts be dumb, Let

p   poco cresc.

all words be mild, All strife re-con-ciled, All pains be-guiled!

poco a poco cresc.   *ff*

Light bring no blind-ness, Love no un-kind-ness, Knowledge no ru - in, Fear no un-do-

p poco a poco cresc.   cresc.   *ff*

-ing: *ritard.*   From the cra - dle to the grave,

f   *f poco rit. ff*

Save, oh! save.   Save, oh! save.

cresc.   *f poco rit. ff*

C. F. S. Co. 1577-4

To Jane Addams and Louise de Koven Bowen.

SUFFRAGE SONG

(Let Us Sing As We Go)

JAMES WEBER LINN.

ELEANOR SMITH.

Copyright 1914 by Clayton F. Summy Co

International Copyright.

C. F. S. Co. 1576-3.

right shall pre-vail o-ver wrong! See! the ban-ner is bright streaming
For the fears of the past lie be-

o'er us, And the barred road lies o-pen be-fore us; Let the
hind us, And its fet-ters no long-er can bind us; Let us

trump-et be blown, Let our pur-pose be known, Put your voice and your soul in the
march with a will Till the trump-et be still In the peace that our strug-gle shall

cho-rus!
find us.

Let us sing as we go, Votes for

Wo - men! Let us sing as we go, Votes for Wo - men! Though the

way may be hard, Tho' the bat - tle be long, Yet our tri - umph is sure; Put your

heart in - to song, In - to cheer - ing and song: Votes for wo - men! For the

right shall pre-vail o - ver wrong!

Hull House Songs and the "Public"

Graham Cassano and Jessica Payette

1   "A Moral Revolution"

Eleanor Smith was director of the Hull-House Music School during Jane Addams's tenure as Head Resident (Addams, 1915: 2). Hull-House music programs were central to the settlement's mission and contributed to the development of talented young working class musicians across Chicago. It was at Hull-House that a young Art Hodes had his first experience jamming with a young Benny Goodman (Vaillant, 2003: 123–124). Smith's importance as a music educator has been widely recognized, and for much of the twentieth century, *The Eleanor Smith Music Course* influenced music curricula for young people all over the United States (Ibid: 107–110). But another aspect of Smith's work remains relatively unknown. In the years between 1900 and 1915, she composed a series of social protest songs Hull-House residents used for political organizing and culture building. They were usually performed in Hull-House concerts attended by neighborhood residents, Hull-House residents, and, sometimes, prominent members of Chicago society. And the performers were often students from the Hull-House Music School, immigrant workers and the children of immigrant workers (Addams, 1910: 378–381; Vaillant 2003: 108). These songs include "The Sweat Shop," about inhumane working conditions, "The Shadow Child," about child labor, "Suffrage Song," about the struggle for voting rights, and "The Land of the Noonday Night," written in solidarity with striking miners in Pennsylvania. In 1915, as a tribute to Hull-House's 25th Anniversary, Smith's political songs were collected in a single folio, with an introduction by Jane Addams. And, as the title indicates, this book was as much a product of collaboration as the earlier *Hull-House Maps and Papers*. Like *Maps and Papers*, *Hull House Songs* replies with one collective voice to the social problems that it addresses.

Jane Addams wished *Hull House Songs* to fill a void hidden in the intersection of American musical and political culture. She differentiates Smith's songs from "old fashioned songs," that "with the exception of those of religion and patriotism, chiefly expressed the individualistic emotions of love, hope or melancholy." Against this old fashioned standard, *Hull House Songs* presents the "imperative" demand "that socialized emotions should also find musical expression" (Addams, 1915: 2). Like nations and religions, movements for social justice require art, and more particularly, song, to express, sustain, and inspire solidarity. Thus, the songbook is intended to provide the "inspiration and solace" that the "manifold movements of our contemporaries...so obviously need" (Ibid). Since the socialized emotions that *Hull House Songs* seek to express emerge from early twentieth century movements for liberation (labor rights and suffrage), it would seem to be a kind of companion to the Industrial Workers of the World's (IWW) *Little Red Songbook* (1909) (Vaillant, 2003: 114). But if Smith and Addams did know of the IWW's songbook, their folio was more a response than a companion. The *Little Red Songbook* was meant to "fan the flames of discontent." Remembering the origin of the book, Richard Brazier writes:

> We will have songs of anger and protest, songs which shall call to judgment our oppressors and the Profit System they have devised. Songs of battles won (but never any songs of despair), songs that hold up flaunted wealth and thread-bare morality to scorn, songs that lampoon our masters and the parasitic vermin, such as employment-sharks and their kind, who bedevil the workers. These songs will...be songs sowing the seeds of discontent and rebellion. We want our songs to stir the workers into action, to awaken them from an apathy and complacency that has made them accept their servitude as though it had been divinely ordained.
> BRAZIER, 2007: 380–381

To this demand for rebellion, a demand that depends upon destroying old myths and lampooning the masters, Jane Addams might respond with an argument she made in *Hull-House Maps and Papers*.

> A movement cannot be carried on by negating other acts; it must have a positive force, a driving and self-sustaining motive-power. A moral revolution cannot be accomplished by men who are held together merely because they are all smarting under a sense of injury and injustice, although it may be begun by them.
> Men thus animated may organize for resistance, they may struggle bravely together, and may destroy that which is injurious, but they cannot build up, associate, and unite. They have no common, collective faith. The labor movement in America bears this trace of its youth and immaturity.
> ADDAMS, 1895a: 194

Jane Addams does not necessarily mean to supplant the IWW; after all, they can begin a "moral revolution." Rather, she argues that any critique of capitalism that depends upon demonizing capitalists remains a partial representation, and produces an incomplete community.

In her settings of the poems for *Hull House Songs*, Eleanor Smith somehow expurgates any reference to class conflict and the privileges of the bosses and capitalists. In fact, she drops some of the most powerful verses from both Morris Rosenfeld's poem "The Sweatshop," and Ernest Howard Crosby's "The Land of the Noonday Night." While the reasons for these changes can't be established with certainty, their representation of labor, capital, and capitalism, corresponds to Addams's attempt to get beyond purely "negating" power to produce a "positive force" for uniting individuals across class lines, and against capitalism's exploitation. While the Wobblies were singing anti-capitalist songs, sometimes demonizing the ruling class, the poems collected in *Hull House Songs* are critiques of capitalism as a system, not capitalists as individuals. Both Smith's compositions, and Addams's essays on labor, attack the systemic elements of exploitation, while, at the same time, attempting to create solidarity between classes (against capitalism). In any case, this was the carefully crafted message behind *Hull House Songs:* Class struggle is against capitalism and exploitation, not against bosses and capitalists.

Addams argues that individuals are products of multiple communities, and thus multiple identities. They can be called forth as "men," as "women," as "white," or "Black," or as "worker" or "capitalist." But broader than these partial identities, Addams argues, is the appeal to the democratic "citizen."

> A workingman [sic] in America who may become a carpenter only as a stepping-stone toward becoming a contractor and capitalist, ... does not respond so easily to measures intended to benefit the carpenter's trade as he does to measures intended to benefit society as a whole; *and it is quite as important that the appeal should be made to him in his capacity of citizen as that it should be large enough to include men outside his class.*
>
> ADDAMS, 1899a: 461; emphasis added

Addams argues that a coherent and consistent critique recognizes capitalism's systemic threat to the community and to democracy, while resisting the urge to lampoon and demonize the privileged classes as bad actors. For Addams, every citizen is equally trapped in an unjust system, and radical social democracy provides the means to restore justice.[1] In this sense, *Hull House Songs* was meant to be a participant in forging a broader set of sympathies

---

1 Sklar, Schuler and Strasser (1998) aptly describe Addams as a "social justice feminist." "In a time threatened by class warfare and marked by violent conflicts between capital and labor, the need for social justice was often explicitly linked to the need for 'industrial peace'" (6).

and identifications across class lines. It imagined a public discourse beyond the clash of class interests. By attempting to forge cross-class solidarities, on the basis of a universal notion of citizenship, the songbook attempted to enact the very public it imagined.

At the same time, while the songbook attempts to build a universal community of citizens, in aesthetic terms both Smith and Addams privileged formal, bourgeois cultural standards and forms of judgment. Folk and popular forms were integrated into *Hull House Songs*, but as subordinate figures in the service of European high culture. Addams and, by implication, Smith, argue for democracy in the workplace and the community, but within the halls of culture, they validate normative standards and formal techniques, over and against the less formalized, and, ultimately, they argue, dangerous, forms found in folk traditions and popular culture.

2   Addams, Sympathy, and the 'Public'

Jane Addams recalls when the cloakmakers were organized at Hull-House in 1892. "The union among the men numbered two hundred; but the skilled workers were being rapidly supplanted by untrained women, who had no conscience in regard to the wages they accepted" (1895a: 189). When Addams and Hull-House hosted the meeting between the male cloakmakers and the women workers, it "was a revelation to all present." On one side stood the male "Russian-Jewish tailors," "ill-dressed and grimy, suspicious that Hull-House was a spy in the service of the capitalists." On the other, the women, "Irish American girls, well-dressed and comparatively at ease" (Addams, 1895a: 189–190).

> They were separated by strong racial differences, by language, by nationality, by religion, by mode of life, by every possible social distinction.... The residents felt that between these men and girls was a deeper gulf than the much-talked of "chasm" between the favored and unfavored classes.
>
> 1895a: 190

Intersecting forms of power and domination shaped the lives of both these tailors and of women workers. Tensions emerging from the demands of masculinity, racial distinctions, and degrees of "Americanization" set the context for their meeting. But in the face of economic necessity, the women and men built bridges across these barriers. Despite their differences,

These two sets of people were held together...by the pressure upon their trade...[by] the economic necessity for combination...[and by] mutual interdependence.... It was a spectacle only to be found in an American city, under the latest conditions of trade-life. Working-people among themselves are being forced into a social democracy from the pressure of the economic situation. It presents an educating and broadening aspect of no small value.

>   Ibid.

Just as Lizabeth Cohen argues that industrial unionism created a new "culture of unity" among otherwise isolated ethnic groups during the New Deal, Addams suggests that this process was beginning in the 1890s at Hull-House (Cohen, 1990). Through trade union organization, old traditional forms of exclusion and domination gave way to new "cultures of solidarity," and workers were "forced into a social democracy" (Fantasia, 1988). This new sense of community transformed the identity of its members. Their association produced a shared identification in which commonality mattered more than difference and unity mattered more than boundaries. International labor solidarity represented "a great moral movement" precisely because it produced new, broader, solidarities, identifications, and communities (Addams, 1902: 175).

Sociologists and historians have long recognized the communal disruptions created by early industrial capitalism (Polanyi, 2001; Thompson, 1966). The transformation of farmers and skilled artisans into wage laborers, rapid urbanization, and the increasing number of women and children drawn into the ranks of wage labor, all disrupted long held traditions and dissolved old communal forms (Stansell, 1987). But this did not simply leave a void. Rather, new working class communities began to emerge. In the United States, with large scale immigration from 1840 to 1924, new immigrant groups were "Americanized" from the bottom up by native born workers, even as these immigrants transformed American communities and very definition of "American-ness" (Barrett, 1992; Roediger, 2005). Addams and Hull-House stood at the very center of this process. But the residents of Hull-House were not passive observers of a spectacle. Rather, they aimed to intervene directly into the construction of these new, broader communities. Above all, as these new communities matured through labor solidarity, it was "the duty of the settlement in keeping the movement from becoming in any sense a class warfare" (Addams, 1895a: 202).

Nonetheless, Addams enumerated at least three reasons why the *interests of labor* (rather than capital) and the interests of the settlement coincided. First, trade unionism is a movement for economic justice: "the labor movement may be called a concerted effort among workers...to obtain a more equitable distribution of the product" (1895a, 187). Second, it is a movement to democratize the industrial workplace: "we contend that the task of the labor movement is the interpretation of democracy into industrial affairs" (196). Third, it creates new forms of broader communal associations, breaking down old barriers and bridging ethnic, gender, and racial divides: "and it is because of a growing sense of brotherhood and of democracy in the labor movement that we see in it a growing ethical power" (202).

In 1899, Addams once again examines the "ethical" power of the union movement, its ability to transform solidarity, and thus the identities of workers themselves. This ethical power, already apparent in the transformative meeting of the cloakmakers' union, emerges in full force with the sympathy strike.

> We see a great sympathetic strike ramifying throughout the entire unions of a trade and its allied trades; we suddenly hear of men all over the country leaving their work, places which they may have held for years, which they know that it may be difficult, and perhaps impossible, again to secure. They certainly do this under some dictate of conscience, and under some ethical concept that stands to them as a duty. Later many of them see their wives and children suffer, and yet they hold out, for the sake of securing better wages for workmen whom they have never seen, for men who are living in another part of the country, and who are often of another race and religion. We see this manifestation, and read about it, and do not make a really intelligent effort to discover its ethical significance.
>
> ADDAMS, 1899a: 458

The "ethical significance" Addams finds in the sympathy strike is precisely the growing sense of solidarity, transcending region, race, religion. Workers engaged in such an action demonstrate that collective attempts to secure social justice transform those involved, giving them a new sense of connection with other agents involved in the struggle, a new sense of collective identity.

But the very promise of new solidarities and identities that the labor movement reveals also demonstrates what Addams sees as the pitfalls of defining the movement in the language of class warfare. "The only danger in the movement, as at present conducted, lies in the fact that it is a partial movement, and antagonizes those whom it does not include" (1899a: 462). Precisely because the movement itself shows the malleability of individual identity through transformed social solidarity, Addams appeals to the interests of the "citizen," regardless of class. In order to become more than a "partial movement," labor needs to recognize that its interests are not class interests, but the public interest. And here the settlement house plays a key role.

"The settlement may be of value if it can take a larger and steadier view than is always possible to the workman, smarting under a sense of wrong; or to the capitalist,...insisting upon the inalienable right of 'invested capital,' to a return of at least four per cent, ignoring human passion" (1895a, 196). But by suggesting that the settlement can take a "steadier view," Addams does not mean to advocate some imagined "objectivity." The settlement is not a neutral arbiter. "The social injury of the meanest man not only becomes [the settlement's] concern, but by virtue of its very locality it has put itself into a position to see, as no one but a neighbor can see, the stress and need of those who bear the brunt of the social injury" (184). While the settlement takes the steadier view, that view emerges from solidarity with the working class.

"It is well, sometimes, to remind ourselves that, after all, the mass of mankind work with their hands" (1899a: 462). Thus, when the labor movement works to advance the interests of the working class, it advances the public interests. Indeed, Addams describes labor as "a great movement toward social amelioration" and compares the "social passion...making for the emancipation of the wage-earner" to the "great social passion" that "insisted upon the emancipation of the slave" (459). Like Marx and Engels (1988: 78), Addams argues that the interests of "working people" represent the most general interests of the society, the public interest. "Probably labor organizations come nearer to expressing moral striving in political action than any other portion of the community, for their political efforts in most instances have been stimulated by a desire to secure some degree of improvement in the material condition of working people" (Addams, 1899a: 459–460).[2] For Addams, labor rights were human rights, and thus the concern of the broadest 'public,' all humanity. Thus, while it is the duty of the settlement to work for the interests of labor, that work involves translating labor's interests into the language of the public citizen (1899a: 451). But she goes further still and identifies the public interests with the interests of labor and the labor movement. This is an identification that is also an appeal. In imagining the American "public," Addams hopes to participate in forging bonds of mutual recognition across class lines.

---

2   In her commentary on Addams's contribution to *Hull House Maps and Papers*, Elshtain (2002) writes: "Jane Addams relationship to Marxism was one of critical engagement.... She gently mocked the utopianism of those Marxist who believed the universe could be cured of all its ills...come the cataclysm of the final revolution. She also opposed the determinism in Marxism and the justification of violence" (60; footnote #2). In a similar vein, Mary Jo Deegan (1988) writes: "Addams remained partial to the socialist vision because of its emphasis on the primacy of economic exploitation and a program for its resolution. Nonetheless, her differences with its methods and underlying principles of addressing economic exploitation caused her to take a separate path" (280).

This mutual recognition requires mutual sympathy. By "sympathy," Addams does not mean "pity." Rather, like her contemporary, Charles Horton Cooley, Addams's use echoes Adam Smith's original deployment of the term (Smith, 1976: 9–26). According to Adam Smith, through sympathy and imagination, we identify with the other, "we enter as it were into his [sic] body, and become in some measure the same person with him" (9). Thus, following Smith, Cooley will define sympathy, "in the sense of primary communication, or an entering into and sharing the mind of someone else" (1902: 102).[3] Recall Addams description of the *sympathy* strike and the way in which it creates new communities and breaks down barriers of race and religion. Workers feel new bonds with one another. They enter into each other's experience and identify with one another. Sympathy is not compassion; rather, it is a primary identification with the other. Through the forging of these sympathetic bonds of solidarity, new communities are born. Addams watched the birth of such a community among the garment workers meeting at Hull-House. Perhaps it isn't surprising that she believed such an expansion of communal boundaries could lead to the creation of a "public" no longer bound by class limitations.

Addams connects the performance of Eleanor Smith's songs directly to this sympathetic creation of new social bonds when she writes: "I recall a creditable chorus trained at Hull-House for a large meeting in sympathy with the anthracite coal strike in which the swinging lines 'Who was it made the coal?/ Our God as well as theirs' seemed to relieve the tension of the moment" (1910: 377). Addams hoped that *Hull House Songs* would contribute to expressing and creating these new sympathetic bonds of solidarity and community. Thus, *Hull House Songs* imagines and expresses a representation of working class community; but in imagining, it also constructs. It constructs an image of working class life, and, at the same time, attempts to create bonds of sympathy across class lines and, so, bring into being the very public it imagines. But in order to ensure that images of class warfare did not rupture this imagined community, the songs' constructions depend upon careful selection and editorial revision of the original poetic sources.

3   Source to Song

By the turn of the twentieth, Morris Rosenfeld (1862–1923) was one of the most popular Yiddish writers in the United States (Miller, 2007). And, apparently, Jane Addams could be counted among Rosenfeld's admirers. In 1901, he read

---

3   On Smith's influence on Cooley's work, see Jacobs (2006).

some of his Yiddish poetry at Hull-House (Polacheck, 1989: 105). Eleanor Smith set one of those poems. Addams recalls:

> Miss Eleanor Smith, the head of the Hull-House Music School, who had put the words to music [for "Land of the Noonday Night"], performed the same office for the "Sweatshop" of the Yiddish poet, the translation of which presents so graphically the bewilderment and tedium of the New York shop that it might be applied to almost any other machine industry as the first verse indicates:
>
> The roaring of the wheels has filled my ears,
> The clashing and the clamor shut me in,
> Myself, my soul, in chaos disappears,
> I cannot think or feel amid the din.
>
> ADDAMS 1910: 377–378

According to Marc Miller, "The Sweatshop" marks a new departure in Rosenfeld's poetry. Rather than concentrating on the external impact of capitalism upon the worker, the poet turns, instead, toward the existential consequences of this "bewilderment and tedium."

> This poem, one of Rosenfeld's finest, represents his first effort at completely focusing on the inner life of the speaker within the all-encompassing confines of the sweatshop.... In "The Sweatshop"... the speaker does not die literally. Rather, his "I" does, namely his individuality, as he slowly becomes a machine.
>
> 2007: 78

And while it is true that Rosenfeld's poem interrogates the psychic cost of sweatshop labor, Smith's setting of the song uses only selected verses, translated by Addams's nephew, James Weber Linn. Linn's translation, presumably guided by Addams's desires, concentrates upon the stanzas that illustrate the degradation imposed upon workers by the machinery of capitalism, turning them into machines. And while Rosenfeld's poem also emphasizes that degradation, and ends with the words "I know not, I care not, I am a machine," the poet's conclusion can be read as *either* an admission of defeat *or* a call for change (Ibid: 84). The degradation imposed by the sweatshop demands resistance: "I will remain forlorn as long as I am silent/ lost, as long as I remain what I am" (Ibid: 83). While Miller detects a subtle transformation in Rosenfeld's political vision at this point in his poetic career, from propagandistic to existential, his poetry continues to be shaped by the language of class conflict and resistance. Rosenfeld describes a worker who looks "at the arena of battle with bitter rage/ with fear, with revenge, with infernal pain," who demands an "end to slavery" in the sweatshop (Ibid: 83). The psychic impact of capitalist exploitation is not simply the deadening of the self, but the fire of rage that can turn into resistance.

But for Addams, such rage could not be productive. The successful labor movement, the successful movement for reform, brings citizens together, despite differences of wealth, race, gender. Before the Wobblies argued that "an injury against one is an injury against all," Addams had already counseled the working class to transcend the idea of class injury.

> The labor movement must include all men in its hopes. It must have the communion of universal fellowship. Any drop of gall within its cup is fatal. Any grudge treasured up against a capitalist, any desire to "get even" when the wealth has changed hands, are but the old experiences of human selfishness. All sense of injury must fall away and be absorbed in the consciousness of a common brotherhood.
>
> ADDAMS, 1895a: 204

Consequently, in James Weber Linn's translation, Rosenfeld's poem loses its bitter edge. Instead, Addams and Smith use it as an occasion for "socialized emotions" to "find musical expression" (1915: 2). Smith's "The Sweatshop" is not an organizing anthem, nor an attack upon class privilege. It is an attempt to make vivid the sweatshop life for those who never set foot in sweatshops. Simultaneously, it attempts to give expression to working class experience for the immigrant workers themselves. It was, after all, members of the Hull-House music school, many of whom were immigrant workers, who sang "The Sweatshop" (Vaillant, 2003: 108). Smith and Addams want to use the song to make working class life a reality for those outside the working class, at the same time that they use art to attempt to shape the working class's perception of itself.

This same intention animates Smith's setting of Harriet Monroe's (1860–1936) poem, "The Shadow Child." The poet had an on-going relationship with the Hull-House Music School. She contributed the libretto to Eleanor Smith's child operetta, *The Trolls' Holiday*[4] (see Payette, this volume). Monroe's importance as a poet has been overshadowed by her importance as the long

---

4   Eleanor Smith, "Eleanor Smith's Brief Autobiography," undated, in *Barbara Shipps Hull House Collection*, Box 1, Folder 3, Richard J. Daley Library Special Collections and University Archive, the University of Illinois, Chicago. Hereafter cited as Smith, "Autobiography."

time editor of *Poetry* magazine and the seminal collection, with Alice Corbin Henderson, *The New Poetry: An Anthology* (1918).[5] She defended modernism in poetry and, in 1918, argued forcefully against a critic's demand that new poetry be socially engaged.

> The poem or picture will stand by its aesthetic adequacy in the triumphant expression of the vision in the artist's soul, whether this vision be minute or cosmic. And if it is aesthetically inadequate, the most illuminating social wisdom will not save it.
>
> 1918: 41

For her own part, however, Monroe's vision could be minute, or, as in "The Shadow Child," cosmic (Monroe, 1914: 84–87). Structured as the dialogue between a mother and her child, both working at factory machines, the poem begins with the evocation of capitalist production as a growling, inhuman monster.

> *Why do the wheels go whirring round,*
> *Mother, mother?*
> *Oh, mother, are they giants bound,*
> *And will they growl forever?*
> Yes, fiery giants underground,
> Daughter, little daughter,
> Forever turn the wheels around,
> And rumble-grumble ever.

This appeal to the image of the mother and daughter assaulted by monstrous machines continues through the poem. "The big wheels grind us in their might/ And they will grind forever." In the poem, as in the song, this image of the struggling mother, and even more, the child, doomed to "feel the sunshine never" attempts to mobilize audience sentiment against capitalist exploitation by envisioning capitalism itself as an assault on mothers and children, and thus upon the community (or public) as a whole.

Here a comparison is useful. Like Eleanor Smith, the Carolina mill worker, Ella May Wiggins, also composed music in solidarity with organized labor. Like "The Shadow Child," Wiggins' "Mill Mother's Lament" takes the form of the dialogue between a mother and her impoverished children (Roscigno and Danaher, 2004: 72). While Wiggins' song does not address child labor, it does critique

---

5   For an overview and analysis of Monroe's poetic and critical writings, see Williams (1977).

the exploitation of working women, and imagines capitalism as an assault on the family. Wiggins used these themes and images to build solidarity among striking workers. And she constructs her lyric's progression upon a foundation of class conflict. The first verse proclaims, "While we slave for the bosses, our children scream and cry," while the last says "But understand all workers, our union they do fear." With this clear contrast between the interests of the workers and the interests of the "bosses," Wiggins demands "Let's stand together workers, and have a union here" (Wiggins, 2014: 99–100).

"The Shadow Child," on the other hand, attempts to translate workers' experiences into a cross-class language. Both the poem and the song aim for the "communion of universal fellowship" Addams advocates in her writing. Like "The Sweatshop," "The Shadow Child" attempts to humanize worker experience for a middle class audience potentially sympathetic to labor reform, while giving voice to immigrant workers' experience of their lives. The aim is not only to build solidarity within a class, but to enable communication across the class divide.

It is only with her setting of Crosby's "The Land of the Noonday Night" that Smith offers the suggestion of the kind of "class warfare" that Addams otherwise discouraged. But even with this radical anthem against the private ownership of public resources, some of the more biting representations of class struggle and inequality disappear as the poem becomes a song. Ernest Howard Crosby (1856–1907) was a popular writer and Christian social activist whose causes ranged from anti-imperialism and anti-racism, to vegetarianism and labor reform.[6] Crosby's poem appears in a variety of sources, including his 1905 collection, *Broad-cast*. But the song, "The Land of the Noonday Night," is copyright 1902, Charles H. Kerr and Co. We mention the copyright date, as well as the press, because these facts lead to Eleanor Smith's probable source, the September 1902 Kerr publication *The International Socialist Review* (Crosby 1902: 133–134). Not surprisingly, perhaps, *The International Socialist Review* seems to have had readers within Hull-House.

Both poem and song were written in solidarity with striking Pennsylvania miners during the 1902 anthracite strike. And Smith's setting, following the ballad form of the poem, has a structure almost like an Appalachian folk song. The song itself describes the struggles and poverty of the miners and the difficulty of their work. And the song, like the poem, ends with a radical rejection of conventional ideas about private property:

---

6   For a contemporary's discussion of Ernest Howard Crosby, see Flower (1901).

Who was it made the coal?
Our God as well as theirs!
If he gave it free to you and me,
Then keep us out who dares!
Let the people own their mines,
Their own by immortal right—[7]
And the right prevail under hill and dale,
In the land of the noonday night.

This plea for public ownership of common resources resonated with both audience and performers. Let me recall, once more, Jane Addams remarks on one
performance of the song:

Apparently the workers of America are not yet ready to sing, although
I recall a creditable chorus trained at Hull-House for a large meeting in
sympathy with the anthracite coal strike in which the swinging lines
"Who was it made the coal?/Our God as well as theirs" seemed to relieve
the tension of the moment.

ADDAMS, 1910: 377

Workers were ready to sing when those songs forged solidarity and an oppositional identity set against an unjust system. And they met in the sympathy
of a common project, the end of private property. Addams and Smith are thus
able to reject capitalism's inequalities while crafting their anti-capitalism message so that it is, indeed, capitalism, as an unjust and unequal system, that
becomes the real opponent, and not its representatives, individual capitalists
and bosses.

Still, Smith cuts Crosby's verses about class conflict and direct action. Missing from the song, for instance:

But the men who own the mines
And who live like kings of old—
Ah! Little they care how their wage-slaves fare,
So long as they get their gold!
And the fire-damp may explode
And a thousand die outright,
For the men come cheap who go down deep,
In the land of the noonday night.

---

7   This line seems to have been altered by Smith. Originally it read "Let the people own their
mines/Bitumen and anthracite."

And, more important still, Smith cuts Crosby's direct invocation of class warfare. Crosby does not call for class warfare; rather, he identifies the fact that it already exists.

> And if in the end we dare
> To assert our just demands,
> Then the courts emit an injunction writ
> To shackle our tongues and hands.
> And if in spite of their frown
> We protest that we will unite,
> Then they lock us up or they shoot us down
> In the land of the noonday night.

Crosby dismissive attitude toward the legal system and the courts was deeply contrary to the vision developed by Addams and the residents of Hull-House. Crosby suggests that the legal system is bought and paid for by the "men who own the mines" and "live like kings of old." But for Addams, strong legal protections were the only way in which an otherwise disempowered working class could reclaim its rights. These expurgated stanzas did not fit with the civil anti-capitalist reforms Hull-House hoped to accomplish by using the state as a battleground for the public (Addams, 1899a: 451).

The words for "Prayer" are drawn from the work of the British poet, Matthew Arnold (1822–1888). Addams calls this song "a prayer to be saved from the eternal question as to whether in any real sense the world is governed in the interests of righteousness" (1915, 2). But in setting this poem, "Stagirius," Smith once again emphasized the desire for civil discourse and mutual understanding across classes. "Let all doubts be dumb, Let all words be mild/ All strife reconciled, All pains beguiled!" The final piece in the collection, "Suffrage Song (Let Us Sing As We Go)," has a lyric by James Weber Linn (1877–1939), who had also provided the translation for "The Sweatshop," and would later write an early biography of his aunt (Linn, 1935). With its conventional verse/chorus structure and marching rhythm, this song, like a Wobblies' tune, does indeed seem to have been written to rally support for a cause, as it may have been performed at conventions of the National American Woman Suffrage Association (NAWSA). Jane Addams served as the organization's vice president from 1911 to 1914 (Brandes, 2016: 1). Communal singing at organizational gatherings and more publicly, in municipal parades and processions, was an important form of activism and camaraderie within the suffrage movement. "Suffrage Song," with its accessible melody and rhythmic mimicking of marching, is a well-preserved example of one of the hundreds of songs that comprise this specialized repertoire (Ibid: 107).

4   Smith's Music: From the "I" to the "We"

Smith's study in Berlin at Theodore Kullak's Neue Akademie der Tonkunst (Elrod, 2001a: 123) provided her both with the opportunity to further refine her craftsmanship and greater exposure to the European canon of art music, which would undergird most of her compositions. While it became increasingly more common for American women of Smith's pedigree to undertake musical study, even in traditionally masculine spheres like composition, most abandoned the profession when the duties of marriage and children arrived. Upon her return to Chicago in 1890, Smith chose to put her training to good use, designing an entire music curriculum that adopted the educational philosophies of Friedrich Wilhelm Froebel (Howe, 2014: 163–164)[8], as well as composing a large number of artistically substantive works that were intended for immediate performance by amateurs, best classified as *Gebrauchsmusik* or "music for use."[9]

Ellen Gates Starr's 1895 report on artistic activities at Hull-House reveals that Smith's primary objective was to endow her students with rigorous musical training, as Starr describes the gifted pedagogue as "a composer and teacher of vocal music who has never compromised her severe musical standards here or elsewhere" (Starr and Addams, 2003: 47). Starr also confirms that Smith sought excellence from her students, requiring them to display continuous progress in order to advance to higher levels in the singing class, as she notes that the

---

8   Froebel was an advocate for early childhood education and the founder of the kindergarten movement, a controversial idea in German-speaking provinces when he died in 1851. It took a large faction of his female students to enact the conversion from theory into practice and to introduce the concept to other countries, like the United States, where it eventually flourished (Alper, 1980).

9   In addition to an impressive number of songs, Smith composed larger-scale works, most notably several operettas for children. These types of pieces are well characterized by the term *Gebrauchsmusik*, which was not coined until the 1920s to distinguish music that had an objective function (e.g. music for social dancing, pedagogical music, or incidental music for the theater) from loftier modern music that was composed as art for art's sake (and, as such, was often unperformed in the composer's lifetime). Only highly ambitious women, the best example being Smith's contemporary Amy Marcy Beach, would attempt to compose in "masculine" genres, like opera and symphony. However, Beach, a child prodigy, had an unusual luxury: she married a wealthy doctor who did not desire children and encouraged her to pursue a difficult career and devote her life to music, regardless of the financial outcome.

oldest singing class, pursuing its third year of study, is comprised of "the comparatively small number of students whose intellect and perseverance have
survived the test; they have had the advantage of an unusual training" (Ibid).

Smith's studies abroad refined her professionalism and compositional interests, and also informed her taste, leading her to highlight the current German
cultural arena in Hull-House programming, as she featured the works of living
German composers, especially Engelbert Humperdinck (1854–1921) and Carl
Reinecke (1824–1910) (Smith, 1916: 8–9). As Derek Vaillant has documented,
the music performed at Hull-House's flagship outreach concerts were planned
as celebrations of multiculturalism, especially the Christmas concert, which
featured a mix of participatory singing and rehearsed ensemble works for children, like Smith's *The Trolls' Holiday* (Vaillant, 2003: 93). Yet Vaillant also points
out that traditional recital and concert programs of European classical music
presented at Hull-House were marketed to potential audiences in a way that
abated any sense of cultural elitism. Smith's approach to concert programming
is historically significant because performances of works by great European
composers (primarily Mozart, Beethoven, and Schubert) were intermingled
with folk music and new works by living composers (Ibid: 100). Furthermore, Smith arranged for English translation of works with text in European
languages; these selections tended to be repertoire composed especially for
amateur musicians and included a sector of high-quality pieces for children
performers, a type of ensemble that was only beginning to be supplied with serious music at the very end of the nineteenth century. Smith's enjoyment and
comprehensive knowledge of both elevated and accessible strains of German
romanticism, combined with her personal desire to contribute works that accurately reflected the emotions and experiences of working-class Americans,
influenced the definitive makeup of the *Hull House Songs* compilation.

Hull House Songs was not conceived as a unified composition; there are not
strong musical recurrences (similar melodic contours or rhythmic patterns) in
the five freestanding songs, and the fact that four of the five songs are marked
with copyright dates of 1914 or 1915 is not necessarily reflective of the original
date of composition (Elrod, 2001a: 110).[10] Instead, *Hull House Songs* displays
a thematic cohesion as Eleanor Smith clearly endeavors to present collective sentiments, which Jane Addams describes as "socialized emotions" in her
preface to the piece. Herbert J. Wrightson recognizes this premise as strikingly
original in his review of the sheet music in *The Musical Monitor*:

---

10   Elrod (2001a) examined surviving Hull House bulletins and concert programs to compile
      a repertoire list. For example, it indicates that "The Sweat Shop" was performed in 1900,
      but the song was only copyrighted in 1914.

> The five Hull House songs by Eleanor Smith are something quite novel. The texts deal with the conditions of the factory worker and that in a very gripping manner, while the music adds its part with singular aptitude. There is nothing at all commonplace about these songs, as anyone will discover at once who tries them over.
>
> 1915: 284

Aiming for a spirit of inclusivity, the five songs align the suppressed voices of all women (including those from privileged backgrounds, like Addams and Smith) with the concerns of the working class, reflecting the ubiquitous realities of many American citizens and immigrants who benefitted from involvement with Hull-House.

The very act of Smith and Addams compiling and publishing a collection is significant regardless of the lack of connective musical reminiscences. Interestingly, Smith seems to deliberately design the collection to accentuate the coexistence of the genres of Lieder (art song, solo vocalist with piano accompaniment) and choral anthems. This defining attribute of *Hull House Songs* captures the communal activism necessary for persuasive human rights advocacy, but also allows both Smith's mature compositional voice and the solo female voice to emerge as an urgent commentator on current social predicaments. By consciously stretching the conventional European generic boundaries, likely for both artistic and practical purposes, Smith displays her own compositional portfolio—a kind of summation of her work as a serious but accessible composer—and Hull-House's commitment to music as a vitalizing and uplifting leisure activity. The placement of the two Lieder at the beginning of *Hull House Songs* initiates a large-scale progression from "I" to "we," as the three concluding songs are less vocally demanding and the straightforward chordal accompaniment suggests that these songs were intended to be sung by a choir.

As an unmarried woman without abundant financial resources to support her artistic endeavors, Smith had no choice but to channel her ambitions as a female composer into the more socially acceptable role of a music educator. The most accomplished of her female contemporaries, like Amy Fay and Mary Carr Moore, who had also studied in Germany, either succeeded as concert performers, or married and composed in their leisure time, showcasing their works at elite social salons and music clubs. Likewise, Smith's career path and lifestyle had a direct impact on her compositional output, which consists primarily of children's songs and pedagogical music. However, her composition of Lieder and other large-scale vocal works broadened the subject matter and performing forces that were typically found in the existing American vocal repertory. The first two pieces in *Hull House Songs* are especially remarkable when compared to art songs by Smith's female contemporaries. Like her colleagues, Smith facilely employs structural frameworks and harmonic devices that are clearly drawn from the German Lieder tradition as an exhibition of musical and cultural refinement. But it is also apparent that she regards the genre as an effective vehicle to dramatically depict the individualistic perspectives of a truly diverse population of Americans and immigrants who she instructed and befriended at Hull-House. Poems about deprivation and struggle were not appropriate for women composers to ponder through music because they were expected to concentrate exclusively on optimistic and decorative topics, as Mary Carr Moore points out in the context of addressing the bigger problem of being discouraged from composing large-scale works, like operas or symphonies: "So long as a woman contents herself with writing graceful little songs about springtime and the birdies, no one resents it or thinks her presumptuous; but woe be unto her if she dare attempt the larger forms!" (qtd. in von Glahn, 2013: 29). The fact that Smith ventures into decidedly "unfeminine" subject matter in order to expose realistic and dispirited reactions to work is a groundbreaking aspect of *Hull House Songs*. This did not negatively affect the piece's reception because early performances were very likely confined to progressive venues where an emphasis on humanitarian issues and the communicative power of art usurped high-society pleasantries and a fixation on the cultivation of elevated musical taste.

The practice of assembling songs into song cycles or songbooks is too complex to be discussed in depth here; let it suffice to say that an array of political, aesthetic, and entrepreneurial circumstances made it attractive to composers and music publishers for commercial and/or ideological reasons. Yet when taking the viewpoints of critics, performers, and listeners into account, the cultural move toward designating a tightly integrated creation as more prestigious, a legacy that still persists in popular music with concept albums, also generally fostered the enlargement of hermeneutical possibilities. Enlightenment ideals propelled the burgeoning of widespread education and literacy, which led to the professionalization of literary and music criticism in the nineteenth century; this in turn resulted in the impetus to read multi-movement musical compositions like novels, and to discuss the narrative modes utilized with thoughtful consideration of how the composer transmits literary properties through music (Reyland, 2014: 203–223).

Some of the most iconic nineteenth-century Lieder are located within longer groupings of songs (*Liederkreis* or song cycles), like Franz Schubert's *Winterreise* (Winter Journey, 1828) and Robert Schumann's *Dichterliebe* (The Poet's Love, 1840), both compositions that explore the intellectual and emotional depth of masculine subjectivity. These collections of German songs, with poetry by Wilhelm Müller and Heinrich Heine, are sung from the perspective of a sensitive male creative being who is in the midst of a crisis ensued by spurned or unrequited love. The narrative unfolds as a lengthy journey, conveyed to listeners by the progression through a long series of songs. The melding of poetry and music work together to suggest that artistic production can function as a coping mechanism for personal shortcomings and internal trauma, but ultimately death is glorified as the only true release. When at the height of their popularity from 1820–1850, German song cycles were typically consumed as *Hausmusik*, absorbed through private introspective study or performed at intimate domestic gatherings rather than formally presented to the public in recital performances at large halls (Tunbridge, 2010: 53). Concerts at Hull-House emulated this dynamic as neighbors were invited into its cozy environs to enjoy the music without the expectation of paying for this enriching experience.

Late 19th-century German song collections, like Gustav Mahler's settings of poems from *Des Knaben Wunderhorn* (The Boy's Magic Horn, 1892–1898), turned to folkloric poetry to portray the experiences of *das Volk*, average German people, some of whom were citizens of a relatively new nation while others observed from within the confines of the Austro-Hungarian Empire. The anonymous stories and verses compiled in the *Wunderhorn* volume were gathered—and often revised or rewritten—on travels by Achim von Arnim and Clemens Brentano between 1805 and 1808, and are particularly remarkable for the inclusion of grim scenarios and oppressed voices that had never emerged so emphatically from German Lieder. Frankfurt School critic Theodor Adorno compellingly contends that Mahler's prolonged attraction to the *Wunderhorn* poems was politically motivated: "To his mistrust of the peace of the imperialist era war is the normal state, and human beings are pressganged soldiers. He pleads musically for peasant cunning against the overlords, for those who desert their marriages, for outsiders, the persecuted and incarcerated, starving children, forlorn hopes" (1996: 46). As a contemporary of Mahler, it is plausible that Smith was familiar with his late romantic style and pursued a similar goal as Mahler in seeking to pay homage to, and simultaneously modernize, renowned classic songs by Franz Schubert, particularly two of his most famous songs that musically dramatize quintessential German folkloric legends by Johann Wolfgang von Goethe. *Gretchen am spinnrade* ("Gretchen at the Spinning Wheel," 1814) and *Erlkönig* ("The Elf King," 1815) were praised as revolutionary and attained masterwork status in part because they projected in art what in the early nineteenth century were the often-neglected emotions of children and women. The voices in Schubert's canonic songs are forerunners to the compendium of riveting *Wunderhorn* vignettes that Mahler crafted as representative of "the people." Schubert's settings, which Smith certainly knew, were likely meaningful and enriching songs for her because she devoted her life's work to precisely these underserved populations (Macleod, 2001: 36).[11]

"The Sweat Shop" and "The Shadow Child," both in the key of G minor and clearly rooted in the German Lieder tradition, seem to be intended as a pair of songs composed for a soprano soloist, though primary source documents indicate that "The Sweat Shop" was sung by Hull-House students as a choral ensemble. In a 1916 article in the *Music Supervisors' Journal* Smith herself designates these songs as a complementary pair and labels them as "modern dramatic labor songs," which she composed to improve upon the content of "spurious labor songs in which labor is only an incident in the conventional love song" (9). Writing in 1901 in response to Smith's forewarning that she was considering resignation from Hull-House, Addams reveals that "The Sweat Shop" was possibly performed by a group of girls and became a pivotal song for musical outreach. For Addams, it was personally emblematic of the magnitude of Smith's contributions to Hull-House: "If you had only written 'The Sweat-Shop' and taught it to the girls, it would be in my mind a complete justification for all the 'room' you ever took" (qtd. in Vaillant, 2003: 104). Furthermore, an article published in the *Brooklyn Daily Eagle* on March 24th, 1901 entitled "Rosenfeld's 'Sweat Shop,' Set to Music by Eleanor Smith, Causes a Sensation in Chicago, The Home of Jewish Poetry," (Illustration 1.1) describes the first performances of the song and its reception:

> The Sweat Shop was first sung before the Arts and Handicrafts' Association, and attracted so much attention there that the Consumers' League—an organization that aims to better the condition of employees generally—expressed a desire to hear it. As before stated [by Smith], the finishing touches had not been put to the music, but it made a distinct hit nevertheless. That was February 15, and since then the poem has become a sort of anthem of the workers in the slums. It is far more typical of existing conditions than "The Man With the Hoe," and it bids fair to have a far-reaching effect.

---

11   Macleod notes that by the late nineteenth century these particular songs were recognized as pinnacles of the Lieder genre and were a standard part of the curriculum at any German Conservatory. Smith included songs by Schumann and Schubert alongside her own in her pedagogical collection entitled *Songs of Life and Nature* (1898).

Although Schubert's *Gretchen am spinnrade* ("Gretchen at the Spinning Wheel," 1814) is a "spurious labor song," it is almost certainly the model for "The Sweat-Shop." Both songs feature a *perpetuum mobile* accompaniment of continual sixteenth notes to represent the unceasing presence of the machine, which is only disrupted when the girl singing becomes lost in her thoughts and questions whether her mind and body will ever be freed from this imprisonment (with Goethe's Gretchen her nervous laboring at the spinning wheel is intertwined with her obsession with Faust and her anxious longing for his acceptance, but it also implies that a life of laboring will be the consequence of her illegitimate pregnancy). Smith sets Morris Rosenfeld's poem to a quintessentially Schubertian modified strophic form, in which the music for each verse of the text is varied to better convey the poetic nuances. The first of three verses (mm. 1–27) describes the deafening and fatiguing effect of heavy machinery upon an individual; the piano and voice introduce the principal accompanimental motive—an oscillating minor second— and the principal melodic motive—a stark triadic outline of G minor—which is repeated four times in the first eight measures. Harmonic movement away from G minor follows these opening gestures, with phrases that end on the major-key regions of D major, the dominant (V, m. 11 and m. 13), and A major, the dominant of the dominant (V/V, m. 19 and m. 23); at this point the music is supplying an optimistic answer

ILLUSTRATION 1.1   Eleanor Smith with Jewish Poets
BROOKLYN DAILY EAGLE (24 MARCH 1901: 23)

to the protagonist's questions—"For whom? For what? Why should the work be done?"—suggesting that the prospect of work may be more beneficial than she is acknowledging.

Again following the framework of *Gretchen am spinnrade*, the climactic second verse (mm. 28–57) expresses the notion of time slipping away and the emotional numbness the girl feels in her heart. Smith captures this intensity by expanding the vocal range to over an octave, with desperate leaps of minor ninths and a minor tenth in the vocal part on the words "It throbs;" "A heart;" and "Their wounds." When compared to the first verse, the harmonic content is much more unstable, rife with chords in second and third inversions, and minor and half-diminished seventh chords. This second section is further differentiated from the outer verses by the addition of an entirely new passage announced by a tempo change to *Adagio* ("slowly," mm. 48–57). At this point the poem's focus shifts outward to the whole community of factory workers, drawing a metaphor with war-wounded soldiers who must fight until the war is won or they die. The concluding third verse (mm. 58–75) is the shortest, with the voice singing in only 12 measures, and the vocal contour depicts the poem's emphasis on "sink" and "fall," spanning from a high G5 (m. 63) down to a Db4 (mm. 67–68). With the introduction of Gb major and minor chords (mm. 67–68) we enter new harmonic territory, perhaps aurally symbolic of a grave as this space below the tonic is now notated enharmonically to distance it from previous chords built on the leading tone of G minor, F#. The song ends with a return to the opening motives, now heard in an extremely low register of the piano. For the conclusion, Smith transfers the opening bars of the introduction down an octave, restricting all pitches to well below C4 (middle C). The brighter sound of the opening, with more energetic octaves in the left hand (as indicated by continual tenuto marks), becomes dull and fades away, creating a very unsettling aura. We will be released from the song's oppressive motives—after umpteen hearings they come to symbolize the drudgery of the factory—but we get the sense that the song could continue ad infinitum. This is further cemented by an incomplete tonic triad in the last measure, in which the third is omitted from the chord, which also deprives the listener of a satisfying resolution.

Harriet Monroe's poem "The Shadow Child" (1909) is folkloric in its enactment of a parent-child dialogue, another poetic topos that Schubert brilliantly dramatized in song in *Erlkönig*. Smith borrows Schubert's idea of representing the voices of different characters with consistent instrumental attributes: throughout the song the top voice of the piano part doubles the child's melodic line as she poses wistful questions while the mother's response, always entering on a low D4 (m. 9; m. 25; m. 41), is accompanied by a descending chromatic line doubled in two octaves of the piano as the accompaniment shifts to a parallel motion figuration. This call and response sequence occurs three times and produces a feeling of stasis as the music for each iteration avoids significant variation and climactic highpoints. In "The Shadow Child" Smith's illumination of the poetry's blurring of hope and despondence is achieved through mode mixture (the mixture of major and minor modes), with passages that blend the pitch content of the keys of G and D minor with G and D major. A prime example of this technique's expressive force is Smith's emphasis on the pitch C# (belonging to the key of D major) on the word "Mother" (mm. 3–4; mm. 19–20; m. 35), which is supported by the continuation of a G ostinato (the tonic) in the bass, forming the jarring interval of a diminished fifth. This recurrent clash on "Mother" perfectly captures the child's awareness of her dire situation, which is only somewhat ameliorated by her mother's attempts to console her without making false promises.

The song's culmination does not arrive until the mother's last response as a glimmer of hope finally appears, marked by a change to a slower adagio tempo (m. 41) and the abandonment of the chromatic figuration in parallel motion. The rhythmic pacing broadens, with the persistent eighth notes slackening into quarter notes, but the prospect of attaining a comfortable life as introduced by the phrase "When we lie down out in the sun" (m. 45), is undercut through the introduction of an unexpected harmonic region (Eb minor) and the arrival of a half-diminished seventh chord, as opposed to the conventional bright major chord, on the word "sun." The song drifts off with an encouraging F# leading tone in the final vocal phrase—"And work no more forever"– however, here the lowering of the dynamics from mezzo forte (m. 45) to triple pianissimo (m. 51) also imparts that faith in the mother's whimsical reassurances slowly fades away.

The inclusion of three songs in *Hull House Songs* that are composed in a choral style is quite representative of the rising popularity of choral music in the nineteenth century as a genre that became increasingly accessible to the middle and lower classes and embraced secular subject matter. Most European choral societies in the nineteenth century espoused highly democratic principles, as evidenced by the formation of gigantic ensembles with up to a thousand singers that were brought together for special events (Di Grazia, 2013).[12] Barbara James and Walter Mossmann (1983) have demonstrated that the practice of mass performance also extended to the forum of political protest as workers' songs were vigorously composed as the 1848 revolutions percolated

---

12   The cover art on Donna M. Di Grazia's *Nineteenth-century Choral Music* (2013) is a reproduction of a famous engraving of an 1857 photograph by Negretti and Zambra, which documents the huge performing forces for the annual Handel Festivals in the Crystal Palace in London.

throughout Germany. The Forty-Eighters, exiled Germans who came to America, brought song repertories that prospered in cities with sizeable German populations, like Chicago. An 1899 article published in the *Chicagoer Arbeiter-Zeitung* entitled "The Purpose of Workers' Singing Societies" asserts that German workers' choruses were founded in Chicago with the goal of renewal in the belief that "The song's might should hold workers from all regions together and inspire them with the great idea which informs the proletariat" (Keil & Jentz, 1988: 285).

The final three songs of *Hull House Songs* are communal portrayals that capture the current predicaments of a wide spectrum of people, ranging from the working class to the Hull-House women themselves. We hear a sonic documentary in "The Land of the Noonday Night" followed by a pensive reflection on spirituality in "Prayer" and an outpouring of optimism for the future in "Suffrage Song." "The Land of the Noonday Night" forms the centerpiece of *Hull House Songs* and perhaps occupies that central position (the third song of five) because it uses musical imagery to poignantly express the demoralization that results from labor exploitation. Smith composed "Noonday Night" as a strophic form, in which all four verses are set to the same melody and accompaniment, to project the text with utmost clarity. Although objectively the most simple and musically unembellished song in the collection, the experience of descending into a mine day after day is vividly portrayed by the declining melodic contours, first heard without voices in the piano introduction. Smith establishes a sense of bleakness by firmly adhering to the key of B minor and maintaining a plodding rhythmic pace to mirror the drudgery of working in a damp, dark environment and the uniform speed that the miners internalized while being transported up and down. In fact, there are only a handful of major chords in the entire song and the final cadence (m. 12) completely avoids the expected movement from the dominant (F# major) to the tonic in favor of plagal movement from E minor to B minor. Smith lingers on the dominant harmony only in the concluding chord of the introduction (m. 4). Surprisingly, the harmony that occurs on the fermata at the midpoint of each stanza (m. 8), which we assume will simply repeat the introduction's overall harmonic trajectory from tonic to dominant, has morphed into an F# minor chord (v), boldly underscoring the poetry's grimness. This is not followed by an accompanimental interlude as one might expect, instead the vocalists launch right into the second half of the stanza, as if too immersed in painstakingly depicting all of the miners' hardships to pause even for a moment.

"Prayer," excerpted from Matthew Arnold's poem "Stagirius" (1844–1849), is the only song in Smith's collection set to the text of a deceased European poet. This verse poem is declaimed from the perspective of Stagirius, who Arnold notes in his 1877 collected edition of poetry was "a young monk to whom St. Chrysostom addressed three books, and of whom these books give an account" (Allott, 1958: 286). Kenneth Allott, an acclaimed scholar of Arnold's work, postulates that Arnold encountered the figure of Stagirius in the work of French critic Saint-Marc Girardin, who offers a synopsis of his story in *Cours de littérature dramatique* (1843–63): Stagirius enters a monastery in the hopes of ameliorating his internal melancholy and unrest through solitary religious contemplation, but is disheartened upon realizing that the superficial dedication of his life to God is not enough to endow him with true inner peace (Ibid: 288–289). This poem, like many of Arnold's great contributions, displays "his perennial concerns with discovering the basis for right action in a difficult world, and with knowing how right action or righteousness bestows its own form of happiness" (Johnson, 2010: 30). This is undoubtedly a quality of Arnold's writing that inspired Addams and her colleagues.

John Henry Raleigh's 1961 monograph explores the great appeal of Arnold's writings to Americans between 1865–1950, and the author asserts that, "no other foreign critic, and perhaps few native ones, have acquired such a reputation and exercised such a palpable influence on American culture" (1). Arnold embarked on a lecture tour of the U.S. in 1883–1884. Although progressive literary figures, like Walt Whitman and Mark Twain, were adamantly opposed to the archaic and formal style of Arnold's work (Raleigh, 1961: 61 and 64), the majority of the American literary establishment in the 1880s praised his approach to literary criticism, even if they were somewhat offended about Arnold's impression of America (Ibid: 68).

Jane Addams studied Arnold's work as it prompted her to think about how she could dismantle the Victorian correlation of culture with class stratification and use her American settlement as a platform to free culture from its association with elitism (Knight, 2005: 89–90). At Rockford Seminary, she read Arnold's cultural theory essay entitled *Culture and Anarchy*, which observes that only culture can abet the rich from becoming entirely devoted to materialism and recommends that the state provide poor citizens with the opportunity to experience culture to uplift them. However, Arnold, after visiting America, published an essay entitled "Civilization in the United States" that declared that America lacked aesthetic "distinction" (Raleigh, 1961: 78), which may have further encouraged Addams and the socially affluent in her generation to assign greater cultural capital to European canonic artworks. Raleigh observes that *The Dial*—a Chicago magazine first published in 1880— "in its early, conservative, New-England loving, Whitman-hating stage, waved Arnold like a flag in defiance of 'low' tendencies in literature and criticism" (1961: 134).

Although not as widely appreciated as his literary criticism, Arnold's four books on religion continued to be read and debated well into the twentieth century. The longevity of his theological thought, and its meaning to American intellectuals and social reform activists, can be gleaned by examining Robert Morss Lovett's 1939 review of Lionel Trilling's *The Mind of Matthew Arnold*. Lovett was a longtime Hull-House resident and this piece lends insight into why Matthew Arnold's ideas were championed by the American Left long after his death (Rodden, 1999: 33). Most importantly, they admired Arnold's statements that in hindsight could be interpreted as anticipating socialism, such as "I am more and more convinced that the world needs to become more comfortable for the mass, and more uncomfortable for those of any natural gift or distinction" (Ibid: 36). Also influential was Arnold's belief that the object of religion is conduct and his identification of this premise as the commonality shared between different world religions. In many of his theological writings Arnold referred to his formula for life, which cites conduct as three-fourths of human life, along with one-eighth art and one-eighth science. This is presented in *Literature and Dogma*: "And as the discipline of *conduct* is three-fourths of life, for our aesthetic and intellectual disciplines, real as these are, there is but one-fourth of life left; and if we let art and science divide this one-fourth fairly between them, they will have just one-eighth each" (Arnold, 1903: 210).

Our brief synopsis of the reception of Arnold's work in the United States offers some insight into why a text by Matthew Arnold was venerated by Addams and Smith and considered worthy for inclusion in *Hull House Songs*. Addams also mused on Arnold's *Literature and Dogma* and his proposition that right conduct is righteousness. Louise Knight suggests the book conveyed to Addams that "the real meaning of Christ's message was to trust one's own moral judgment" (Knight, 2010a: 45) and she deduces that Addams valued this book because "it was the message that her father had taught her as a child and that Emerson in his essays, in his secular way, had taught her too" (Ibid). Addams describes the function of the excerpts from Arnold's "Stagirius" in *Hull House Songs* as "a prayer to be saved from the eternal question as to whether in any real sense the world is governed in the interest of righteousness" (1915: 2). Addams's tone seems to imply that constant meditation on this question is anti-productive to her work and the continual striving for a universalistic mindset grounded in humanistic compassion is perhaps the most valiant way to combat stringent religious dogma and prejudicial preconceptions. This statement is unquestionably paraphrasing Arnold's ideals concerning what constitutes a "liberalized, literary Christianity," which many American cultural authorities singled out as one of the most far-reaching components of Arnold's work in the late nineteenth century because he argued that a universalized concept of morality should be regarded as the cornerstone of all religions (Raleigh, 1961: 55). Smith seeks to illuminate Arnold's plea for a unified concept of individual agency and to generate a modern sensibility by steering her music for "Prayer" away from archaic Christian liturgical models, instead utilizing an abundance of chromatic mediants, all varieties of seventh chords, extended tertian chords, and chordal parallelism to replicate the vibrant soundscape of early-twentieth century French impressionism and American popular music idioms.

"Prayer" is another modified strophic form with three verses that are separated by short instrumental interludes. Smith musically renders the poetry's grandeur, evoking a vast span of time and space, by journeying to more wayward harmonic regions from the tonic key of C major, most of which are associated to the tonic by mediant (III, VI, iii, or vi; movement to a new key that is located a third away from the tonic) and chromatic mediant relationships (a chromatically inflected third away from the tonic, e.g. bVI). However, after the first statement of the pivotal words that bind all three verses, "Save, oh! Save," initially accompanied by D minor chords (mm. 11–12), the return to the key of C major is always strongly bound to this text (mm. 28–31; mm. 70–73). The second verse diverts from the melody of the first verse at measure 42 when the text turns to address adversity and unrest. The flurry of activity in the accompaniment, intensified by quick scalar patterns in the bass, barrages through a series of phrases in mediant and chromatic mediant keys, arriving in D minor for the beginning of the third verse (m. 54). The mood suddenly changes in the third verse as Smith composes energetic jazz-inflected harmonies and a profusion of seventh chords to match the prayer's conclusion, which contains the statement of a series of uplifting maxims that are further vitalized by syncopated block chords in the piano accompaniment (mm. 59–66). The coda (mm. 67–77) commences abruptly with a striking textural change as *a cappella* voices enter with the "From the cradle to the grave, Save, oh! save" refrain on the pickup to measure 68, initiating a final majestic cadence in the key of C major.

"Suffrage Song (Let Us Sing As We Go)," a rousing and optimistic march in the key of C major, closes *Hull House Songs* with a jubilant tone. Many early twentieth-century suffrage songs are contrafacts: new lyrics sung to the melodies of traditional hymns and patriotic songs, like "America" and "Battle Hymn of the Republic" (Rehm, 2011: 94). In her study of suffrage music Elizabeth Wood discovers that the practice of devising contrafacts also influenced original compositions, like Smith's "Suffrage Song," as composers sought to emulate the traits of iconic nationalistic songs, or familiar hymns, like "Onward

Christian Soldiers." Wood notes that the style of many of the songs is indicative of the middle-class background of the lyricist and composer.

> On the one hand, and more numerously, are the orderly, conventional borrowings and arrangements of traditional song tunes, ballads, hymns, and patriotic or military march tunes, to which were attached new, mostly uplifting and devotional words penned by women and men in the movement. Many betray in earnestly didactic literary style their religious, middle-class origin and are not as easy to perform (or suited to the untrained voice) as the "barrack-room" ballad style of labor and strike songs.
>
>   1995: 611

The production of original suffrage compositions by American women appears to increase after the success of British composer Ethel Smyth's 1911 hit "The March of the Women" (Brandes, 2016: 106–108). The majority of the American suffrage sheet music that was published from 1911–1918, when the movement gained momentum and approached its culmination, featured new music and lyrics. Interestingly, none of the music for these songs was composed by men, and collaboration with male lyricists was rare, found only in "Suffrage Song" and Elsa Gregori's "Women's Political Union March," set to Henry Grafton Chapman's lyrics (Ibid).

With lyrics by James Weber Linn, "Suffrage Song" is an example of a typical suffrage anthem penned by a male poet. By focusing on "us," as opposed to a feminine "I" or references to "sisters" or "daughters," the imagined collective that emerges from Linn's lyrics does not overtly exclude men from participating in the suffrage movement, and this perhaps prompts Smith to champion the strength of this consolidated group through masculine musical rhetoric. Smith employs the traditional ternary form used for military marches: march (mm. 1–12, verses 1 and 2); contrasting trio (mm. 13–22, verses 3 and 4); march (mm. 23–38, verse 1 repeated). She adopts referential devices from other famous suffrage songs including conventional martial codes for emboldening the troops, especially the mimicking of trumpet calls in measures 14 and 16 of the trio and the frequent breaks on the third beat (beginning in m. 2) where the punctuating clash of the cymbals would typically ring out.

The energetic momentum is maintained throughout the entire song by the fixture of a lilting rhythmic pattern on the weak beats (beats 2 and 4): a dotted eighth note followed by a sixteenth note, present at least once in every measure except the concluding two measures. The strong metric regularity that presses forward truly qualifies as a musical metaphor representing the act of not backing down until the aim is accomplished. The contrasting trio is strongly differentiated from the outer march sections by modulation to the key of E minor and by the decreased volume that shifts to a much quieter dynamic range than the march. The trio conveys a more serious tone for the text's reminiscence of years past that were fraught with obstacles, but Linn maintains the present tense throughout to sustain the idea of steady progress. Interestingly, the song's most repetitive and outwardly rousing phrase, "Votes for Women," tends to be harmonized with a first inversion tonic triad containing an E in the bass (this first occurs in measure 4). Smith reserves the union of voices with a tonic C in the bass for the two-measure tag that closes out each of the framing march sections—"For the right shall prevail over wrong!"—and thus stresses that the issue of suffrage is not just of pertinence to women, but is a worthy cause for all citizens who wish to fight for the greater good.

Although we have no extant documents in which Eleanor Smith explains her compositional aims and discloses whether her song collection is purposefully arranged in a particular order, the musical and poetic trajectory of *Hull House Songs* directs the listener's course. The experience of hearing a vast array of perspectives, ranging from a solitary juvenile voice to a collective of laborers to a community of worshippers, allows for a moving depiction and commemoration of the variety of people who learned their voices mattered at Hull-House. And, whether intended or accidental, the sequence of songs moves the listener from the isolated and alienated "I" of "The Sweatshop" to the communal "We" that sustains "Suffrage Song." In this sense, *Hull House Songs* echoes Jane Addams's attempt to build a universal community beyond the boundaries of class exploitation and resentment.

5   Finding Her Voice

Both materially and symbolically, *Hull House Songs* gives voice to the working class. This materiality takes form in the space of the performance, as they songs are sung by working class artists, often to working class audiences. In this material space, the songs symbolically construct an image of community that includes the working class, but reaches toward a broader public through bonds of solidarity and sympathy. But, in giving voice to class experience, the songbook simultaneously attempts to mediate that experience, and offers a construction that emphasizes social solidarity rather than class conflict. Just as Addams and Smith hope to mediate class conflict, while imposing the settlement's point of view, they also privilege the settlement's cultural perspectives. Eleanor Smith's style emerges from bourgeois high art, and both her compositions and her pedagogy reinforce bourgeois artistic standards and cultural attitudes, even as they search for working class agency.

Hull-House residents idealized high culture, as well as "authentic" folk culture, as artistic antidotes for the moral breakdown produced by industrialization (Cassano, this volume). In the first volume of her music course, Smith includes a large number of European traditional songs. These simple melodies will "help to improve the intonation and perfect the rhythmic sense of the children" (Smith, 1908: iii). In addition, such material helps "form a link between our pupils and their forbearers" (Smith, "Autobiography"). With this latter remark, Smith evokes one of the major concerns of Addams's theories of popular culture. For Addams, the modern city isolates immigrant children from their traditional culture, leaves a vacuum in place of that culture, and subsequently fills the vacuum with the dreck of modern, commercialized words, songs, and films (Cassano, this volume). This commercialized culture emphasizes sensuality and degrades solidarity. By creating a cultural bond between American-born children and their Old World parents, folk music combats the forces of spiritual decadence. Folk music then becomes a two-fold tool: on the one hand, it builds cultural continuity across generations; on the other hand, in its simplicity, it prepares the student for more difficult, and 'serious,' musical education. But the folk music Smith transcribes and teaches is de-contextualized and transformed. As it was taken out of the "village," the village (the indigenous folk style) has been taken out of the music.

Even as she drew upon folk sources, Smith hoped to transform both the students and the songs through formal training. In her emphasis upon training, she and Jane Addams drew a sharp line between the music performed by formally trained artists, on the one side, and popular, *commercial*, art forms on the other. Addams (1910) mentions a student from the music school, a "Bohemian girl, who, in order to earn money for pressing family needs, first ruined her voice in a six months' constant vaudeville engagement, returned to her trade working overtime in a vain effort to continue the vaudeville income" (381). In a similar vein, Smith tells the story of "Rosie."

> She was seventeen and sang with a voice like a steam whistle. In her village, she told me, all the girls would walk down the street arm-in-arm all singing, the louder the better. Rosie apparently wished to learn to sing... The restoration of the wreck of a fine voice offered a combination of problems too fascinating for me to resist and Rosie and I entered in a long series of struggles.
>
> SMITH, "Autobiography"

While Rosie's folk and community traditions represent source material, she required training and method in order to restore "the wreck of a fine voice." In her home village, "the girls would walk arm-in-arm down the street in the evening all singing, the louder the better." It was this village habit and cultural practice that gave Rosie a "voice like a steam whistle." And, in order for her voice to become "smooth and agreeable," she had to repress her initial cultural training. In a quite literal sense, Rosie had to give up her village, her traditions, her peasant habits, her past... in order to become "agreeable." To the extent that Rosie's new voice meets bourgeois cultural standards, becomes agreeable, Smith's educational practices *Americanize* the girl.

Part of the task of the settlement is to translate folk forms and styles into the formal categories of European musical training and public performance. Through this formalization, Smith and Addams argue, the diversity of ethnic and racial stock achieves a common American-ness. Thus, musical training itself is a kind of Americanization, forming bonds of sympathy and identification across racial and ethnic boundaries in order to produce a larger, synthetic culture. At the same time, this Americanization through "high culture" necessarily posits the superiority of formal European and American training methods over ethnic and popular styles. These ethnic and popular voices could be included in the community Smith and Addams imagined, but always as subordinate to the normatively sanctioned styles associated with bourgeois culture. Thus, the "public" imagined by both Smith and Addams was rooted in a basic solidarity with working class interests and values, but its categories of judgment, taste, and training, were drawn from the "top down" (Mink, 1996).

But Smith's emphasis upon formal training did not simply represent acquiescence to bourgeois artistic ideology. Rather, like Addams, Smith used musical training as a weapon against capitalist exploitation. For Addams, the venues of commercial culture, and the entertainments they served, represented another form of exploitation that paralleled workers' exploitation at the job (Cassano, this volume).

> Apparently the modern city sees in these [working class] girls only two possibilities, both of them commercial: first, a chance to utilize by day their new and tender labor power in its factories and shops, and then another chance in the evening to extract from them their petty wages by pandering to their love of pleasure.
>
> 1972 [1909]: 8

The culture industry produced by capitalism disabled workers by "pandering to their love of pleasure," fused them with their sensuality, and thus eliminated the possibility of agency. Workers were exploited at work, and then seduced and silenced by the entertainments they purchased with their pay. Eleanor Smith argues that music, and musical pedagogy, creates new capabilities in students, thus enabling them to find a voice for resistance. Smith recalls Rosie's own self-discovery through music: "I found one very high tone which she had never known she possessed and very slowly and patiently we worked down into the other registers of her voice until it was all smooth and agreeable in quality." After all their laborious efforts, however, Rosie found the chance to sing "for real money" too tempting to refuse. "Two months after her departure she returned with her voice in tatters" (Smith, "Autobiography"). Smith connects the ruin of the girl's voice to its commercial exploitation. Just as education creates capacity, exploitation endangers those new capacities. If folk music represents untutored culture, popular, commercial music represents the destruction of all culture and all capacity. Thus, for Smith, bourgeois artistic education engenders agency.

Here we need to step back from our role as analysts, and write, instead, from our phenomenological perspectives as musicians. The authors of this chapter have very different musical experiences. One has a scholarly background in classical European music, the other knows music primarily as an amateur performer. But what we have in common is the experience of discovering, for the first time, a new musical capacity. That moment, when we find a note we did not know we possessed, when we cover a scale that seemed out of reach, or master a composition that appeared, at first, unimaginably difficult, a new, visceral power is produced. What had seemed impossible eventually becomes a part of the practice regime, a routine. And when the impossible becomes routine, the world opens. Music may seem to be simply one fragment of subjective experience, but its practice can serve as allegory and guide for pedagogy. The experience of musical mastery creates a confidence that potentially enables agency well beyond the bounds art. To the extent that Eleanor Smith awakened new capacities within her students, her vocation was fundamentally political as well as pedagogical. In a very real sense, then, *Hull House Songs* was written to give Rosie, and other working class students like her, a voice, and through that voice, a sense of agency. At the same time, the text gave voice to the women residents of Hull-House, to their politics, as well as to their cultural attitudes.

Jane Addams, Florence Kelley, Julia Lathrop, Eleanor Smith, and the other residents shared a commitment to social justice. They formed a "professional women's commune" that allowed for lines of activity and forms of behavior that challenged the dominant culture's normative constraints upon women, even as they accepted the dominant culture's definition of "high art" (Deegan, 1988: 48). While they guided the perspectives of workers away from class conflict, and attempted to educate their aesthetic tastes, it was nonetheless through their roots in the neighborhood and community that the Hull-House residents found their collective voice. The title *Hull House Songs* represents the rooted-ness of the manuscript in that community. Each composition was written to be performed in Hull-House, by workers, for the neighborhood. Hull-House, as an institution, gave Eleanor Smith access to students, to performers, and to an audience. In turn, Smith attempted to use her artistic voice for the community. Her songs were written to interact with the struggles that animated the neighborhood. Because the songs interacted with those struggles, *Hull House Songs* is more than a work of art. It is documentation of the impact of the industrial revolution upon citizens and workers, and a record of their too easily forgotten resistance.

But by the time the folio was published, Addams and the other Hull-House residents no longer seemed so centrally concerned with organized labor and capitalist exploitation. On the eve of the U.S. entry into the First World War, Addams's turned her attention to international issues, and, especially, the prospects of war and peace. The roots of Addams's shift in interest can already be found in her writings on labor. With the bloody destruction of war, the community of national "citizens" Addams evoked in 1899 perhaps appeared too small. Just as Addams hoped with that word to forge a community broader than the class differences between labor and capital, during and after the World War she imagined a "public" broader and deeper than the arbitrary limits of national borders. While this internationalist perspective always included Addams's support of international labor solidarity, her struggle for peace, her international travels, and, after the war, her fight for her own reputation during the Red Scare, eclipsed Hull-House's efforts within the labor movement (Sklar, Schuler, and Strasser, 1998). By 1915, the poems, the lives, the strikes, and the performances, documented by the songbook were memories. *Hull House Songs* represents a passing moment in the labor movement's and Hull-House's intersecting histories. Perhaps the passing of that moment also helps explain the shadows that concealed these songs for too long.

CHAPTER 2

Hull House Songs and Jane Addams's Political Aesthetic

Graham Cassano

1   Introduction

Workers' songs, written in a classical idiom, influenced by romanticism, but decidedly modern, with a woman composer mining a field overwhelmingly dominated by men, perhaps it is hardly surprising that Eleanor Smith's *Hull House Songs* would disappear from print, leaving only an echo behind, a few faded recordings, and a few copies of the folio in specialized libraries and archives. Had she written in a different context, it's possible that Smith would be remembered as an influential composer. Smith left a mark, and her influence in contemporary music education continues to be felt. But as an artist, as a composer, as a modernist collaborator with some of the most important poets of her day, Eleanor Smith remains largely unknown. What Smith accomplished with *Hull House Songs* was the synthesis of art and politics. Her compositions were political art; art with political purpose integral to the aesthetic intentions. Smith suggests this interpretation in her own self-assessment from 1916. After describing a program of "authentic" labor songs from various national folk traditions, Smith warns:

> Much more numerous are those spurious labor songs in which labor in only an incident in the conventional love song. Two modern dramatic labor songs figured on this program. These were "The Shadow Child" and "The Sweat-Shop" by Eleanor Smith.
>
> SMITH, 1916: 9[1]

Adding her compositions to the list of authentic labor songs, Smith makes it clear that hers are not "spurious labor songs." The political themes and content are fundamental to the structure of music, and to the function of the work as art. Songs like "The Shadow Child" or "Land of the Noonday Night," are not, like "Gretchen at the Spinning Wheel," simply observations of the human condition

---

1   Jessica Payette directed my attention to this quotation from Smith.

or the tragic entanglements of love (Cassano and Payette, this volume). All of the *Hull House Songs* contain *demands*, and, as such, represent calls to action, not occasions for passive observation.

Jane Addams, too, recognized that *Hull House Songs* represented a particular kind of political art, meant to have particular political, as well as aesthetic, affects. In the preface, Addams argues that *Hull House Songs* had a purpose beyond simply aesthetic comfort. Through these songs, the "socialized emotions" find expression and the "manifold movements of our contemporaries" find inspiration. Nonetheless, the precise nature of the connection between art and politics remains obscure. Although Smith herself left no fully formalized aesthetic theory through which we can understand her artistic aims, Addams developed precisely such an aesthetic theory. Smith was not simply Addams's acolyte. But Smith's long residence at Hull-House put her into close contact with Addams's ideas, and, judging from the writing the composer did leave behind, those ideas influenced Smith's artistic aims.

This chapter examines two of Addams's books in order to explore her aesthetic theories, *The Spirit of Youth and the City Streets* (1972 [1909]) and *The Long Road of Woman's Memory* (1916). Neither of these works seems immediately concerned with enunciating an aesthetic theory, but, I will argue, both nonetheless do so.

The Spirit of Youth and the City Streets is most obviously about the rise of early twentieth century popular culture and youth culture. But in crafting her discussion of popular culture, Addams uses an idealized image of "high culture" to critique the vulgar arts of the street. In the course of the book's narrative, Addams posits a number functions for art. Art sublimates dangerous sexual instincts and lifts the audience above the senses. Art becomes the basis for popular moral codes. And art becomes an occasion for conversation and thereby builds social solidarity. The first function of art Addams posits does not fully address the aims of *Hull House Songs*. Yet it is the romantic notion of the redemptive possibilities in high art that dominate *The Spirit of Youth*. This romantic conception of art as "higher imagination" potentially depoliticizes aesthetics. But when the political content of *Hull House Songs* is disregarded, something is lost even in the description of artistic content.

The Spirit of Youth was published several years before *Hull House Songs* appeared as a folio, but *The Long Road* appeared in print directly after *Hull House Songs*. It is in *The Long Road,* not *The Spirit of Youth,* that Addams fully develops her theories of the relationship between art, solidarity, and culture. As with *The Spirit of Youth*, the subject animating *The Long Road* does not, at first, seem relevant to aesthetic theory. Instead, the text takes up the question of memory and its selective capacity. Yet the occasion for this examination of memory is the story of the "Devil Baby," an urban myth that Addams equates to a kind of popular folk mythology or poetry. So Addams returns to an interrogation of aesthetics. Art, like memory itself, has the potential to mediate solidarity and forge connections between social actors. These bonds of solidarity enable political action. And, quite unlike her earlier work, *The Long Road* depicts agency within communities of working class women, traditional women and modern "factory girls."

Both texts represent interventions, but of very different kinds. *The Spirit of Youth* is a critique of popular culture, and, by implication, of working class mores. The author's voice is stern; the cultural attitudes she represents are bourgeois, though clearly philanthropic. Moreover, *The Spirit of Youth*, together with its companion volume, *A New Conscience and An Ancient Evil* (1912a), represent working class youth as lacking agency, the passive playthings of sinister commercial forces and faceless industrial processes. On the other hand, through their combined solidarity, and their newly forged cultural bonds, the figures of youth who populate *The Long Road* resist capitalist exploitation.

This difference does not represent an evolution in Jane Addams's consciousness. Rather, a continuity unites these seemingly contradictory representations. Both *The Spirit of Youth* and *The Long Road* argue that capitalist cultural forms induce sickness and disable agency. And both argue that the solution to that sickness is social integration and solidarity. In *The Spirit of Youth* that solidarity appears as working class conformity to bourgeois cultural standards, inculcated through education and through the work of social settlements. In *The Long Road*, however, Addams examines working class solidarity built from the ground up, among traditional immigrant women, and among women factory workers fighting capitalist exploitation.

This final contradiction renders visible one of the difficulties inherent in Hull-House's culture of class mediation. Addams herself emphasized the mediate position Hull House occupied. "The settlement may be of value if it can take a larger and steadier view than is always possible to the workingman, smarting under a sense of wrong; or to the capitalist... insisting on the inalienable right of 'invested capital, to a return of at least four per cent, ignoring human passions" (Addams, 1895a: 196) To say that Addams recognized her mediate position is not to suggest she fully understood that position. Nonetheless, it was precisely this in-between-ness that allowed for Addams's modulation between voices, positions, and value schemes. Because the world they constructed was a subculture separate from—but related to—both middle class and working class Chicago, Addams and the other Hull-House residents modulate between learning from working class practices and attempting to impose middle class judgments upon workers.

Nonetheless, Jane Addams's partial identification with young working class women allowed her to take their industrial work and political activity as a model for modern women, even as she distrusted the commercial and popular culture that helped create solidarity among those women. However, Addams's identification did not extend to Chicago's working class Black population. As I will argue in the "Coda" to this chapter, Addams's portrayed Black culture as pathological, and she remained largely blind and deaf to the cultural work of African Americans in literature and music. In a series of invidious comparisons, Addams whitens new immigrants from Southern and Eastern Europe through the rhetorical denigration of working class Black Americans. Even as she attempted to build bridges to (and between) working class immigrant and white communities, Addams's class biases and unconscious white supremacy became a veil that concealed the realities of Black Chicago from her sociological gaze. While she was an advocate for civil rights and an early member of the NAACP, the color-line nonetheless shaped Addams's work, her vision, and her interaction with Chicago's neighborhoods (see Schultz, Chapter 7, this volume).

2   *The Spirit of Youth*: Against the Culture Industry

On the one hand, *The Spirit of Youth* depicts itself as a celebration of the possibilities of youth and the newly emerging Twentieth Century urban youth culture. On the other, Addams insistently attacks popular culture, or, more specifically, commercialized youth culture. Thus, the text simultaneously celebrates an idealized youth, and yet dismisses the form their culture actually takes. However, Addams's critique is not aimed at youth themselves, but at the purveyors of commercialized decadence. In this sense, Addams presents the early architecture of the "culture industry" argument (Adorno and Horkheimer, 2007).

> Quite as one set of men has organized the young people into industrial enterprises in order to profit from their toil, so another set of men and also of women, I am sorry to say, have entered the neglected field of recreation and have organized enterprises which make profit out of this invincible love of pleasure.
>
> ADDAMS, 1972 [1909]: 6

Urban youth are victims of a kind of cultural exploitation. At work they experience the exploitation of the industrial process; and then, with their wages, they willingly expose themselves to emotional exploitation by the culture industry.

What Addams says of the so-called "factory girls" applies equally to their male counter-parts.

> Apparently the modern city sees in these girls only two possibilities, both of them commercial: first, a chance to utilize by day their new and tender labor power in its factories and shops, and then another chance in the evening to extract from them their petty wages by pandering to their love of pleasure.
>
> 1972 [1909]: 8

At least three factors make this urban culture industry possible: First, the industrial revolution creates unparalleled independence for working class youth. "Never before in civilization have such numbers of young girls been suddenly released from the protection of the home... Never before have such numbers of young boys earned money independently of family life, and felt themselves free to spend it..." (Addams, 1972 [1909]: 5) Second, these working class youth are immigrants, second generation children of immigrants, and migrants from rural America, cut off from traditional cultural practices, and the culture industry fills that void. Third, the abiding, instinctual, and erotic love for pleasure dominates the youthful mind. Traditional culture sublimates those sexual energies; art sublimates those sexual energies. But the dance hall, the gin palace, and the nickelodeon, pander to the sensuous and stimulate dangerous instincts.

Thus, as her book critiques the culture industry, Addams posits two idealized points of comparison that highlight the degrading conditions created by that industry: folk-culture and high (as opposed to both folk and commercial) art. As with Smith, according to Addams folk culture forms an important link with the past. But folk culture also becomes the mirror of a degraded urban present.

> The public dance halls filled with frivolous and irresponsible young people in a feverish search for pleasure, are but a sorry substitute for the old dances on the village green in which all of the older people of the village participated.
>
> 1972 [1909]: 13

Despite her admiration of folk forms, Addams also recognizes that such forms no longer meet the needs of industrial, urban society. But neither, she argues, are working class youth in a position to create new cultural forms to fill new cultural needs. "We cannot expect the young people themselves to cling to conventions which are totally unsuited to modern city conditions, nor yet to be equal to the task of forming new conventions through which this more agglomerate social life may express itself" (Addams, 1972 [1909]: 15).

An idealized culture of the "higher imagination" (19) represents the other point from which Addams surveys the degradations of popular culture. This idealization comes across most clearly in Addams's attack upon "street music."

> We are informed by high authority that there is nothing in the environ-ment to which youth so keenly responds as to music, and yet the streets, the vaudeville shows, the five-cent theatres are full of the most blatant and vulgar songs. ...The street music has quite broken away from all con-trols, both of the educator and the patriot, and we have grown singularly careless in regard to its influence upon young people... we constantly permit music on the street to incite that which should be controlled, to degrade that which should be exalted, to make sensuous that which might be lifted into the realm of the higher imagination.
>
> ADDAMS, 1972 [1909]: 18–19

Popular cultural practices "debase existing forms of art" (18) by turning young people toward the vulgar and sensuous. On the other hand, high art lifts the subject into the imagination, and she is thereby freed from sensuous reality, and thus, capable of self-control. Further, the fact that contemporary culture has "broken away from all controls, both of the educator and the patriot," sug-gests an educational mission is implied by this opposition between high art and debased forms of culture. If the city itself sees in young people only op-portunities for commercial exploitation, it is the task of the educator, and the Hull-House resident, to help create the necessary—, but non-commercial—common culture that will unite this newly "agglomerate" and polyglot working class without degrading them. Finally, it is important to note that in building this common culture, Addams reserves a special place for music as the cultural practice "to which youth... keenly respond."

Since *The Spirit of Youth* appeared well after Smith had begun composing the material that would become *Hull House Songs*, it seems likely that Addams imagines Smith's work as the kind that lifts the listener into the "realm of the higher imagination." But before exploring this realm, let me return to one of the unexamined concepts encountered above: "this invincible love of plea-sure." If the function of appropriate cultural practice is to induce the "control" that debased forms of art find anathema, what precisely, is being controlled?

In *The Spirit of Youth* working class young people are not agents. They are victims of the industrial process. They are victims of the purveyors of com-mercial culture. And, importantly, they are victims, in part, because they are automatons controlled by unguided sexuality. The "fundamental susceptibility of which we are all slow to speak" represents an equally fundamental danger to social solidarity (Addams, 1972 [1909]: 25). This "emotional force which seizes" youth, "when it does not find the traditional line of domesticity, serves as a cancer in the very tissues of society and as a disrupter of the securest social bonds" (15). Unguided youthful sexuality destroys normative bonds and disrupts the smooth functioning of the social system. Thus, for the sake of the youth, as for society as a whole, sex must be controlled.

Addams celebrates the "spirit of youth" because it opens the world to new possibilities. But in the promise of this spirit, she finds danger. Because for the young person the world is new, and the senses are open, she/he is particularly liable to become a plaything for "the newly awakened susceptibility of sex" (26). Addams continues:

> ...this instinct ruthlessly seized the youth at the moment when he was least prepared to cope with it; not only because his powers of self-control and discrimination are unequal to the task, but because his [sic] senses are helplessly wide open to the world.
>
> 26

By way of contrast, Addams returns again to folk culture. In the traditional village, this youthful sensuousness is carefully channeled into traditional lines of domesticity, as with Addams's imagined village dance.

> Chaperonage was not then a social duty but natural and inevitable, and the whole courtship period was guarded by the conventions and restraint which were taken as a matter of course and had developed through years of publicity and simple propriety.
>
> 13

But in the modern city, these traditional lines of simple propriety are largely unavailable. Supplanting traditional practices, the culture industry profits by "over-stimulating" the senses of an already overly sensual subject.

> The newly awakened senses are appealed to by all that is gaudy and sensual, by the flippant street music, the highly colored theater posters, the trashy love stories, the feathered hats, the cheap heroics of the revolvers displayed in the pawn-shop windows. This fundamental susceptibility is thus evoked without a corresponding stir of the higher imagination, and the result is as dangerous as possible.... *the senses become sodden and cannot be lifted from the ground.*
>
> ADDAMS, 1972 [1909]: 27; emphasis added

Thus the spirit of youth, as an open and sensuous approach to the world, becomes the danger of sensuousness, and, in particular, senses so sodden by stimulation they cannot again be lifted to higher imagination. The subject is fused to her desires and the immediacy of her environment. Here, education must step in as mediator and Addams proposes a "top-down" aesthetic theory. In place of a sodden aesthetics that panders to sensuality, Addams argues for the necessary sublimation of "this fundamental instinct through the [higher] imagination" (29). To gain control of dangerous sexual impulses, the educator needs to "substitute the love of beauty for mere desire, to place the mind above the senses" (30).

Against the "dumb and powerful" sex impulses, the mind achieves elevation over the senses through erotic diffusion.

> Every high school boy and girl... will declare one of their compan- ions to be "in love" if his fancy is occupied by the image of a single person about whom all the newly founded values gather, and without whom his solitude is an eternal melancholy. But if the stimulus does not appear in a definite image, and the values evoked are dispensed over the world, the young person suddenly seems to have discovered a beauty and significance in many things—he responds to poetry, he becomes a lover of nature, he is filled with religious devotion or with philanthropic zeal. Experience, with young people, easily illustrates the possibility and value of diffusion.
>
> ADDAMS, 1972 [1909]: 29–30

By eroticizing the world, art frees the young person from imprisonment within the boundaries of sensuality. When "in love," for instance, the definite image of the beloved pins the subject to experience and to sensuality. All "newly found- ed values" gather about this image of the beloved, and without it, the subject plunges into melancholy. In like fashion, the "flippant street music" and col- ored theater posters propel the self ever toward a sensuality that becomes sodden and disruptive. It reduces the self to a "degenerate" subject, "over- mastered and born down" by enslavement to brute experience (28). Against this fusion to the sensuous, the aesthetic impulse scatters erotic force by cov- ering the world in a web of the beautiful and the sublime. Through the diffu- sion of sexuality, Addams hopes to defuse sexuality. The mastery of the sexual impulse ensures "freedom for the young people made safe only through their own self-control" (45). Thus, if dumb sexuality produces servitude, the "higher imagination" gives voice to a free self, master of her senses and her sexuality.

Here we encounter the first political function of art that Addams posits: While commercial culture debases the subject and fuses her to experience, authentic, high art diffuses erotic impulses, and so defuses the dangers of sexuality. In short, high art functions as a form of social control by potentially enabling the subject to control, repress, and sublimate her own dangerous sexual desires. Further, by guiding sexuality and enabling self-control, (proper, mediated) aesthetic experience also helps ensure the security of normative social bonds. But this first proposition on the function of high art does not fully account for *Hull House Songs*. Smith's songs certainly aspire to the kind of style found in songs by Schubert, Mahler, and Beethoven (see Cassano and Payette, this volume). It is also possible that the audience experienced the songs through a kind of diffusion that raised them above immediate experience of the sensuous world. Thus, to a degree, the songs may conform to Addams's theoretical proposition. But they also exceed the limits of that proposition. After all, both Addams and Smith argue that *Hull House Songs* have unique political content, and that lived experience is integral to their aesthetic impact.

Indeed, in her preface to the songs, Addams suggests that their political content is fundamentally important to their artistic meaning. First she introduces the songs as "giving expression to the type of emotional experience which quickly tends to get beyond words" and as "affording an escape from the unnecessary disorder of natural life into the wider region of the spirit" (Addams, 1915: 2) And, yet, while presumably any art would provide such an escape, Addams simultaneously emphasizes the importance of *this* folio's counter-hegemonic political content. "Because old fashioned songs... chiefly expressed the essentially individualistic emotions of love, hope or melancholy, it is perhaps all the more imperative that socialized emotions should also find musical expression, if the manifold movement of our contemporaries, are to have the inspiration and solace they so obviously need" (Addams, 1915: 2). Here we begin to see a tension in Addams aesthetic theory, between the romantic idealization of art as "higher imagination" and the modernist conviction that art should be a critical, political force. The higher imagination lifts the subject above the senses, "giving expression" to the highly individualized "emotional experience which quickly tends to get beyond words." Rather than aiming only at wordless experience, however, *Hull House Songs* seeks to give expression to the "socialized emotions," through music, words, and the accompanying conversation that produces intersubjective solidarity.

The theory of erotic diffusion represents only one aspect of Addams's aesthetic approach. Art may elevate the audience, but it also has far more prosaic functions. In particular, it helps establish social codes and cultural mores.

While *The Spirit of Youth* presents culturally normative art as a scene of instruction, and insists upon the necessity of the educator in the cultivation of working class tastes, Addams also recognizes the stirrings of a new culture, from the ground up. "Thousands of young people in every great city are either frankly hedonistic or are vainly attempting to work out for themselves a satisfactory code of morals" (1972 [1909]: 159). Without the tutelage of reformers and settlement house workers, "young people themselves are working out a protective code" (45–46). The theater and the early five-cent film play a special role in this new working class "code of morals." Theater allows workers to make sense of their fragmented lives and the otherwise bewildering experience of the city. It offers them narrative schemas and imaginary templates through which they can judge their own experiences. After describing a series of these narratives, Addams asks: "Is it not astounding that a city allows thousands of its youth to fill their impressionable minds with these absurdities *which certainly will become the foundation for their working moral codes and the data from which they will judge the proprieties of life?*" (1972 [1909]: 79–80; emphasis added).

Thus, Addams reveals another political function of aesthetics in social life: Drama and music teach workers moral and emotional boundaries, and produce "working moral code[s]" that interpret the bewildering urban data that constitutes the subject's experience. In the modern city, since "the only art which is constantly placed before [their] eyes... is a debased form of dramatic art, and a vulgar type of music..." (1972 [1909]: 87–88), the moral codes that emerge are necessarily "debased" and "vulgar." Culture provides templates for understanding the world. Popular culture provides precisely such templates, and those templates emerge from song narratives, five-cent plays, and movie scripts.

For many of the working class youth Addams knew, the five-cent theater, in particular, provided a new collective mythology that bound them together in a common culture. This culture was established and elaborated through the interactions and discussions inspired by the play or the moving picture.

> Hundreds of young people attend these five-cent theaters every evening in the week, including Sunday, and what is seen and heard there becomes the sole topic of conversation, forming the ground pattern of their social life. That mutual understanding which in another social circle is provided by books, travel and all the arts, is here compressed into the topics suggested by the play.
>
> ADDAMS, 1972 [1909]: 86

Conversation, inspired by "topics suggested by the play," produces the "ground pattern" of social life and "mutual understanding." Consider the "more agglomerate social life" (15) Addams encountered in early twentieth century Chicago: immigrants, the children of immigrants, native born workers, migrants from the country, all with different cultural conventions and points of reference. Popular culture provided the narratives that allowed these diverse groups common material for interaction, and through conversation, solidarity emerged. This theory of the function of art stands in stark contrast with Addams's original notion that art raises the subject above the senses. In this context, art anchors the self to the social world by intertwining self and other, through word and gesture.

The Spirit of Youth and the City Streets thus posits several propositions concerning the political functions of art. First, Addams suggests that the function of art is to channel dangerous erotic impulses by elevating the aestheticized subject above the senses. Addams never fully defines this realm of "higher imagination," other than to suggest it diffuses the sexual impulse by eroticizing reality itself. Further, Addams argues that working class youth waste their aesthetic impulses upon commercial entertainments, and that it is the task of the educator and the settlement house worker to train working class youth in the appreciation of high art.

If Addams first statements on art might account for the style of *Hull House Songs* as music, and as poetry, but not its political contents, its particular function as *political art*, her remarks about the importance of the five-cent theater for youth culture open the path to understanding this function of the work. While Addams bemoans the fact that in the emerging twentieth century working class culture, films and plays become the "sole topic[s] of conversation," and form the "ground pattern of [working class] social life," she simultaneously acknowledges the importance of this aesthetic function. Artistic experience becomes the occasion for conversation and "mutual understanding." These conversations produce solidarity, group mores, and engender further interactions. As myth, ritual, and formal religion once provided the cultural patterns that enabled interaction, in early twentieth century Chicago, the nickelodeon supplants the cathedral and the synagogue. Thus, Addams posits art as a basis for social solidarity. But with this argument, the educator no longer seems so central. Young people begin to create solidarities on their own, using commercial art as their common ground. When popular art becomes an occasion for culture building, the working class becomes the agent of that transformation. That agency, however, remains conditioned by the purveyors of commercialized vice, and dependent upon an imagination so sodden that it cannot be lifted from the ground. For Addams, then, the agency of these youthful bearers of mass culture is an illusion.

3   *The Long Road of Woman's Memory*: The Devil Baby

In *The Long Road of Women's Memory* (1916), Addams more fully interrogates this function of art as the production of mutual understanding and solidarity through conversation. *The Long Road* appeared just after the publication of *Hull House Songs*, and like the songbook, it serves as a moment of reflection upon the past. In addition, Addams makes clear in the introduction that this volume, primarily focused upon older working class women, is a kind of companion volume to *The Spirit of Youth* (Addams, 1916: x). Yet there are important differences between the two books. While *The Spirit of Youth* focused upon the necessity of training and teaching workers, *The Long Road* has few scenes of top-down instruction. Instead, the later book is most obviously about what Addams *learns* from working class women. This is Addams at her most personal. Gone is the sometimes scolding tone of works like *The Spirit of Youth* and *A New Conscience and an Ancient Evil* (1912a). In its place is a sense of learning from workers' lives, their bodies, and their memories.

Addams situates her inquiry at the boundary of philosophy and social scientific research. She begins by noting in her conversations with older women a certain tendency to the "transmutation of their [past] experiences" through "a power inherent in memory itself" (Addams, 1916: ix). Memory orients life, but memory is inherently unreliable. It colors the past, romanticizes, and thus makes life tolerable even for those who live in perpetual poverty and misery. Further, Addams argues that this power of memory is a kind of aesthetic power: "...it was the Muses again at their old tricks,—the very mother of them this time—thrusting their ghostly fingers into the delicate fabricate of human experience to the extreme end of life" (1916: x). Memory, as the mother of all art, has the aesthetic capacity to transmute past experience to meet present needs. While Addams's sample for this power is largely taken from those in their later years, when she calls it a power inherent in memory itself, she suggests this human process takes place throughout the life-course, from youth, until the end of life. This idea, that memory changes depending upon the present needs of the organism, sounds much like the pragmatic theory of memory elaborated by William James (1987). Indeed, Addams situates her own text in this pragmatic philosophical tradition when she writes, "while I may receive valuable suggestions from classic literature, when I really want to learn about life, I must depend upon my neighbors, for, as William James insists, the most instructive human documents lie along the beaten path" (Addams, 1916: xi).

Her invocation of James also makes it clear that Addams's explorations are more than simply empirical investigations. They are empirical investigations structured by a sociological theory. As Addams puts it:

> To my amazement, their reminiscences revealed an additional function of
> memory, so aggressive and withal so modern, that it was quite impossible,
> living as I was in a Settlement with sociological tendencies, to ignore it.
>
> ADDAMS, 1916: xi.

Thus, Addams offers a theoretical exploration of the selective and constructive powers of memory, based upon William James' pragmatism, intermingled
with her own "sociological tendencies." While Addams finds that memory has
a tendency to soften "the harsh realities of the past," that same force "exercises a vital power of selection which often necessitates an onset against the
very traditions and conventions commonly believed to find their stronghold
in the minds of elderly people" (1916: xi–xii). The elderly are presumed to be
more traditional in their mores and outlook, but contemporary necessity
sometimes challenges those traditional beliefs. And when traditions begin to
crumble in the face of a new moral schema, the elderly do not abandon their
previous values and their history. Rather, they re-imagine them, or re-orient
their interpretations of the past. According to Addams's evidence, present social necessity constantly remakes the past world, and thus opens the way for
modern challenges to outmoded and ill-adapted traditions of domination and
solidarity.

This transmutation of memory takes place in social contexts, through social
interaction, and especially through conversation. Addams goes much further
with her next proposition, that

> *mutual reminiscences perform a valuable function in determining anal-*
> *ogous conduct for large bodies of people who have no other basis for*
> *like-mindedness.*
>
> 1916: xiii; emphasis added

In other words, the discussion of shared memory, like the discussion of art,
can build bonds of solidarity. Memory transmutes the past. But this transmutation is a collective, shared process, and the product is like-minded mutual
understanding. Only through collectively shared memories, narratives, experiences, can social movements find the basis for collective social transformation.
Memory, the mother of the Muses, reimagines the past in order to create real
social bonds in the ever-recurrent disappearing present.

The Long Road is about memory, but it also about art. What unites the two,
in this context, is narrative. Not all art contains narrative, but nor does every
memory. Instead, memory, like art, inspires narratives built by conversation
(with oneself, with others). Narratives, even fictional narratives, bring the self
into the world of others and potentially produce wider solidarities. Addams

develops this proposition through a story about a story that reveals these fundamental functions of art, myth, and memory: the Hull-House "Devil Baby."

The Hull-House Devil Baby was, perhaps, the first documented urban myth of the twentieth century. Addams uses the story to illustrate the collective social power of narrative—about art, about myth,—to provide the raw material for community formation. She recalls, "for six weeks from every part of the city and suburbs the stream of visitors to this mythical baby poured in…" (1916: 3). Different ethnic communities produced different variations of the story, but the basic outline remained relatively stable:

> The Italian version, with a hundred variations, dealt with a pious Italian girl married to an atheist. Her husband in a rage had torn a holy picture from the bed-room wall saying that he would quite as soon have a devil in the house as such a thing, whereupon the devil incarnated himself in her coming child. As soon as the Devil Baby was born, he ran about the table shaking his finger in deep reproach at his father, who finally caught him and, in fear and trembling, brought him to Hull-House.
>
> ADDAMS, 1916: 3

In form and effect, the story of the Devil Baby is quite like the narratives at the nickelodeon. Themes of sexuality, religion, modernity versus tradition, paternal responsibility and maternal agency; these were working class concerns also dramatized in the five-cent theater. For the young audience, these fictions became the raw material for culture building. For older, traditional women, through conversations about the Devil Baby social memories were awakened and transformed.

While Addams seems mildly amused by the chaos of the Devil Baby days at Hull House, she does not pass the kind of withering judgment upon the story that she passes upon the plays of the nickelodeon. In fact, she takes the myth as evidence of the continuing power of old world peasant traditions.

> …the story constantly demonstrated the power of an old wives tale among thousands of men and women in modern society who are living in a corner of their own, their vision fixed, their intelligence held by some iron chain of solid habit. To such primitive people the metaphor is still the very "stuff of life," or rather no other form of statement reaches them; the tremendous tonnage of current writing for them has no existence.
>
> 1916: 4–5

Perhaps it is precisely the fact that Addams sees these "primitive" women as chained to solid habit that allows her to shed her role as instructor. These women will hear no lessons. More than that, the Devil Baby confirms their traditional principles, fears, and expectations. That mythological confirmation becomes a resource for agency. Addams describes them as "all alive and eager; something in the story or in its mysterious sequences had aroused one of those active forces in human nature which does not take orders, but insists only upon giving them. *We had abruptly come into contact with a living and self-assertive quality*" (1916: 7; emphasis added). The Devil Baby story endowed these traditional women with agency, or, more correctly, with an insistence that their voices mattered. Consequently, Addams steps back from her vocation as teacher, and instead, listens to these active, assertive, traditional women.

> During the weeks of excitement it was the old women who really seemed to have come into their own, and perhaps the most significant result of the incident was the reaction of the story upon them. It stirred their minds and memories as with a magic touch, it loosened their tongues and revealed the inner life and thoughts of those who are so often inarticulate.
> 1916: 8

The direct effect of the Devil Baby story was to loosen the tongues of the older women who arrived at Hull House searching for the story's truth. Mythology, like art, breaks through the shell of isolation and, at least potentially, leads the self toward others with whom she can share her stories, her memories, and her hopes. Addams postulates that the Devil Baby myth had this impact upon traditional immigrant women because it made sense of their traumatic experience. In a modern urban environment that challenged their traditional values, the Devil Baby story promised a moral universe that still made sense (again something this urban myth had in common with the early nickelodeon).

> In the midst of their double bewilderment, both that the younger generation was walking in such strange paths and that no one would listen to them, for one moment there flickered up the last hope of a disappointed life, that it may at least serve as a warning, while affording material for an exciting narrative.
> 1916: 22

The Devil Baby was a morality tale for the amoral modern city. Perhaps more important, however, was the fact that *the story gave these women a voice.* Silenced by age, displaced by a younger generation that no longer holds traditional values, and seemingly irrelevant, these older women are forgotten by their community. The story of the Devil Baby "put into their hands the sort of material with which they were accustomed to deal" (1916: 8). And by re-telling the Devil Baby narrative, they find authority and agency. "That the old women who came to visit the Devil Baby believed that the story would secure them a hearing at home was evident..." (1916: 22).

This power of narrative, to pull the self out of herself and bring her into community, appears most clearly in the sad story of bedridden old woman who "refused to believe that there was no Devil Baby at Hull-House, unless 'herself'[Addams] told her so" (1916: 15–16). For several pages, Addams struggles with her own conscience. She understands the importance of the myth for her old friend, but hesitates to tell an outright lie.

> But the story of a Devil Baby, with his existence officially corroborated as it were, would give her a lodestone which would attract the neighbors far and wide and exalt her once more into the social importance she had had twenty-four years before when I had first known her.
>
> 1916: 17

Addams brings out the power of myth with full force in this passage. The story of the Devil Baby would be a "lodestone," would restore the old woman's social importance, would bring her back into society and banish her lonely isolation. As she nears her friend's home, Addams asks herself again, "why not give her this vivid interest and through it awake those earliest recollections of that long accumulated folk-lore with its magic power to transfigure and eclipse the sordid and unsatisfactory surroundings in which life is actually spent?" (18). Addams never actually makes a decision regarding this dilemma. Instead, she writes, "my hesitation was enough" to shatter the old woman's hope (1916: 20).

Art, myth, and narrative bring the self out, and into contact with others, and the world. When the old woman lost hold of the myth, she was "violently thrown back into all the limitations of her personal experience and surroundings, and that larger life she had anticipated so eagerly was as suddenly shut away from her as if a door had been slammed in her face" (1916: 20–21).

4   Hysteria/Solidarity

The Spirit of Youth and *The Long Road of Woman's Memory* not only provide alternative theories of the political function of art. They provide alternative perspectives on working class cultural forms built from the ground up. In terms of its political function, *The Spirit of Youth* considers political art primarily as "high art" that uplifts the audience, frees them from fusion to immediate sensuous desires, and so instills a degree of social control and individual agency. Ideally, art functions as an integrative force, reinforcing social cooperation and mediating normative interactions. But, Addams argues, popular, commercialized art has a disrupting impact upon normative social bonds, and threatens the smooth integration of the social order. Thus, a top down aesthetics emerges from the text. Working class aesthetic tastes and cultural formations need education by settlement house workers, school officials, and middle class reformers. Further, to the degree that working class youth build a culture, from the ground up, so to speak, their reliance upon popular and commercialized forms and tropes hopelessly contaminate that attempt. The result is a corrupt and corrupting youth culture of licentiousness that fuses young workers to their senses and thereby disables agency.

On the other hand, in *The Long Road*, Addams idealizes the impact of the Devil Baby myth upon traditional women. While the tropes that constitute the Devil Baby story could have been lifted from a nickelodeon moving picture, Addams recognizes that the story, and its truth content, is less important than the impact it has upon the women she knows. It brings them out of themselves, restores some of their cultural status, gives them an irrepressible sense of agency. This function of art hardly appears in *The Spirit of Youth*. The Devil Baby creates bonds of community by inspiring conversation. Working class cultural narratives, even trite myths like the Devil Baby, can be mobilized by social actors as material for engaging with others and for understanding social reality. As in *The Spirit of Youth*, popular art re-enforces "primitive" moral codes and superstitious, but it also gives marginalized women power.

Addams remains blind to the possibility that commercialized art forms like music and early cinema could provide that same resource for working class youth. On the one hand, Addams bourgeois cultural tastes, her prior training, and her aesthetic prejudices would perhaps deafen her to the power of proto jazz as it was gestating in early twentieth century Chicago. And for similar reasons, she may not have been able to see the artistry in early cinema (although, truthfully, in 1909 cinema had more charm than artistry). These questions of education and attitude aside, Addams had theoretical reasons for rejecting the music of the streets and the shadow plays in the nickelodeons. Because they emerged from the commercial motive, with only the intention of selling as many tickets as possible, Addams argues that they necessarily appeal to the most base and sensual aspects of the audience.

Indeed, Addams goes further. City life is bewildering for the new immigrant, for the rural migrant, for the young person, for the worker, even for the upright bourgeois citizen. Culture and institutions need to counter that bewilderment by creating a sense of unity, solidarity, and purpose. Commercial art, however, contributes to disintegration by fusing the self with her desires. The result is "moral breakdown." In this sense, commercial art (morally) sickens its audience.

This contrast between healthy solidarity and the sickness induced by commercialized culture parallels two representations Addams offers of the life of working women: one set of women, in *A New Conscience and An Ancient Evil*, show tendencies to moral and emotional breakdown; the other set, in *The Long Road*, find the resources to resist that breakdown.

A New Conscience and An Ancient Evil represents Addams's assault on prostitution and "commercialized vice" (1912a: 97). At the same time, the book offers more general reflections on the political economy of women's labor in the early twentieth century. Because commercialized vice (sex work, drug use) finds shelter among the vulgar entertainments of the youth, *A New Conscience* also continues Addams's critique of popular culture and serves as a companion to *The Spirit of Youth*. Commercialized vice is the necessary double of commercial culture. Like the earlier text, *A New Conscience* sets modern urban problems in relief by comparing the city to an idealized traditional culture. Since commercialized vice requires the commodification of young women, it is one consequence of the breakdown of traditional culture, and, Addams argues, one necessary result of women entering the waged workforce.

As in *The Spirit of Youth*, Addams ascribes a lack of agency to the working class as a whole, and to young working class women in particular. Young working class women and men lack self-control, and no adequate social control exists. Thus, when women enter the workforce, their economic freedom becomes dangerous. Women working in cafes, dance halls, and department stores, not only sell their wares, they sell themselves. Appearance, comportment, and even flirtation, are requirements of the job. For instance, in the case of a restaurant worker, "a certain amount of familiarity must be borne lest their resentment should diminish the patronage of the café" (Addams, 1912a: 69). Service work turns women themselves into the commodities on display.

Addams holds special scorn for the social environment of the department store. "It is perhaps in the department store more than anywhere else that every possible weakness in a girl is detected and traded upon" (Ibid: 64). The particular danger of the department store comes from the fact that it presents the wealth of the city to a girl too poor to afford its bounty.

> The department store has brought together, as has never been done before in history, a bewildering mass of delicate and beautiful fabrics, jewelry and household decorations such as women covet, gathered skillfully from all parts of the world, and in the midst of this bulk of desirable

> possessions is placed an untrained girl with careful instructions as to her
> conduct for making sales, but with no guidance in regard to herself.
>
> 1912a: 65

Bewildered by commodities she covets, but "without adequate clothing" (66),
nor sufficient training in self-control, the "shop girl" is a weak vessel, easy
prey for devising men and deceitful women. Service work leads women to
unsavory companions and unhealthy entertainments and so leads to moral
breakdown.

While Addams fears for the fates of shop clerks and waitresses, she is somewhat more sanguine with regard to factory girls.

> All girls who work down town are at a disadvantage as compared to fac-
> tory girls, who are much less open to direct inducement and to the temp-
> tations which come through sheer imitation. Factory girls also have the
> protection of working among plain people who frankly designate an ir-
> regular life in harsh, old-fashioned terms.
>
> 1912a: 71

Both because of the nature of the work itself (it does not require "a certain
amount of [emotional] familiarity" to run a machine), and because of the
stricter standards of old world working class communities, "factory girls" have
a certain degree of protection from commercialized vice. Even here, however,
in her relative approbation of factory work, Addams finds disabling dangers
confronting working women.

> Yet in spite of all this corrective knowledge, the increasing nervous en-
> ergy to which industrial processes daily accommodate themselves, and
> the speeding up constantly required of the operators, may at any mo-
> ment so register their results upon the nervous system of a factory girl as
> to overcome her powers of resistance.
>
> 72

As a result of capitalist production techniques, and especially the ever-present
"speed-up," a woman worker may become "overwrought," her "mental balance" plainly disturbed (73). Factory work potentially causes nervous breakdown and hysteria. "The study of industrial diseases has only this year begun
by the federal authorities, and doubtless as more is known of the nervous and
mental effects of over-fatigue, many moral breakdowns will be traced to this
source" (73). By definition, the hysterical, exhausted woman lacks agency. She
becomes easy prey for suggestion and loses herself.

It is already easy to make the connection in definite cases: "I was too tired to care," "I was too tired to know what I was doing," "I was dead tired and sick of it all," "I was dog tired and just went with him," are phrases taken from the lips of reckless girls who are endeavoring to explain the situation in which they find themselves.

> 73–74

Nor does Addams confine her discussion of the pathogenic impact of factory labor to women workers. Men, too, experience conditions of factory work as bewildering, resulting a nervous strain, and "moral breakdown." In *The Spirit of Youth*, she describes the experience of young male factory workers:

The modern factory calls for an expenditure of nervous energy almost more than it demands muscular effort, or at least machinery so far performs the work of the massive muscles, that greater stress is laid upon the fine and exact movements necessarily involving nervous strain... The demands made upon his eyes are complicated and trivial, the use of his muscles is fussy and monotonous, the relation between cause and effect is remote and obscure.

> ADDAMS, 1972 [1909]: 108–109

These pathogenic work conditions have a necessary consequence. Young factory workers "are driven into all sorts of expedients in order to escape work which has been made impossible because all human interest has been extracted from it" (Addams, 1972 [1909]: 129). In order to escape the emotional and physical strain produced by working conditions, young men turn to commercialized culture and commercialized vice. Thus Addams is able to "trace the connection between the [pathogenic] monotony and dullness of factory work and the petty immoralities which are often the youth's protest against them" (1972 [1909]:107). Precisely because factory work denies the body and the intellect, workers rebel by immersing themselves in the sensuous escapes of commercialized vice, whether that vice be in the dance hall, the nickelodeon, or the brothel. Capitalism induces moral breakdown as a necessary by-product of the commodity.

For all workers, then, factory labor has an incapacitating impact upon their bodies and their minds. This leads to their pursuit of illusory freedom through the pleasures of popular culture. In addition, women service workers, bewildered by the enchantments of commodified society, experience another sort of hysterical fascination that leads to damaging desires, unsavory companions, and liability to suggestion. Whether factory worker or department store clerk, however, capitalist labor conditions, and the commercial culture that capitalism produces, sickens workers and disables agency.

Now consider Addams's radically different depiction of "factory girls" in *The Long Road*. *The Spirit of Youth* and *A New Conscience* bemoan the loss of traditional forms of social control, and argue that young girls' freedom from family restraint and opinion imperil them. Yet this same freedom from familial control enables garment workers to strike in *The Long Road*.

> During the long strike these young women endured all sorts of privations without flinching; some of them actual hunger, most of them disapprobation from their families, and all of them a loss of that money which alone could procure for them the American standards so highly prized.
>
> 1916: 96

Despite the disapproval of their families, these young women resist. And, in striking, they demonstrate the new zones of freedom available to modern women. Addams does not attempt to hide her admiration for the strikers. She recognizes that it is their new social and economic freedom from familial domination that makes this social movement possible. And she sees a stark difference between these modern factory girls and their traditional families. Their mothers, Addams argues, might find sustenance in domestic responsibilities and child-care.

> But such girls as the strikers represent are steadily bending their energies to loveless and mechanical labor, and are obliged to go on without this direct and personal renewal of their powers of resistance. They must be sustained as soldiers on a forced march are sustained, by their sense of comradeship in high endeavor.
>
> 1916: 97

These young women have "tasted... freedom from economic dependence," discovered solidarity, and have "equipped themselves with a new set of motives." They are not the potentially hysterical factory workers who inhabit *A New Conscience*. They are not the helplessly sensuous young people debased by popular culture who populate the pages of *The Spirit of Youth*. Politically active agents, shaped by machine production, buoyed by solidarity, these working class women were "mark[ing] out a cultural terrain distinct from familial traditions and the customary practices of their ethnic groups" (Peiss, 1986: 47).

While Addams never denigrates traditional mothers, she argues that "the very power of resistance in such a socialized undertaking as a strike, presents a marked contrast in both its origin and motives to the traditional type of endurance exercised by the mothers and grandmothers of the strikers" (Addams, 1916:

96–97). During the strike, "some of the young women involved were sitting in the very chairs occupied so recently by the visitors to the Devil Baby" (1916: 96).

> My conversations with these girls of modern industry continually filled me with surprise that, required as they are to work under conditions unlike those which women have ever before encountered, they have not only made a remarkable adaptation but have so ably equipped themselves with a new set of motives.
>
> 98

This "new set of motives" emerged from new solidarities of work and struggle that crossed traditional divisions of gender, race, and nationality.

> Organizing with men and women of divers [sic] nationalities they are obliged to form new ties absolutely unlike family bonds. On the other hand, these girls possess the enormous advantage over women of the domestic type of having experienced the discipline arising from impersonal obligations and of having tasted the freedom from economic dependence, so valuable that too heavy a price can scarcely be paid for it.
>
> 100

There is a necessary distance between this new proletarian culture and traditional cultures that emphasize family bonds and obligations. In particular, this new culture arises among free women, economically independent, an economic independence "so valuable that too heavy a price can scarcely be paid for it." Here Addams argues that this economically independent working woman is a distinctively modern type, adapted to the rigors of the urban, capitalist environment. She goes even further, arguing that despite the fact they work "under conditions unlike those which women have ever before encountered," they have adapted to those conditions well enough to resist their exploitation.

While *A New Conscience* depicts in women factory workers a tendency to hysteria and moral breakdown, *The Long Road* answers with counter-point:

> Even the re-strained Greeks believed that when the obscure women at the bottom of society could endure no longer and "the oppressed women struck back, it would not be justice which came but the revenge of madness." My own observation has discovered little suggesting this mood, certainly not among the women active in the Labor Movement.
>
> ADDAMS, 1916: 101

Throughout *The Spirit of Youth* and *A New Conscience*, workers appear as either, isolated and lonely, or, surrounded by unsavory companions. But in *The Long Road* Addams sees working women struggling for their rights, and building mutual solidarity. This mutually supportive working class culture protects women from the deleterious effects of machine production. As with the story of the Devil Baby, Addams returns to the idea that solidarity pulls women from their isolation, opens doors. By depicting this development among working class women, their agency and autonomy come into focus. Solidarity prevents madness.

Jane Addams's nephew, James Weber Linn, tells a story that illustrates the complexity of her responses to working class cultural development. In doing so, he also provides some historical context for the garment workers' strike described in *The Long Road*:

> One of the most dramatic and yet Addams-like accomplishments of the year was her intervention in the garment-workers' strike. On September 29th [1909] a sixteen-year-old girl, a "seamer," walked out of one of the shops...because five weeks before her foreman had ordered her pay reduced a quarter of a cent per garment. She did not think of herself as a "striker," or even know there was a garment-workers' union. But nineteen other girls followed her out; the news spread; and within three weeks almost every garment-worker in the city was out...
>
> LINN, 1935: 240

The garment strike began with the action of a 16 year old "factory girl," one of the very girls to whom Addams assigned such a dependent, secondary position in texts like *The Spirit of Youth* and *A New Conscience*. Linn points out that while Addams mediated the strike, her social theories continued to develop. "And yet not her doing but her thinking marked those days. For it was just at this time that she was bringing out *The Spirit of Youth in the City Streets* [sic], and *Twenty Years at Hull House*" (Linn, 1935: 241). Even as she listened to workers, Addams pursued her cultural project of imposing middle class morality and aesthetic judgements upon the working class. Perhaps it is difficult to understand how Addams could watch a 16 year-old worker begin a walk-out that eventually encompassed 90,000 workers throughout Chicago, and yet that same year publish a book about the children of the working class depicting them as if they were helpless playthings of passion and peer-pressure. Part of the answer to this difficulty is, perhaps, that young people were, and are, both agents of their destiny, and victims of their social, cultural, and biological circumstances. But, of course, that is true of any social subject. In this context, we need to return to Addams's invidious aesthetic classifications. Folk culture and high art represent the ideals that demonstrate the degradations of popular culture. In another Manichean maneuver, Addams idealizes labor solidarity and culture building as the absolute other of commercialized youth culture. Labor culture restores the autonomy perpetually endangered by popular, commercial entertainments. Labor solidarity prevents both the nervous exhaustion produced by the speed-up and the moral breakdown provoked by popular culture. Yet even as she celebrates working class agency through collective resistance, Addams remains unwilling or unable to see that the cultural practices she condemns could become sources of working class solidarity, and thus contribute to the solidarity of the labor movement (Peiss, 1986: 45–51).

5   Conclusions

Jane Addams provides at least three theories of the political function of art: 1) Art lifts the [working class] audience above their senses, frees them from the immediacy of experience, and so instills a degree of self-control; 2) Art inspires conversation, mediates interaction, becomes the raw material through which bonds of solidarity are forged, and provide the schema through which social reality is interpreted; 3) commercial art degrades the self, fuses her to her senses, and disables agency. From Addams's perspective, then, *Hull House Songs* encapsulates the settlement's aesthetic mission. Composed in a challenging style, necessitating formally trained singers and musicians, and demanding an attentive audience, *Hull House Songs* represents the "high art" Addams celebrated. At the same time, the political and sociological themes of the songs attempted to inspire discussion and solidarity. At least some of the songs that constitute the folio were composed for particular occasions, with particular political intentions. So Addams recalls a "creditable chorus trained at Hull-House" singing "Land of the Noon-Day Night" at a large rally "in sympathy with the [Pennsylvania] anthracite coal strike" (1910: 377). Thus *Hull House Songs* aims at the paradoxical task of raising the audience above its senses, and, simultaneously, fusing that audience to an experience of sympathetic community *in the world*. Perhaps the songs achieve that effect. In any case, Addams would share Smith's judgment that these are "authentic" labor songs, and not the spurious productions of commercialized popular culture.

Nonetheless, this aesthetic position leaves Addams deaf to the music of the streets. It's worth returning to the passage cited above from *Twenty-Years at Hull-House*, and recalling it at length:

> Mr. William Tomlins early trained large choruses of adults as his assistants did of children... It was in connection with these first choruses that a public-spirited citizen of Chicago offered a prize for the best labor song,

> competition to be open to the entire country. The responses to the offer lit-
> erally filled three large barrels and speaking at least for myself as one of the
> bewildered judges, we were more disheartened by their quality than even
> by their overwhelming bulk. Apparently the workers of America are not yet
> ready to sing, although I recall a creditable chorus trained at Hull-House…

The competition Addams discusses was open to the entire country, but even
just in Chicago, as Addams points out in her work, there were large Irish
communities, Italian communities, Black communities, Scottish and Polish
and Russian enclaves. Demographics alone makes Addams's argument that
the "workers of America are not yet ready to sing" nearly impossible to accept at face value. Add to this the prior existence of labor songs from the mid-
Nineteenth Century, like "The Factory Girl's Song," and it becomes clear that at
least some workers were ready to sing, and ready to use song for protest and
solidarity, long before Jane Addams took up residence at Hull-House.[2] But Addams was unable to hear their songs. Or, perhaps more charitably, she did not
know how to *listen* to workers' songs. Even as she crossed cultural boundaries, there were aspects of working class cultural life that remained beyond her
competence as a participant observer.

Much of this chapter has pointed to limitations in Addams's work, her idealization of folk culture, high art, and labor culture, and her demonization of
commercialized, popular, culture. Addams's argument anticipates the work
of many anti-capitalist critiques of U.S. culture, most notably Adorno and
Horkheimer's (2007) work on the culture industry. But some labor historians
have resisted the Manichean division between popular, commercial culture
and the political culture of the labor movement. These historians argue that
since at least the 1840s, working class women and men from diverse ethnic,
regional, racial, and national boundaries had been forging bonds of community through the pursuits of popular, commercial culture. This solidarity of
the streets was separate from, but still related to, solidarity at the job. Workers
were able to resist capitalism in part because of bonds forged outside of work
(Stansell, 1987; Peiss, 1986; Rosenzwieg, 1983; Cassano, 2015). When historian
Kathy Peiss writes that, in the early Twentieth Century working class women
were "mark[ing] out a cultural terrain distinct from familial traditions and the
customary practices of their ethnic groups," she adds the important modifier,
"signifying a new identity as wage-earners through language, clothing, and
social rituals" (1986: 47). This new, empowering cultural identity contributed
to women's agency when they stood against capitalist exploitation. While

---

2 See the broadsheet from the 1830s, "The Factory Girl's Song," archived by the Smithsonian:
   http://americanhistory.si.edu/collections/search/object/nmah_1445159.

Addams understood that young working class women were marking out this cultural terrain, she could not see the connection between fashion, music, slang, and class politics. She was unable to recognize that the working class solidarity she encountered among striking workers emerged, in part, from their solidarity in leisure, sexuality, and entertainment.

Nonetheless, in this interrogation of Addams, I am in danger of seeming to suggest that *Smith's* compositions in *Hull House Songs* should be something other than what they are. All compositions are located within a tradition or a genre framework through which the compositions makes sense of the world. Smith, for her part, made no apologies about situating her work in the tradition of European classical Lieder (Cassano and Payette, this volume). Her re-interpretation of that tradition through a political lens gives her work a particular, unique, and consequential point of view. While Jane Addams's aesthetic theories may not account for the linkage between *popular* (commercial) art and political solidarity, they provide a language for understanding Smith's songs. *Hull House Songs* uses art to forge bonds of solidarity. As art, it imagines the community it hopes to create. In that sense, as with much of Jane Addams's work, Eleanor Smith's *Hull House Songs* is a signifier searching for a signified.

6   Coda: On "White Slavery," Black Culture, and Gershwin

Eleanor Smith composed the material for *Hull House Songs* when Chicago was emerging as a center of American life. Jazz was migrating up the Mississippi river, blues was migrating with country workers as they moved into factory life, and Black cultural production was remaking the city's popular music (Gioia, 2011; Kenney, 1993). Perhaps not surprisingly given her training, Smith does not acknowledge these new cultural forms, and her compositions draw almost entirely from the European tradition. Most of her compositions precede the jazz age, and she shows little interest in the syncopations of ragtime. Jane Addams, however, is interested in popular music, at least to the extent that it represents a danger to the youth. True, Addams central critique of popular music emerges from her more general distrust of the commercialized culture industry. Nonetheless, much of Chicago's early twentieth century popular music was derived from African American forms like ragtime and blues. So when Addams writes in 1909 that through "flippant street music," the "senses become sodden and cannot be lifted from the ground," it's hard not to hear an implicit attack upon African American musical forms. Indeed, Addams only specific acknowledgement of the importance of African American musical traditions comes in her praise for George Gershwin's *Porgy and Bess*, a problematic portrayal of Black culture, adapted and composed by two Americanized Jewish brothers. This reference points to a deeper contradiction in Addams's work. While Hull-House may not have been officially Jim Crow, the 'color-line' divides Jane Addams's cultural imagination, blinds her to Black cultural originality, and leads her to denigrate Black culture itself. Addams's use of language makes this imaginary color-line visible, but never more so than in her attempt to operationalize the phrase "white slavery" in *A New Conscience and An Ancient Evil*.

When Jane Addams used the term "white slavery" as a euphemism for sex work, or, in her words, prostitution, she recognized it as a problematic figure of speech. Nonetheless, she justified her use of the term on two grounds. First, currency: the term was widely used by opponents of the organized sex industry. Second, the term was based on the analogy with the great moral crusade of the 19th century, the anti-slavery abolition movement (Addams, 1912a: 3–13). For Addams, liberating young women from the sex trade was as much a civil rights crusade as the anti-slavery movement, and, as with slavery, the abolition of "white slavery" (not the regulation of prostitution as sex-*work*) had to be the goal. Throughout *A New Conscience and an Ancient Evil*, Addams thus uses "white slavery" in order to inflame her readers and spur on a moral crusade against "this twin of slavery, as old and outrageous as slavery itself and even more persistent" (4).

Yet the term also serves another racial function. *A New Conscience* tells story after story of poor and working class young women forced into the sex trade. Some of these women are native born, Anglo and Irish Americans. Some are southern Europeans, some Russian, Bohemian, and Jewish. By capturing the experience of all these women with the term "white slavery," Addams potentially had a subtle impact upon her middle class readers' racial thinking. At a time when the boundaries of whiteness were being contested, and large segments of the Anglo-American population regarded southern Italians, Jews, and Bohemians as not-white, Addams's *term* was an *argument*. If these women were captured by *white* slavery, then they were, by definition, *white*. As in so many other ways, Hull-House contributed to the whitening of the new, post-1890 immigrants through Jane Addams's use of the term "white slavery" to describe sex-work. But this whitening of the new immigrants came at the expense of the Black community. Both immigrants and Black Americans were stereotyped as having supposed cultural deficits. But when the two groups were compared, immigrants were often found to be culturally superior to Black Americans. Jane Addams played a vital role in valorizing immigrant identity, and, at the same time, valorizing white culture as superior to both immigrant and, especially, Black, culture (Roediger, 2005, Mink, 1996, Barrett, 1992, Cassano, 2015).

In her longer books, Addams seldom addressed the problems of the Black community in Chicago. However, *A New Conscience* provides an extended discussion of the causes of Black prostitution. As if catching herself, Addams does not use the word "white slavery" to describe African American sex workers. Instead, she refers to the "high percentage of colored prostitutes," or the "large number of colored girls entering the disreputable life" (1912a: 119). She never specifies the exact "high percentage" of Black women in the sex industry, but the very fact that she refers to this "high percentage" makes her use of "white slavery" all the more problematic.

Addams discusses multiple causes for prostitution in the Black community, including poverty, segregation, and racism. But the most important single cause, she argues, is a culture of poverty in the Black community caused by the legacy of slavery. Black Americans, Addams argues, have been socialized into cultural practices (especially child-rearing practices) that re-enforce and reproduce their economically impoverished conditions. "The negroes themselves believe that the basic cause for the high percentage of colored prostitutes is the recent enslavement of their race with its attendant unstable marriage and parental status, and point to thousands of slave sales that but two generations ago disrupted the negroes' attempt at family life" (1912a: 119). Addams does not identify who within the African American community believe that "the basic cause for the high percentage of colored prostitutes is" the legacy of slavery. In all likelihood, Addams knew Black Chicagoans who held such views. Equally likely, these Black Chicagoans came from a middle class background and understood as much about Black working class life as middle class white Chicagoans understood about white working class life (which is to say, not much). Through a lens distorted by middle class biases, Addams thus argued that slavery created pathological values for [working class] African Americans, and this culture reinforced the cycle of poverty. By articulating this popularly held theory, Addams meant no racism. She was a racial liberal. But what matters from the rhetorical point of view is the racialized function this argument has in Addams's work.

Pointing once more to the supposed pathological character of the Black community, she writes: "The community forces the very people who have confessedly the shortest history of social restraint, into dangerous proximity with the vice districts of the city" (1912a: 119). Addams never fully explains the term "social restraint" in *A New Conscience*, but returns to the idea in *The Second Twenty Years at Hull-House* (1930). *The Second Twenty Years* begins the discussion of race-relations and Hull-House after 1924, when "the industrial needs of war-time and the immigration restriction following the [First World] war, resulted in a great increase of Negroes in the urban populations throughout the country" (Addams, 1930: 396). Addams goes on to highlight the impact of racial prejudice and the resulting residential segregation. Segregation, she argues, has pathological effects on the Black community. "Whatever may be the practical solution it is still true that a complete segregation of the Negro in definite parts of the city, tends in itself to put him outside the immediate action of that imperceptible but powerful social control which influences the rest of the population" (396). Then Addams offers a comparison:

> One could easily illustrate this lack of inherited control by comparing the experience of a group of colored girls with those of a group representing the daughters of Italian immigrants or any other South European peoples. The Italian girls very much enjoy the novelty of factory work, the opportunity to earn money and to dress as Americans do, but only very gradually do they obtain freedom in the direction of their own social affairs. Italian fathers consider it a point of honor that their daughters shall not be alone upon the street after dark... The fathers of colored girls, on the other hand, are quite without those traditions, and fail to give their daughters the resulting protection.
>
> 397

This supposed lack of social restraint on the part of Black Americans is not the result of a corrupt biological heritage. Addams goes so far as to say that "the civilizations of Africa are even older than those in Italy" (1930: 397). Rather, this lack of restraint, she argues, is the legacy of the "chattel slavery" that destroyed African American traditions and left pathology in the place of family values. What is particularly of note in this passage is the way in which Italians and other immigrants are valorized in comparison to African Americans. In so far as the whitening of new immigrants meant their normative acceptance by the native born white community, that acceptance came at the expense of African Americans. Italian fathers supposedly know how to raise their daughters. "The fathers of colored girls," Addams argues, have no tradition of restraint and thus "fail to give their daughters the resulting protection." While Addams softens the white supremacist argument of D.W. Griffith's *Birth of a Nation* (1915), the same stereotypes about Black Americans haunt both her text and his film. As in Addams's book, Griffith represents African Americans as lacking social restraint, as uncontrolled, and potentially savage. Through comparison to supposedly more "primitive" Blacks, Italians and southern Europeans begin to appear white.

Despite what Addams sees as the pathological impact of slavery upon Black culture, she finds at least one aspect of that culture worthy of preservation, "the melodies which we have learned to call the only American folk-songs and which have become the basis of the Negroes contribution to American music. Perhaps because an oppressed people have always been sustained by their dreams the spirituals became the support of their failing spirits" (Addams, 1930: 399). At least here, in their contribution to *folk* music, Addams recognizes African American agency. She even acknowledges that American cultural change is in "an ever-increasing respect coming from the Negroes own achievements in the arts" (399). Then she cites her only specific example of such an achievement:

> Through their plays they have found the stimulus for conduct in the very field where it was possible to make the initial step toward social efficiency. It may be significant that the curtain falls on an advanced play like "Porgy" while the Negroes of Catfish Row are singing, "I'm on my way".
>
> ADDAMS, 1930: 399–400

No doubt, *Porgy and Bess* was an advanced play, in the sense that an all-Black cast (rather than whites in blackface) portrayed the characters. And, no doubt, between *A New Conscience* and *The Second Twenty Years*, Addams's views on race evolved.[3] But, like the Gershwins' imitation of Black dialect, Addams's views remained fundamentally constrained by racialized preconceptions about the Black community and by her unconscious white supremacy. Her primary points of reference were working class immigrant neighborhoods, and to the extent she saw the Black community at all, it was as an invidious point of comparison that whitened those European immigrants. Thus, when Addams searches for a symbol of Black musical culture, she reaches to Gershwin, a Jewish American who achieved normative acceptance (whiteness) in part by appropriating Black cultural productions and transforming them into what he imagined to be more "serious" music, accompanied by dialect that has more than a hint of minstrelsy.

When Addams uses Gershwin to signify Black music, she effectively renders Black culture producers invisible. In like fashion, despite Addams's argument that a high percentage of Black women enter sex-work, the term "white slavery" effectively renders those women invisible. Black Americans disappear into their imagined vicious neighborhoods and their supposedly pathological communities. When working class African Americans occasionally appear in her work, Addams views them through the lens of class bias and racial stereotype. If she asserts in her writings that African Americans have the "shortest history of social restraint," then, likely, she passed this supposition on to the newly whitened immigrants with whom she worked. While immigrants may have learned the goals of democracy and (potential) racial equality from Addams, they also learned to view African Americans as culturally primitive, and as inhabiting

---

3   Addams's use of the capital in "Negro," unlike her usage in earlier works, where she writes "negro," suggests, at the very least, the increased influence of W.E.B. DuBois. In a footnote on the first page of *The Philadelphia Negro*, DuBois wrote "I shall... capitalize the word [Negro], because I believe that eight million Americans are entitled to a capital letter" (DuBois 1996 [1899]: 1).

a pathological community. At the same time, Addams's middle-class readership learned that immigrants may appear racially primitive, but compared to
her representation of Black Americans, the immigrants are actually civilized.
Thus, Addams simultaneously promoted her unconscious white supremacy
to immigrants, and whitened those immigrants in the eyes of her native born
middle-class readers by denigrating Black Americans and erasing Black cultural producers (on the broader cultural process of immigrant whitening through
invidious comparisons to Black culture, see Cassano, 2015: 84–104; Roediger,
2005).

But let me return to one of the central themes of this chapter: Jane Addams's
argument that shared narratives, and common cultural forms, promote social
solidarity. In her work at Hull-House, Addams did much to build communities
between immigrant groups and native born Americans. But, as Lunin Schultz
demonstrates (Chapter 7, "Hull-House and 'Jim Crow'," this volume), African
Americans rarely participated in Hull-House's rituals of community. While Addams believed in racial equality, she did little to build bridges between working
class Blacks and working class whites in her Chicago neighborhoods. Perhaps,
like many progressive whites, she simply acquiesced to the hard color-line that
already existed in the minds and in the practices of many native born whites
and many new immigrants from Europe. If so, her acquiescence may well have
been shaped by her sense that African American working class culture was
pathological and, therefore, dangerous to social solidarity. On the other hand,
African American cultural production demonstrates that Addams may have
been correct about the social functions of art. During the first decades of the
twentieth century, the popularity of African American art forms, and "vulgar"
"street music," based on ragtime, blues, and jazz, probably did more to promote interracial solidarity than all the settlement workers and social reformers
in Chicago.

CHAPTER 3

Eleanor Smith's Operettas for Children

Jessica Payette

1 Introduction

The Hull-House Music School and its director, Eleanor Smith, garnered much public attention for the implementation and sustainment of a strenuous curriculum, which Smith modeled on her professional training in Germany. The Hull-House music students who reached the highest levels received a musical education similar to that which Smith had attained abroad. Yet the School also gained further recognition in Chicago and beyond through superb student performances of Smith's original dramatic compositions, which have not been studied in depth. This chapter examines these works—*The Trolls' Holiday* (1905), *A Fable in Flowers* (1918), and *The Merman's Bride* (1925–28)—and illustrates their centrality to the settlement's artistic projects, as they portrayed the varied identities and pressing concerns of the Hull-House community on stage.

Harriet Monroe's and Eleanor Smith's *The Trolls' Holiday*, a staged operetta for children, was the first newly composed dramatic work to premiere at Hull-House in May 1905 with additional performances mounted the following November (*Hull House Bulletin*, 7/1, 1905–06: 18).[1] It was the first in a series of operatic works that Smith composed that were prepared as special productions to expand the horizons of Hull-House music students by offering them the experience to acquire and strengthen singing, acting, and movement skills, thus moving beyond the standard recital or concert format. Addams and Hull-House artistic personnel truly believed that one of the most valuable forms of assimilative pedagogy was achieved through having children rehearse and execute large-scale collaborative artworks, as theater scholar Melanie N. Blood observes: "At Hull-House, Addams, Pelham, and Nancrede viewed dramatic production primarily as an educational tool, a way of integrating immigrants into the American cultural mainstream and of demonstrating the success of their assimilation through the mechanism of public performance" (1996: 50).

---

1 The *Bulletin* states that *The Trolls' Holiday* was "a little operetta given by the Hull-House Music School six times in May and again in November."

Smith's adept musical directorship and enthusiasm for contributing original music to large-scale dramatic productions never waned throughout her career at Hull-House. The 1934 edition of the *Hull-House Yearbook* concisely enumerates the operatic works that were staged at Hull-House and notes that all of the settlement's artistic divisions contributed to meet the significant demands of staging a full-length production.

> The Music School has rendered Reinecke's *Snow White*, and his *Enchanted Swans*, also *A Masque of the Seasons*, and three original cantatas for which the music was composed by Miss Eleanor Smith, and the librettos by residents of Hull-House. The first of these was entitled *The Trolls' Holiday*, the second, *A Fable in Flowers*. A third, *The Merman's Bride*, was given numerous performances in which members of the Dramatic Clubs assisted. The music was sung in the gallery of the theatre, accompanied by pantomime on the stage. It was composed by Eleanor Smith and dramatized by Edith de Nancrede and Mabel Katherine Pearse. All the performances of cantatas, including tableaux and dances and setting, taxed the entire artistic resources of the settlement.
>
> 21

As will be examined later in the chapter, reviews that appeared in Chicago's major newspapers reveal that these productions were not amateurish plays presented by children in a school gymnasium, but well-rehearsed and carefully conceived artworks that attracted attention because of the high caliber of performance.

At this time, operettas were especially popular musical works for juvenile and amateur performers that were presented to celebrate ethnic heritage and, in the case of Eleanor Smith's works, to introduce children to culturally esteemed art forms, like opera, and to build community morale through the newly composed libretti that allegorize social dynamics in the Hull-House neighborhood. Operettas from Central and Eastern Europe—such as the Croatian operetta entitled *Caricine Amazonke*—were imported to the United States and often performed by amateur groups in Chicago, like the Zora Croatian singing club. Newly composed operettas, such as Michael Gold and Rudolph Liebich's *The Last Revolution*, were composed as propagandistic entertainment for political gatherings in Chicago. Firsthand accounts in the immigrant newspapers of Chicago often stress that the whole point of staging a dramatic musical performance is to convey the prestige of a long-standing cultural lineage to immigrant audiences, or to use music to comment on social issues.

Eleanor Smith's operettas most certainly adhere to this model as she privileges European folklore and Germanic musical formulae in her American works that are composed especially for children performers. At her core Smith is fundamentally steeped in German compositional technique, but it is apparent that she integrates contemporary American styles more frequently as she matures as a composer. Although we know very little about Smith's professional relationships with esteemed musical figures in Chicago, or her personal investment in and experiences with labor activism outside of Hull-House, some insight into the creative personnel and themes of productions at Hull-House can be gained from the accounts of musical performances that were recorded in Chicago's journalistic media, and from the work and viewpoints of Smith's collaborators.

Surprisingly, Eleanor Smith's first large-scale dramatic work, *The Golden Asp*, a secular cantata, premiered at Hershey Music Hall (20-24 W. Madison) in December 1883, four years prior to her travels to Germany for advanced music study and ten years before she arrived at Hull-House in 1893. The *Chicago Tribune* deemed this performance, which the twenty-five-year-old Smith conducted, important enough to warrant a full-length music review ("Music: *The Golden Asp*," *Chicago Tribune*, 23 December 1883: 14). The critic reports that the piece was heard by "a very large audience" and scored for four vocal soloists, chorus, and two pianos. Smith is commended on "her first debut as a composer," but the review is peppered with the typical gendered discourse of the time that asserts that the work of female composers is unoriginal and implies that women should contemplate whether they are up to the feat of composing large-scale works. For example, the critic offers some back-handed complements, stating that "it was certainly an ambitious undertaking for a young lady who has hardly finished elementary studies," and "Miss Smith has used the reminiscences of the works of others with considerable skill, even if she has not developed any originality, and her treatment of her subject shows a high degree of taste." However, this review is quite telling because it stands out as an anomaly in comparison to reviews from later in Smith's career, which almost uniformly praise Smith's compositional voice and originality. This suggests that Smith's juvenile compositions, prior to completing advanced studies in Germany, may have been quite different from her mature compositions that she created for Hull-House.

Meticulously tracking this development is rather difficult as it appears that only a few fragments of Eleanor Smith's first operetta, *The Trolls' Holiday*, survive (Hull-House Collection, Box 52, Folders 588 and 590). However, quite a lot of information about the production can be gleaned from Harriet Monroe's libretto (reprinted in the Appendix) and the press coverage. Smith's subsequent staged works, her second operetta entitled *A Fable in Flowers* and *The Merman's Bride*, which she categorizes as a cantata, were composed much later in her career and are better preserved (Eleanor Smith Papers, Box 2, Folders

71 and 129). My study of these works reveals that a collaborative network of creative women at Hull-House felt impelled to devise new artworks for children to diversify the existing repertoire, offering alternative scenarios to the fantastical fairy tale plots that dominate the European operettas that were performed at Hull-House. Hull-House's newly composed dramatic works presented Progressive Era themes to local audiences in stories that were transmitted through live performance. Newspaper articles and archival materials from the University of Illinois-Chicago's Hull-House Collection and Eleanor and Gertrude Smith Papers, as well as the *Chicago Tribune*, facilitate the construction of a fascinating history that provides information about the artistic and social significance of these productions.

2   The Romantic German Operatic Tradition: *Gesamtkunstwerk* and *Märchenoper*

At the turn of the twentieth century, the entire enterprise of American musical drama—works performed at the opera house, on Broadway, or in immigrant theaters, especially Yiddish—was influenced by the compositional techniques and theoretical principles of German Romantic composer Richard Wagner (1813–1883). Most important to the modern development of opera and operetta, Wagner coined the term *Gesamtkunstwerk* (a "complete artwork," or an "all-encompassing union of the arts") to describe his approach to operatic production in which he sought to utilize all of the arts collectively as a means to propel the drama forward and to endow performances of his works with an impressive monumentality. Both Smith and Jane Addams attended performances of Wagner's operas in Europe and were exposed to legitimate realizations of *Gesamtkunstwerken* and affected by the profound messages that are transmitted through the union of music, poetry, set design, dance, and special effects, as will be discussed momentarily.

Furthermore, with regard to the *Ring Cycle*, Wagner campaigned for societal redistribution of wealth by transferring Fichte's and Hegel's ideas about materialism—subsequently reformulated in Marx and Engels's *Communist Manifesto*—into his libretti for the *Ring Cycle*, which concludes with the demise of the Gods (who represent the aristocracy) as their castle, Valhalla, goes up in flames (Scruton, 2016). Today Wagner's operas are regarded as emblematic of "high art," but Wagner tried to appeal to the sensibilities of "the People" (*das Volk*), average German citizens, by employing all of the arts in combination to produce a stark visual, literary, and musical contrast between the lofty dwellings of the Gods and the industrial underworld of the working classes. This encouraged audiences to envision a modern German state that rejected aristocratic rule and class stratification.

The reception of Wagner's operas today cannot be entirely divorced from Hitler's appropriation of the works for Nazi ideology. However, at the turn of the twentieth century, cultured women, like Addams and Smith, viewed Wagner's work as progressive and capable of highlighting, and combatting, societal disequilibrium. Music historian Shannon Green recognizes that "in the U.S., Wagner represented 'music as uplift,' a philosophy resonant with many middle-class American women, including the settlement music educators" (1998: 19). Furthermore, Victoria Bissell Brown (2004) notes that Addams's diaries from her European grand tour (1883–85) frequently address plays and operas that she attended and reveal that "at age twenty-four, Jane Addams's passions were not excited by love stories but by 'scenes among gods and giants' in which she perceived individuals, including strong females, struggling to advance human progress out of 'mere goodness'" (142). Addams commented specifically on Wagner's *Tannhäuser*, summarizing the opera as "a 'powerful' story of a man 'who is down trying to work his way up'" (Ibid).

Classical music is now regarded as "high" culture that primarily attracts an elite clientele. Lawrence Levine (1988) argues that the association of operatic and symphonic music with upper-class patronage did not occur in America until well into the twentieth century. During the transitional time around the turn of the twentieth century, many average Americans had access to high culture without ever setting foot in an opera house or concert hall. Similar to the increasing impetus to program high art in casual venues today, they experienced it at civic programs or at performances hosted by clubs that were organized by different ethnic groups. In Chicago, conductor Theodore Thomas's concert program of Wagnerian overtures, presented at outdoor "summer nights" concerts from 1877–1890 (Vaillant, 2003: 37), exemplifies how Wagner's music crept into American popular culture. Thomas even complained that Wagner's emotive compositional style—often described as "narcotic" due to Friedrich Nietzsche's assessment—dissuaded the public from recognizing the merits of other great composers, like Brahms: "Wagner to some extent interested the people, but he had also accustomed them to strong doses of excitement, and contrast, and everything without these tonic properties was regarded with indifference" (qtd. in Vaillant, 2003: 44).

Thus it is not surprising that Addams and Smith were quite familiar with Wagnerian works and strove to realize similarly ambitious artistic statements at Hull-House. They conceived of the student productions as localized

Gesamtkunstwerken that sought to socialize the community's children through the staging of allegories of real-world scenarios. In her description of the collaborative labor that fosters the production of Hull-House operettas Addams even refers to the Wagnerian principle of *Gesamtkunstwerk*:

> Sometimes all the artistic resources of the House united in a Wagnerian combination; thus, the text of *The Trolls' Holiday* was written by one resident, set to music by another, sung by the Music School, and placed upon the stage under the careful direction and training of the dramatic committee; and the little brown trolls could never have bumbled about so gracefully in their gleaming caves unless they had been taught in the gymnasium.
>
> 1910: 226

It is entirely appropriate for Addams to stress the operetta's German romantic roots. In 1905, when *The Trolls' Holiday* premiered, Hull-House was the only American settlement house that offered advanced artistic training in all of the performing arts (music, theater, and dance) and that possessed the financial resources, primarily provided by Mary Rozet Smith, to purchase materials for the participants in the dramatic clubs who specialized in stage design and carpentry to create high-quality set design, lighting, and costumes (Green, 1998: 199 and 204).

In this sense the operettas were indeed monumental institutional undertakings made all the more impactful by placing children performers in the spotlight (Illustration 3.1). As will become clear in my discussion of Smith's operettas, they are conceived in the same spirit as Wagnerian operas: to reflect current-day societal dilemmas and to influence public thinking on these matters. This is manifested in the original libretti by Harriet Monroe, Caroline Foulke Urie, and Smith herself that represent neighborhood social dynamics and impart feminist pragmatism akin to the way that it is conveyed in the speeches and essays of Addams and her associates, which assert, "the kind of social change advocated could not be paternalistic in nature. Policies and programs would not be effective in solving social problems unless they were defined, directed, and implemented in direct relationship with, and in the common interest of, the poor, immigrants, women, children, and the laboring classes they were intended to serve" (Williams & MacLean, 2016: 110). Smith's attempts to serve these populations and to express feminist pragmatism through music led her to spearhead the composition of new operettas that introduce strong female characters and modern Progressive Era ideals into the framework of the prevailing German fairy tale operetta.

Several late romantic German composers who drew inspiration from Wagner wrote operettas specifically for children, a repertoire that was distinct

ILLUSTRATION 3.1   Jane Addams with Children Performers in *The Merman's Bride*, 1928
SOURCE: JANE ADDAMS MEMORIAL COLLECTION (JAMC), SPECIAL
COLLECTIONS, DALEY LIBRARY, UNIVERSITY OF ILLINOIS AT
CHICAGO.

enough from standard opera to warrant its own generic category of *Märchen-
noper* ('Fairy-tale opera'). Nineteenth-century German *Märchenopern* featured
children as performers in varying capacities: in some works all of the parts are
sung by children, whereas in others the children's roles are confined to the
chorus. The *Märchenoper* that has best withstood the test of time is Engelbert

Humperdinck's *Hänsel und Gretel* (1893), which employs a children's chorus to simulate the celestial voices of fourteen angels. Humperdinck established a compositional framework that was adopted for subsequent *Märchenopern* in which he adeptly fused Wagnerian leitmotives (recurrent musical signifiers that represent a person, object, place, idea, or emotion) with German folk songs (Glauert, "Hänsel und Gretel").

German émigré conductors who resided in the United States were quick to introduce the genre of *Märchenoper* to American audiences and located suitable works in English by American and British composers. Professor Gabriel Katzenberger, who served as the supervisor of music in the Chicago schools until 1899, directed children's operettas in Chicago ("Kipling in the Schools," *Chicago Tribune*, 11 October 1899: 16). Katzenberger presented *Golden Hair and the Three Bears*, the first children's operetta that received press coverage in Chicago, at the Schiller Theater in December 1892. The event was promoted as a preview of the children's chorus that would join with over 2,000 adult voices at the World's Fair to form the German-American World's Fair Chorus ("Children Sing in an Operetta," *Chicago Tribune*, 26 December 1892: 9). Boston composer John Astor Broad, who served as an organist and director of music at several Boston and Worcester churches, published the score for this "juvenile operetta" in 1879 and it was performed frequently in communities throughout the United States and the United Kingdom in the late nineteenth century.[2]

Eleanor Smith was particularly fond of Carl Reinecke's musical fairy tales, composed between 1876 and 1878. In her 1916 article entitled "The Music of School Entertainments" Smith advocates for the educational value of mounting large-scale dramatic works with children and she discusses the merits of specific repertoire that she has selected for Hull-House performances. Smith mentions that Reinecke's *Snow White* (Op. 133) was performed at Hull-House in 1914 and that plans were underway to mount his *The Enchanted Swans* (Op. 164) later in 1916. Smith expressed admiration for Reinecke's literary aptitude and his creation of an inviting musical atmosphere for children.

> The music of both cantatas is in Reinecke's happiest vein. It is romantic but restrained. Its musical thoughts are delightful and expressed with that perfection of workmanship so characteristic of this composer. The

---

2   Many notices in music journals apprise readers of upcoming performances and thus attest to the popularity of *Golden Hair and the Three Bears*. For example, see the 1 February 1897 issue of *The Musical Herald*, which praises a performance by Miss Wilkinson's junior choir at the Kendal Town Hall (p. 62). The 1 May 1908 issue of the same journal notes, "*Golden Hair and the Three Bears* has been successfully given by the Uttoxeter R.C. school children" (p. 141).

librettos of both works are better constructed and more sensible than most librettos, but needless to say, they have suffered at the hands of the translator.

8

These works, for which Reinecke doubled as librettist under the pen name of Heinrich Carsten, constitute a separate generic category from his standard operas, which were not successful in Germany. The musical fairy tales include spoken recitation and advanced music for vocal soloists and large choruses. Interestingly, Smith did not stage *Glückskind und Pechvogel* (*Good Luck and Bad Luck*), Reinecke's only *Märchenoper* that includes a specific designation recommending that children sing the lead roles, but it is likely that her knowledge of his entire output and musical philosophy impacted principles that Smith adopted from his compositional approach.

In his writings Reinecke, an esteemed professor at the Leipzig Conservatory from 1860 to 1902 and teacher to the likes of Edvard Grieg and Max Bruch, frequently discusses how children have the ability to become increasingly cognizant of important aesthetic properties from engaging with serious artworks and he advocates for composers to respond by creating sophisticated artworks for children. This Germanic philosophy of *Bildung* (self-cultivation through exposure to culture and education) encourages the formation of strong aesthetic values in the training of juvenile musicians, in addition to technical skill. Smith endorses this *Weltanschauung* in her autobiography, as she advises that, "its disciples should early be given the best music possible. Good taste and the enjoyment of the finest music is best implanted in early youth" (1). This pedagogical stance is clearly reflective of her experiences in German institutions and likely fueled her sustained interest in composing difficult, large-scale works for children performers throughout her career.

It is also significant that Reinecke's compositional approach, in particular, became well known in the United States through the publication of many of his essays in English translation in American music journals, like *The Etude*. The magnitude of Reinecke's influence in the United States is revealed in a 1906 profile on the composer in *The Etude*'s "Children's Page" segment, which designates him as "A Musician Who is a Friend of Children." The article declares that "most of the young readers of *The Etude* have played or sung at least one of Carl Reinecke's compositions for children, and doubtless learned them with great pleasure" and it avows that "his happiest work" contains "descriptive fairies and goblins" ("Children's Page," *The Etude* 24/8, August 1906: 496). In Reinecke's preface to *Glückskind und Pechvogel*, he even explicitly addresses the technical limitations that confront the composer when writing for young singers and notes that he composed alternative *ossia* passages in the score to guarantee that children's voices would be accommodated:

> In order to render this Fairy-Opera easily available for children, the greatest possible attention has been paid to the capabilities of the executants' voices; the compass of an octave is seldom exceeded, and even where an exception is made to this rule, small notes are inserted, to be used in case of necessity. The part of the King can be sung by a child, whose voice is limited to the middle A.
>
>   2

The notion of revising fairy tales to make them more palatable to juvenile readers was also a prolonged concern in the nineteenth century. Folkloric scholars, as well as psychoanalytic disciples of Freud, most notably Bruno Bettelheim, have stressed that fairy tales and folklore offer children the opportunity to vicariously experience other children's agency, as they are obliged to use critical-thinking skills to outsmart malicious adults or demons and avert crisis. Jack Zipes's prolific scholarship on the manifold social functions of fairy tales in Western society explores how the content, dissemination, and reception of fairy tales changed throughout history. In the nineteenth century this occurs largely in response to the formalization of educational structures and the burgeoning study of child psychology.

> The Grimms purposely changed their fairy tales between 1819 and 1857 to make them more instructional and moral, and other writers worked to create tales more appropriate for children, not realizing that often, in seeking to protect children, we harm them most. [...] At the same time, many writers during the latter half of the nineteenth century, such as George MacDonald, Lewis Carroll, and Oscar Wilde, used the fairy-tale-for-children form to question the overly didactic tales. The result in Western countries was the split and the commodification of the fairy tale. The split was complicated because the divide was not only between the literary fairy tale for adults and the wholesome tale for children, but also between 'proper' and 'improper' traits. One thing was clear—the 'proper' fairy tale for children had become a hot commodity used expressly to socialize children in families and at schools.
>
>   1997: 5

Zipes differentiates between literary fairy tales, devised and preserved by the ruling classes, and folk tales, predominantly an oral tradition accessible to all classes, and observes that increasing commercialization, even in the early twentieth century by the book publishing and toy industries (luxury items that only the upper-middle and affluent classes could afford), resulted in the sanitization of classic literary fairy tales: "In short, by institutionalizing the literary fairy tale, writers and publishers violated the forms and concerns of non-literate, essentially peasant communities, and set new standards of taste, production, and reception through the discourse of the fairy tale" (Zipes, 1995: 24). One ramification of this institutionalization in twentieth-century youth culture was an increased emphasis on feminine objectification—facilitated by the new technologies of photography and film—and marrying well (upward mobility), as Marcia Lieberman argues in her seminal essay "Some Day My Prince Will Come" (1972). However, other scholars point to fairy tales as ideal templates for feminist rewriting, which was already a common practice in the Victorian era. For example, author Anne Thackeray Ritchie's collection *Fairy Tales for Grown Folks* (1868) was directed toward adult female audiences and replaced the palatial settings and magical intervention in literary fairy tales with contemporary domestic interiors and realistic events. They contained a "restrained but explicit criticism of pretentiousness, materialism, and the restricted situation of women in Victorian society" (Barzilai, 2008: 810). Ritchie's retelling of "Beauty and the Beast" challenges the traditional patriarchal scheme: the narrator is an elderly, unmarried woman and both the Beast character and Belle's father are "decidedly subservient to stronger females" (Auerbach & Knoepflmacher, 1992: 16).

Similarly, the original operettas and cantatas that were created for the Hull-House community are also notable for their female authorship and reviewers recognize that they sensitively present allegories of the immigrant experience and offer optimistic responses to neighborhood and global crises, namely World War I. However, the inclusion of assertive female characters and progressive feminist attitudes in the operettas was not often addressed in the reviews and will be examined more thoroughly in this chapter. We can surmise that Smith and her collaborators were not content with dramatizing well-known fairy tales, and thus utilized the folk tale model for the scenarios that they created. Zipes classifies these stories as having "themes and characters that were readily recognizable and reflected common wish-fulfillments" (1995: 24). This narrative type provided the scaffolding for socializing immigrant children into the Progressive movement, allowing them to value the participatory culture of the performing arts and realize that both domestic and civic/political challenges are a natural part of life and can best be overcome through logical reasoning and collaborative problem solving. I believe that Smith's works challenge literary fairy tale themes and imagery. By 1900 classic fairy tales were marketed to young girls to reaffirm that their dreams for the future would be best fulfilled by marriage, and they also continued to present both the happy couple and the nuclear family unit as entities that are isolated from both the nation and the local civic community. The Smith operettas especially resist what Zipes refers to as "the privatization" of the literary fairy tale by offering children who did not have an abundance of material play objects at home the opportunity to tell a story and by depicting a larger community that supports the protagonists and the nuclear family.[3] In speeches Jane Addams employed the image of the tightly-integrated and unified vocal chorus as an analogy for the Nineteenth ward's potential for harmonious collectivity, comparing the Hull-House neighborhood to "a rendition of the Hallelujah Chorus in which one would surely appreciate all the solo voices but in the end it would be the joining of the voices that 'produced the volume and strength of the chorus'" (Williams & MacLean, 2016: 113). This promotion of social harmony is also accentuated in Smith's operettas as the child protagonists are supported by larger masses of children in the chorus and succeed in triumphing over adversity, resisting exploitation, and acting as a motivating force to renew joy in their parents' marriages.

3   The Collaborative Artistic Networks of Women in Chicago

In her impressive catalog, *American Women Playwrights*, Frances Diodato Bzowski lists over 12,000 plays by approximately 2,000 American women that were published in the first three decades of the twentieth century. In her preface to the catalog, Bzowski emphasizes that a number of factors made the turn of the century a very dynamic time for American women to address issues that were central to their own lives in theatrical works.

---

3   In his essay "Breaking the Disney Spell" Zipes draws attention to the class stratification that was exacerbated by the gap between the literate and non-literate at the end of the nineteenth century. We know that access to print culture was one of the reasons that immigrants and their children visited Hull-House, and must keep in mind that children's books and toys were likely not found in low-income neighborhood households in the early twentieth century: "Such violation of oral storytelling was crucial and necessary for the establishment of the bourgeoisie because it concerned the control of desire and imagination within the symbolic order of western culture. Unlike the oral tradition, the literary fairy tale was written down to be read in private, although, in some cases, the fairy tales were read aloud in parlors. However, the book form enabled the reader to withdraw from his or her society and to be alone with a tale. This privatization violated the communal aspects of the folk tale, but the very printing of a fairy tale was already a violation since it was based on separation of social classes. Extremely few people could read, and the fairy tale in form and content furthered notions of elitism and separation" (24).

As New Women, they found their voice in an era that accepted a woman's right to express herself. And this new personal freedom occurred at the same time that the little theatre movement provided countless opportunities for women to write plays and to see them performed. Hardly any sizable community was without some kind of amateur theatre at this time. Also, it was an age of pageantry, when cities and communities, as well as the women's movement itself, utilized spectacle and drama".

vii

As first-hand accounts and historical records document, women were the most numerous contributors to artistic production, patronage, and arts education in Progressive Era Chicago. However, as I gather and assess the historical documents over a century later, it is evident that some women in artistic networks were more motivated than others to lay the foundation for a posthumous artistic legacy and thus explain the significance of their output in greater detail. Harriet Monroe, now regarded as a poet possessing average capabilities, writes extensively about herself and her work because she wants to share with her readership stories about her poetic subject matter and the difficulties that she confronted as a female poet. On the other hand, Eleanor Smith, acknowledged by many as a very talented composer, and someone who was obviously exposed to the voluminous literature authored by the Hull-House founders and residents, did not have the time, or did not wish, to discuss her compositional activities in depth. Thus, as will be summarized below, Monroe's account of her artistic work and her residency at Hull-House serves as a case study, offering insight into the career of a financially self-sufficient American woman in the arts circa 1900.

Although there is no evidence that Eleanor Smith attended any Chicago salons, we know that Addams and Monroe circulated among this crowd and viewed the salon as a prime venue to campaign for women's rights, and in Monroe's case, to demonstrate women's aptitude in creative fields. The voicing of these principles allowed for the broader recognition of feminist issues in the bourgeois salon and the cultivation of a thriving arts scene at Hull-House that was staffed entirely by women. While founding and overseeing Hull-House Jane Addams was an active participant in Chicago's salon culture, frequenting The Little Room and the Cordon Club, and it is important to observe that from the beginning she created the infrastructure for professional-grade performances—as well as spaces within Hull-House to support an artists' colony and a salon dynamic—in a very unlikely place: the middle of an urban slum. Edith de Nancrede, director of children's dramatic activities at Hull-House from 1902–36, even credits Addams as "one of the very first people to found a 'little theater' in this country. Because she believed so much in the

great educational value of drama, she built the Hull-House Theater in 1901"
(1928: 23).

A whole gamut of creative individuals, many women among them—Enella
Benedict, Clara Laughlin, Harriet Monroe, Elia Wilkinson Peattie, and Edith
Wyatt—chose to make Hull-House their home for short- or long-term residencies and this offered a benefit that the downtown salons could not provide:
the opportunity to build relationships with each other and with the neighborhood visitors who congregated at Hull-House in their leisure time and, in some
cases, relied on Hull-House to alleviate complete financial despair through its
contributions to their basic needs, like meals or childcare. Wallace Kirkland, a
social worker and photographer who lived at Hull-House, remarks on this special community in his unpublished memoir: "Hull-House residents came from
many walks of life. They were people who worked in other parts of the city,
who wanted to live and share their talents with the less fortunate people of the
neighborhood. They were doctors, lawyers, college professors, school teachers,
social workers, students, musicians, actors, writers, poets, artists, politicians.
Some lived in single rooms, others in apartments" (quoted in "The Many Faces
of Hull-House," *Chicago Tribune*, 8 October 1989: section 13, p. 20).

Addams and Harriet Monroe met at The Little Room, an intellectual Chicago salon that was founded by Monroe's sister, Lucy. The group, which literary scholar Sidney Bremer deems as "probably the most important attempt by
Chicago's literary women to join with male colleagues on both professional
and social grounds" (1989: xv), began gathering in 1893. Joan Stevenson Falcone
characterizes the group of Chicago women writers who met at The Little Room
as a "sisterhood," and examines Elia Wilkinson Peattie's novel *The Precipice* to
argue that their work presents an optimistic view of the opportunities afforded
to women in Chicago while that of contemporaneous male authors, like Sinclair Lewis, tends to focus on the grittiness of industrialization and ill effects
of capitalism (1992: i). Peattie, one of the first women to be hired as a journalist by the *Chicago Tribune* and *Omaha Herald*, met Willa Cather, Hamlin
Garland, and Harriet Monroe at professional functions prior to attending The
Little Room salon (Ibid: 45–46; 51) and credits the eclectic membership with
generating "a rarefied bohemianism" (Peattie, qtd. in Falcone 1992: 54), likely
the byproduct of an improvisational atmosphere where impromptu dancing
and zany plays, such as a dramatization of "The Bird Center" cartoons, reigned
supreme (Morgan, 1918: 190).

The Little Room initially gathered in sculptor Lorado Taft's studio and later
convened in the Fine Arts Building to discuss art and literature and to entertain
distinguished artists who visited Chicago from other cities (Morgan, 1918:

188). Unlike the Cliff Dwellers Club, a prominent salon that did not welcome women, The Little Room was open to both sexes, with the stipulation that one had to create something—artistic, philanthropic, or entrepreneurial—to be granted membership, as an anonymous poem, housed in the Chicago Historical Society collections, dictates.

> To this mysterious Chamber
> the 'hoi polloi' ne'er come;
> one can cross the portal
> Unless some work he's done—
> some stunt in art or poesy,
> or maybe writ a tune,
> Ah! Then he may find entrance
> into The Little Room.
>
> Qtd. in STILSON, 2006: 68

The group met after the Chicago Symphony's Friday matinee performances and sought to encourage conversation between artists, businessmen, and community leaders (Pinkerton & Hudson, 2004: 204).

In 1902, The Little Room regressed into a bourgeois social club as the women's organizational roles were entrusted to male officers who eventually, in 1906, decided that spouses could be added as associate members, "confusing the status of the professional women who were attempting an extension of family-like dynamics beyond the private home" (Bremer, 1992: 105). The Little Room's emphasis on its membership's diverse creative activities was negated as wives who did not engage in creative work, and who may have shifted the conversation away from intellectual discourse, could attend the gatherings (Miller, 1991: 224). Partly as a result of this shift toward a more conservative social sphere and the increasing male domination of the salon's affairs, Jane Addams became a member of the Cordon Club. The Cordon Club was founded in 1915 as the feminine counterpart to the Cliff Dwellers Club and limited its membership to 400 "literary, artistic, professional, and inspirational women" ("Cordon Club Name Explained," *Chicago Tribune*, 27 May 1915: 5). Elia Wilkinson Peattie's bylaws further stress the club's promotion of women's empowerment: "To establish a common meeting place for lovers of independence and self-expression, whose vocations permit excursions beyond domestic bounds" (Ibid).

Harriet Monroe is a good example of a literary woman who prided herself on advocating for the advancement of women in poetry and remained independent despite significant obstacles, such as hostile criticism from men and bouts of poverty. Before taking up residence at Hull-House, Harriet Monroe was on a quest for poetry to be recognized as a civic art, and her poems were set to music for two very important events: the dedicatory programs of the Auditorium Theater in 1889 and the World's Columbian Exposition in 1893. Frederick Grant Gleason, one of Eleanor Smith's composition teachers, set Monroe's *Auditorium Festival Ode* to music and George W. Chadwick composed the music for her *Columbian Ode*. Monroe's lengthy *Auditorium Festival Ode* traces the history of Chicago and advocates for the cultivation of harmonious relations between the civically-minded upper class and the working class, as musicologist Mark Clague notes: "The Association worked to undercut an increasingly militant labor movement by using culture's ideological tools" (Clague, 2002:13). Unlike the *Columbian Ode*, it was conceived operatically, with recitatives and arias, and sung in its entirety. Monroe's conclusion for the piece explicitly focuses on improving relations between Chicago's socio-economic classes by pinpointing greed as a potentially destructive civic catastrophe, comparable to the Great Fire, which had been depicted earlier in the work (16). Clague details how the *Auditorium Ode* presents a narrative of Chicago's historical events, ending with the work's commentary on the present moment: "In the minds of the Auditorium's patrons, then, Greed was a real plague in the city. To combat it, Auditorium leaders sought to establish a philanthropic tradition in Chicago and foreground the plight of the working class" (18).

During the lead-up to the World's Fair performance Monroe proved difficult by disregarding contractual stipulations and demanding payment for her work prior to its evaluation by an expert, and by unsuccessfully demanding royalties for the reprinting of the twenty-eight-line excerpt that was distributed to the choir for rehearsal (Massa, 1986: 56). Despite these outbursts, Monroe's poetry for the World's Exposition was reviewed in the local and national press, and in keeping with the prevailing prejudices of the time, weaknesses of the poetry were attributed to her sex. The reviewer for *The Literary World* remarks that:

> A great poet like Lowell would have given verses filled with significant and ideal comment upon the progress of American civilization—sentences which should illuminate the national history and long remain valuable. But such a poem would have been the work of a man well acquainted with political philosophy and aware of the tendencies of the country. In criticism of this artistic work by a feminine hand it would be unjust to judge it by what it is not, instead appreciating it for that which it is.
>
> "The Colombian Ode," 19 November 1892: 23–24

Surprisingly, Monroe believed that the Ode did not earn a lasting place in the American poetry canon because it did not effectively capture the rhetoric of Progressivism, as the "finale of the Ode did not seem too hopeful" (1938: 122). Although Monroe would not rise to national prominence until after the founding of *Poetry* in 1912, she quickly assimilated into elite literary circles in Chicago after the World's Fair (Miller, 1991: 163). At this time, in an effort to reap more financial profits from her literary work, Monroe turned her attention to art criticism, along with prose and playwriting, first publishing short stories and then securing a volume with Houghton, Mifflin & Co. entitled *The Passing Show*, a book compilation of five plays by Monroe that was published in 1903. Monroe's libretto for *The Trolls' Holiday* falls into her post-"Colombian Ode" period when she was trying her hand at many diverse literary genres in an attempt to achieve wider recognition. Jane Addams's correspondence with Monroe just prior to the premiere of *The Trolls' Holiday* suggests that she was eager to introduce Monroe and Smith to other artistic Chicagoans.

> My dear Miss Monroe,
>   Won't you come to dinner on Saturday at quarter past six, we are inviting a few actors and musical folk and must insist upon the author and composer as chief guests.
>
> Always faithfully yours,
Jane Addams
Jane Addams Digital Edition: 13 May 1905

3.1   The Trolls' Holiday

Monroe was a temporary Hull-House resident for three months in 1905 when she mapped out a vision for *The Trolls' Holiday* with Smith and oversaw the production of several of her plays by the Hull-House Players (Pinkerton & Hudson, 2004: 169). Monroe's and Smith's *The Trolls' Holiday* was directed by Edith de Nancrede, head of children's dramatics clubs at Hull-House, with set design and costumes by Enella Benedict and other resident artists. According to Pamela Elrod, *The Trolls' Holiday* had a cast of around sixty children and young adults, who were either Music School students or Hull-House residents, and ranged from age five to twenty (2001a: 56). Little is known about most of the performers, except the names of the cast and the fact that *The Trolls' Holiday* was revived at Hull-House in May 1923 with Louis C. Alter, the original Troll king, reprising his role. The *Chicago Tribune* mentions that Eugene Carroll had performed in the chorus of the original performance and would return with a leading role in the remounting (see cast lists in *Hull-House Bulletin* 7/1, 1905–06: 18; "Hull House Music Students to Revive *Trolls' Holiday*," *Chicago Tribune*, 3 May 1923: 23).[4]

While growing up in Chicago, Harriet Monroe (1860–1936) regularly attended operatic performances and thus acquired firsthand knowledge of the structure and pacing of iconic European operatic libretti (Miller, 1991: 25). Her knowledge of operatic dramaturgy and themes are aptly displayed in the libretto for *The Trolls' Holiday*, as will be discussed in detail below. In her autobiography Monroe recounts the circumstances surrounding the genesis of the work and reveals why the score was never published.

> One little episode of dramatic success gave me much pleasure. During a short residence at Hull-House, I was asked by Eleanor Smith, composer and head of the music school, to write the text—the dialogue and songs—for a children's operetta. So I wrote a fairy-and-moral comedy, *The Trolls' Holiday*, based remotely on Norwegian myth; and it was given with Miss Smith's beautiful music by the Hull-House children and young people in May 1905. The performance was charming beyond all expectation. The seven-year-old hero, and indeed other children, were worthy of Hollywood, and the play worked out to a happy and exciting climax. This pretty thing was given many times, and repeated with a new cast in later seasons, and one would think it might be used by many schools. But the music publishers said it was too difficult for most children and impossible for grown-ups; so it is still unpublished.
>
> 187–188

In keeping with Jane Addams's effort to showcase the Old World cultural heritage of immigrant communities (see Lunin Schultz, "Democratizing Mass Culture," this volume), Monroe turns to Scandinavian folklore as the source material for her libretto. It is unclear precisely which Norwegian folktales Monroe drew from, but she explores the opposition of humans versus trolls, a defining characteristic of Scandinavian folklore that led to its global popularization. Monroe's dramaturgical concept is adapted from Norwegian folktales that illustrate the benefits of coexistence among outwardly dissimilar factions and cultivating neighborly courtesy. In many of these stories humans exhibit caution around supernatural trolls, but at the same time they develop

---

4   Eugene Carroll and his four siblings participated in music and drama at Hull-House. Eugene had a career in radio and then, briefly, in television with a role in the NBC production of *Fibber McGee and Molly*, a short-lived adaptation of the popular radio series. For more information on the upbringing of the Carroll children see the Eleanor Carroll Farwell Oral History transcript, University of Illinois–Chicago, OH-052.

a "friendly coexistence" with the under earthlings (Lindow, 2014: 58), often resulting in scenes of "neighbors helping one another" (Ibid: 62). Trolls may help humans by offering them transport and aiding with the harvest while humans may help trolls fix tools, provide firewood or food for troll children, or lend luxurious items for weddings and celebrations. Monroe's scenario also offered the opportunity to creatively design the movement and costumes of the chorus of trolls, comprised of the smallest children.

Although little else is known about the details of Eleanor Smith's collaboration with Harriet Monroe, a synopsis of the plot of Monroe's libretto is provided in several reviews. The libretto, which was criticized by the *Chicago Tribune* reviewer as lacking "striking literary beauty," is an adaptation of a Norse legend that explores themes of parental neglect; the power struggles between humans and trolls (which can be interpreted more broadly as "others" who infringe on the community's stability); arranged marriage; and music's persuasive rhetorical power. A synopsis of Monroe's scenario follows, as it appeared in the *Chicago Tribune*:

> The scene is in Norway, and the time is the summer day when the Trolls—the underworld elves—are permitted to come to the earth's surface. The peasants gather on the green, and against the advice of the wise old "Grannie" of the community, leave their children playing there alone. The Trolls appear, cast the spell of sleep over the little ones, and carry off Solvy, a spirited youngster, who has been naughty. The parents, returning, discover Solvy's loss. Meia, the sister of the stolen lad, undertakes to journey to the land of the Trolls, there to reclaim her brother. She goes, accompanied by the lover, Peik, but he may venture only to the entrance to the enchanted kingdom. Meia is seen as she meets the Trolls, and Peik is carried by them back to the upper world. She finds her brother, but may not go to him. While lamenting, she is approached by Ripple-Winkle, a water sprite, who, taking the viol Meia carries, sings into it a charm which makes its music potent over all the Trolls. Armed with this, Meia goes to the palace of the Troll king and there is taken for the mortal who is destined to wed the crown prince—a union which must occur once every hundred years if the Trolls are to preserve their identity. Meia refuses to wed and escapes with Solvy. They come to their home and parents again, and are followed thither by the Trolls, who plead for a maiden who shall wed their prince. Meia's music renders the elves powerless and they are transformed into stone for having ventured to the upper world on a day other than their holiday.
>
> HUBBARD, "News of the Theaters: *The Trolls' Holiday*," *Chicago Tribune*, 5 June 1905: 9

What the *Tribune* reviewer unfortunately overlooked about Monroe's libretto is that it intentionally embraces one of opera's enduring themes: the power of music to persuade and influence the decisions of those in control. In fact, this aspect of the plot harkens back to the very first operas, which date to the early seventeenth century, and present adaptations of the Orpheus myth. In the first surviving Italian operas, composed by Jacopo Peri and Claudio Monteverdi, Orpheus, the Greek God of music, journeys into the Underworld to retrieve Eurydice, his wife, who has died from a snake bite. Orpheus plays his lyre for Hades in order to gain entrance to the Underworld. Hades is so moved by Orpheus's musical lament for his deceased wife that he allows Orpheus to take Eurydice with him: she is to follow behind him as they ascend up to earth and he must not turn around to look at her until they have made it back. Unfortunately, Orpheus cannot resist the temptation and he glances back at Eurydice. She is whisked away and Orpheus dies trying to go back into the Underworld to rescue her again.

As a children's story *The Trolls' Holiday* is not tragic like the Orpheus myth, but Meia's ability to save her brother and triumph over the trolls by playing her violin is akin to Orpheus's performance for Hades. Aslog, the mother of Meia and Solvy, is distraught when she learns that Solvy has been kidnapped by trolls and exclaims, "Oh, woe is me! How could I leave my children alone on the troll day? (Monroe, 1905: 15)." But Granny advises the adults that Meia is the only one equipped to take on the trolls because she can gain entrance to the troll country by singing (17). Thus the theme of music as a means for rhetorical vibrancy and empowerment emerges as one of the operetta's most important messages. This is reinforced in Monroe's libretto as the water sprite, Ripple–Winkle, magically transports magnificent tunes into Meia's viol: "Come, pretty maiden, and take back thy viol from me. The drip of its music, more potent than thunder, shall charm the beasts out of the earth and the fish from the sea. Thy voice will bring to it the paddling of oars that shall carry thee where thou wouldst be—the rising and falling of oars to a shore where the heart is free" (Monroe, *The Trolls' Holiday*: Act II).

The operetta's themes, which are not discussed on a sophisticated level in any of the surviving reviews, seem almost premeditated to encapsulate Addams's belief that "music is perhaps the most potent agent for making the universal appeal and inducing men to forget their differences" (Addams, 1910: 380). In an address to the National Education Association Smith even claims that music is more meaningful and therapeutic for the lower classes.

> But music is, as it has always been, the chief delight and solace of the
> poor, and her most ardent votaries, as well as those high in her service,

have always been the poor. A realization of this fact, and the conviction that music has supreme power to refine and elevate those who embrace it, lay at the foundation of our efforts to create a democratic school of music.

SMITH, 1912: 1015–16

The Trolls' Holiday features numerous scenes in which laborers sing for diversion from work and rely on children to lead the songs, including the very first which contains "a song to begin the day with" (see Appendix). Furthermore, Meia's musical proficiency enables her to travel to remote territory and eases her communication with groups of people who are different from her, signaling to the children in the show that music may grant them access to adventure in foreign realms (whether real or imagined). The plotline allegorically illustrates both the capacity of musical proficiency to psychologically transport musicians to a higher spiritual plane and to potentially offer opportunities to physically move beyond the neighborhood environs through social mobility.

Furthermore, in *The Trolls' Holiday* Monroe and Smith privileged the perspectives of young girls, as opposed to lovesick teenagers seeking romantic partners, in order to enlarge the spectrum of feminine character traits associated with young girls: Meia is an active and intelligent heroine who can navigate the trolls' domain on her own. In 1892, Eleanor Smith wrote an article entitled "Music for Young Girls" in which she draws attention to the insensitivity of assigning young women singers passionate love songs about romantic emotions that they have not experienced.

> I have often seen a damsel of fifteen, to whom Heaven has given a voice, making wry faces over words of her songs which to her innocent mind were very distasteful; and I believe that, unless the young singer has been encouraged to regard her song texts as of no more dramatic importance than the vowels of her solfeggio, she will always have an instinctive shrinking away from the expression of emotions of which she knows nothing.
>
> 454–455

Smith predicts that once archaic musical pedagogy practices are discarded composers will write more music for young people.

> When the old superstition that children's voices should not be trained dies out completely, when more well-schooled musicians shall see the necessity of teaching children what they can so easily be taught, then the

attention of the composers will be called not only to the child's song but to the necessity of writing more especially for young girls.

455

As we know now, Smith responds to the dearth of children's repertoire by contributing many works and methods books for young musicians and she targets the gender issues that she outlines in this article by featuring courageous female protagonists in *The Trolls' Holiday* and other operettas. Monroe and Smith, both fiercely independent women, openly glorify the virtue of feminine self-sufficiency, as intimated above by Ripple–Winkle when he encourages Meia to search for a place where her heart is free. In Act Two, while on her journey through the land of the trolls, Meia shuns the prospect of arranged marriage to the wealthy crown prince. Then, at the end of the operetta, Meia sings a "rollicking duet" with her purported love interest, Peik, each asserting their desire to live alone.

[Dialogue]

Meia:	Ah, but I should be free – free to come and go through all the palaces under the sun. That's more than you will do for me!
Ulva:	Free!
Peik:	Well, go back to your base-minded little prince then! Run away!
Meia:	Tomorrow, Peik.
Peik:	I haven't a single jewel.
Meia:	Beads and shells!
Peik:	Nor ever a palace, -
Meia:	The forest, the sky, and a cot to be warm in!
Peik:	And I shan't share you with any other man!
Meia:	What others are there for me?
Peik:	Nor let you go roaming around the world.
Meia:	Away from you!
Peik:	Just an everyday common lot ours will be, and you an everyday hardworking woman –
Meia:	But with a song in the work!

[Duet]

Meia:	With a cot and a garden And a chicken or two –

Peik:	And a girl like a rose on my heart –
Meia:	With a cow and a dairy
	And plenty to do –
Peik:	And a man to do his part –
Meia:	But what need of a man?
Peik:	Oh what need of a wife?
Both:	I shall live in content
	The most rapturous life!
	We shall live all alone
	Oh the merriest life!.

MONROE, The Trolls' Holiday: Act III

Unusually, rather than raving about the solo vocalists and their numbers, the reviews of performances of *The Trolls' Holiday*, as well as Smith's later operettas, always comment on the quality of the numbers that she composed for chorus and their execution. A reviewer for the *Chicago Tribune* writes, "Despite the very creditable work of three or four of the young people, the chief merit of the performance lay in the spirit of the singing of the chorus. It is obvious that Smith works 'from within.' Nothing so fresh and spontaneous and unspoiled could have been achieved by the methods of the ordinary automatic trainer" (*Chicago Tribune* review qtd. in *Hull-House Bulletin* 7/1, 1905–06: 18). An unlabeled press clipping in the Jane Addams Papers reinforces this: "As a chorus the entire company sang well. Tuneful melodies, wrought into intricate and weird yet beautiful harmonies, gave opportunity to all to give of their best" (Unknown source reprinted in Elrod, 2001a: 239). This review also observes that the children transcend the misery of impoverishment through art: "Besides bringing into the limelight several future prima donnas—who can both sing and act—it proved that in the slums there is talent that is both willing and ready to learn."

The only surviving numbers from Smith's score for *The Trolls' Holiday* are choral pieces from Act I: "It's Summer Today" and "Come with Me." Monroe's libretto indicates that there are three additional choral numbers in Act I, two choruses sung by the trolls in Act II, and four choruses (sung by village residents, children, and trolls) in Act III of *The Trolls' Holiday*. The surviving excerpts illustrate Smith's ability to design harmonic contrasts that support the text and to craft artful melodies for children, as noted by W.L. Hubbard in the *Chicago Tribune*.

For this pretty story Miss Smith has supplied a succession of musical numbers which are attractive beyond the average. They are in every instance melodious and essentially singable, and they are harmonized in a manner which, while skillfully avoiding the difficult and intricate, still lends them musical interest and individuality. Many of the melodies have a distinctly northern turn, and their treatment has been in several instances in keeping with this national character.

"News of the Theaters," 5 June 1905: 9

"It's Summer Today" (Illustration 3.2) is the first choral number in the piece and expresses the excitement that Norwegian (and Midwestern) children experience as the summer solstice approaches. Smith composes a small ABA' ternary form in which the middle section modulates from A♭ major to A major and changes meter from a lilting 6/8 to a brisk 4/4. This corresponds to shift in the text in which the "troop of children," as they are called in Monroe's libretto, divert their attention from expressing glee at the wonders of nature's playground and momentarily convene as a military regiment: "We are soldiers with drum and a gun, A marching to Battle! Come join in the fun!." The vocal melody in the framing A sections of this song is quite unusual for a children's tune because it very rarely emphasizes or rests on the tonic note, A♭. Instead, the vocal line outlines an F minor[7] chord while the accompaniment sounds an open fifth drone on the tonic (A♭–E♭) in the bass for most of the number, a standard feature of European folk music. This sets the mood for a whimsical adventure that is intensified by unconventional chromatic inflections, like the recurrent B-natural in the harmony (a good example of a "weird, but beautiful harmony").

In "Come with Me," the second number for chorus in *The Trolls' Holiday* (Illustration 3.3), the group of village children pretend to be fairies floating in the sky. In this number Smith abandons the stylized folk music idioms of "It's Summer Today" and adopts the qualities of dreamy songs from contemporary Broadway shows, like "Moonbeams" from Victor Herbert's *The Red Mill*. A typical device in songs from this era is the use of the harmonic progression I-vi-ii-V (mm. 10-16), which Smith uses to accompany the long-held sustained notes in the vocal part (half notes in measures 12 and 16). This ascent leaves the listener yearning to reach the high F in measure 17. Delaying the flow of constant eighth notes in this passage creates a sense of suspended hovering as the singers slowly ascend to the high F in the vocal part on the words "Fly o'er the housetops and up to the stars."

4   *A Fable in Flowers* and *The Merman's Bride*

In 1918, Eleanor Smith composed another operetta entitled *A Fable in Flowers* with her younger sister, Gertrude. Caroline Foulke Urie, the author of the

ILLUSTRATION 3.2   "It's Summer Today," choral number from *The Trolls' Holiday* by Eleanor
Smith, 1905
SOURCE: HULL HOUSE COLLECTION, SPECIAL COLLECTIONS,
DALEY LIBRARY, UNIVERSITY OF ILLINOIS AT CHICAGO.

libretto, became involved with educational initiatives at Hull-House in 1910
and was the head of the Montessori school at Hull-House from 1916–19. The
Chicago Tribune reports that Edith Nancrede designed the settings and costumes and Mabel Pearse choreographed the dances ("An Operetta in Hull

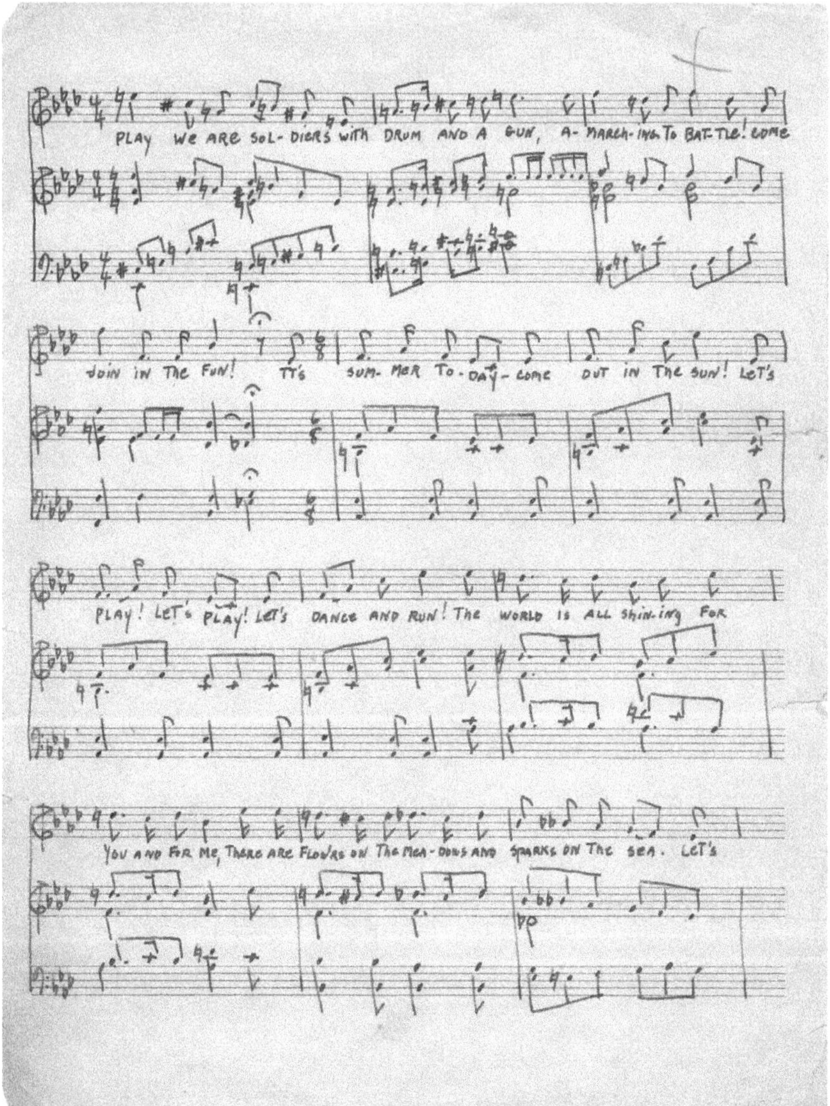

ILLUSTRATION 3.2 (continued)

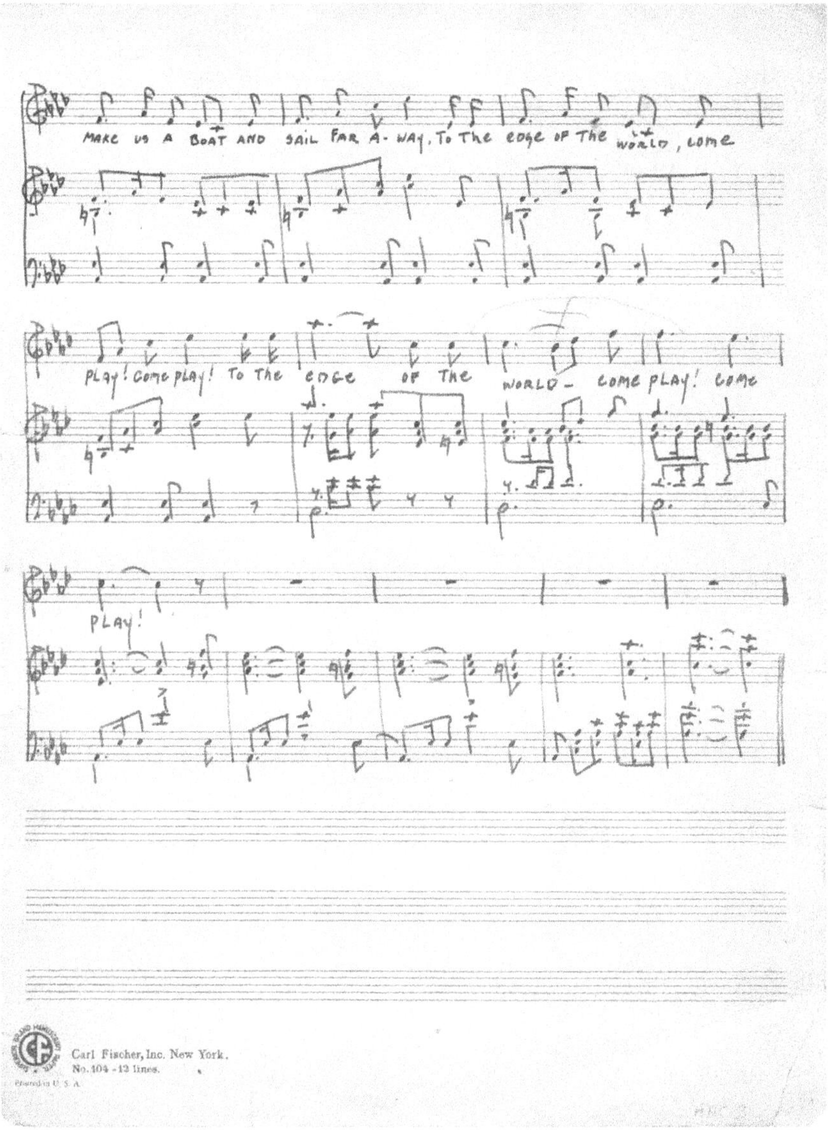

ILLUSTRATION 3.2 (continued)

ILLUSTRATION 3.3   "Come with Me," choral number from *The Trolls' Holiday* by Eleanor
                      Smith, 1905
                      SOURCE: HULL HOUSE COLLECTION, SPECIAL COLLECTIONS,
                      DALEY LIBRARY, UNIVERSITY OF ILLINOIS AT CHICAGO.

Carl Fischer, Inc. New York.
No. 104 - 18 lines.
Printed in U. S. A.

ILLUSTRATION 3.3   (continued)

House," *Chicago Tribune*, 18 February 1918: 11). The piece premiered at the Hull-House Theater on 23 February 1918, while the First World War was still raging, and the operetta was performed five times; subscription seats were available at the last performance on March 17th, which was a benefit for the Red Cross ("Urie-Smith Operetta Sung in Hull House," *Chicago Tribune*, 25 February 1918: 11). This operetta also enjoyed a 1936 revival at Hull-House as indicated on a program in the Hull-House Collection dated 4 June 1936 (Box 34, folder 337).

Urie (1873–1955) graduated from Bryn Mawr College in 1896 and was a devoted Quaker and an outspoken pacifist. She married Dr. John Francis Urie in 1910. Examining Urie's libretto, published by the Hildman printing company in 1918 as a freestanding literary text, illustrates that the story promotes the protection of American natural resources and civilian life. Harriet Monroe provides a plot synopsis and offers enthusiastic praise in an undated "Letter to the Editor" that was published in the *Friday Literary Review*:

> A pageant of the seasons in which the characters are Mother Earth and her children, the winds and rains, the trees and flowers, the birds, butterflies, insects, etc., all personified by human children, from 5 years old to 20, or more. This sounds formidable, I admit, but the theme is so skillfully handled by the poet and composer, and so bewitchingly acted and sung by the hundred or more people, little and big, in the cast, that the performance races along all too rapidly, with dramatic variety in its action and never a slow moment to interrupt its beauty.
>
> Eleanor Smith Papers, Box 1, Folder 36

The reviewer for the *Chicago Tribune* praises Urie's libretto: "Mrs. Urie's libretto is well nigh entirely in rhymed verse, with sparse passages of spoken dialogue. Her verses 'sing'; that is, they lend themselves easily and smoothly to singing, they are bright and clear in idea, with a quality of unexpectedness in meter and rhythms. They have been set by the Misses Smith to light, ornate music, which, like the text, sings ("Urie-Smith Operetta Sung in Hull-House").

A Fable in Flowers, which strongly conveys the values of the Progressive movement even during the late stages of the Great War, is an early example of children's musical literature that advocates for pacifism and humanitarianism through its personification of nature ("Mother Earth") as a caring, maternal figure. A lengthy review published in *Social Progress* suggests that the theme of trust in maternal guidance is one of the operetta's most important messages. Of course, this was a particularly relevant subject after the U.S. entrance into World War I in April 1917. Described by reviewer Elisabeth Miller as "a pageant of seasons," *A Fable in Flowers* depicts Mother Earth sending her flower children out into the world during the spring, summer, and autumn seasons.

The flower children encounter insects, butterflies, and birds and they are subject to the harsh elements as heat, winds, rain, mists, and a blustery storm, threaten their well-being. Finally, as winter approaches, the North Wind and the East Wind perform a wild dance that "scatters the flower children, blowing them off the stage" (Miller, 1918: 318). Although none of the commentary on the work explicitly draws this connection, the Mother Earth character may be a portrayal of Jane Addams as she was one of the most prominent American women who campaigned for pacifism prior to and during World War I.

In essence, *A Fable in Flowers* allegorically depicts that Mother Earth's faith in the ability of the flower children to adapt to their natural environment will be the societal cornerstone that will allow future generations to overcome the devastation of war. Religious studies scholar Elizabeth Agnew illustrates that Addams's justification for her pacifist position is grounded in the "romantic strain of antiwar evolutionism, which pointed to altruism and mutual support in nature to assert the human potential for cooperation in countering class and state violence" (2017: 9). After the conclusion of the War, Addams formalized her pacifistic thought in *Peace and Bread in Time of War* (1922), a text that Agnew argues is strongly influenced by Georg Freiderike Nicolai's *The Biology of War* (1915, English translation 1918). Addams reinforces Nicolai's assertion that animals do not kill members of their own species as a means of evolutionary survival, but instead they survive by better adapting to the environment (Agnew, 2017: 13). She reminds readers that human evolution advanced with the development of tools and cooperation, not with weapons, and writes that cooperation "is older and more primitive than mass combat, which is an outgrowth of the much later property instinct" (Addams qtd. in Agnew, 2017: 13).

Score excerpts from *A Fable in Flowers* support this reading. When compared to the manuscripts from *The Trolls' Holiday*, which feature text written in capital letters, it is difficult to discern whether Eleanor or Gertrude Madeira Smith penned the manuscript. This opening prologue establishes that Mother Earth is extremely concerned about the loss of life that has occurred due to the War and she strives to protect her flower children, or fellow citizens, by advocating for peace. The scene is conceived holistically as one flowing stretch of music comprised of smaller units; musical transitions connect the sung dialogic exchanges between the flower children and Mother Earth (Hull-House Collection, Box 52: Folder 594). The scene begins with a frightful cry from the flower children: "Ah! What was that? A cry in the dark! Danger is near us, listen! Hark!." Reminiscent of the style of representative cinematic music, Smith composes menacing tremolos in the key of D minor to indicate that a storm is on the horizon. A short musical interlude, which maintains an unsettling dominant pedal A in the bass, precedes the entrance of Mother Earth, who confirms that there is chaos raging outside: "Out in the night the wild storm giants go forth to fight! High on the galloping winds they ride, wasting and ruining far and wide. Their cloud battalions go thundering by to quench the sun and darken the sky." (Illustration 3.4)

This passage introduces emphatic war imagery that appears throughout the rest of this scene, and continues throughout the operetta. The hyper-dramatic opening section suggests that the work is intended as an allegory for wartime

ILLUSTRATION 3.4   "Prologue," from *A Fable in Flowers* by Eleanor and Gertrude Madeira
Smith, 1918
SOURCE: HULL HOUSE COLLECTION, SPECIAL COLLECTIONS,
DALEY LIBRARY, UNIVERSITY OF ILLINOIS AT CHICAGO.

ILLUSTRATION 3.4 (continued)

sentiment to illustrate that feelings of fear and insecurity, likely deeply felt by many of the women and children comprising the audience and performers, can be overtaken by optimism and collective strength.

After putting the flower children to sleep with a lullaby in the key of G major, Mother Earth reverts to a gloomy C minor to voice her own concerns in an aria that functions as a soliloquy (Illustration 3.5). Again, the symbolism quite obviously pertains to World War I and also projects evolutionary rhetoric that places an emphasis on the continuity of life.

When fields are bleak and branches bare
And winter and death are everywhere
Deep in the earth beneath the snows
Is a Mother heart that stirs and glows
And keeps long vigil in Death's domain
To make all ready for spring again
For Winter and Death like a dream will pass
Like shadows of cloud on the sunlit grass
And Life will triumph through travail and strife
For the will of the world is Life, is Life

The aria begins with hollow, widely-spaced chords in the accompaniment to create a mood of desolation and emptiness. This texture prevails as the text's focus on winter and death dominates most of the aria, and it is generally paired with an emphasis on the low register of the singer's voice. Smith draws our attention to the phrase "And Life will triumph" by creating a sudden shift in the metric grouping, moving from a duple to a triple subdivision of the beat, accompanied by a modulation from C minor to E♭ major and a robust chordal texture. This excerpt is certainly one of Smith's most powerful solo arias; it displays a similar poignancy in response to current social predicaments as *Hull House Songs* and suggests that the young adults who played the leading roles in the Hull-House operettas were capable singers.

Lastly, Eleanor Smith composed both the libretto and score for *The Merman's Bride*, excerpts of which were presented at Hull-House and the Chicago Intersettlement Music Festival in 1925 (Moore, "Children Stage Intersettlement Music Festival," *Chicago Tribune*, 7 June 1925: 26). The complete work premiered in 1928, with performances in May and November (Elrod, 2001b: 812).[5] Smith conceived the story as an adaptation of "The Forsaken Merman," which is a Danish or German folk tale, but commentators clearly viewed it as an allegory of present-day issues. *The Merman's Bride* is staged, but Smith classifies the work as a cantata, not an operetta, possibly because the vocal soloists do not act on stage. It is scored for two pianos, string quartet, four solo voices, a chorus, and actors and dancers to mime the characters of the story (Elrod, 2001a: 81). The singers and musicians performed offstage in the theater's balcony while the actors and dancers were the primary focus on the main stage (Illustration 3.6).

---

5   Albert J. Kennedy (1929) cites specific dates: "Three years ago in May *The Merman's Bride* had its first performance. The work was repeated in November, 1925 and again in May and November, 1928. The writer was privileged to attend the performances of November 10 and 11, 1928" (91).

It is unclear whether Smith was familiar with Matthew Arnold's 1853 poem with the same title. In "The Forsaken Merman" a Merman marries Hannele (the character is called Margaret in the Arnold poem), a human woman, who descends under the sea to wed the Merman and lives happily there for seven years in a castle with her husband and their three children (Illustration 3.7). Extremely homesick, Hannele hears bells ringing on Easter Day and asks her husband to

ILLUSTRATION 3.5   "When Fields Are Bleak," aria from *A Fable in Flowers* by Eleanor and
Gertrude Madeira Smith, 1918
SOURCE: HULL HOUSE COLLECTION, SPECIAL COLLECTIONS,
DALEY LIBRARY, UNIVERSITY OF ILLINOIS AT CHICAGO.

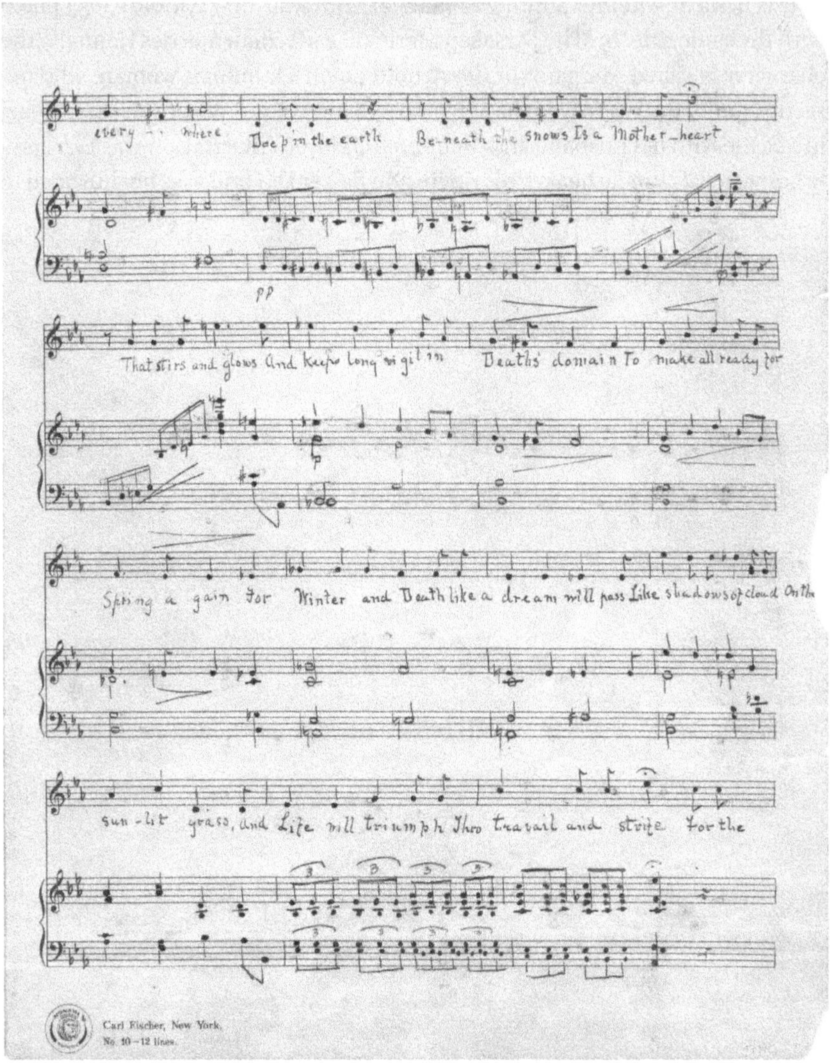

ILLUSTRATION 3.5 (continued)

ILLUSTRATION 3.5   (continued)

ILLUSTRATION 3.6   Dancers in *The Merman's Bride*, 1928
SOURCE: JANE ADDAMS MEMORIAL COLLECTION (JAMC), SPECIAL
COLLECTIONS, DALEY LIBRARY, UNIVERSITY OF ILLINOIS AT
CHICAGO.

permit her to return to earth for a day to visit her parents and friends. While attending church Hannele obtains spiritual fulfillment and cannot bear to return to a life under the sea. The Merman and the children frantically call to her from outside of the church, but Hannele is preoccupied with scripture and does not even notice. In this tale, the female character uncharacteristically deserts her husband and children because she feels stifled by her futile existence under the sea.

Matthew Arnold's poem, told from the Merman's perspective, portrays Margaret (Hannele) as cold and selfish, as conveyed by the poem's final lines:

Over banks of bright seaweed
The ebb-tide leave dry.
We will gaze, from the sand-hills,
At the white, sleeping town;
At the church on the hillside—
And then come back down.

Singing, "There dwells a lov'd one,
But cruel is she.
She left lonely forever
The kings of the sea…"
ARNOLD, 1922 [1853]: 22

ILLUSTRATION 3.7   Hannele and Her Children in *The Merman's Bride*, 1928
SOURCE: JANE ADDAMS MEMORIAL COLLECTION (JAMC), SPECIAL
COLLECTIONS, DALEY LIBRARY, UNIVERSITY OF ILLINOIS AT CHICAGO.

This story is darker and less optimistic than those dramatized in Smith's other works, but its themes of combating feminine despondence through emancipation must have resonated with her as she chose this text, adapted from an unknown literary source, to set to music with her own lyrics. In Smith's operetta Hannele does return to her family, but Albert J. Kennedy's discussion of the production in *Neighborhood* (1929) reports that Smith's "music mirrors the brooding tragedy, perhaps unsolvable, which is the story" (93), and thus does not downplay the depiction of the painful emotional distancing of Hannele from her husband and children.

Kennedy, an esteemed researcher of the settlement house movement, continues with more detailed information about *The Merman's Bride*, which was not reviewed by the *Chicago Tribune*. Similar to remarks made about the premise of *The Trolls' Holiday*, Kennedy observes that the themes of the folk tale relate fittingly to the lives of participants at Hull-House.

> The germ of the libretto Miss Smith found in an old folk tale, known under the title of "The Forsaken Merman." Certain it is, however, that in passing through Miss Smith's mind, the story has come to have a curious affinity with the social forms and the temper of the folk life on Halsted Street. It moves with the simple swift directness of life itself, echoing its imperious demands on the body and the emotions. It neither preaches nor teaches. The characters are, if you will, the victims of forces which, when all is said and done, are themselves.
>
> 92

Kennedy elaborates further and explains that the piece speaks to couples and families in the neighborhood who overcome the challenges of domestic ennui by heeding their children's needs and upholding the nuclear family:

> Thus do they marry on Halsted Street, and children come, and love grows thin and wan, and sounds and odors and associations of other days imperiously call. But the even more imperious will of the children, for the most part, whips the parents into the ancient and traditional family mold.
>
> 93

Like other commentators Kennedy praises the high quality of Smith's music, calling it "thoroughly and profoundly original," and specifying that there is "no harking back to older modes or composers, no ghosts rise upon the current of the melodic stream" (93). Writing in the late 1920s, when the American art music repertoire had undergone significant expansion by composers like John Philip Sousa and George Gershwin, Kennedy places more emphasis on Smith's crafting of an American style, proclaiming that it is "deeply American [...] a kind of writing that is slowly but surely bringing us to that definitive musical idiom which will be as distinctively ours as are those of France and Italy and Germany" (93). Kennedy also waxes ecstatic about the choral numbers, reporting that "the choruses are the most beautiful and moving of all... into them Smith has put her most original and charming melodies, her subtlest rhythms and her swiftest and most provoking changes of tonality" (94).

Smith's large-scale operatic compositions offer valuable insight into how Progressive Era women valorized, and collaboratively implemented, art as a pedagogical necessity for children at Hull-House. It is obvious that as they envisioned the operettas they felt it imperative to create new scenarios to better depict the world of their students. In keeping with John Dewey's notion that children profit from hands-on experience (Provenzo Jr., 2009: 484), they also clearly believed that children benefitted from the challenge of performing full-length productions comparable to those of adults: the libretti and music are very difficult and their apparently brilliant execution is a testament to the women's rigorous training and rehearsal methods. In fact, in her essay "The Play Instinct and the Arts" Addams confirms that Hull-House's emphasis on the arts was devised in tandem with Dewey's discoveries.

> The early School of Education at the University of Chicago, founded by John Dewey, demonstrated that a child, after an historic period had made itself at home in his imagination, would whole-heartedly live in that period for weeks at a time. He energetically dug, built, wove and cooked, sometimes according to his need in a primitive hut, at other times in a moat surrounding a medieval castle. But because this fresh imaginative life with its instinct for play is, in a sense, the mission of art itself, we have found at Hull-House that our educational efforts tend constantly toward a training for artistic expression—in a music school, a school of dramatics, classes in rhythm and dancing and the school of the plastic and graphic arts.
>
> 1930: 808

Eleanor Smith's forgotten operettas, which at the time of their premieres were recognized as consummate artworks for children, truly substantiate Addams's affirmation that "From time to time in moments of depression or of exhilaration over some public undertaking to which the residents were committed, we have urged Miss Smith to phrase in music the social compunction which at the moment it seemed impossible to express in any other way" (Elshtain, 2002: 427). My examination of Smith's operettas authenticates that these elaborate productions were indeed intended to serve as commentary on local and global issues and to portray women as active contributors to society, breaking from the fairy-tale topoi of princesses being whisked away by wealthy suitors that dominated romantic opera and ballet. Similar to the opening songs of *Hull House Songs*, Smith relies on dramatic music to bring to life the predicaments of female and juvenile characters in the operettas and she does not sanitize their emotional travails. As has been discussed, the characters not only represent the neighborhood's workers and communal networks, but they also possess attributes that seem to reflect facets central to Smith's identity and that of her Hull-House colleagues.

In their depiction of domestic spheres, the operettas feature few paternal figures (this could be for practical purposes as there were more female singers available for the demanding protagonist roles than male) and contain undertones of resistance to heteronormativity and marriage, which several scholars have established as an important, but largely unspoken, value of some Hull-House women (Hamington, 2010: 21–22). For example, in *The Trolls' Holiday* Meia rejects an arranged marriage and envisions her future as a free, independent woman, unbound to a husband. Her mother, Aslog, is a single mother and relies on the community to look out for her children. In *The Merman's Bride* Hannele is trapped in an unhappy marriage and sacrifices her own emotional health for the sake of her children. Neither Jane Addams, Harriet Monroe, nor Eleanor Smith openly discusses her sexual identity, but all profited from intellectual, and possibly intimate, relationships with women. Louise W. Knight argues that Jane Addams's same-sex relationships with Ellen Gates Starr and Mary Rozet Smith shaped her social theory and outlook on life: "Addams thought about, and explored, three functions of love: intimate love; affectionate, cooperative love; and love of humanity, sometimes called love of the stranger" (Knight, 2010b: 182). In essence, the lives of these women were largely detached from the masculine realm of economic opportunism and unburdened by contemporaneous masculine expectations of women, namely child-bearing.

All of Smith's operettas articulate this "love of the stranger" philosophy as they sought to help Chicago citizens of all classes recognize that a broadened understanding of maternalism could serve as a catalyst for wide-scale social reform. Maternalism could take the form of reconceptualization of the settlement as a multifaceted space that would benefit urban professionals as well as the poor, nurturing disadvantaged children through the arts, and it could even help to alleviate violent global conflict through advocacy for pacifism. This veneration of maternalism was achieved not only through the operetta's thematic messages, but also through public recognition of the talents and expertise of the women who brought them to the stage and served as the maternal figures for the productions.

CHAPTER 4

Eleanor Smith and Her Circle: Female Patronage, Cultural Production, and Friendship at Hull-House

Rima Lunin Schultz

1   Introduction

For almost fifty years Eleanor Smith (1858–1942) directed the Hull-House Music School. Through its portals hundreds of neighborhood children were introduced to the great canon of Western musical culture. They were taught to read and write music; they participated in choral groups, cantatas and operettas and became familiar with a classical music repertoire. They also learned ethnic folk songs and dances of their own and their neighbors' backgrounds. Many studied instruments and participated in ensembles. Some were asked to play in the Hull-House symphony orchestra alongside professional musicians. Smith, who composed the music for the *Hull House Songs*, several cantatas, and a number of operettas was aided in her work by talented teachers and supported by the collaborative efforts of two extraordinary Hull-House women: artist Enella Benedict (1858–1942), who headed the Hull-House art studios and Art School for more than four decades, and Edith de Nancrede (1868–1936), the director of children's and young adults' theatrical productions, who came to Hull-House in 1897 while a student at the Art Institute of Chicago and remained at the settlement until her untimely death in 1936. Music, art, and drama students tended to develop relationships with their teachers over many years. They knew Hull-House primarily from these long-term associations. A music student recalled, "You see, we never got too close to Jane Addams although we saw her quite a bit. But she was always busy—either going places or probably out of town" (Eleanor Carroll Farwell Oral interview transcript, July 14, 1981, 10, Hull-House Oral History Collection). Nancrede, Benedict, and Smith *were* Hull-House to them as much or more than Addams. Yet Smith, Benedict, and Nancrede have been treated as secondary or tertiary residents marginally related to the reform activism associated with the progressive movement (Davis, 1967).

Few historians have made the connection between its innovative cultural pedagogy and its reform politics and, instead, have focused on the latter, emphasizing the way the settlement run by women empowered female social feminism, advanced professional careers, promoted women's trade unionism, and engendered the emerging welfare state (Sklar, 1985; Muncy, 1994; Payne, 1988; Gordon, 1994; Fitzpatrick, 1994). Overlooking the settlement's cultural leaders is surprising because for quite some time there has been a focus on Hull-House as woman's space, but even here the focus has been on the political or redemptive, not the performative (Sklar, 1985; Spain, 2001; Hayden, 1995). James Weber Linn, most likely with his Aunt Jane Addams's help and her approval, since she read the draft of the manuscript before she died and annotated it (Linn, 1935: vii-viii), also chose six women of the many who were resident at Hull-House, as those closest to Addams: Ellen Starr, Julia Lathrop, Alice Hamilton, Florence Kelley, Louise Bowen, and Mary Rozet Smith (129–150). Enella Benedict and Edith de Nancrede are mentioned in passing and Eleanor Smith is not mentioned at all. This certainly can account for the erasure of Eleanor Smith and her circle from the history of Hull-House; after Linn's, no serious biography of Addams is written until 1973 when historian Allen F. Davis published *American Heroine: The Life and Legend of Jane Addams*. Eleanor, Edith, and Enella are not mentioned at all by Davis. Addams recognized the cultural work that had been accomplished by Smith and her circle in *The Second Twenty Years at Hull-House's* (1930) chapter, "Play Instinct and the Arts," but the sense of friendship and the excitement of innovation of the early years is absent. Only when you read the collection of oral interviews of former students does the cultural work come alive. One of the few books to capture this is Shannon Jackson's *Lines of Activity* (2000) which relies on interviews. This chapter attempts to recapture the initial enthusiasm and creativity that led to the large body of work produced by Smith with the collaboration of Benedict and Nancrede. They were the architects of the less examined but nonetheless *major* work of the Hull-House founders: the experiment with new democratic roles for art, music, dance, drama, crafts, literature, and storytelling in American life. Although these women worked in cultural and educational institutions run by men during most of their careers, they found at Hull-House, working with co-founders Jane Addams (1860–1935) and Ellen Gates Starr (1859–1940), and the financial support of Mary Rozet Smith (1868–1934) and Louise deKoven Bowen (1859–1953), something otherwise missing: an environment that *empowered* them and *unlocked* the creativity of themselves and their students. Other institutions, like the public schools, offered the opportunity to work with the children of immigrants, but under bureaucracies such teachers as Smith did not control.

This chapter introduces the three women biographically and in the context of Chicago as a center of a thriving women's political culture in the Progressive Era (Flanagan, 2002; Schultz, 2001: xxvi-xxviii) that nurtured the work undertaken at Hull-House. Addams's and Starr's early efforts to bring the arts to the poor immigrants of Chicago's industrial West Side (Boris, 1986; Horowitz, 1976) were met with enthusiasm as social feminists volunteered at the settlement, became residents, and used their talents in a collaborative effort. Hull-House soon became a community of women and men, led by women and funded primarily by them (Sklar, 1990; Schultz, 2001: 817–819; Alter, 2001: 101–106; Glowacki, 2001: 202–205), based on shared values and female friendship. Soon Hull-House became a center for innovation and a clearing house where new ideas and praxis of play, performance, and the use of dance, art, music and drama developed alongside social and political campaigns (Jackson, 2000; Tomko, 1999; Vaillant, 2003). Eleanor Smith and the Hull-House community were involved with the work of progressive education reformers Francis W. Parker and John Dewey (Durst, 2010: 109–112), but Hull-House's pedagogical and cultural innovations were dominated by the women.

2   The Biographies of Eleanor Smith and Her Circle

Who were the three women who spent their lives teaching neighborhood children music, art, and drama at Hull-House? Very little has been written about

ILLUSTRATION 4.1   Eleanor Smith with students at the Hull-House Music School, c. 1920
SOURCE: JANE ADDAMS MEMORIAL COLLECTION (JAMC), SPECIAL
COLLECTIONS, DALEY LIBRARY, UNIVERSITY OF ILLINOIS AT
CHICAGO.

them (Ganz, 2001: 75–77; Jackson, 2001: 618–620; Elrod, 2001b: 810–812). Eleanor Smith was born in a small town, Atlanta, in central Illinois, but moved
with her family to Chicago. She was the second of seven children; her sister
Gertrude Madeira Smith was a pianist and taught at Hull-House where she
lived for many decades. As with many families from small Midwestern locales
who had roots in New England and New York, the Smiths were culturally sophisticated. Her family, she recalled, "were all musical people, the forbears on
both sides...being devoted to the art in one way or another" (1909: 112). Her father's family came originally from New England, and there was a remote great-
grandfather who was known locally as a composer. "However, being a Puritan
minister, he confined himself to psalm-tunes" (Ibid). The maternal line was of
"that mixed blood which is supposed to make musicians. They were Danish,
with German, French and a slight flavor of the Jewish somewhere in the past"
(Ibid). Smith's musical abilities in childhood and adolescence were largely self-
taught (Elrod, 2001b: 810). She displayed a remarkable ear, teaching herself to
play the piano duplicating melodies and harmonies with great accuracy (Ibid).
Her father, like John Huy Addams, Jane's father, was an early and ardent supporter of Abraham Lincoln (Ibid), again keeping with the patterns of culture
and politics that emanated from New England and forged the abolitionism of
the upper Midwest. When Willard Newton Smith moved his family to Chicago
in the 1860s (her sister Gertrude was born in 1868), the city was emerging as an
impressive metropolis growing rapidly after its Great Fire in 1871 and flourishing culturally with energy and drive ready to establish museums, concert halls,
academies and conservatories to vie with those in the eastern cities (McCarthy,
1982). Her father was in the choir of the First Presbyterian Church (Otis, 1924).
First Presbyterian was the "hub" of elite culture at the time and its music program was ambitious for the young city (Stevenson, 1907). It was in this milieu
that Smith, at the age of eighteen, began formal musical training with voice
and composition lessons. "Troubled with very poor vision and a possibility of
blindness, Smith was sometimes forced to use her eyes for only a brief period
each day" (Elrod, 2001b: 810). However, she was intensely ambitious and committed to music composition. Her enrollment in the Hershey School of Music
coincided with the arrival of Frederic Grant Gleason on its faculty. Gleason had
studied in Leipzig and had a reputation as "a futurist, an impressionist... holding ideals as to the future of music which were somewhat revolutionary" (Otis,
1924: 165). Smith's ambition to be a composer of serious music strengthened
and while still at the Hershey School she composed *The Golden Asp*, which premiered in 1883 (Payette, this volume). Concurrently she trained to be a music
teacher and graduated from the Cook County Normal School during the period
of Col. Francis Wayland Parker's leadership. Called the "father of progressive

education," by John Dewey (Cremin, 1964: 21), Parker had been successful as superintendent in Boston and Quincy, Massachusetts, where he inaugurated changes in the public schools. He left the east to take charge of the teachers' training institution in Chicago with goals of carrying out the same kinds of radical changes—rejecting rote learning, ending harsh discipline, introducing music and art in elementary education, and unleashing children's natural creativity. Having previously visited schools in Prussia, Switzerland, and Holland, "he based his educational reforms especially on the work of Pestalozzi and Froebel" (Corcoran, 2005: 73). He turned Cook County Normal into a laboratory, an "open-minded setting where faculty planned teaching, evaluated curriculum, shared ideas" (Ibid). This exposed Smith to the latest educational theories. Froebel had emphasized music education in the formative years of a child's cognitive and spiritual development and this fit with Parker's ideas. Believing that the schoolroom should "nourish rather than kill" the natural qualities of which every child was endowed, Parker was especially interested in stimulating creativity through the arts and music using the child's natural spontaneity (Curti, 1959: 381). Teaching under Parker for several years, Smith became interested in the training of children's voices (Anonymous, 1909: 112–113). Smith felt she needed more advanced training and left for Germany. In Berlin, she studied composition under Moritz Moszkowski and Ludwig Bussler and singing under Julius Hey (113). She also traveled extensively in Europe and in England, visiting choir schools to learn as much as she could about methods for vocal instruction of children.

> While abroad I did everything possible to get hold of the secrets of the choir-masters, especially to find out how the wonderful quality of the boys' voices is achieved and preserved. I had letters to Albert Becker from my friend, Dr. Langhans, the critic. Herr Becker was at the head of the Dom Chor, one of the greatest in the world, and taught as well at various of the boys' high schools. I called on this gentleman, who, by the way, was an eminent composer. He gave me permission to attend his rehearsals and lessons. This, however, had to be withdrawn, as the high powers considered it most indelicate for a woman to wish to attend rehearsals and lessons where males alone were pupils and performers.
> ANONYMOUS, "Interview with Eleanor Smith," 1909: 113

Smith said she had better luck in South Germany where she spent five or six weeks observing the Cathedral choir at Regensburg, the renowned choir of the great Cecilian movement that had led in the reform of Catholic church music.

While at this place I made up my mind on one point, and that was that there was ground for original research and study in the matter of voice training among children. For, while the quality of the children's voices was wonderful in the choirs, it was very bad in the schools, and classes taught by the same people who had apparently achieved great results in the choirs. My conclusion was that only rare and lovely voices were secured for the choirs, and these voices are carefully preserved and their owners given fine musical training. But as to the ordinary and spoiled voice, this training did not touch it. 'He that is filthy, let him be filthy still,' seemed not the intention, but the fact.

ANONYMOUS, "Interview with Eleanor Smith," 1909: 113

Smith also listened to many choirs in England, but they did not compare with the Dom Chor in Berlin, or the Thomas Chor in Leipzig, either vocally or musically (113).

During her three-year sojourn in Berlin her musical friends encouraged her plan of founding a music school that would provide an all-round training.

We agreed that there was need of a school where there should be co-operation between the teachers of singing and piano—that 'one hand will watch the other,' as the Germans have it—that ability to sing will help piano-playing, while the mastery of the piano is of immense value to the singer. Singers are constantly being blamed for their lack of general musical culture, and pianists are too often over devoted to the technical side of their art. I had many valuable suggestions from wise and learned friends, and one of these was Miss Amalie Hannig, a teacher of piano at the Klindworth Conservatory.

ANONYMOUS, "Interview with Eleanor Smith," 1909: 113

In 1892, Smith invited Hannig to leave Germany and relocate in Chicago and become part of the pioneering music school at the settlement. The two women shared a love of music and similar pedagogical philosophies and they began to construct a music curriculum that would incorporate their ideas about the cognitive, emotional, and spiritual development of children as well as their understanding of technical aspects of musical training.

Concurrently Smith sought professional employment outside of the settlement. With her reformer's zeal to disseminate her philosophy about music education, at the invitation of Col. Parker, Smith took charge of the Vocal Department of the Cook County Normal School in 1897, and in 1902, accepted

John Dewey's invitation "to teach music to aspiring teachers at the University of Chicago's School of Education and to assist him in revising curriculum for music education" (Elrod, 2001b: 811). In addition, she taught at the Froebel Kindergarten College and the Chicago Kindergarten College, which at times were housed at Hull-House. She authored many books of vocal music for children, among them the multi-volume *Eleanor Smith Music Course* published by the American Book Company (Bryan and Davis, 1990: 103).

The Hull-House Music School, however, was Smith's priority and in reading between the lines, one detects her ongoing effort to make the case for the sort of musical training with professional staff she envisioned. A perfectionist, demanding excellence from her students, staff, and most of all, herself, Smith fought to expand the music school and to provide adequate compensation for the music teachers who, like herself, were independent, self-supporting women without privilege. "Eleanor Smith is again on the warpath about Miss Jones," Addams wrote Mary Smith. "She says Miss Jones would come for $10.00 a month and do lots of teaching of a most valuable sort" (Addams to Mary Rozet Smith, 1898).[1]

Eleanor Smith's brief autobiographical writings do not indicate any conflict over her choices to forego marriage and travel as a single woman in Europe, unaccompanied by a relative or friend. Nor did it seem strange for Amalie Hannig to relocate in Chicago and join Smith at Hull-House. More middle-class and privileged women were remaining single, a trend started before the Civil War, but the highest percentage of women who never married occurred among those born between 1860 and 1890 (Palmieri, 1995: 17). Smith, who did not come from wealth, expected to teach and support herself even as she pursued the dream of becoming a composer. It was Addams's social network and her ability in finding patrons to pay for these initiatives that may have made Hull-House so attractive. Eleanor became friendly with Mary Rozet Smith and her family and may have lived with the Smiths off and on before moving to 12 Walton Place, the Smith family residence in Chicago, on a permanent basis from 1924 to 1934. The Smith family provided a cushion tempering the demands and stresses caused by life in the impoverished world of workers' and immigrants. It was one of the unstated, hidden contradictions of Addams's avowal to share the common lot. Eleanor Smith benefited from friendships with rich women as did many of the middle-class Hull-House residents including Ellen Gates Starr and Edith de Nancrede. This tension between the plight of the working poor

---

1   All quoted correspondence in this chapter and the chapters that follow written by Jane Addams or sent to Jane Addams can be found in the Jane Addams Papers (microfilm collection).

ILLUSTRATION 4.2   Eleanor Smith and her patron, Mary Rozet Smith (unrelated), c. 1896
SOURCE: JANE ADDAMS MEMORIAL COLLECTION (JAMC), SPECIAL
COLLECTIONS, DALEY LIBRARY, UNIVERSITY OF ILLINOIS AT CHICAGO.

and their own privileges—albeit the result of patronage—may have had in Eleanor's case, such a deep impact that it translated into the compositions of the
Hull House Songs. Addams always understood that there was a real difference
between her residency and her neighbors in the Nineteenth Ward.

Of course, there was always present the harrowing consciousness
of the difference in economic condition between ourselves and
our neighbors. Even if we had gone to live in the most wretched
tenement, there would have always been an essential difference
between them and ourselves, for we should have had a sense of
security in regard to illness and old age and the lack of these two
securities are the specters which most persistently haunt the poor.
Could we, in spite of this, make their individual efforts more effective
through organization and possibly complement them by small efforts
of our own?

> ADDAMS, 1910: 133–134

Dr. Alice Hamilton contended that Walton Place was a refuge for Addams,
"who could hardly have carried on had she not been able to slip away from the
West Side [Hull-House's location] now and then" (1995: 67). The same could be
said for Eleanor Smith.

Enella Benedict, like Addams, came from an upper-middle-class, Protestant
background. How much money either woman controlled during her lifetime
is easier to pin down in the case of the latter, for we know little about the personal life of Enella Benedict. Both women had fathers who were Illinois pioneer entrepreneurs, civic minded, and politically active (Brown, 2004: 13–23;
Ganz, 2001: 75). Addams's father had a role in developing Cedarville, Illinois,
and served as a State Senator, and was a booster for rail lines, banks, and other
economic improvements (Brown, 2004: 15, 18–21). Enella's father, Amzi Benedict, was a Chicago cloth merchant as well as a founder and mayor of the elite
suburb of Lake Forest (Ebner, 1989). After studying at the School of the Art
Institute of Chicago and in New York, Benedict traveled to France for advanced
training in painting, "despite the isolation there of female art students, who
paid higher fees and received less rigorous instruction" (Ganz, 2001: 76–77). Her
teachers in Paris—Jean-Paul Laurens, Jules Lefebvre, and Benjamin Constant—
were realists, fine draughtsmen and colorists who produced historical works
and portraits. "As realists, they instilled in Benedict a style of precision but also
a philosophy of the relevance of art to the social, political, and economic events
of the time" (Ibid). Returning to America, she found opportunities for artists
were limited, especially for women. In a pattern resembling Eleanor Smith's
early years in Chicago, Enella Benedict pursued her career goals, continued to
exhibit her paintings, taught at the School of the Art Institute, the hub of art education in the Midwest (Moser, 1990: 194–195), and found opportunities where
she could implement her belief in the social value of art (Addams to Linn, Feb.
12, 1889, Feb. 19, 1889). Benedict did not immediately move into Hull-House
with Starr and Addams, who she had met when the three women roomed at

ILLUSTRATION 4.3 Enella Benedict, c.1920
SOURCE: JANE ADDAMS MEMORIAL COLLECTION (JAMC), SPECIAL
COLLECTIONS, DALEY LIBRARY, UNIVERSITY OF ILLINOIS AT CHICAGO.

a boarding house in a fashionable Chicago neighborhood, but she did begin
teaching art classes and she set up her own studio which was the first of many
studios Hull-House furnished for artists in the neighborhood. Benedict's bedroom at the settlement was considered plain, and she painted in the studios
she shared with others, not in her private space. Addams likened these studios
to the ones found in the Latin Quarter in Paris (1910: 374) and Benedict found
friendship and support to live in Chicago as freely as if she had remained in a

foreign city when she took up residence at Hull-House and established its Art School in 1893 (Ganz, 2001:76). She also had garnered some local recognition for her paintings. "The Singing Spinner" had been awarded the first prize at the fifth annual black-and-white exhibition of the Chicago Society of Artists (Cameron, 1893: 298–299). Benedict's painting, "Counting the Ships"—which depicted a Dutch peasant girl in a blue dress against grey rocks, looking out to sea—hung in one of the seventy-four galleries of the Palace of Fine Arts at the 1893 Columbian Exposition (Ibid). Just as Eleanor Smith had arrived at Hull-House as a seasoned music practitioner, a composer-in-residence, Benedict, who remained a working, artist-in-residence for over forty years, already had earned a reputation as an artist and teacher. Evening classes with live models made Hull-House an art center as much or even more so than the construction of the Butler art galleries (Schultz, Chapter 6, this volume). Equally significant for her future work at Hull-House was Benedict's ongoing connection with the School of the Art Institute. First as a student, and then as a faculty member, Benedict was in the center of the debate over art pedagogy and the influences of educational theorists including Froebel and Pestalozzi. She likely worked with one of the key figures in the art education movement, Josephine Locke, an art educator both in the Chicago public schools and at the School of the Art Institute (Corcoran, 2005: 64). Addams, Starr, and Benedict met Locke in 1889 (Addams to Linn, Feb. 12, 1889, Feb. 19, 1889). Although Benedict did not evolve her style, she was open to the experiments with modernism embraced by her students (Glowacki, 2004: 25). By 1899 she had begun organizing exhibits of the work of her students and neighbors (Jackson, 2000: 254) and had transformed the project of bringing art to the neighborhood to one that saw the neighbors engaged in the production and exhibition of art.

Edith de Nancrede more closely approximates the image historians have constructed of the settlement house resident than either Benedict or Smith, who were specialists in their fields and had well-defined goals for their work at Hull-House. In 1896, Nancrede came as the consummate generalist, young and unfinished in terms of a career. Nancrede, younger than the other women, had studied in Rome for two years before taking classes at the School of the Art Institute (Jackson, 2001: 618). Perhaps at the instigation of Enella Benedict, Nancrede began to volunteer at the settlement. Although she had started out contemplating a career in painting, Nancrede soon found herself initiating collaborative projects that brought music, dance, art, and drama together. She joined the new theater ensemble as one of two residents who acted in plays. Given the responsibility of supervising social clubs for young boys, she was immediately thrust into the daily activities with the neighborhood's children. Her innovative work with these social groups became her greatest contribution to the settlement and its cultural production.

ILLUSTRATION 4.4 Edith de Nancrede, c. 1929
SOURCE: JANE ADDAMS MEMORIAL COLLECTION (JAMC), SPECIAL
COLLECTIONS, DALEY LIBRARY, UNIVERSITY OF ILLINOIS AT CHICAGO.

Nancrede also found a way to integrate the arts, music, and drama departments through a creative fusion that produced the annual Christmas tableaux. She had been influenced by the artistry of *"tableaux vivants"* or living
pictures, which had become popular in the United States in the nineteenth
century (Elbert, 2002). As a student of art history, she found this reproduction
of art a way to engage the Hull-House neighbors in their cultural roots that

ILLUSTRATION 4.5   Christmas celebration in Bowen Hall, c.1930s
        SOURCE: JANE ADDAMS MEMORIAL COLLECTION (JAMC), SPECIAL
        COLLECTIONS, DALEY LIBRARY, UNIVERSITY OF ILLINOIS AT CHICAGO.

was performative rather than didactic. The elaborate Christmas tableaux were inaugurated in 1897, about one year after Nancrede's first introduction to the settlement.

> "We sang on the stage proper," remembered Eleanor Carroll, "and then overhead were the tableaux where Miss Nancrede spent a lot of time working. And Miss Gertrude Smith [Eleanor's sister] helped out on it, and there were a couple of other residents... I think Miss Benedict helped a little. She was an artist... [who would] give pointers on how the angels would look. But Miss Nancrede, of course, had all the knowledge of that. She knew just how to dress them."
>
>   ELEANOR CARROLL FARWELL Oral Interview transcript, July 14, 1981: 11,
>   Hull-House Oral History Collection

The daughter of a prominent surgeon who was on the faculty of the University of Michigan's Medical School, Nancrede had enough money to travel and study, but once she settled at Halsted and Polk her dual life as a working woman and a Hull-House resident and drama director began in earnest. Initially working as a volunteer in 1897, Nancrede moved into one of Hull-House's newly renovated single rooms when her application for residency was accepted in 1898. "She earned money for her room and board by teaching art at several North Shore private schools and later the [University of Chicago's] University School for Girls, maintaining a balance of paid employment and volunteer settlement work until the end of her life" (Jackson, 2001: 618). It was a difficult balance to achieve and her students recognized it. Nicolette Malone, who had been

Nancrede's student and, then as a young adult had become her assistant, attributed her death to overwork:

> She was very young when she died, 59, but you see we didn't have all the
> penicillin and all the antibiotics you have now, she had strep infection ....
> [and] lasted four days ...see it was the end of the season, her resistance
> was pretty low, she was worn out. * * * ** Besides teaching away from
> Hull-House, she had all these rehearsals... we would have six plays, so she
> would be rehearsing one play, getting the scenery ready, getting the cos-
> tumes ready and then teaching... she was just worn out. It was our sixth
> play—and then she had dancing classes on Saturday, 1:30 through 6:30.
> This was her whole life, her whole life.
>
> NICOLETTE MALONE Oral Interview transcript, March 10, 1980: Part I, 8, Hull-
> House Oral History Collection

In later years Nancrede was paid a modest stipend for her Hull-House work,
but not enough for her to forego her other positions. Her work at the settlement, like Smith's and Benedict's went far beyond the narrow definition of a
"job." For the Hull-House women professionalism was not equated with a pay-
check. From the start, seasoned residents seemed to know that Nancrede had
the settlement spirit. The absence of such a quality made some recruits unsuit-
able to join the community. "We have another resident whom we hope to have
soon in the crèche cottage," Addams wrote Mary Rozet Smith. "She frankly acknowledges that she is 'self centered,' no one disputes her. But I pity her from
the bottom of my heart. If the children can't help her nothing human can"
(Addams to Mary Rozet Smith, December 1892). In their judgments of new residents, the Hull-House women were constructing this new female personality.
It was not the self-effacing helpmate or the silent, selfless religious worker. The
new settlement woman had talent, training, even expertise. But not because
she had personal ambition: to claim "authorship" for the kind of cooperative
activity that the cultural productions entailed would have been antithetical
to the settlement mission. Addams cultivated what she called the settlement
spirit, a kind of disinterested selflessness that promoted social progress rather
than individual authorship or personal ambition. When one resident worried
about her own career advancement as a physician rather than her *usefulness*
in an underserved community, Addams thought she "ha[d] not the settlement
spirit" (Addams to Mary Rozet Smith, Feb. 2, 1895). She liked the way Canon
Samuel Barnett, warden of Toynbee Hall, insisted that "we must sacrifice the
very feeling that we are sacrificing" (Addams, 1970 [1932]: 125). Nancrede exemplified this model. "A woman who, as journalist and Hull-House resident

ILLUSTRATION 4.6 Edith de Nancrede and her drama club at the Bowen Country Club Camp,
Waukegan, Illinois, c. 1925
SOURCE: JANE ADDAMS MEMORIAL COLLECTION (JAMC), SPECIAL
COLLECTIONS, DALEY LIBRARY, UNIVERSITY OF ILLINOIS AT CHICAGO.

Francis Hackett recalled, was 'skilled in vanishing from the successes she con-
trived'" rhetoric and theater scholar Shannon Jackson writes that Nancrede
"solidified the esprit de corps of the group of hardworking reformers" (Jackson,
2001: 620). A former member of one of the Hull-House drama clubs described
the settlement spirit that prevailed as a "kind of complete devotion and serious
concern, the ability to give up everything for a community" (Alex Elson Oral interview transcript, October 12, 1980: 10–11, Hull-House Oral History Collection).
He felt it was "a rather rare kind of quality...typical of that group [Hull-House
residents] that "couldn't be recaptured" (Ibid) after the shift to professional
social work in settlements had occurred. Almost nothing is known about Edith
de Nancrede's personal life. One of her students recalled that Nancrede's friend
Alice Crocker, a Hull-House resident, who seemed to disturb Eleanor Smith,
helped with the theatricals Nancrede produced. One summer Eleanor Carroll, a
prize piano student and one of Nancrede's drama club enthusiasts, vacationed
with Edith and Alice. To her students she appeared to have no private life at all
but poured her energy into working with them. Eleanor Carroll's experience
was not unique; talented students were incorporated into the friendship circle.
This was not done in any inappropriate way. It was part of the mimetic pedagogy that Hull-House's unorthodox women developed, perhaps unintentionally.
In blurring the lines between the personal lives of the cultural pedagogues and
the formal teaching, they had created ever-widening circles of inclusion in this
new educational space the settlement ideology had constructed.

3   The Settlement Spirit and Female Friendship

Scholars have looked for reasons why Hull-House was so successful in its collaborative approach to cultural work. Shannon Jackson found, for example,
that "Nancrede's presence contributed to the emotional bonds of friendship
and mutual support that maintained the settlement" (2001: 620). There was
something about her personality and the manner she had developed in relationships within the settlement household. While there has been a focus on
Mary Rozet Smith's role in Jane Addams's life, less is known about how she
similarly provided friendship and support for many at Hull-House and especially for Eleanor Smith. Alice Hamilton, who had deep connections in both
households, considered Mary "the most universally beloved person I have ever
known... [who] left a deep mark on all her knew her even slightly, for she had
a genius for personal relations" (Hamilton, 1995: 67). Early on, as this chapter
has described, Eleanor Smith had become a close friend of the Smith family
and of Addams who expressed affection and admiration for "Sister Eleanor."

Often referring to her as "Lady Eleanor," the term "Lady" being reserved by Jane only for such close friends and allies as Florence Kelley and Mary Rozet Smith, Eleanor had become a significant member of the *chosen* household of Jane Addams's and Mary Smith's. She was one of the intimates, a small group who spent time at the Smith residence at 12 Walton Place and over the four decades of friendship, traveled to vacation spots in Maine, Arizona, California, and Europe. Letters between Mary and Jane offer an insider's perspective on the private world inhabited by this double household: the circle of cultural leaders at the settlement who were also members of the private household. For Eleanor, who Jane Addams referred to as a "house companion," living with Mary Smith's family appears to have been a critical factor in her longevity with the music school (Addams to Lida Heymann, Feb. 22, 1924). Eleanor seems to have supplemented Mary's role as caregiver for her elderly parents and aunt as the latter developed asthma and suffered from frequent bouts of bronchitis and other maladies, including periods of depression. Curiously, Eleanor also suffered from fatigue, depression, and illness and took her "turn" as the invalid needing support. (This was true of Jane Addams, too, whose variety of medical problems were increasingly debilitating requiring periods of convalescence either in watering holes of the privileged, or often, at 12 Walton Place.) Eleanor was also prone to nervous exhaustion and poor health. For a rest cure, in 1899 she sojourned with Mary Smith in Europe for almost four months. "I cannot tell you how relieved I am about E. Smith—I had gotten to imagine dark events" (June 24, 1899), Jane had written Mary. Substitutes took over Smith's music school responsibilities (Addams to Mary Smith, July 25, 1899), and Addams "almost wish[ed]" Eleanor and Mary "were going to take the Norway trip and keep on a boat going in and out of the fiords for weeks—perhaps the sea air is what she [Eleanor] needs & nothing else will do" (July 28, 1899). By September Addams remained concerned about Eleanor's health and wished "she might be persuaded to stay over for the winter" (Addams to Mary Smith, Sept. 4, 1899).

These periodic journeys away from Hull-House continued, but so did Smith's strenuous teaching schedule. The weave of work and rest, made possible by the generous patronage and friendship of Mary and her wealthy family perhaps explains how Eleanor could be so prolific and focused for so many decades. Her health issues aside, in 1925, Eleanor at age sixty-seven was, according to Mary Smith, still capable of "slaving over her new cantata to be given with Miss Nancrede's pictures next week" (Mary Smith to Lillian D. Wald, April 25, 1925). There were to be all sorts of May Day celebrations as well, and Mary wrote: "It promises to be quite lovely." The two households surrounded Eleanor with support and keen anticipation for the new cantata. She was Hull-House's composer-in-residence, director of music programs, and leading cultural figure.

ILLUSTRATION 4.7   Mary Rozet Smith, c. 1893–96
SOURCE: JANE ADDAMS MEMORIAL COLLECTION (JAMC), SPECIAL
COLLECTIONS, DALEY LIBRARY, UNIVERSITY OF ILLINOIS AT CHICAGO.

The extended household at 12 Walton Place not only offered more refined
creature comforts not available in the residences at Hull-House, but a kind of
unconditional love and an affirmation of the reform work undertaken at the
settlement that Addams's own family never fully provided. This may have been

true for Eleanor Smith too. Lacking Eleanor's own words, we will never know definitively what "house companionship" entailed. Many letters indicate how Eleanor became a trusted and respected member of the households at both 12 Walton Place and in the community at Hull-House. However, there may have been subtle tensions under the surface as well.

Mary Smith had become Jane's closest friend, replacing Ellen Starr in that role (Schultz, 2001: 817–819). A letter inviting Addams to take a four-month trip with the Smith family to Europe reveals how the circle of friendship tied the residents, volunteers, and supporters together. Mary deftly incorporated Eleanor, Amalie Hannig, and Jane into her travels abroad with her own family members just as she integrated them in the family occasions at her family's homes at Walton Place and in Winnetka. These domestic arrangements were in keeping with upper-middle-class lifestyles in Victorian society and initially aided in Jane Addams's efforts to garner support from middle-and-upper-middle -class women and men for Hull-House and its reform agenda. Not so veiled hints of the Smith family support for Addams's plans to add new space to the settlement house complex were part of the teasing banter of the letter Mary had written extending the invitation to travel:

> Will you go in [sic] a nice little "tour" with the Smiths in May? You can go for as long or short a time as you like, go anywhere you please and visit settlements and philanthropists to your heart's content.
>
> If you will go we will take the quickest and steadiest steamer there is. You can come home in time for part of the Summer School and soon after Stanley's [Addams's nephew who lived at Hull-House] school is over. Mother and Father are going to abide quietly in one or two spots and I am prepared to go anywhere from the North Cape to Greece as occasion may offer. This is a very fine plan and you'd better consider it. I will offer you bribes to the extent of my fortune. I'll even build a third floor on the Butler Gallery if you'll come. Otherwise I won't.
>
> If it's more convenient you might come over with Miss [Eleanor]Smith and Miss [Amalie] Hannig and bring Stanley.
>
> The trip would be very edifying for him. If you'll come this time I will stop being injured about the time you wouldn't and I will promise to be as gentle as a dove.
>
> Always yours
> Mary R.S.
> MARY ROZET SMITH to JANE ADDAMS, February 1896.

The elder Smiths—Mary's parents—were picking up the tab, presumably, since Addams, Hannig, and Eleanor Smith were not able to pay for such an extended tour, one of the highlights being a stay at Bayreuth, Germany, for the summer opera festival (Addams to Sarah Alice Addams Haldeman, March 16, 1896).

Mary and Jane were developing their own relationship, a network of support for Addams's visionary plans, and, unconsciously, a version of family life for single women with careers and for same sex partners. It was an adaptation of traditional domesticity by incorporating Victorian extended family relations rather than extinguishing them. While there is incomplete information about Eleanor Smith and her family, she followed a pattern that was emerging at Hull-House: her sister's son, William Chenery, was a Hull-House resident as a young adult ("Bill" [William Chenery] to Eleanor Smith, Dec. 31, 1930).[2] Edith de Nancrede's sister Katherine married Irving Pond, the brother of one of Jane Addams's most trusted advisors and the Hull-House architect Allen B. Pond. The examples are too numerous to cite here. Jane Addams's nephews and nieces lived at Hull-House for different periods. Stanley, mentioned in Mary Smith's travel invitation, became Jane Addams's ward after the death of her sister, and he grew up at Hull-House along with his sister, Esther, also under Jane's guardianship. Residents from the early years sent their daughters and sons to Hull-House to experience settlement life. This mix of friends and relatives counteracted the tendencies toward institutionalism and professionalism and kept Hull-House as Addams's "home." It meant that disagreements could be personal even though longtime resident Alice Hamilton thought that for a community largely of women, there was a high level of privacy and individual autonomy for residents (1995: 61). There were also disagreements. The disagreement that Eleanor Smith and Jane Addams had in 1899 over the right proportions of popular and highbrow music to be featured in Hull-House concerts, which was reported in the Chicago-based journal, *Music* (Vaillant, 2003: 102) was one example of conflicts over goals and pedagogical philosophies. Two years later Smith apparently wrote Addams a disturbing letter in which she threatened to leave the settlement house. Coming after her celebrated composition and recital of "The Sweat Shop," this shocked Addams (Addams to Eleanor Smith, August 6, 1901) who had come to value the music school and see it as a central piece of the overall settlement program. Addams's letter (we do not have Eleanor's) reads much less like the plea of the powerful and famous head resident hoping to keep a valuable staff member in place and more as a misunderstood intimate friend and ally in the settlement's sisterhood. "Your letter quite hurt my feelings in spite of its sweetness and sincerity," (Addams

---

2 Jane Addams Papers (microfilm collection).

to E. Smith, Aug. 6, 1901) Addams began. She chastised Eleanor for thinking that quantity rather than quality was a criterion for worthiness in her eyes— perhaps alluding to the fact that the Music School engaged a smaller group of students than did the social and drama clubs or other activities. "If you had only written 'The Sweat Shop' and taught it to the girls, it would be in my mind a complete justification for all of the 'room' you ever took" Addams claimed. And she made clear that the music school had become "more a part of the House than it used to be and a very fine and important part" (Ibid).

Unlike other institutions or associations, the "glue" that held disparate and often independent, strong-willed women of talent together at Hull-House were the bonds of female friendship and the construction of the two chosen households—12 Walton Place and Polk St. and Halsted. After making her argument for why Eleanor should stay at Hull-House, Jane turned to the deeper emotional plea:

> I hope the household [Mary Smith family, etc.] is jolly and comfortable as can be in the mountains [on vacation in August]. I remember our day in the house very vividly. Please give my love to all the members, and do send me a little line saying that you understand and are coming back, not because I insist upon it (and I am not going to give you up without a fight—I warn you now) but because it does seem a little like home so much so that you will stop calculating how "profitable" you are and will come back to it because you belong to it whether you know it or not.
>
> ADDAMS TO ELEANOR SMITH, August 6, 1901

4   The Settlement Idea and Educational Objectives

Smith and her associates in art, music, and drama were able to directly address the pedagogical contradictions inherent in the goal of the socialization of immigrants and workers. For these highly trained practitioners, it was to be a pedagogy that was authoritative *and* democratic: that balanced the highest aesthetic and technical standards which they imposed, with respect for cultural and social differences and the developmental needs of the child. Eleanor Smith called the pedagogy "wise guardianship" (1914: 1014). She and her circle of Hull-House cultural workers were social reformers engaged with Jane Addams in socializing democracy as well as being creative artists and educators. Their creative achievements have meaning precisely in the context of the social movements in which they were engaged. The most important of these was the redefinition of the nature of childhood and the relationship that art and music had to the cognitive, physical, emotional, and spiritual development of the child. Hull-House became a center for experiments in early childhood education which dovetailed with the creation of a curriculum of art, music, and drama.

Stressing another aspect of the language of domesticity and female friendship, historian Dorothy Ross emphasizes that Addams's construction of social democracy at Hull-House on a domestic model "placed Addams in tutorial relation to her immigrant neighbors and brought into play domesticity's parental model of moral training" (1998: 241). Addams struggled "to both act the part of the parent and recognize the egalitarian claims of the child" (Ibid). She attempted, Ross contends, to reconcile the conflict by redefining leadership: "Leading here is a form of 'training,' and it operates by drawing out the child/ immigrant's own social impulses. Addams struggled to reconcile the hierarchical authority and the mutuality of interests the process assumes and requires" (Ibid). Speaking of the difficulties the settlement encountered in reaching adults in the neighborhood, Addams told the Chicago Woman's Club, "If education is, as Froebel defined it, 'deliverance,' deliverance of the forces of the body and mind, then the untrained must first be delivered from all constraint and rigidity before their faculties can be used" ("Outgrowths of Toynbee Hall", December 3, 1891, JAP). Addams's struggle, more theoretical than practical, was shared by the women cultural workers whose daily activities were an ongoing effort to balance the parental and the democratic.

Introducing the concept of choice in a group of children or young adults, as Edith de Nancrede did, was a break from the traditional classroom protocol. Bringing this level of child-centered pedagogy to working class and immigrant students was key, in the minds of Smith and her circle, to developing a democratic cultural program. The "wise guardianship" (1914: 1014) expressed by Smith and concurred in by Nancrede indicated the assertion of parental authority. This was, however, a new conception of "parental" as ideas about the rights of children to freedom from labor and access to education came into conflict with traditional views of the child as property of the parent. Hull-House's pedagogy was radical even as it was parental. Chicago drama critic James O'Donnell Bennett wrote that Nancrede "believed in 'the amazing rightness' of the boys' 'taste in choosing plays for performance'" (qtd. in Jackson, 2001: 620). Theater historian Shannon Jackson writes that Nancrede "led by encouraging the actors to form their own interpretations of the characters they played" (Ibid). Eleanor Smith was adamant about the indispensable role that traditional neighborhood families played in motivating or supporting the education and uplift of their children (1914: 1015), thereby implicitly identifying their agency in the educative process, but such engagement was mediated by

Smith's expertise and, in the context of Froebelian theories, the dual education of the child and the parents. The limits of this mediation, of course, were the exigencies of economic conditions that ruled family life.

Addams, Ross contends, argued that "the philanthropist [educator/social reformer] must 'discover what people really want' and then provide the channels in which their 'moral force' can flow. Underpinned by the 'multitude,' progress will be 'slower perpendicularly, but incomparably greater because lateral'" (242). Addams here is expressing her overall belief in social evolution that bordered on the metaphysical (1930: 7). What kind of channels were to be provided, of course, was a serious question for the cultural workers, and there were times when Addams's priorities and Eleanor Smith's differed substantively. Eleanor Smith's vision of a democratic music school sometimes clashed with Jane Addams's agenda. Addams saw music, as she did the arts and drama, as a tool of outreach as well as the great universal solace and uplift of people, and an opportunity of escape from weariness (Addams, 1910: 371–399). She wanted to secure for working people the opportunity to know the best art. She also wanted to demonstrate to immigrants that there were people in America who cared for great art. She hoped Hull-House could offer an opportunity of escape from dreariness. Smith shared many of these thoughts but was dedicated to "making musicians" (1914: 1014) out of the talent she believed resided in the unlikeliest of places, the urban slum. She wrote that "the conservation of talent seem[ed] an important matter" and she was highly critical of a society that had much to say "about the conservation of our natural resources," but very little to say "for the nurture of artistic resources, so precious to older nations" (Ibid). Smith considered public schools as "the only democratic ground for the fostering of talent" yet "too often [schools] fail[ed] in this regard" (Smith, 1914: 1014). The Hull-House Music School was to accomplish this fostering of talent and light the way for the public schools. In the meantime, the three women who labored each day contended with students whose immediate futures often were bleak. To insist as Eleanor Smith did, that these "tender shoots" needed "wise guardianship" from well-trained teachers even though their young voices were "bound in so many cases to extinguishment later in the dust and heat of factories and workshops" (1914: 1014) was imbedded in her philosophy that equated music with air and water as life saving and the nurture of it in all people the duty of citizens (Ibid). Contemporaries in the settlement movement had mixed reactions to the cultural work at Hull-House, not unlike Addams and Smith and her associates. Was the work intended to foment change? Was it to find and promote the talented few? As one observer of social settlements opined: "Settlement clubs are to touch the single cases; not to give the mass of men better conditions under which to live, but to help a few to defy conditions" (Jenison, 1906: 91). Addams often commented that those who signed up for the classes and participated in the clubs were the better element, the ones with more ideals, the people who do not need new thoughts so much, who are already progressive, who will find things anyway; that they are at Hull-House at all proves that they have reached out for the best thing that they knew. But, as one of the residents commented, "this is only a partial view. It is like keeping bread from a man who is hungry, and looking for one who has no appetite. No doubt the latter is the sicker man; he needs labor laws and sanitary commissions. But there is still the hungry man and the bread" (Jenison, 1906: 91).

In 1931 Addams was preparing a Carnegie Foundation grant proposal. The settlement house needed funds to maintain their programs and Addams asked Smith, Benedict, and Nancrede to provide data. The women protested that they had not kept statistics on students, so from memory they pieced together the highlights of almost forty years of work. You see, they explained, their work had not been about producing great musicians or successful actors or artists. That did happen, but it had never been the goal. Nor had it been Addams's goal. Addams, instead, found enormous pleasure and success in a different kind of achievement: "We have in Hull-House a music school in which some of the foreign-born children have been pupils for twelve years. These children often discover in the neighboring foreign colonies old folk songs which have never been reduced to writing. The music school reproduces these songs and invites the older people to hear them; their pleasure at such a concert is quite touching as they hear the familiar melodies connecting them with their earliest experiences; reminiscent perhaps of their parents and grandparents" (1908a: 59). Social adjustment of families and the solace and pleasure of familiar melodies produced had become more important to Addams than Eleanor Smith's goal of providing as many students as the school could serve, a thorough education in classical music. Eleanor Smith understood that studying music composition, voice, and piano were prerequisite for doing the "simple" act of transcribing oral traditions to written musical compositions.

5   Conclusion

The settlement movement adopted Smith's music reform (Smith, 1914: 1015; Ramsey & Ramsey, 1933: 21). She, like Jane Addams, understood the limits of what settlement houses could accomplish and sought to transform music programs in public schools. "As imperfect as is the music of the schoolroom, it is the one widespread popular agency which can be enlisted for the making of the musician" and could counter the "music of entertainment... almost always debasing..."(Smith, 1914: 1015). Smith joined associations of music teachers, wrote about her ideas in professional journals, and published textbooks to further her reform agenda.

Smith, who found abundant talent, motivation, and love of music among working-class and immigrant families, saw proper instruction of even greater value in their lives than perhaps of the privileged. "It is sad to think of what becomes of all the tender shoots which might flower so sweetly in the schoolroom under wise guardianship. Bound in so many cases to extinguishment later in the dust and heat of factories and workshops, these ideal strivings might long survive if teaching were better and music more pure" (Smith, 1914: 1014). These were radical ideas about how the cultural resources of society should be apportioned. Smith's pedagogical experiences taught her to respect poor people's love of the best in music, which distinguished her from many reformers whose condescending attitudes toward the masses presumed the opposite. Smith realized her successes were not possible without the cooperation and enthusiasm of parents (1015). "The greatest advantage which we enjoy in our work," Smith told the National Education Association in 1914, "is the sincere love of music which we meet in parents and pupils" although she admitted that there was also "the realization that music lessons for children, like Nottingham lace curtains and plush furniture for the parlor, stand for a certain social advance" (1015). Her immigrant neighbors were aggressive in their efforts to get ahead. This understanding allows us to rethink the relationship between reformers and neighbors. It brings up the question of social control and offers evidence for the "agency" of the immigrant families whose quest for betterment and social advancement is often absent in history books. The Hull-House children who as adults had the opportunity to comment on their esteemed teachers all remarked on the unfailing dedication and professionalism the women demonstrated. They indicated how the seeming lack of other interests made them feel as if they were important and worthy of the very best instruction and they brought them into the circle of the residential community. "Miss de Nancrede would say, 'well you are staying tonight for the rehearsal, so come down to resident's dinner with me.' I was frightened because there were all of these brilliant people around me. I would just sit and listen and not say one word because they were all doing such wonderful things" (Nicolette Malone, Oral interview transcript, 1980: Part 1, 22–23, Hull-House Oral History Collection). Youngsters were brought into the private world of female friendship and patronage in the settlement's socialized domesticity which came to include Nicolette Malone, who grew up in the neighborhood and became Edith de Nancrede's assistant. These settlement women—so different from their own mothers and the teachers in public or parochial schools—had liberated themselves from one kind of family claim—private and often oppressive in its bourgeois isolation, and in the Hull-House world constructed new relationships and new identities for themselves and for their students. "You might have found me [listed] as Immaculate, see because... when I went to school my mother must have told the nun I was Nicolette... and they called me Immaculate. Miss de Nancrede says [sic] 'what is really your name?' and I said [sic] 'It is Nicolette,' so she says [sic] 'we are going to start calling you by your right name and it is going to be Nikki, and it is short'" (Nicolette Malone, Oral interview transcript, 1980: Part 1, 32, Hull-House Oral History Collection).

The pedagogy of Eleanor Smith, de Nancrede, and Benedict worked in large part because they inadvertently created schools of refinement and social mobility in a neighborhood where many families already were striving for self-betterment. Against the insistent claims of Eleanor Smith and her circle, and Jane Addams, that the schools were not trying to make professionals out of the young people, or steer them toward careers, in many cases they did just that. The immigrants and their children who "bonded" with Hull-House became educated and middle class; their own words reflect this process indicating the way in which this turning away from the narrowness of the local and embracing an expansive world view indicated the successes the settlement had in developing connections—literal and figurative—to opportunities, people, places, ideas and advancement outside the scope of the neighborhood. These were transformative experiences for individuals. Hull-House pedagogy developed a variant on the assimilation process. It was a combination of paternalism and immigrant agency. Addams hoped to realize a socially ethical democratic community through the interactions of the different groups, social & economic classes, races who were encouraged to know each other and recognize their commonalities, both of human needs and of the qualities of human nature. The role of the settlement (and of Addams and other social reformers) was to lead by example and to construct public and semi-public spaces for association and civic engagement, and for social adjustment. What Edith de Nancrede understood, perhaps far better than Jane Addams, was that the neighborhood people *craved art* before and after the reformers arrived to demonstrate the value of art. She found that the young men and women who had been members of her social and drama clubs for ten, fifteen, even twenty years, never lost interest in the "art" side as they grew older. "On the contrary," she wrote Jane Addams, "it is the only thing that continues to hold their interest. It is the older ones who are the most intensely interested, in not only the acting, but in the scenery, costuming and light effects" (Nancrede to Addams, August 13, 1931). She had expected, originally, that the clubs would disband after the members "were thoroughly grown up and married" (Ibid), and she even "tried [to disband] the oldest group, thinking the younger ones needed her time more." After a year, the group reorganized. "I am convinced ... that the great contribution that Hull-House makes to the neighborhood is along the 'art' lines. I am so convinced, that as you know, I am willing to give all my time energy and strength to it," (Ibid) she wrote Addams. "One has only to go to their homes to see the effects. You would be amazed at the charming apartments ... most of my older young people have. You will find that the majority of them go to all the good plays that come to town and to concerts and lectures" (Ibid). And she quoted from one of her students: "Hull-House shows the neighborhood that there is another way of life." It is, of course, much more complicated to extrapolate from this what results can be determined for the progress of the community along the lines of social democracy as Addams had outlined in *Democracy and Social Ethics* (1902). There is substantial evidence that the work of Eleanor Smith and her circle had a deep, positive, and lasting effect on the individual lives of countless families and their children for over half a century.

CHAPTER 5

Cultural Pedagogy at Hull-House: Shaping Ethical Behavior through Performance

Rima Lunin Schultz

1   Introduction

Jane Addams identified the religious impulse in her generation to make social service express the "spirit of Christ" without dogma or sectarianism (Addams, 1910: 122) in her 1892 Plymouth Conference presentation, "The Subjective Necessity for Social Settlements," which she included as a chapter in *Twenty Years at Hull-House* (1910) because it continued to be vital and to resonate with the approach she and her colleagues in the social settlement movement embraced. Religion was not the only motivation by any means, as Addams herself indicates (115–122). Yet it became a source of culturally universal symbols to the women who joined Addams at Hull-House and who were a generation raised on Christian principles but challenged by new ideas in the humanities, and the biological and social sciences in the theories of Charles Darwin, Frederick Froebel, Auguste Comte, John Ruskin and Karl Marx. In their search for ways to connect with the new immigrants and workers, as Addams put it, to avoid "shut[ting] one's self away from that half of the race life … away from the most vital part of it" (1910: 116–117) they used many of the tropes of religion always attempting to universalize the message. Eleanor Smith identified this motivation when she wrote about establishing a democratic school of music at the settlement (Vaillant, 2003: 110). This chapter describes both the innovative opportunities and the limitations of pedagogy by focusing on the usages of Christian art, music, and drama in Hull-House's cultural work. It also examines the inner tension felt by the women reformers as they mediated between the top-down authoritative voice of European Christian hegemonic cultural forms and standards and the impulse to work democratically and cooperatively with their neighbors and students, learning as much as teaching.

2   Cultural Work and Religion at Hull-House

Eleanor Smith, along with Ellen Starr and Jane Addams believed that the arts were a means of education capable of connecting uneducated or unlettered people to history, to the great ideas of philosophy and religion in an age when traditional religion no longer reached the masses. The arts had the ability to contextualize or historicize contemporary conditions and to shape ethical behavior. One is reminded that the last of the five songs in the *Hull House Songs* is "Prayer" written by Eleanor Smith who chose from *Stagirius* by Matthew Arnold for her text. In her preface to the *Hull House Songs*, Addams endorses Smith's adaptation of Arnold because "Prayer" speaks to righteousness in the context of a "liberalized, literary Christian universalized concept of morality" as "the cornerstone of all religions." In keeping with the settlement's approach to religion which was the *performance* of religious values and ideals with no references to denominational or sectarian dogma, the verses do not mention a god at all. As Jocelyn Zelasko has written in this volume: "Religious affiliation is completely irrelevant. The prayer asks for all of us to be saved from our anguish, tribulations, strife, and pain. Additionally, without the mention of a god, the prayer could be a mantra asking to be saved from the hate, anger, and bitterness between groups of people" (Zelasko, this volume). Smith expresses Jane Addams's philosophy of reconciliation of class disputes epitomizing the goal of using the arts as vessels of moral and ethical values rather than the limited or worn-out methods traditional religions in their sectarian and divisive discourses offered. Addams carried her message to religious organizations and alliances and joined liberal religious societies in efforts to reform traditional Protestantism (Schultz, 2015: 207–219). Smith hoped to provide music for Sunday schools and church services that followed her theories on voice development as well as reflected her work with children from diverse cultural backgrounds. Finding a lack of quality in the content and composition of hymns sung in Sunday schools she wrote *The Children's Hymnal* with Charles H. Farnsworth and C.A. Fullerton (Elrod, 2001b: 812).

Addams self-consciously identified the cultural work at Hull-House with religious ideas that were Christian, however. Comparing Hull-House to settlement developments in New York, Addams privately wrote, "We are modest enough to think that ours is better, is more distinctively Christian, and less Social Science" (Addams to Mary Catherine Addams Linn, March 13, 1889). Ellen Starr, at the time a devout Episcopalian, even defined the settlement's objective of establishing true social relations with their neighbors "[as] almost sacramental... the visible means and channel of a spiritual grace" (Starr, 1895b, n.p.). In preparing to put their plan for a "Chicago Toynbee Hall" in place Addams and Starr had imbedded themselves very comfortably in the Protestant establishment in Chicago gaining approval for their new work from such clergy luminaries as the Rev. David Swing and the Rev. Frank W. Gunsaulus. Both men had the support of the wealthiest capitalists in the city—those identified with liberal Protestantism and aware of the importance of finding methods to reach

the masses with messages pitched toward mediating class conflict.¹ Eleanor
Smith and her family belonged in this cultural milieu (Schultz, Chapter Four,
this volume). From its first days, the settlement's material culture was the art
of Western Christian religious themes; theatrical productions frequently had
Christian themes; history and literature lectures and classes privileged the
Western European canon and stressed the methodologies and disciplines of
high culture, as did the music that was taught and the concerts that were offered for the neighbors under Smith's direction. A simple explanation for this
Christian and European content might be that the immigrants in the neighborhood came from European countries where these traditions had long histories.
This was only partially true, since in its early years the settlement's programs
were well attended by Eastern European Jews.²

A better explanation is that Addams, Starr, and Smith relied on the only
cultural materials they understood and had spent their adult years studying in
the United States and in their travels and, in the case of Smith, extensive studies abroad. Their tastes and ideas about art and culture were formed by this
Eurocentric, Christian culture; their trips to Europe were heavily motivated by
the opportunities to inhabit these cultural spaces which were seen through the
moral aesthetic of John Ruskin, William Morris, and Matthew Arnold. It was
also European culture seen through the eyes of an American Protestant cultural sensibility that disdained Catholic practices, found the Vatican aesthetically
vulgar and morally corrupt, and had interests only in early Christian artifacts,
medieval saints and works, and Renaissance art and the societal relationships
and roles of those times as respecting artisans and their craft (Addams to Hal-
demann, Feb. 12, 1888; Addams to J. Weber Addams, Feb. 17, 1888; Scambray,
1976: 156–171). Typical of their enthusiasm for European culture was the excitement experienced when Addams and Eleanor Smith, joined by Mary Rozet
Smith, enjoyed the summer performances at Bayreuth, Germany (Chapter
Four, this volume).

---

1   See: Rima Lunin Schultz, "Garnering Support for Hull-House from the Clergy," http://hull-
    house.uic.edu/hull/urbanexp/main.cgi?file=new/subsub_index.ptt&chap=7.
2   It is worth noting that Addams does not comment on the Christian flavor of Hull-House
    programs or compare the Jews in the vicinity of Hull-House with the significant Jewish popu-
    lation in Whitehall, East London, the locale of Toynbee Hall. Neither, by the way, do the Bar-
    netts of Toynbee, even though Charles Booth includes information on the East London Jews
    in his voluminous study and, of course, Addams, 2007 [1895], *Hull-House Maps and Papers*,
    includes a chapter on the Jewish ghetto in Chicago (96–106). The Jews in East London estab-
    lished a substantial religio-cultural infrastructure, as do the Chicago Jews.

ILLUSTRATION 5.1   Jane Addams with Chi-Rho pin prominent, 1892
SOURCE: JANE ADDAMS MEMORIAL COLLECTION (JAMC),
SPECIAL COLLECTIONS, DALEY LIBRARY, UNIVERSITY OF
ILLINOIS AT CHICAGO.

3   Hegemonic European Christian Art as "Ethical Culture"[3]

Her own search for the ethical way of life had taken Addams through a process
of historical reconstruction. She offered her neighbors the cultural material for
a similar process: Christian themes were displayed in art reproductions on the
walls of all the rooms, in the choice of children's plays and literature; in the annual singing of carols, and decorating with Christmas trees, and in the religious
art of the "living pictures," the Christmas tableaux, which were the highlight
of the Winter season, and had been perfected by the trio of Eleanor Smith,
Enella Benedict, and Edith de Nancrede. They gave the settlement house continuity and a cultural unity that, Addams argued, was not sectarian and did not
force dogma or doctrine or even prayer, let alone conversion, but rather, were a
source of ethical and moral teachings to inspire her neighbors.

An article in the January 1897 *Hull-House Bulletin* describes one of the religiously inspired theatricals that was offered to the public, as well as the scenes
from the miracle play that was performed:

> The Christmas play this year, 'Longfellow's Golden Legend,' was given
> three times to various audiences and the scenes from the miracle play
> oftener. The latter consisted of the Annunciation; the Angels of the Seven
> Planets, bringing their characteristic virtues to earth and forming the Na-
> tal Star; and of the Nativity. They were done with a great deal of care and
> artistic merit. The scenes of the 'Golden Legend' were laid in Germany in
> the 14th century. The piety of the peasant Gottlieb and his wife, the un-
> selfishness and devotion of the beautiful Elsa, the struggle of the prince
> to overcome his weakness and self-absorption ought to remain with us
> as helpful experience and *remind us* that the *object* of the early medieval
> plays *was to give religious instruction.*
>
> HULL-HOUSE BULLETIN, January 1897: 6; emphasis added

Years later Addams explained to a conference of social workers: "One of the
first plays we gave was Longfellow's 'Golden Legend.' This play is one in which
the good angel is dressed in white, and is never wrong in anything, and the bad
angel is clothed in red, and is never right. There is no mistake about it. It is all

---

3 I am using this term to clarify what Addams hoped to achieve in using the hegemonic or
   canonical works of Western culture in a non-creedal framework. I am both distinguishing
   this effort from the Ethical Culture Society's aims but suggesting that Addams was trying
   to do something akin to Felix Adler, of whom she often associated with in liberal religious
   alliances.

very plain. It was played for several years until the performers declined to go on with it. It was hard on their feelings as upon those of the audience" (quoted in "The Third Monthly Conference," *Charities*, March 29, 1902: 284–286). Addams says no more about why the young actors refuse to do the play. She uses the story to emphasize the consummate engagement young people have in play acting. The young Hull-House actors were so involved they crossed the "line" separating the theatrical from daily life and rebelled against the rigid portrayal of good and evil. Theater, Addams tells us, was an intense experience in the Hull-House community. It was moral drama in which the neighbors and the residents performed; it was a way of expressing truths about real life better than other methods or approaches.

Children from the neighborhood, including those from Jewish families, participated in the Christmas plays as actors and also took part in choral singing. A great deal of preparation and thought went into the productions with Eleanor Smith, the head of the music department, Edith de Nancrede, the head of the children's drama clubs, and Enella Benedict, the head of the art school, who worked on set design, bringing their professional skills to the event. The pageant was not meant to be a religious service or ritual, but a *cultural* experience with ethical significations. Jane Addams, who rejected Americanization programs that forced a premature assimilation or acculturation, conceived such plays as opportunities for moral fables that also bridged the traditional cultures of the European immigrants and helped preserve their rich heritages. They were chosen from all European traditions seemingly without preference for one nationality over others. A review of *Hull-House Bulletins* illustrates the range of plays and music performed. American identity would be shaped in the context of respect for the customs of Christmas, for example, from many nationalities. Cultural differences could be respected and exchanged while an appreciation of the unity underlying these differences could be displayed. This fit with her notion that immigrant neighborhoods were political and social spaces where universal values replaced xenophobic feelings based on old traditions of religious and ethnic hatreds. Choices of plays were based on the potential they had for socialization of differences and for moral uplift (Jackson, 2000; Hecht, 1983).

We have three "eyewitness" accounts of how Jewish neighbors viewed the Christmas activities at Hull-House. "Several days before Christmas 1896 one of my Irish playmates suggested that I go with her to a Christmas party at Hull-House," Hilda Satt Polacheck remembered in her autobiography which she penned in 1953 (1989: 51). Hilda, a Jewish immigrant from Czarist-controlled Poland in the Pale of Settlement, explained that she never went anywhere on Christmas Day because she was afraid that she "might get killed" (52). She then asked her Irish friend if there would be any other Jewish children at the party and she was assured that there had been Jewish children at the parties every year and that no one ever got hurt. Hilda came to the party and realized that the kind of religious intolerance and bigotry, including violence, that Jews experienced in her native Poland during the Christmas and Easter seasons did not occur in the United States, at least not at Hull-House: "We were all poor. Some of us were underfed. Some of us had holes in our shoes. But we were not afraid of each other. What greater service can a human being give to her country than to banish fear from the heart of a child? Jane Addams did that for me at that party" (Ibid).

However, there was much more to the story. Hilda also recalled the confusion and intergenerational conflict her assimilation into Hull-House's all embracing but hegemonic cultural environment caused her. "While I felt that I had done nothing wrong or sinful by going to the Christmas party, I still hesitated telling Mother where I had been. I was glad that she did not ask me" (52). Hilda's story challenges us to dig deeper for the immigrant voices. As one of the "transfigured few,"[4] Hilda's identification with the progressive narrative of Hull-House and Jane Addams was almost total in its screening out of any discordant or oppositional narrative. (Weiner, 1989). Initially the Satt family were relatively prosperous, Hilda's father a self-employed craftsman. Her mother was a housewife and Hilda attended public school. Only after the unexpected death of the breadwinner did Hilda and her family experience the crushing exigencies of poverty. Hilda at age thirteen left school and began work in a knitting factory. Four years of work radicalized Hilda, who was fired for her attempts to organize her fellow workers. The settlement was as "an oasis in the desert" of monotony and exhaustion of factory work" (Polacheck, 1989: 68).

"At Hull-House no religion was introduced into any of the clubs or classes, with the one exception of the annual Christmas party," Hilda explained, "which became a sort of folklore tradition. The religious side of Christmas was left to the various churches. The feature of the Hull-House Christmas party centered around the trees and the songs and the candy and popcorn balls" (Polacheck, 1989: 103).

There were, however, religious tensions that were unstated but, according to another Hull-House girl, Dorothy Sigel, were negotiated somehow by the

---

4   Jane Addams used this term (Addams, 1900: 423) to refer to the eager, upwardly mobile, English-speaking immigrants who she believed would have sought out educational and cultural benefits for themselves even without Hull-House. She was grateful for their participation and certainly mentored them, but she was frustrated with the settlement's inability to reach the more ordinary working people, especially adults, whose dull lives she wished to inspire.

residents who were sensitive to possible criticism or opposition from Jewish parents. Sigel never appeared in the cantatas or living pictures, but there were Jewish boys and girls who did. She had the feeling that Jane Addams or Edith de Nancrede "just kind of stepped around that situation" and made sure that a Jewish girl did not portray the Virgin Mary, or that some of the boys did not "depict the Three Wise Men" (Sigel, Oral Interview transcript, 1981: 3–4, Hull-House Oral History Collection).

Sadie Ellis [Garland Dreikurs], the daughter of Jewish immigrants from the nearby Maxwell Street neighborhood, had a mother who feared the Hull-House settlement as a place where her daughter would meet Catholics and maybe even end up marrying an Italian. "It was sure that I would come to no good end—an awful place, Hull-House. So many things happened there that were strange to them [her parents]. I defied them" (Dreikurs, Oral Interview transcript, 1980: 4, Hull-House Oral History Collection).

Sadie Ellis took art classes at Hull-House and was mentored by Enella Benedict's protégé Emily Edwards, who was teaching art at the time that Sadie first arrived. She, like Hilda Satt Polacheck, found intellectual stimulation, progressive politics, and the beginnings of a lifetime career as an artist and therapist. She eventually returned to Hull-House as a resident, after marrying the artist Leon Garland.[5]

The experiences of Jewish youth at Hull-House were multi-faceted. The warm mentorship of adults who were not Jewish became part of a liberating, cosmopolitan experience rather than a Christian evangelizing experience. Having a Texas-born artist recognize her talents strengthened Sadie Ellis'

---

5   Emily Edwards (1888–1980) was an artist, art historian, teacher, and cofounder of the San Antonio Conservation Society. She was born in San Antonio. Texas, on October 7, 1888. Her mother died in 1895. From 1898 to 1902 Emily and her three sisters boarded at the Ursuline Academy, where her talents as an artist were first apparent. She studied drawing with sculptor Pompeo Coppini. In 1905 she moved to Chicago, where attended the Art Institute of Chicago and studied with Enella Benedict, Ralph Clarkson, Harry Walcott, and John Vanderpoel. In 1906 she began working at the institute and she also taught classes at Hull-House. From 1915 to 1917 she taught at the Francis Parker School. She returned to San Antonio in 1917 to teach art. She taught at Hull-House again before returning to San Antonio in the early 1920s. Her studies in the summers with Diego Rivera stimulated an interest in Mexican murals, and Edwards subsequently spent ten years in Mexico. She published a pamphlet, (Edwards, 1932) on Rivera's frescoes in Cuernacaca. During the 1930s Edwards established a modest reputation as an artist, exhibiting watercolors and color-block prints in Texas and New York. In the late 1930s she moved to Chicago to head the art program at Hull-House. Sadie Ellis Garland's life was changed by her participation in Hull-House (Sokol, 2013). After Leon's death, Sadie married Rudolph Dreikurs, who had joined the settlement community. A refuge from Hitler's Germany, he was a practicing psychoanalyst interested in adolescent behavior. Sadie began to do art therapy.

ability to see herself away from the culturally homogeneous zone of her Jewish neighborhood. In this respect, Hull-House liberated youngsters from their neighborhood identities. This was true for Catholics, too. Instead of reinforcing traditional Catholic identity, participating in the "living pictures" and the cantata for Christmas displaced family and local parish or neighborhood loyalty and identity with thoughts of the larger world and the possibilities of finding one's place in it. Some began to think about travel away from home for college; others found new friends beyond their "block"; and many found in the Hull-House residents mentors who competed for their affection.

Florence Giovangelo Scala,[6] who by the 1960s had become a community activist on the Near West Side, grew up Italian Catholic. The daughter of an immigrant tailor, whose ties to church and community never wavered, Scala explained the power of the settlement's influence in terms of the class, education, and diversity of the colony of residents within. Her participation in the arts at Hull-House, especially the theater, had a major influence in her life thru her young adult years. She noticed how those in the neighborhood who didn't participate in Hull-House didn't change: "Ordinarily you just grow up, have a nice time with your friends. You'd get married, and you have children. And your life, unless you reach out, it's going to just be right here. And so your world is very small" (Scala, Oral Interview transcript, 1982: 4, Hull-House Oral History Collection). This was what happened to so many of the girls that she grew up with. "But there [at Hull-House] I got to see a lot of other things." She saw residents and volunteers who were upper middle class and educated. And she began to understand what college might mean. "And so my own horizons were being extended just by being there" (Ibid). She met many residents over the years, having begun her relationship with Hull-House at the age of ten. While the youngsters like herself were overwhelmingly Italian, few of the residents were. "The people [residents] who were at Hull-House [1928–1961] were all Anglo Saxon or they were Jewish. There were blacks. There were not many

6   Florence Giovangelo Scala was born on September 17, 1918 to Alex and Teresa (Scardepane) Giovangelo in Chicago, Illinois. She studied subjects such as urban planning at the University of Chicago and Northwestern University. Florence Scala was a Hull-House participant from the age of 10; she was in the youth theater groups during her adolescence, and then, as a young woman, volunteered at Hull-House from 1934 to 1954. Active in her community, Scala served as secretary and treasurer of the Near West Side Planning Board, 1949–1958, and secretary of the Near West Side Conservation Community Council, 1957–1959. Florence Scala is best known for her impassioned struggle to defend her neighborhood from urban clearance make way for a new Chicago campus of the University of Illinois. She became co-chair of the Harrison-Halsted Community Group in 1961 and ran for Alderman of the 1st Ward of Chicago in 1963 as an independent candidate against the political machine. Scala endured ridicule, threats, and several bombing attempts, but remained outspoken.

Latinos, but there were such a variety. It was comparable to what this neighborhood was like. Which was primarily Greek, black, and what was left of the Irish who had not already moved out and Italians. At Hull-House you had a cosmopolitan mix [of residents], but all of them were highly educated, most of them coming out of a middle class, or upper-middle class backgrounds" (Scala, Oral Interview transcript, 1982: 5, Hull-House Oral History Collection).

Had Scala remained "local," which meant retaining Italian Catholic affiliations almost exclusively, she would have experienced the diversity of the neighborhood differently. That was the difference Addams was trying to achieve. Having the Christmas "living pictures" tableaux at Hull-House contextualized the message vastly differently than a performance by one of the neighborhood churches of similar material. Florence Scala was able to see her neighborhood through the lens of the democratic cosmopolitanism and Christian humanism that Addams preached and the settlement house "performed," but neither she nor her brother Ernest Giovangelo, or any of the other neighbors also active at the settlement, were asked to serve in any leadership role by Addams, although occasionally they were asked to assist the residents in giving music lessons or helping run the theatricals (Schultz, 2008). As we shall see in the discussion

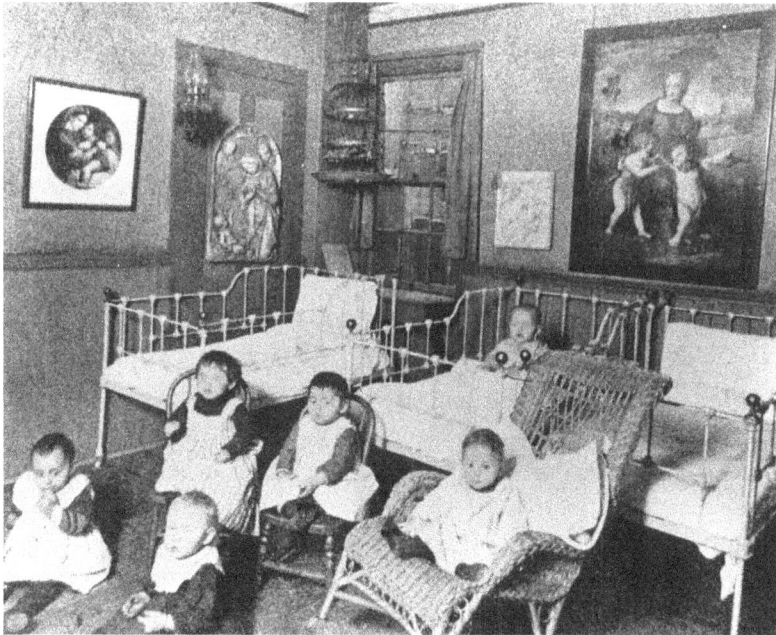

ILLUSTRATION 5.2   Room in the Children's Building at Hull-House, 1895
            SOURCE: JANE ADDAMS MEMORIAL COLLECTION (JAMC), SPECIAL
            COLLECTIONS, DALEY LIBRARY, UNIVERSITY OF ILLINOIS AT
            CHICAGO.

of Edith de Nancrede's pedagogical methods, the young people in the neighborhood with talent and drive learned mimetically, taking on the values and
the techniques of the residents who were mentoring a life style, including attitudes about religion, through the activities of cultural production.

There were other ways in which religious ideas were transmitted at Hull-
House without reference to denominational creeds and without prayer. One
significant way was through the use of art and literature that had religious
themes. Paintings of the Madonna and Child adorned the walls of the crèche
and the children's rooms; plays and books on moral and religious themes were
part of settlement life. Addams's goal in offering this cultural and aesthetic
environment was not to "preach" a specific religious doctrine or evangelize,
but to demonstrate "the conception of life which the settlement group holds.
The demonstration is made not by reason, but by life itself" (Addams, 1899b:
37[327]). As Addams restated this concept, Art was used to express the meaning of life "in forms of activity" (36[326]). Stories of how the children in the
crèche physically interacted with the three-dimensional murals or friezes on
the walls—touching and kissing the Madonna and child—circulated among
reformers and reflected the earnest faith the settlement residents had in the
efficacy of a kind of aesthetic environmentalism. Ellen Starr reflected this in
her assessment of the results of the cultural space Hull-House was providing,
that "when one sees how almost miraculously the young mind often responds
to what is beautiful in its environment, and rejects what is ugly, it renews courage to set the leaven of the beautiful in the midst of the ugly, instead of waiting
for the ugly to be first cleared away" (Starr, 1895a: 165).

When Jane Addams and Ellen Gates Starr envisioned the neighborhood surrounding Hull-House, they first imagined it as a place where there was a complete absence of art.

Yet we know that the ethnic groups in these neighborhoods attended religious services in churches filled with Christian art. They created street pageantry in their festivals and parades. They played music and organized bands
for their fraternal organizations, and they created and participated in family
and social circles where music and food and traditional ritual were cultural
expressions. Addams apparently did not see a relationship between these activities and the work lives of her neighbors. If the solace of art could only be
experienced through craftsmanship, the unskilled worker without the opportunity for craft work, was torn asunder from art. Why Addams did not see these
other activities as replacements where artistic expression and the joy of cultural exchange was occurring remains a mystery. Initially, at least, her public
statements and writings portray her immigrant neighbors without aesthetic
outlets. Contemporary newspapers and the Catholic press featured articles

ILLUSTRATION 5.3   Ellen Gates Starr, co-founder of Hull-House, c. 1889
SOURCE: JANE ADDAMS MEMORIAL COLLECTION (JAMC), SPECIAL
COLLECTIONS, DALEY LIBRARY, UNIVERSITY OF ILLINOIS AT
CHICAGO.

about the cultural and religious activities of Italians ("Italians In Parade," *Chicago Tribune,* September 23, 1895: 8; Prindiville, 1903: 452–461). Yet Addams did not relate these activities as a form of art used to express the meaning of life. Perhaps she believed that the Roman Catholic Church, often at the center of these activities, was oppressive in its authoritarianism thus precluding congregants from fully or freely experiencing art by living it, since they had not "created" it through their own initiative and craftsmanship. The ethnic parish Catholic churches in Chicago were paid for by the congregants, not the American hierarchy or the international church. Thus the "little people," if they happened not to be craftsmen bricklayers, stonemasons, or artisans fabricating stained glass windows (and many immigrants did this kind of work) were making weekly contributions to pay for the construction of these edifices. The notion that Addams and Starr had about the lack of partnership between immigrants and the churches was not the reality (Skerrett, 2001: 22–63).

The same could not be said for the festes and other communal activities which, in the case of Italian immigrants, often represented popular forms of religion unsanctioned by the church authorities. Such activities in the New World, signifying attachments to local or regional religions of place and fraternal fellowship, were subversive acts, "forbidden" by the American priests, and misunderstood by reformers like Jane Addams (Orsi, 1988).

Addams, instead, declared the results of the settlement's efforts to disseminate good art in the neighborhood to be successful and inspirational, and she reported her "findings" to the world of Progressive reformers and friends of the settlement's efforts through newspaper and magazine articles. "There is abundant testimony," Addams wrote "that the lectures and pictures have quite changed the tone of ... [Ellen Starr's students'] minds; for they have become, of course, perfectly familiar with the photographs of the best things, and have

ILLUSTRATION 5.4   Interior decoration in a Hull-House parlor, c. 1895
SOURCE: JANE ADDAMS MEMORIAL COLLECTION (JAMC), SPECIAL
COLLECTIONS, DALEY LIBRARY, UNIVERSITY OF ILLINOIS AT CHICAGO.

cared for them, not 'as a means of culture,' but as an expression of the highest human thought and perception" (Addams, 1895b: 615). Addams was happy to report that "one of the Hull-House students had bought from her scanty earnings a number of classic works of art which will make her house really charming when she is married next fall, and more than that will be to her the same vital connection with the minds 'who have transfigured human life,' as a fine library is to the student who has time for constant reading." Another example was the transformation of a worker's little parlor "by the Fra Angelico over the mantel and the Luca della Robbias on the walls," and "a few doors down the street a tiny bedroom has been changed from a place in which a fragile factory girl slept the sleep of the exhausted, into one where she 'just loves to lie in bed and look at my pictures; it's so like Art Class'" (Addams, 1895b: 615).

Addams and Starr did come to recognize that immigrants craved art in their homes of their own workmanship. "I have never seen in a city anything in the way of decoration upon the house of an American citizen which he had himself designed and wrought for pleasure in it," Starr observed. "In the house of an Italian peasant immigrant in our own neighborhood, I have seen wall and ceiling decorations of his own design, and done by his own hand in colors. The designs were very rude, the colors coarse; but there was nothing of the vulgar in it, and there was something of hope" (Starr, 1895a: 169).

This theorizing about art and labor relates to the role of religion at Hull-House. Starr and Addams were grounded in the moral writings of the nineteenth century and could not think about or imagine the development of character in the human being without there being available an aesthetics of high European culture that would lead or motivate inspiration and idealism. Eleanor Smith's training in Froebel's educational theories underscored this concept of human development requiring access to high cultural forms, specifically music. The aesthetic underpinning this pedagogy was religiously based in most representations of Western art and culture. The awakening of the child's reasoning and moral senses required exposure to ideals of the good, beauty, virtue, and truth that were imbedded in the aesthetic of Western religious art. This necessitated an early experience with art that embodied these ideals. In Hull-House this meant Madonnas in the crèche and children's rooms. It meant religious tableaux and reproductions of the great Renaissance artists. It naturally followed that religious themes would be instructive, not for their specific doctrine, but for their embodiment of moral parables.

The imposition from top down of European high culture, presumably in keeping with the national origins of the immigrants, was also a preventative measure. Addams and Starr were dismayed to learn that the most successful of the Italians in the neighborhood had adopted store-bought clothing, cheap and vulgar goods in the eyes of cultivated American middle-and-upper-class ladies who had sojourned in Rome and Tuscany, and in little sun-drenched villages. Settlement houses were positioned to be the first line of defense against an assimilation of immigrants by the crude commercial culture of the city. Eleanor Smith was horrified by the kinds of street sounds or commercial music her students heard daily. Not only was the city threatening of the immigrant's well-being because of terrible housing and unhealthy and dangerous jobs, but it was an aesthetic nightmare in the introduction of badly and cheaply produced ready-made goods, bad music, and cheap amusements. In the hunt for the "right" neighborhood for the settlement house, Addams had written her sister about a location she liked:

> It was exactly as if we were in a quarter of Naples or Rome, the parents and the children spoke nothing but Italian and dressed like Italian peasants. They were more crowded than I imagined people ever lived in America, four families for instance of six or eight each, living in one room for which they paid eleven dollars a month, and are constantly afraid of being ejected. Yet they were affectionate and gentle, the little babies rolled up in stiff bands and the women sitting about like mild eyed Madonnas. They never begged nor even complained, and in all respects were immensely more attractive to me than the Irish neighborhood I went into last week with a Mrs. Estes.
>
> JANE ADDAMS to MARY CATHERINE ADDAMS LINN, March 13, 1889

The Hull-House women found the immigrants not yet Americanized to be purer, more innocent, even more culturally authentic, and blessedly untouched by the vulgarity and crassness of American popular culture. Eleanor Smith wrote that "music is, as it has always been, the chief delight and solace of the poor, and her most ardent votaries as well as those high in her service have always been the poor" (Smith, 1914: 1015–1016). How might the children be saved from the "attractions" of the prevailing street culture so that the integrity of their culture could be refined and guided by the best in music, art, and drama? Smith's answer was simple. Realizing this natural interest in music poor and working-class neighbors exhibited, "this fact, and the conviction that music has supreme power to refine and elevate those who embrace it, lay at the foundation of our efforts to create a democratic school of music" (1016). The settlement house programs, however, had to direct "the poor" from the "cheap music" of the street.

Settled in Halsted Street, the following Spring, Addams and Starr invited the press to observe an Italian night at the settlement. "The night was very interesting," Ellen wrote in a letter. "There were a great many children, babies even, & some of the women wore bright kerchiefs on their heads. The rich & vulgar Italians are taking to coming, sporting diamond crosses. I hope something will come of it. We put them on the back seats, & the peasants to the front" (Ellen Gates Starr to Mary Houghton Starr Blaisdell, 18 and 22 May 1890). Renaissance paintings of the Madonna and Child graced the interior space of Hull-House as an aesthetic challenge to the gross commercial culture enveloping the new immigrants and, as well, denoted concepts of love, family, and idealism that the two women understood were universally "religious." So too were the concerts and musical choices made by Eleanor Smith an antidote to vaudeville and the music of entertainment, "almost always debasing" (1914: 1014).

True to the nineteenth-century sensibility, Smith, Starr and Addams could not imagine that such visual representations could offend non-Christians and traditional Christians. To many conservative Protestants, social settlements were not Christian enough (Stebner, 1997: 34–35). Many Roman Catholics believed settlements were engaging in Protestant proselytizing (Skok, 2007: 65–90). Addams saw no contradiction in the appropriation of Christian art in a settlement identified as independent of any denominational religious affiliation. Smith's "Prayer" may well have been composed in the absence of this kind of nondenominational religious cultural expression that Addams promoted and rationalized as non-evangelizing. In line with this argument, Addams believed that it was important for the *socialization* of the immigrants that they experience the moral parables in the context of the settlement house rather than their own nearby parish churches. In this she was implicitly arguing that for religious art to reflect ethical and moral themes there needed to be a cultural space that was nonsectarian, neither Protestant nor Catholic. The settlement, which in this era approached the more modern conception of the "public square" in the United States, created the space where immigrants could experience a "higher form of life."

Addams saw nothing in the neighborhood that united the disparate groups: "How should a little colony of south Italians become Americanized?" she asked in 1894.

> They saw nothing but the baser elements of American society. They did their work under an Italian padrone and there was nothing to bring them into contact even with their employers. The Polish and Russian Jews Americanize very rapidly, but as before there is nothing to bring them into a realization of a higher form of American life. The Bohemians are clannish. The Canadian French have their own churches, their own stores and have little to do with anything around them. The Irish are another

class that quickly become molded into American ways and manners, especially into our corrupt politics, but there is nothing to unite all these people.

ADDAMS, 1894: 98

Did the neighbors who attended the dramas, listened to the music, celebrated the Christian holidays, even participated as actors and musicians, find the framing of folk and fairy tales, and the display of high culture which was filled with Jesus' birth, the Virgin Mary, and countless renditions of the Madonna and Child objectionable? Addams was asked about the "religious question" by another settlement head resident and answered her: "We find each year that it is more possible to discuss frankly religious problems and differences, because our neighbors have constantly less fear that we will proselyte them" (Addams to Katharine Coman, Dec. 7, 1891). To the reformers at Hull-House, the absence of any creed or requirements to sign a pledge or "convert" made the settlement's approach tolerable but still "religious" as a place of deeds and performances that enacted ethical behavior and promoted a higher moral life. More to the point, the most "Christian" expression artistically was the annual "living picture" tableaux held in the great Bowen Hall.

The idea that settlements could retain their status as unaffiliated and non-religious yet celebrate Christmas was widespread during the Progressive Era, cautioning us to understand that the concept of cultural pluralism is a recent idea in American history.[7] For example, in an article about Chicago's flourishing settlement houses, Northwestern University's Settlement claimed that

All festivals and holidays are provided for and observed... already preparations are going forward for Christmas. *There is no direct religious teaching.* [Italics added.] The aim is to so raise the tone of living and of actuations that whatever the religion professed it will be more conscientiously practiced. The result of the work of this settlement is said to be most encouraging. Not only is there a marked advance in the habits and manners of those families connected with the settlement, but a constantly increasing desire for improvement.

"Work for the Poor," *CHICAGO TRIBUNE*, Sept. 16, 1894: 33

Probing for reasons behind the use of religious pageantry and music, Toynbee Hall's Samuel A. Barnett's writing may provide some answers. He wrote about

---

7   The longevity of the tableaux at Hull-House should be noted; the tradition continued after Addams's death, kept going by a few former students who now worked for the settlement. Many of the characters had participated in the living pictures for 10 to 12 years (Cousin Eve. December, 28, 1941. Writer's Yule Cards Bigger and Brighter. Clipping Hull-House Collection).

ILLUSTRATION 5.5 A "Living Picture" from the Christmas Tableaux at Hull-House, c.1925
SOURCE: JANE ADDAMS MEMORIAL COLLECTION (JAMC), SPECIAL
COLLECTIONS, DALEY LIBRARY, UNIVERSITY OF ILLINOIS AT
CHICAGO.

how East End Londoners were deeply affected by musical productions of religious themes when conventional church services did not reach them: "Creeds
have ceased to express men's inner reverence. Music is a parable, telling in
sounds which will not change of that which is worthy of worship, telling it to
each hearer just in so far as he by nature and circumstance is able to understand it, but giving to all that feeling of common life and assurance of sympathy which has in old times been the strength of the church" (Barnett, 1899: 503).

Even more subversive to ethical values was the development of a commercial and popular culture that, from the point of view of Addams and other

reformers, had enormous power over the masses. For Jane Addams, who agreed with Barnett about the continued need for music as parable, drama was also a parable for universal religious and ethical values and for the modeling of civic righteousness. Different from other contemporary moral reformers, Jane Addams uniquely understood that the power of the commercial theater was being squandered. Although she participated in the efforts of reformers to combat the evils of vulgar entertainment and the premature sexualization of youth with legislation and censorship, her efforts at Hull-House centered on developing constructive substitutes that actually used drama and music to uplift and channel the energies and sexuality of youth. She considered the type of dramatic art being placed before young people to be "debased" and made even worse by the "vulgar type of music" that accompanied it (James, 1998: 292–293). She thought that popular theater encouraged audiences to be "passive and idle" and vulnerable to "exploitation through cheap entertainments" that mushroomed in cities throughout the United States at the turn of the century. Cheap theater relied on plots that focused on revenge, a problem that was a concern to reformers who feared "inter and intra-ethnic rivalries and tensions" (James, 1998: 292–293). Worse, Addams believed that popular theater sensationalized "robbery, sexual molestation, assault and murder," and was a serious threat to the social order. Kathy Peiss has demonstrated that "dark and malevolent motifs" were not the only sources of concern to reformers; comedies posed additional problems. Popular among the working classes and regularly featured in vaudeville shows, comedies were subtly subversive as they mixed the sentimental with the sexually suggestive (Peiss, 1986: 144). Ellen Starr, Eleanor Smith, Edith de Nancrede, and Enella Benedict were the talented co-workers whom Addams relied on to implement her goals. In the Music and Art Schools, the social drama clubs established by Nancrede, and the allied work that took place in the Labor Museum, Hull-House became a model of a new kind of cultural pedagogy. Historian Derek Vaillant finds Eleanor Smith to have "demonstrated a particular ability to balance high aesthetic and technical standards with a genuine regard for the multiple cultures joined by music" that gathered at Hull-House (2003: 110).

4   The Cultural Work of Edith de Nancrede

A visual artist by training, Edith de Nancrede became a Hull-House resident in 1897; her first responsibilities at the settlement were to initiate programs for the Boys' Club (Jackson, 2001: 618–620). Soon Nancrede broke new ground when she experimented with social clubs that made use of drama and other arts to encourage group cooperation, to acquaint young people with the works of "high culture," and to draw on the children's immigrant culture for theatrical inspiration. She, like Smith, immediately noticed how engaged the children and their parents were in the pursuit of drama and music. Nancrede had a major role in developing the interdisciplinary approach of Hull-House productions, a good example of which is *The Trolls' Holiday* (1905), written by poet Harriet Monroe (a short-term Hull-House resident), set to music by Eleanor Smith, and with a set designed by Enella Benedict, which was constructed in the Hull-House shops. The production was accomplished through the cooperation of the settlement's art school, music school, shops, dramatic clubs, and the movement and gymnastic classes of Mary Hinman and Rose Marie Gyles (Odom, 2001: 395–398; Schwendener, 2001: 335–337).[8]

Nancrede saw great potential in the children and young adults who came to Hull-House from the neighborhood and found, almost by accident, the key to a pedagogy that used theater to inculcate the moral aestheticism of bourgeois culture to combat the deleterious effects of commercial theater and movies on the lives of young people. Training in music, art, dance, and drama was to begin early, as young children were organized into small groups and taught the rudiments of movement, elocution, and voice. Nancrede worked with children primarily who had studied voice with Eleanor Smith.

Looking back at her work, Nancrede was struck by "how right Miss Addams was in believing what most people now concede—that the drama is of the utmost value in educating and developing the young" (1928: 24–25). After twenty years of work with children, Nancrede had six groups, in all two hundred and forty members. Her social drama clubs had the power to hold a group together from childhood through adolescence and into maturity. The only other department at the settlement house which held people from childhood to adulthood was the music school, but in fewer numbers than the dramatic clubs, and very rarely with the boys. Acting had appeal for boys and young men, and in each of the groups they usually outnumbered the girls.

Were the "lifetime" members of Nancrede's drama clubs the factory workers of concern to Jane Addams, the working people she believed needed to have their monotonous jobs made meaningful through a connection to the history of the art and craft? Were they "the poor" that Eleanor Smith insisted were the most "ardent" votaries of music? Did the plays provide an antidote to the ugliness and dullness of their lives? Not enough data is available to draw any statistical analysis of the students enrolled in the Hull-House programs as to class and income. Nor is there enough of a sample to comment definitively

---

8   Jessica Payette's chapter in this volume discusses the production in detail.

about the results of the cultural programs. Our knowledge is limited to some suggestive oral interviews of individuals whose lives were shaped, according to their own assessments, by the settlement, and to the comments of the practitioners of the cultural pedagogy. Nancrede knew that many of the young people in the older clubs had left school at the age of fourteen, and their chief intellectual stimulus since then had been gained with the plays at Hull-House. "Someone once expressed amazement at the unusually large vocabulary of a certain young man who had left school at fourteen. But it was not really surprising when one considered that he had memorized hundreds of lines of such authors as Shakespeare, Sheridan, Galsworthy, Shaw, Yates, Housman, Barry, O'Neill, and Granville Barker" Nancrede explained (1928: 24–25). There were, however, many members of the social drama clubs whose formal education far exceeded the compulsory age of fourteen. They came from workers' and small shopkeepers' families, but many graduated from college and professional schools. Several of them considered the Hull-House programs instrumental in their personal and professional careers. Nancrede perhaps made too little of the link between the refinements and enrichments of the drama clubs and the social mobility experienced by her students. It was true that few became professional artists, actors, or musicians; but many entered the middle class and had productive careers in education, law, social work and other fields. Ironically, the pedagogical philosophy embraced by Addams, Nancrede, Benedict, and Smith almost intentionally downplayed any focus on preparation for professional careers and, most likely, ignored the strong pattern of social mobility (Nancrede to Jane Addams, August 13, 1931; Enella Benedict to Jane Addams, August 13, 1931) that students participating in the music, drama, and arts programs experienced. Eleanor Smith's accounts emphasize the parental enthusiasm for the acquisition of music training at the same time that she rather dramatically expressed her dismay at the lack of preparation or background most of her students exhibited when they first arrived at Hull-House (Smith, 1914: 1015). Both statements can be true, of course. Overall, the drive to get ahead, to master language, music, art, and drama, to climb out of poverty and achieve the American dream did not come from the settlement house alone but from the tenements and workers' cottages. The cultural workers were an important factor in the construction of the dream for many who saw for the first time a different or alternative lifestyle and absorbed aspirations and goals that set them apart from others who lived in the same neighborhoods but were not influenced by the cultural and social idealism of the progressive reformers led by Addams.

Nancrede indirectly instructs us about this reality when she reflects on the incredible attraction the theatricals held for the young women and men who had been her students from childhood. In this she confirmed Addams's observation of the importance of drama in the lives of ordinary people. The plays were elaborate productions because the young people had acquired tastes for beautiful and imaginative settings, and incidental music. Much of the production costs were buried since the music and art departments cooperated and many of the actors were also trained in the Hull-House schools of music and art and contributed these talents along with the acting responsibilities voluntarily. Nancrede and her actors all worked during the day, so the painting of scenery and the experimenting in lighting, as well as all rehearsing, were done at night. The settlement house only had funds for the plays given by children under the age of fourteen. This meant that the young adult groups struggled to keep afloat (Nancrede, 1928: 25).

The social drama clubs were mixed, boasting as many as nine different nationalities. This was unusual because most of the clubs at the settlement were either all-Italian or all-Jewish (Nancrede, 1928: 26). Folk dancing and rhythmic dancing formed a very important part in the training of the younger students as did vocal training with Eleanor Smith. Nancrede saw the whole process as using "drama in awakening and stimulating interest in intellectual and beautiful things and, ultimately... of freeing people from inhibitions and repressions" (28).

Addams and Nancrede called these productions the people's theater because neighbors—children and adults—were the actors and assisted in the construction of sets. Did the people choose the plays? Did the drama groups make their own decisions about casting? "I think casting was pretty much a unilateral decision that Nancrede made based on her knowledge of various people and where they fit into the parts of a play. There was no democratic aspect whatsoever. She made the decisions on casting and I would say also pretty much on the selection of plays" Alex Elson recalled (Oral Interview transcript, 1980, Hull-House Oral History Collection). Elson was one member of a large Russian Jewish family that was interested in Hull-House. His father came to the United States as a young man and had returned to Russia, married Alex's mother, and then several years later, the whole family returned. Alex's father had read about Jane Addams. The Elson family lived about a mile or so from Hull-House and Alex's oldest brother started going to Hull-House to take art lessons. Then his older sister began taking music lessons and in time all of his siblings—there were eight in the family—were involved in various activities at Hull-House. "Almost all of us went to the music school in one way or another, or singing classes, or taking lessons in instruments. Two of my brothers became very much interested in the violin, one of my brothers became a professional violinist, played in various symphony orchestras" (Ibid).

Alex Elson, like Hilda Satt and Sadie Ellis, had talent. All three came to know the Hull-House community and Jane Addams well as adults. Alex worked at the settlement when he was going through college and law school (Oral Interview transcript, Nov. 11, 1982, Hull-House Oral History Collection). These

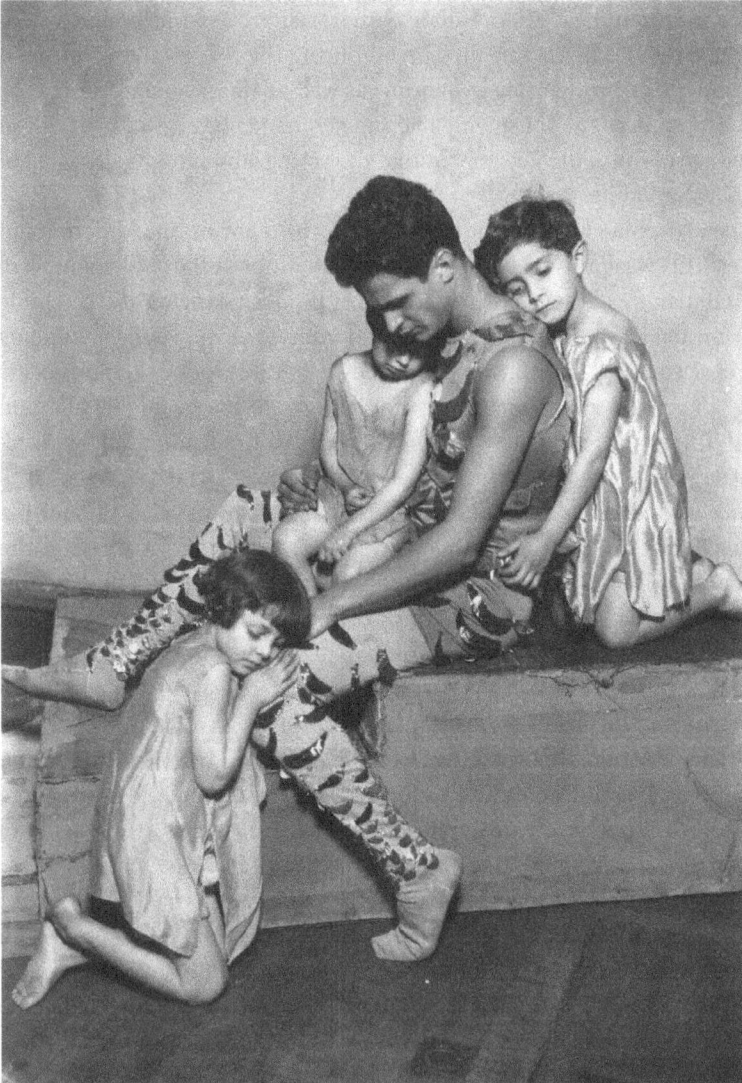

ILLUSTRATION 5.6   Alex Elson as King Merman in *The Merman's Bride*, 1928
SOURCE: JANE ADDAMS MEMORIAL COLLECTION (JAMC), SPECIAL
COLLECTIONS, DALEY LIBRARY, UNIVERSITY OF ILLINOIS AT
CHICAGO.

were the "transfigured few" that had the capacity to take full advantage of exceptional opportunities to work with talented teachers. Alex's brother was taught violin by a violinist who was performing with the Chicago Symphony Orchestra. "The remarkable thing about it as I look back," Elson said, "was the diversity of background from which the kids came, the mixture of all sorts of nationalities and religion and what not. I would say that in our group we had a predominance of Italians, but there were Poles, Irish, Jewish, Russian-Jewish. Various nationalities that came from different levels, there were some from working class families, most I would say came from working class families at different levels of culture. It happened in my family, my father was a highly educated person at the time he was growing up. He worked in a cigar factory, but he was by training and education a scholar and a Hebrew scholar in the old country and when we came here he could not make a living like this so he went to work in a cigar factory. But books played a very important part in his life and our lives and music and the theater were all very close to us" (Alex Elson, Oral Interview transcript, 1982, Hull-House Oral History Collection).

Alex Elson had a sense that his family's experience was out of the ordinary. He suspected that some of the kids in the program "were close to delinquency at the time" (Ibid). Elson was correct in his speculation. William John Granata had, in many ways, just as close a relationship with Jane Addams as Alex. He had the nickname, "The Greek," although he was Italian. Wallace Kirkland, who directed Hull-House's boys' club programs for almost fourteen years (1922–1935), considered "Greek" one of Edith de Nancrede's favorites. "She had great hopes for Greek, that when he was graduated from college he would become an influence for good in the city (Wallace Kirkland, "William John Granata, 'The Greek,'" n.d., Wallace Kirkland Papers). Kirkland, a social worker, had written his thesis on "Utilizing Gang Control in Boy's Work." He had argued that "the most effective means to influence the behavior of working boys was not to sepa-rate them based on categories such as age, size, or ability, but rather to use their own groupings, by gangs, and allow them to determine their activities based on their interests. Kirkland was able to apply this theory in his own work with the Hull-House Boy's Club" (Jordan, Wallace Kirkland Papers Inventory: n.p.).

The "Greek" came from a large Italian family in the neighborhood and his world was tough, gang-ridden, and his and his siblings' struggles to overcome the streets were challenges the settlement house was willing to take on in their support of him. Like so many of the neighborhood families in the 1920s and 1930s, the Granatas were plagued with economic struggles and inadequate city services forcing them to deal with daily indignities of living in a district that had been designated a "slum" and not a place of value. With the in-creased gang violence and crime in the Al Capone-Prohibition era, Hull-House more than ever offered shelter and, "as Greek put it 'Hull-House shows the neighborhood that there is another way of life'" (Wallace Kirkland, "William John Granata, 'The Greek,'" n.d.). The Granata family had successes, perhaps not as grand as the Elsons, but certainly respectable advances. The Greek became a lawyer, just as Alex Elson; his oldest brother served as a U.S. Congressman and a state senator; another brother joined the police department and became a detective; and a third brother became a certified public accountant (Ibid).

Greek and his brothers remained "neighborhood" people and the Elson family moved on, most of them geographically as well as culturally, and became the democratic cosmopolitans Addams had envisioned. Alex, who managed to keep his ties to the social justice goals he had developed, continued to live elsewhere in Chicago, but made urban justice issues his concern, returning to Hull-House settlement as a trustee.[9] The Greek followed his brother into local politics. In a run as the Republican candidate for Circuit Court Clerk in the October 1948 election, he was brutally killed just as he returned to his building after campaigning all evening (October 8, 1948. Assassins Slay Candidate in Loop. *Chicago Sun-Times*, Hull-House Collection, Spec. Col. Daley Library, Box 51, folder 553. October 23, 1948; Inquest in Granata Death Continued for More Investigation. *Chicago Tribune:* n.p.).

The Greek's world was split: Hull-House created an environment in which a tough kid could take dancing lessons and be the favorite of Nancrede, one of the close-knit group that went on picnics, enjoyed nature walks, summered at the Bowen Country Club camp[10] in Waukegan, Illinois, and, at the same time, remain a member of the West Side Sportsmen's Club, which met at the settlement house. It was one of a number of community groups or societies that rented space at Hull-House for a nominal fee. The clubs allowed groups of young people to socialize, use the settlement's athletic facilities, and enjoy the legitimacy and prestige of Hull-House and, however, to be self-initiated. In late 1931, when the Sportsmen's Club's questionable ties to criminal behavior

---

9   Living until the age of 103, he practiced law in Chicago for 70 years; was one of the founders of the National Academy of Arbitrators; served as chair of the American Civil Liberties Union (March 15, 2008. Death Notice. *Chicago Tribune*).

10   This was the camp built by Louise deKoven Bowen in 1912 in memory of her husband Joseph T. Bowen. Located in Waukegan, Illinois, conveniently on a train line from Chicago, it served thru the 1960s as a place of repose and renewal for adults in the neighborhood as well as a camp for children where arts and crafts, sports, drama and dance continued the programs at Hull-House, but in an environment free of the social constraints as well as congestion and evils of city streets. Here campers enjoyed roomy quarters that often were more comfortable than life in crowded apartments in the neighborhood and ate in the dining room on proper Blue willow-patterned china. Here early efforts at racial integration were part of a more self-conscious social engineering that Addams and Bowen did not feel was possible at Hull-House.

in the neighborhood were reported to her by insiders in the Juvenile Court system, Addams decided to terminate their lease. Addams was recovering from an operation performed at Johns Hopkins Hospital, Baltimore, and too weak to travel to Stockholm to receive the Nobel Prize for Peace that had been awarded her. From her hospital bed she was eager to keep the allegations secret and ended the lease with what appeared a flimsy and not credible reason: that the settlement needed the space. Granata, now a lawyer and brother to a local state senator, was asked by the West Side Sportsmen's Club, of which he was no longer active, to vouch for them and appeal to Addams to reverse her decision. Addams and her tight little circle of trusted confidants wanted none of the accusations made public and kept the information from even other Hull-House residents as well as The Greek. Granata understandably saw the termination of their relationship with Hull-House as a public repudiation, a rejection by Addams of her "beloved" neighborhood and himself. There were intimations of a public meeting to air the matter.

Granata had no compunctions about directly appealing to "Miss Addams," even as she remained hospitalized. This presumption on his part may be read as evidence of the remarkable relationship Addams had with her neighbors. She had invited the neighbors in; she had encouraged them to study art, music, and drama. She had valued *them* even as she had envisioned *their social uplift* in the context of an incompletely explored assumption about the validity of bourgeois values and the virtues of a largely top-down cultural pedagogy.

Addams might have been trying to protect the settlement house, and the members of the club, especially the Greek's association with them, by quietly ending the relationship. She might have been protecting the probation officers and Hull-House staff who had received "classified" information which they ought not to have known about. What is true of the situation is that she had invested a great deal of herself in retaining a real bond with The Greek. That relationship evidenced her claim to having achieved true social knowledge. She also had a desperate need to protect the institution she had built from scratch as both hers and the settlement's identity had been forged together. Those surrounding the seriously ill woman—her partner, Mary Rozet Smith who was in Baltimore with her, and her closest colleague who remained on the scene at Hull-House, Louise Bowen—knew that the letters and telegrams sent by Granata had to reach Addams in her hospital bed.

One could read her efforts to manipulate what could become a terribly embarrassing, volatile situation as the self-protective and defensive "cover-up" of an old woman who did not want the world to know that Hull-House's children, now grown-up, had not escaped the perils of the neighborhood environment. Or, that the settlement house was harboring active gang members. Worse, it could be interpreted as a signal that the pedagogy did not work.

Addams knew that Hull-House had not been able to marshal the public opinion capable of local political reform. The neighborhood had deteriorated. "Slowly through the years one is forced to recognize that the increase of crime is connected with the general state of political corruption throughout the community as a whole," Addams asserted, "for no social institution can escape from the community which gives it birth and which either promotes or retards its operation" ("Miss Addams Gives Views on Chicago Gang Disorders." *The Sun*, Baltimore, Jan. 18, 1932: 12). All the cultural activities, the best art and music, the beautifully composed *Hull-House Songs* by Eleanor Smith, the great theatrical productions—the Greek had starred in the French comedy by Moliere, "The Bourgeois Gentilhomme"—could not protect against the street and the general impact of the Great Depression (Addams to West Side Sportsmen's Athletic Ass., Dec. 4, 1931; Granata to Addams, Jan. 11, 1932; Addams to Granata [drafts] Jan. 15, 1932; Granata to Addams, Jan. 11, 1932).

The public spectacle and embarrassment to Hull-House did not happen; nor did criminal prosecution against any of the Sportsmen ever occur. After a ninety-day extension of the lease, the settlement house helped the club relocate to other space in the neighborhood. The Greek remained faithful to Hull-House and, after the death of Edith de Nancrede, who had cultivated the potential talent she saw in him, William John Granata became the chairman of the memorial fund in her honor. Alex Elson was a member of the memorial fund committee (Granata to Marion Young, April 13, 1940).[11]

As early as 1902, Addams had been aware of the contradictions inherent in the largely top-down approach to theater productions and rather defensively addressed a conference of charity and settlement house workers upon the subject "What the Theater at Hull-House Has Done for the Neighborhood People." She immediately turned the question around and told her audience "what the people of the neighborhood have done *with* the theater at Hull House, *for the theater has been turned over to the people, and they for the most part have been actors upon the stage*" (qtd. in "The Third Monthly Conference," *Charities*, VIII, no. 13, March 29, 1902: 284). [Italics added.] How far the theater was controlled by the neighbors was a sensitive point. To Addams it was of utmost importance to emphasize agency in her neighbors' involvement. Addams explained that theater had been established at Hull-House "because of the influence this institution had upon the working people, all of whom attend as frequently as they are able to afford the small admission fee charged at the cheaper places of amusement." From her earliest excursions into the neighborhood, Addams had been profoundly moved by the realization of how strong an influence commercial theater was in the life of ordinary working

---

11   Marion Young Collection, Chicago Public Library.

boys and girls. She would express this again in essays and in her major work, *The Spirit of Youth and the City Streets* (1909). "[The theater] forms to some extent their concept of morality, and in a greater degree shapes their outward manners and conduct. It rivals the schools in its influence, which, indeed, is protracted far beyond the school age" Addams told the charities' workers. In her explanation of Hull-House's theater work, however, a top-down pedagogy is apparent, although clothed in a more interactive performance setting, accomplishing what a more traditional instructional approach could not achieve:

> The theater at Hull-House has been a ready and potent means of *training the young people of the neighborhood in manners and personal refinement and courtesy,* a result which could not have been achieved by direct instruction with this end in view. The theater has been as well a means of education in the broader sense. It has been the *means of connecting the lives of the people with the life of the world*, not only with that outside of their present environment, but with historical events and achievements. It has served *to break up the feeling of isolation.*
>
> Quoted in "THE THIRD MONTHLY CONFERENCE," 1902: 284; emphasis added

Addams's use of the word "isolation" has meaning in the context of the opposite condition, which is to be engaged as a social person. Isolation can occur in a crowded flat or apartment in a congested block, or even a beehive of workers in a sweatshop. It is the absence of social connectivity leading to ethical behavior required by the conditions of industrial society. Addams imagines the *right* kind of drama can develop these connections among people and promote social progress and social citizenship. Again, the socially relevant theater experience provides useful context for the interpretation of the fable or story and leads to a wise conclusion on the part of working people and their children. For example, the movies were places where adolescents and young adults "can satisfy the craving for a conception of life higher than that which the actual world offers them. In a very real sense the drama and the drama alone performs for them the office of art as is clearly revealed in their blundering demand stated in many forms for 'a play unlike life.' The theater becomes to them a 'veritable house of dreams' infinitely more real than the noisy streets and the crowded factories" (Addams, 1909: 75–76). Tragically, in Addams's view, the subject matter of *commercial* theater was mostly amoral or immoral and worthless for providing material for the development of good character and citizenship. "Seldom" Addams tells us, "do we associate the theater with our plans for civic righteousness, although it has become so important a factor in city life" (83–84).

5   Searching for A Democratic Pedagogy: The Evolution of the Labor
         Museum

Jane Addams and Ellen Starr were never satisfied with the programs Hull-
House had established in the humanities, the fine, arts, and the performing
arts. The major goal was to democratize culture as a necessary stage in the
evolution of society. This meant devising ways to transmit quality humanities
education outside of universities to the working people in their neighborhoods and to the public schools. The early efforts at Hull-House, which included college-type courses, were discontinued when universities formalized
college extension (Addams, 1900: 423). The Butler Art Gallery project closed
after not more than five years of existence when it became possible for working people to visit the Art Institute on Sundays when admission was free. Its
space was then used for additional art studios. From 1895 until 1900, when the
Labor Museum was opened, there was a progression toward creating space at
Hull-House for neighborhood people to work in industrial shops and at hand-
icrafts while the colony of resident artists flourished (Michael, 2005. Recovering the Layout of the Hull House Complex. http://www.uic.edu/jaddams/
hull/urbanexp). The two trends were complimentary. In this manner, Addams and Starr were constructing a non-elitist, differently gendered version
of the artist in her/his studio; Ellen Gates Starr's evolving pursuits in the labor
movement and in her bookbindery modeled this conception more than any
of the other resident artists. She was also the resident who experienced the
most inner turmoil and conflict over the imperfect relationship of art and labor actualized by the settlement. She was deeply troubled by the failure of
the settlement to develop a communal "religious" community to support the
labor activism and militant politics she believed necessary to heal industrial
society.

      Sharing studio space with the neighborhood people in unstructured as well
as formal classes meant that the art studios were open to Hull-House residents
and neighbors who found time to pursue art interests. The Chicago Society
of Arts and Crafts, organized in 1897 at Hull-House, respected the textiles,
metalwork, and woodwork crafted by the neighbors; when the Art Institute of
Chicago began to have annual arts and crafts exhibits, local artisans exhibited
alongside the society's entries on an equal footing (Catalogue, 1904: 53–55).
Courses were offered, but the focus and "production" of culture, especially in
the fine arts, in this early period expressed the experiences of the residents
more than those of the neighbors. This would change by the 1920s when former art students began to teach and in their social realist paintings reflected

the social justice concerns of the settlement's philosophy of art and labor through the lens of workers and immigrants.[12]

Resident artists had captured their own Hull-House "colony": Alice Kellogg Tyler painted portraits of Jane Addams and Mary Rozet Smith and Cornelia De Bey, feminist physician who was part of the Hull-House circle. Frank Hazen painted Jenny Dow, who taught kindergarten.[13] Slowly the neighborhood intruded the inner-most space of the colony of women and men. Enella Benedict painted the portrait of "Edith" (Edith Redding[14]) a neighborhood girl who came to classes and activities. Benedict also painted a scene of men on an employment line capturing in one of her impressionistic canvasses the dire economic crisis that descended on the neighborhood in the depression of 1893–97.

All the artists taught "classes filled not only by young people possessing facility and sometimes talent," but also, which impressed Addams, "by older people to whom the studio affords the one opportunity of escape from dreariness; a widow with four children who supplemented a very inadequate income by teaching the piano, for six years never missed her weekly painting lesson because it was 'her one pleasure'; another woman whose youth and strength had gone into the care of an invalid father, poured into her afternoon in the

---

12   William Jacobs, Morris Topchevsky, Leon and Sadie Garland—all who had taken art lessons at Hull-House, produced socially relevant art that could be identified with the emerging Cultural Front aesthetics that would become more fully articulated at Hull-House in the late 1930s: Jacobs (Jewett, June 16, 1929: 17; Jacobson, 1933); Topchevsky (Bulliet, 27 June 1936: 27; Jewett, 4 May 1935: 17); Leon and Sadie Garland (Sadie Garland Dreikurs Oral Interview transcript, June 24, 1980, Hull-House Oral History Collection; Sokol, 2013: 2–12).

13   Alice Kellogg Tyler's portraits of Addams and Mary Rozet Smith deserve their own study. Tyler, whose life was cut short, had already achieved national attention at the time she began to paint in the Hull-House studio (Bowie, 2001: 468–470). See Addams's correspondence (Jane Addams to Mary Rozet Smith, March 23, 1898; Alice Kellogg Tyler to Jane Addams, [?] 1898; Jane Addams to Sarah Alice Addams Haldeman, March 5, 1898). Kellogg Tyler painted De Bey's portrait, a study of a feminist whose mannish attire indicates the unconventional gender roles in the Hull-House colony. Hazen is discussed in Boris, 1986: 46. For De Bey: Schiltz & Sinke, 2001: 214–216.

14   Nowhere in Addams's writings or in the "folklore" of Hull-House do we learn that the red-haired beauty in her white confirmation dress, was the daughter of a local Irish Catholic saloon keeper, educated by Catholic teaching sisters, who later entered the order of the Sisters of Charity of the Blessed Virgin Mary (BVMs). My colleague Ellen Skerrett learned of the identity of "Edith" when she presented a paper in Dubuque, Iowa, to a history meeting of the Sisters of Charity of the Blessed Virgin Mary (BVMs). Sister Mary Healey, BVM, recognized the slide of Benedict's painting of "Edith" as a portrait of Sister Sariel, BVM. See: Sister S. Sariel Redding File, Mount Carmel Archives, Dubuque, Iowa.

studio once a week, all of the longing for self-expression which she habitually suppressed" (Addams, 1910: 373–374).

More than skills or occupational benefits that the classes offered, the unstructured time for art and craft work in shops and studios by ordinary people exemplified Addams's and Starr's efforts to democratize culture. Both women envisioned a society where the expression of traditional arts and crafts provided solace and gave meaning to workers' lives otherwise involved in jobs, and even careers, that were alienating. "Perhaps the most satisfactory results of the studio have been obtained through the classes of young men who are engaged in the commercial arts, and who are glad to have an opportunity to work out their own ideas," Addams felt (1910: 373–374). "This is true of young engravers and lithographers; of the men who have to do with posters and illustrations in various ways. The little pile of stones and the lithographer's hand-press in a corner of the studio have been used in many an experiment, as has a set of beautiful type loaned to Hull-House by a bibliophile" (374–375).

Soon, Addams tells us, "the work of the studio almost imperceptibly merged into the crafts and well within the first decade a shop was opened at Hull-House under the direction of several residents who were also members of the Chicago Arts and Crafts Society. This shop... [was] not merely a school where people [were] taught and then sent forth to use their teaching in art according to their individual initiative and opportunity, but where those who had already been carefully trained, [might] express the best they can in wood or metal" (Addams, 1910: 375). These developments were the precursors of the Labor Museum.

The shops like the art studios provided "restorative power in the exercise of a genuine craft" (376). Addams told the story of a young Russian who, "like too many of his countrymen had made a desperate effort to fit himself for a learned profession and who had almost finished his course in a night law school" (375). She explained how he

> used to watch constantly the work being done in the metal shop at Hull-House. One evening in a moment of sudden resolve, he took off his coat, sat down at one of the benches, and began to work, obviously as a very clever silversmith. He had long concealed his craft because he thought it would hurt his efforts as a lawyer and because he imagined an office more honorable and "more American" than a shop. As he worked on during his two leisure evenings each week, his entire bearing and conversation registered the relief of one who abandons the effort he is not fitted for and becomes a man on his own feet, expressing himself through a familiar and delicate technique.
>
> ADDAMS, 1910: 376

The shops had the additional virtue of providing Addams access to relationships with neighborhood people who had remained hard to reach. Confessing that she had found it difficult to come into "genuine relations with the Italian women and... *they themselves so often lost their hold upon their Americanized children"* (1910: 235). [Italics added.] Addams conceived of the Labor Museum as space to accomplish both goals: her own need for connection and her "overmastering desire to reveal the humbler immigrant parents to their own children" (255).

> It seemed to me that Hull-House ought to be able to devise some educational enterprise which should build a bridge between European and American experiences in such wise as to give them both more meaning and a sense of relation... The occupation of the old woman [spinning on traditional wooden spindles] gave me the clue that was needed. Could we not interest the young people working in the neighborhood factories in these older forms of industry, so that, through their own parents and grandparents, they would find a dramatic representation of the inherited resources of their daily occupation. [sic] If these young people could actually see that the complicated machinery of the factory had been evolved from simple tools, they might at least make a beginning toward that education which [educational reformer] Dr. [John] Dewey defines as "a continuing reconstruction of experience." They might also lay a foundation for reverence of the past which Goethe declares to be the basis of all sound progress.
>
> ADDAMS, 1910: 236–237

It suited Addams's rhetorical needs to locate the origin of the Labor Museum in the desires of the very people she found most difficult to bring into the orbit of the settlement house. As her reference to John Dewey implies, Addams drew upon many sources in her quest for a method or strategy to engage workers and their families in a process of acculturation.[15] Mary Hill, a resident at

---

15   Addams had identified pedagogical problems with immigrants and their children in a
      speech to the National Education Association in 1897: Reading her analysis of the predica-
      ment of the families makes clear that many of her ideas expressed in the Labor Museum
      and its complex programs and activities were brewing in her mind as early as 1897, and
      perhaps earlier. She begins by articulating what she believes is a widely held assumption
      among educators, which she also holds, that "whatever may be our ultimate conception
      of education, and however much we may differ in definition... we shall probably agree
      that the ultimate aim is to modify the character and conduct of the individual, and to
      harmonize and adjust his activities; that even the primary school should aim to give the

Hull-House, and a protégé of John Dewey, connected Dewey's experiments with industrial education to the Labor Museum. Both Addams and Dewey conceptualized a new kind of school where children and adults would learn from the arts and industries of the past in order to respond to the changing reality of industrial America.[16]

Addams conceived the museum—so named because she felt adults would feel more comfortable with exhibits and activities that were not in places called "classrooms" and she wanted to avoid the feeling of children's lessons or instructions (Washburne, 1904: 572–573)—to have five departments: textiles, metals, wood, grains, and printing and binding. Later she added a sixth section focused on pottery. The elders of the community were to be the teachers as they brought their craft equipment into the museum spaces, which also served as the industrial shops.

All the departments placed the congruent labor processes into a historic sequence. There were live demonstrations, displays of specimens of materials exhibited in raw form, and then as they changed during the different stages of production. There were maps and diagrams, photographs and paintings illustrating the kinds of labor involved in each industry. Efforts were made, when possible, to coordinate the displays and lectures with the growth and history of Chicago and the development of its industries (Addams, 1901–02: 1–2).

The Weaving or Textile Room was the most well-developed section of the Labor Museum.[17] In it the history of the craft was charted from the construction

---

child's own experience a social value; and that this aim too often fails of success in the brief sojourn of the child of the foreign peasant in the public school" (Addams, 1897: 105). Addams indicated that John Dewey was working on similar pedagogical problems at the University of Chicago. One of Dewey's students, Mary Hill, was resident at Hull-House. At both places Hill was experimenting with Labor Museum pedagogy (Durst, 2010: 104–109). In addition, Addams had been impressed with Patrick Geddes's use of exhibition rather than traditional classrooms, to acculturate traditional Scottish townspeople in his urban planning initiatives. Geddes overall vision was of evolutionary social progress, stemming from his science and sociology interests. Addams also had absorbed ideas of Comte and Darwin (Bryson, 1936: 343–362). Geddes visited Chicago in 1899: "We expect Mr. Geddes tomorrow to spend a week with us and we hope for much wisdom" (Jane Addams to Helena S. Dudley, Chicago, March 28, 1899). Addams and Geddes in Paris, where Addams spent time in Geddes' exhibition & school at the Paris Exposition 1900 (Jane Addams to Mary Rozet Smith, June 14, 1900).

16   Mary Hill letter (Durst, 2010: 106).

17   Addams went to great lengths to develop the weaving room. She sent Hull-House residents George E. Hooker and Mary Hill to Wisconsin to visit woolen and knitting mills (George E. Hooker to Gerard Swope, Nov. 9, 1900. Mary Hill Swope Papers, University of Illinois—Chicago).

End of Textile Room – Labor Museum

ILLUSTRATION 5.7   The textile room in the Hull-House Labor Museum, 1900
SOURCE: JANE ADDAMS MEMORIAL COLLECTION (JAMC),
SPECIAL COLLECTIONS, DALEY LIBRARY, UNIVERSITY OF
ILLINOIS AT CHICAGO.

of baskets and mats through the production of cloth on a fly shuttle loom. A timeline illustrating the longevity of the traditional methods of weaving impressed visitors as did the textile room's exhibit that illustrated the long span of time that the stick spindle had been in use. The point, of course, was to demonstrate how recently steam-power had revolutionized textile production. Many European traditions were displayed and during the first year the museum added Navajo and Turkish looms to its collection.

A series of lectures on industrial history with a discussion of labor conditions in different periods and their effects on workers ranged from slave labor during the Roman Empire to the industrial revolution and rise of trades unions among textile workers in England. The museum organized several evening gatherings where poems and literary works were read and discussed with textile workers.

The Labor Museum expanded its programs after it moved into the remodeled gymnasium building on the corner of Polk Street in 1901. The displays were installed throughout the first floor of the building and in two rooms on the second floor. Pictures illustrating textile production, including two reproductions of the French painter Jean-François Millet's famous images of spinners decorated the rooms and the Field Museum of Natural History loaned an extensive collection of textiles including specimens of raw materials, examples of finished goods, and implements. Specimens from China, Japan, and India made the display worldwide (Luther, 1902: 7–8; Washburne, 1904: 576). After the close of the 1904 Louisiana Purchase Exposition in St. Louis, a group of Philippine objects that had been exhibited there came into the museum and included native fibers, baskets, looms, agricultural tools, and models of spinning processes and a sugar-cane mill (Washburne, 1904: 576; *Hull-House Bulletin*, 1905–06: 15–16).

The Labor Museum also had a kitchen with an old-fashioned fireplace, modeled on the kind used in Colonial American homes. Modern kitchen equipment was used for the cooking classes in contrast to the colonial. The first floor also contained the room where work in wood, metal, and clay was carried out. On display were antique wooden tankards and "Viking bowls" made by Norwegians. Copper pieces from Russia, Italy, and England and photographs of famous examples of metalwork, as well as drawings illustrating the modern smelting processes that took place at the Calumet mines, just south of Chicago, were also on exhibition.

The art studio moved into the renovated building to be near the industrial shops and the Labor Museum. In a collaborative fashion, Enella Benedict contributed sketches of sheep-shearing and spinning in the North Carolina mountains to the textile room and drawings of workers in the copper foundries of northern Michigan to the metal department.

The printing and binding departments were the last sections added to the museum. The *Hull-House Bulletin* explained that this ordering was logical: "As the need of books came into man's life later than the necessity for means of feeding, clothing, and housing himself, this department of the labor museum naturally follows those of the grains, textiles, wood and metals." The bindery exhibit was Ellen Starr's bookbinding workshop. The walls of the bindery were decorated with framed samples of fine printing, including arts-and-crafts style pages printed at the Kelmscott Press and the Doves Press in England, and a replica of John W. Alexander's frieze illustrating the history of the book, based on his original mural at the Library of Congress. The printing shop, installed in the room next to the bindery, featured a hand-press. There were also photographs of historic typography and facsimiles of illuminated manuscripts, and a copy of B.J.O. Norfeldt's series of four prints entitled "The Wave," which illustrated the production of a colored wood-cut (Washburne, 1904: 574).

In framing the discussions of labor conditions with literary culture, and in taking an historicist approach in explicating labor conditions, Addams continued to mediate between workers and the middle classes through well-tempered bourgeois art and literature sentiments that balanced messages of protest and hope. Thus, in her explanations of the Labor Museum for her

middle-class readers she evokes George Eliot, reproaching herself that no contemporary "poet or artist has endeared the sweaters' victim to us as George
Eliot has made us love the belated weaver, Silas Marner" (Addams, 1910: 240).

It made sense, then, for the Hull-House Music School to offer a program of
labor songs for the Labor Museum. Eleanor Smith put together a collection of
folk-songs including songs related to the textile industry ("Art and the Labor
Museum," *Hull-House Bulletin* Autumn 1900: 9 and Semi-Annual 1902: 13; Washburne, 1904: 580). (Smith's adaptation of Rosenfeld became "The Sweat Shop
Song" included in the *1915 Hull House Songs*.) There was also a series of lectures
on industrial history with a discussion of labor conditions in different periods
and their effects on workers ranged from slave labor during the Roman Empire
to the industrial revolution and rise of trades unions among textile workers
in England. The museum organized several evening gatherings where poems
and literary works were read and discussed with textile workers. Addams
considered Hauptmann's drama "The Weavers," which was presented in the
Labor Museum, as "the most striking picture" of the period when steam was
first introduced. Once again literature was used to express great truths about
the laboring of the people. At the same time, there was room at Hull-House
for a committee of garment workers' in the neighborhood to discuss the latest
efforts to unionize and deal with recalcitrant owners who refused to accept
collective bargaining. What value the museum and shops had for workers and
their children has been hard to gauge. Ellen Starr gives us an opposing view to
Addams's overwhelmingly positive construction.

6   Ellen Gates Starr and The Contradictions of Art and Labor

Ellen Starr was a discordant voice from the start. She did not agree completely
with the direction that Hull-House settlement was taking. It seemed Starr almost immediately felt the contradictions that Addams later alluded to when
she wrote "how difficult it... [was] to put a fringe of art on the end of a day
spent in a factory" (Addams, 1910: 375). Addams, however, proudly displayed
the arts and crafts produced in the shops at the 3rd annual exhibit of held at
the Chicago Institute (1904: 53–55). Ironically, the contradictions were to become most obvious to Starr in the way her own work in the Labor Museum's
bookbindery seemed at times irrelevant to her actual labor union activities
and socialist politics. She rationalized that her work provided opportunity, albeit limited, to illustrate products of unalienated work and that in her bindery
she was demonstrating work done in the "'spirit of the future'—that is, in a
spirit allowing for self-expression" (qtd. in Boris, 1986: 180).

ILLUSTRATION 5.8   Ellen Gates Starr, left, and her student Peter Verburg, right, seated
in the bookbindery, c. 1890s
SOURCE: JANE ADDAMS MEMORIAL COLLECTION (JAMC),
SPECIAL COLLECTIONS, DALEY LIBRARY, UNIVERSITY OF
ILLINOIS AT CHICAGO.

In 1892, Starr had accused Hull-House of being merely "an excuse for the things
we ought to do and be and don't and aren't" (qtd. in Carrell, 1981: 320). She worried about the contradictions of offering bourgeois culture to workers but not
sharing power with them. "If we don't wish working people to stand upon the
same ground with us, if we believe that there is an eternal distinction, if we
believe in caste, no matter how we disguise it, then why shouldn't we let them
alone? Why insult people by saying to them, 'you are different, you will be different always, you can never be as we, knowing false and true, beautiful and
ugly, but we wish to be kind to you, we want you to enjoy in your poor capacity,
what you are capable of enjoying, and so we come and give you this and this'"
(qtd. in "Chicago's Hull-House" 1895b: n.p.).

Starr's 1895 contribution, "Art and Labor," discussed earlier, was anti-
capitalist and anti-modernist in tone. Starr had warned that it was not enough
to fight for wages, you had also to fight for the soul of man against the commercial and industrial world that was crushing him. She was uncomfortable with
a maternalist argument that an educated and cultivated class should guide
the tastes of the uncultivated but succumbed to such an arrangement. The
Chicago Public School Art Society, born out of Starr's determination to bring
objects of beauty into all the places she could, was a top-down organization

that assumed the role of arbiter of taste and disseminator of bourgeois art. The activities in the Labor Museum, the arrangement of artifacts, and the interpretation of the presentations were controlled by Hull-House residents and staff.

Starr's own complicated feelings about her loyalties surfaced as she began to feel a closer relationship to the working class and to those bright, ambitious young men and women who were attempting to better themselves. On one hand, her art history lectures, her Shakespeare club, or reading books like *Romola* to a small group of school teachers and white-collar workers thirsty for enrichment and cultivation had value to them. In many respects she was more like these young women than she was like Enella Benedict, whose wealth and education in European art schools and at the Art Institute had led to her position on the faculty of the School of the Art Institute and her professional work as an artist. Ellen had her own yearnings and ambitions. She had decided to go to England in 1897 and study the art of book binding with the leading arts and crafts practitioner, T.J. Cobden-Sanderson. Perhaps, as well, it was an effort to become more authentic in her relationship with workers (Bosch, 2001: 840). After fifteen months as an apprentice in his shop, Starr returned to Hull-House where she set up the bindery and began to teach a small number of students.

One of the great differences between Addams and Starr was that of their class positions. Issues of financial dependence had plagued Starr from her college days when she was able to complete only one year at the female seminary. Addams remained to finish college while Starr taught school and dreamt of more ambitious plans. The friendship, sustained by copious letters and infrequent visits, was fueled by Ellen's admiration and love for Jane. As much as Ellen brought to the relationship—actual independence and courage in living on her own in the big city of Chicago—Jane always had the upper hand as a young woman of wealth and superior rank. Addams's "patronage" of Starr had made possible the schoolteacher's European travels and the opportunity to leave a prosaic existence where she had deferred to her students—the daughters of the elite. Instead, she joined in the adventure of co-founding a cultural and social institution soon to have worldwide connections. The imbalance and subsequent dependency of Starr was understood by both women. "I have thought of the possibility of my dying [before] the experiment [Hull-House settlement] is in full sway," Addams wrote her sister Alice. "As Ellen has given up her regular teaching and trusts all her future to the affair, I should like her to be given $1500.00 enough to support her for a year or more until she could get back into her regular work. I have now made a will and... know you would see to that for me" (Addams to Sarah Alice Addams Haldeman, Aug. 31, 1889).

To complicate this class difference between the two, which one can argue further pushed Starr in the direction of radical social action, Addams began to depend on her new friend, Mary Rozet Smith, a wealthy, comely young woman who began volunteering at the settlement. She, with her upper-class family in tow, were willing to use their money to "clothe in brick and mortar" the expansionary dreams of Addams's cultural agenda (Schultz, 2001: 817–819) and especially Eleanor Smith's music school project (Schultz, "Eleanor Smith and Her Circle," this volume).

Addams felt comfortable with capitalists—the enlightened and well-intentioned.[18] She shared the "colonizers" outlook that supported the American way of developing "undeveloped" regions and lifting up populations with education and cultural programs, but in her anti-militarism, preferred international associations and cooperative ventures that often hid the cultural hegemonic values inherent in the power imbalances. Building up an institution that modeled appropriate working-class cultural life had become Addams's passion. This drift toward institution-building was not shared by Starr whose bindery room seemed to offer scant comfort but, rather, felt incomplete as she imagined a socialist and religious cooperative workshop buzzing with activity. Starr's frustrations with teaching bookbinding and with the slow progress made in advancing the overall cultural and economic interests of the working class were further exacerbated by her basic disagreement with Addams about the need for revolutionary change in the social system. For Starr, nothing short of a religiously-inspired radical conversion to communitarian or socialist values would address the deep injustices caused by capitalism. Like her hero, William Morris, Starr married her own artistic expression and belief in socialism only to find that the contradictions were too dramatic. Expensive materials

---

18   Addams's closest associates other than the Hull-House residents were her board of directors and they included the richest people in Chicago: Julius Rosenwald, a variety of McCormicks and Blairs, who married Bowens and all were investment bankers; Charles L. Hutchinson, banker, commodities trader, and cultural philanthropist, also was a director. Just a note to contextualize class further, at Jane Addams's 70th birthday party, hosted by soon to be Secretary of the Treasury Henry Morgenthau, was in attendance none other than John D. Rockefeller, Jr. The party took place in Bar Harbor, Maine, where Addams and her partner Mary Rozet Smith, the daughter of Chicago wealth, summered. "Honor Jane Addams on her 70th Birthday. J.D. Rockefeller Jr. and others Join in Praise at Morgenthau Luncheon at Bar Harbor. Distinguished guests voiced high tribute to JA, founder of Hull-House at a luncheon given in honor of her 70th birthday at their Harbor Summer home, Mizzentop. Among those who praised JA were Morgenthau, Dr. Francis G. Peabody, Harvard; Dr. Robert M. Hutchins, president of the U of Chicago; Arthur Henderson, son of the British Minister of Foreign Affairs; Dr. Richard C. Cabot of Boston and John D. Rockefeller, Jr." (Sept. 7, 1930, *The New York Times*: 20).

and long years' training achieved great art at a cost beyond the means of workers. Ultimately, Starr was only able to train a handful of students in the craft[19] and the cultural world inhabited by artists and artisans in which she traveled and in which she exhibited her decorative and expensive rare books was becoming increasingly more remote from the picket lines she also inhabited in support of striking garment workers and waitresses.[20]

Starr had begun to take labor's side in an activist way during an 1896 garment workers' strike (Starr to Henry D. Lloyd, March 12 & April 17, 1896[21]) in Chicago and she continued to advocate for workers becoming more passionate and personally engaged than Addams, whose interest in mediation and arbitration efforts had surfaced in 1894 with the Pullman strike (Smith, 1995: 255–258). Addams's classic "A Modern Lear" was too controversial to be published until 1912, even though it was an attempt to understand Pullman and the complexity of the human situation in which he found himself with his workers (Smith, 1995: 258). Abjuring the cant of class conflict, Addams turned to lectures on mediation and spearheaded political efforts to institutionalize collective bargaining through legislation. She, not Starr, was called to resolve labor conflicts. In contrast, the 1910 garment workers' strike consumed the energies of Starr in a manner that frightened Addams, who by then had become a national leader in reform politics and whose relationship to the local scene had shifted. "I am sorry and ashamed to be so far out of the strike but at the present moment there is nothing to be done but to distribute the relief to the strikers as wisely as we can," Addams wrote in a letter to her family. "Sister [Ellen Gates] Starr is becoming very overwrought and has had one or two fits of sobbing that have rather alarmed us all" (Addams to Mary Rozet Smith, Nov. 22, 1910). Addams concluded that there was "every reason for worry over the strike" but that there was very little chance for arbitration.

Starr remained involved with the strikers organizing relief for families. Before the strike, she had spent several months in Italy building up her spiritual strength by visiting with the Benedictines and Franciscans and acknowledged to her friends that the months in Italy "made it possible for me to do this" (Starr to Charles Wager, 1910[22]). The contradictions here are obvious. For all of Starr's earnestness and her distress over her class position, the emotional differences

---

19   In 1904 Starr's pupils Peter Verburg and Mary Kelley exhibited bound volumes (1904, Third Annual Exhibition: 53–55).

20   Starr was one of the founding members of the Chicago Society of Arts and Crafts (Boris, 1986: 33, 45–46). When the arts and crafts community, Byrdcliffe, was established in Woodstock, New York, in 1902, Starr was a visitor (Green, 2004b: 56–81).

21   Ellen Gates Starr Papers, Sophia Smith Collection, Smith College.

22   Ellen Gates Starr Papers, Sophia Smith Collection, Smith College.

between the two women could not mask the greater affinity they both had for bourgeois culture. Even more of a contradiction was the ability both Starr and Addams had to escape from the neighborhood and they never shared the daily bone-grinding poverty that defined sweatshop and factory workers' lives. Starr's discomfort with the contradictions that were expressed in the way the settlement movement developed did not cause her to break with Addams, or to give up fine art book binding or even change her ideas about cultural pedagogy. As historian Suellen Hoy informs us "Until she closed her bindery in the 1920s, Starr earned a good part of her living by binding and ornamenting books" (Hoy, 2010: 5–7).

At the same time, her radicalism was becoming more public. On March 6, 1914, at age fifty-five, Starr was arrested and brought to trial on a charge of disorderly conduct stemming from her behavior on the picket line at a waitresses' strike in Chicago ("Ellen G. Starr's Trial on Today," *Chicago Tribune*, March 4, 1914: 7). She had shouted at the police, who she believed had unjustly arrested three waitresses on picket duty, "I am a citizen and as such protest this arrest." The crowd became excited and it was reported that they shouted: "Kill the police." After eight hours' deliberation, a jury found her innocent (Carrell, 1981: 357–358). Within a few months of her trial Starr sailed to Europe to make another tour of the medieval shrines, revisiting Assisi and the Benedictine monastery at Monte Cassino. Renewed and strengthened in her idealism, the next year, during the Amalgamated Clothing Workers of America strike when over 1,700 strikers were arrested and two were killed, Starr herself was arrested several times for "inciting a riot" and insisted on a jury trial to bring the facts to the public (McCreesh, 1985: 218–220). She had thrown herself into the fray with Sidney Hillman and Bessie Abramowitz, the rebels who had broken with the American Federation of Labor (AFL) and were leading the Amalgamated. Starr debated Samuel Gompers, president of the AFL, in the pages of the *New Republic* (McCreesh, 1985: 218–220; Hoy, 2010: 17). He was the most powerful union leader in the country. Gompers told Starr to stay out of labor's business. Starr blamed the initial loss of the Amalgamated on the "heavy hand of Mr. Gompers" (qtd. in McCreesh, 1985: 218–220).

Starr's plunge into a deeper and more catholic devotional life that served to pull her out of recurring emotional depressions, was also an expression of her lifelong search for fellowship and salvation (Carrell, 1981: 398–400; Starr to Wager, Feb. 12, 1917).[23] In contrast to Addams, Starr was searching for

---

23   Ellen Gates Starr Papers, Sophia Smith Collection, Smith College. Among her periods of
      depression, in 1896, after a garment workers' strike, the first in which she was actively

something close to a sacramental community, a version of "social holiness" beyond "personal holiness" that would also reconcile her individuality as an artist
with her desire to identify with workers (Starr, 1895c: 1–3).[24] Shortly after the
Garment Workers' Strike in 1910 Starr had joined the Socialist Party, and fit in
with the Marxist, hard-line, predominantly immigrant organization. Although
middle-class social workers were discouraged from joining, by 1915 Starr was
serving on the Cook County Socialist Party's executive committee (Carrell,
1981: 357). She did this even while deepening her commitment to Christianity. For Starr, her labor union radicalism seemed to draw her more deeply into
her faith, or perhaps, the arduous task of standing up for the workers against
the wealthy and powerful could only be endured by her through the strength
of her religious convictions. It was her vision of the implementation of the
social gospel here on earth that continued to inspire and sustain her as much
as the realities of oppressive conditions stirred her rebellion. When she ran
for alderman of the Nineteenth Ward as a socialist in 1916 she explained her
credo:

> I became a Socialist because I was a Christian. The Christian religion
> teaches that all men are to be regarded as brothers, that no one should
> wish to profit by the loss or disadvantages of others [...] that none should
> enjoy "two coats" while others are coatless. Civilized life is in grotesque
> contrast to all this. Only socialism promised to put down the mighty from
> their seats and to exalt the humble and meek; to fill the hungry with good
> things and to send the rich, if not quite "empty" away, at least relieved of
> some of their unnecessary and arrogant fulness [sic].
>
> Clipping, "Why I am A Socialist," February 10, 1916, ELLEN GATES STARR PAPERS,
> SOPHIA SMITH COLLECTION

---

involved, Starr became exhausted and left for New York for a prolonged period. In 1907,
she collapsed from nervous exhaustion, spent a month in a sanitarium, and spent 1908
abroad, living in relative isolation on a farm in Ireland. Starr describes her conversion to
Roman Catholicism (Starr, 1924: 167–200).

24   Starr most likely was disappointed in the other group to which she attempted to meld
     art and labor: the Chicago Society of Arts and Crafts. Historian Eileen Boris found that
     "By 1910 it [the Chicago Society for Arts and Crafts] had dwindled to 26 members, who
     concentrated on running their own studio-shops rather than promoting cooperative ven-
     tures. Crafts workers increasingly were alumni of the School of the Art Institute, which
     had replaced Hull House as the center of the movement in Chicago. With this shift, the
     crafts—while flourishing as profession, personal avocation, and part of an appealing
     lifestyle—lost their more intimate relation to the reform impulse" (Boris, 1986: 51).

ILLUSTRATION 5.9   Ellen Gates Starr, age fifty-seven, 1916
SOURCE: JANE ADDAMS MEMORIAL COLLECTION (JAMC), SPECIAL
COLLECTIONS, DALEY LIBRARY, UNIVERSITY OF ILLINOIS AT CHICAGO.

7   Jane Addams and Industrial Education: Contextualizing Factory
        Work and Elevating Craft at the Labor Museum

Starr remained conflicted about the craftsman ideal and attempts at cultural
expression by working people in the top-down and controlled atmosphere of
Hull-House, its Music School and operettas, and she moved further into the
trenches of class warfare. Addams moved toward institutionalizing cultural
production and the settlement ideal of social amelioration as the answer to
industrial conflict. She identified this as much more than the conflict between
labor and capital in the workplace. Addams saw the disintegration of traditional family life, especially among immigrants, as intergenerational conflict
exacerbated by the too-early employment of children and adolescents, and
further negatively impacted by the attractions of popular culture. The museum's workrooms and classes became models she used in advocating industrial
and vocational education.

   Addams was critical of the public schools, as was Eleanor Smith when she
examined the way in which music was taught. Both women, as Ellen Starr advocated in her Chicago Public School Art Society, worked with organizations to
reform curriculum. Trying to get to the root of the problem of alienated labor,
Addams, writing about foreign-born children in the primary grades, questioned whether anything had been done to give boys who stayed in school until the required age of fourteen a consciousness of their social value. "Has the
outcome of the processes to which he has been subjected adapted him to deal
more effectively and in a more vital manner with his present life?" (Addams,
1897: 104–112). Addams attempted to do just this for young men and women in
the programs of the Labor Museum. The pedagogy of the Labor Museum was
based on Addams's belief that:

> Industrial history in itself is an interesting thing, and the story of the long
> struggle of man in his attempts to bring natural forces under human con-
> trol could be made most dramatic and graphic. The shops and factories
> all about him contain vivid and striking examples of the high develop-
> ment of the simple tools which his father still uses, and of the lessening
> expenditure of human energy. He is certainly cut off from nature, but he
> might be made to see nature as the background and material for the hu-
> man activity which now surrounds him. Giotto portrayed the applied arts
> and industries in a series of such marvelous beauty and interest that ev-
> ery boy who passed the Shepherd's Tower longed to take his place in the
> industrial service of the citizens of Florence. We, on the contrary, have

succeeded in keeping our factories, so far as the workers in them are concerned, totally detached from that life which means culture and growth.

JANE ADDAMS, 1897: 108–109

Addams envisioned public schools as social centers that dealt with the larger issue of socializing work. She lobbied for curriculum to bridge the gap between traditional customs and youth's embrace of popular culture by valorizing craftsmanship, folk music and dance, and theater of the immigrant generation and developing historical perspective while at the same time learning science, hygiene, and household skills for urban living (Fones-Wolf, 1983: 43).

Work was at the center of the Labor Museum not as an antiquarian obsession with craft, as latter-day pro-labor New Dealers including Charlotte Carr[25] would contend, but as an approach to socialize and humanize industrial occupations. Addams had become aware of the realities of workers' families' lives just as Starr. Central to her concern was the woeful inadequacy of educational preparation for workers' children.[26] Workers' children rarely attended high schools and for students who had no intention of attending college, high schools offered little in the way of training for jobs anyway. At the same time, families encouraged their post-grammar school sons and daughters to find whatever work was available. To Addams the long-range outcomes of this custom were dire, consigning young people to lives of insecure employment, low wages, and the sort of hollowness of spirit that led to negative habits and even criminal activity as the culture of the streets provided gratification (Addams, 1972 [1909]: 107). She wrote:

As it is possible to establish a connection between the lack of public recreation and the

vicious excitements and trivial amusements which become their substitutes, so it may be illuminating to trace the connection between the monotony and dullness of factory work and its petty immoralities which are often the youth's protest against them.

ADDAMS, 1972 [1909]: 107

---

25   Charlotte E. Carr, headed Hull-House from 1937 to 1942, at the height of the settlement house's engagement with the New Deal Popular Front and Cultural Front movements. See Lunin Schultz's Chapter Six in this volume.

26   Addams was so concerned about the fate of young girls, fourteen years and older, that in 1912 the Hull-House Trade School for Girls was opened and used the area of the industrial shops and other classrooms. Dressmaking was featured and girls were placed in dressmaking shops after completing a summer course. By 1915 a new department, The Hull-House Design Shop, prepared girls to work in children's clothes shops.

And the remedy, which the Labor Museum was created to provide, was to equip the apprentice with "the informing mind":

> [A] certain trade school for girls, in New York, which is preparing young girls of fourteen for the sewing trade, already so overcrowded and subdivided that there remains very little education for the worker, is conquering this difficult industrial situation by equipping each apprentice with 'the informing mind.' *If a child goes into a sewing factory with a knowledge of the work she is doing in relation to the finished product; if she is informed concerning the material she is manipulating and the processes to which it is subjected; if she understands the design she is elaborating in its historic relation to art and decoration, her daily life is lifted from drudgery to one of self-conscious activity, and her pleasure and intelligence is registered in her product.*
>
> ADDAMS, 1972 [1909]: 119–120; emphasis added

Classes and apprenticeship training became important pieces of the programs offered at Hull-House, part of a complicated equation that balanced demonstrations by immigrants "performed" to develop intergenerational understanding and respect of old world customs with the new vocational knowledge that aided first and second-generation daughters and sons to enter the American economic system. Addams's views of vocational guidance and industrial curriculum differed from both the plans put forward by business interests and those developed by organized labor precisely in this idea of connecting current skill learning with the history and art of craft.

Marion Foster Washburne, a writer knowledgeable about current reform ideas in education, visited the Labor Museum in 1904, and came away impressed. She was attentive to the kinds of students in the industrial shop classes, some who were "saved from clerkships, according to their instructor." These classes were "a small attempt to stem the current... [trend toward] work of the middlemen, and away from the industries and constructive hand-work. Numbers of the pupils are errand-boys, office-boys, and delivery-boys, who are earning a precarious living and learning very little which can permanently benefit them. They come here Saturday evenings and work; they learn to design a little; they gain some idea of a genuine beauty not based upon display; and they acquire a respect for good workmanship and good workmen" (Washburne, 1904: 571).

This effort to develop a kind of apprenticeship system in the industrial shops which would combine skills and understanding of tools and materials, with an historical context for the industry and for the development of the labor movement, was being done, seemingly, outside of the trades unions. But Washburne reported that, after taking classes, one office-boy had given up his job and "became apprenticed to a skilled metal worker, and is now in a fair way to master a paying and progressive trade." Washburne outlined that the students in the industrial classes sold the product of their labor, which were on exhibition in cases. "A small percentage of the selling price is returned to the [Hull] House, although it is not as yet nearly enough to pay for the cost of the material and the use of the machinery" (Washburne, 1904: 571).

Addams incorporated the immigrant women and men who regularly "performed" their artistry and crafts in the Labor Museum, in the education of young boys and girls. This was an innovation pedagogically. The elders took on young men and women as "apprentices." The products of the work were made available for sale, with the same split between the House and the artisan. There are no statistics to measure how much any artisan "earned" or how many students transitioned into a permanent industrial job. The dissemination of the craftsman ideal to the youth of the neighborhood was much more important to Addams than running industrial shops that saw a profit or adapting youth to fit the specific employment needs of industry. Washburne detected the anti-commericalism of the Labor Museum explaining that "[t]he sale of the work is encouraged more to hold the interest of the boys and to stimulate them to better craftsmanship than for any other reason" (571).

The Labor Museum and Industrial Shops were inaugurated by Addams at the peak of the arts and crafts movement in Chicago and at a time when "exhibition" to educate the public on industrial conditions, model housing, and municipal planning was a key strategy of reformers and practitioners of the new fields of sanitation, urban planning, and public health. It was also a period in which middle-class native-born Americans were not convinced that the "New Immigrants" were assimilable. The charts that demonstrated the continuity and similarity of craft in the history of industry also depicted universality among the different ethnic groups whose techniques were both culturally specific and part of the universal story. There was a positive response from middle-class visitors, a key piece in Addams's agenda. Addams expanded programs, added classes, and collected more artifacts and encouraged the collaboration of all the other departments of the settlement house in this pursuit of an educational medium that would successfully connect immigrants and their children in a positive way to the long history of industrialism, and as well, connect Americans with their new neighbors.

In the Labor Museum we see the pattern of cultural pedagogy applied to craft and industry where it first had been implemented in theatrical and musical performances by Edith de Nancrede and Eleanor Smith. The use of literature, music, and art of mostly European and Christian sources to historicize work, with contributions from Nancrede, Smith, Benedict, and Starr, is emblematic of the shared cultural values imbedded in their pedagogy. The variations of subject or medium should not confuse us from seeing how each department separately and all departments collaboratively sought ways to democratize culture by fostering access and opportunity of poor and working-class immigrants and their children to the high culture that was increasingly the province of a propertied elite and their progeny. Eleanor Smith spoke directly to these issues when she advocated for high quality instruction in music programs in all public schools. Just as Ellen Starr could not imagine the production of art occurring in an unjust and inhumane society, Eleanor Smith questioned whether the United States could be a successful nation if its social fabric did not contain systems in place to foster musicianship. Writing in 1914, one year before the anniversary publication of *Hull House Songs*, and at a time of impending world war, she thought it "doubtful whether the simplicity and ideality of the good musician was ever more needed in the world than they are today" (1914: 1017). It was not only a matter of "paltry ideals [being] a cord for the strangling of genius" but fear that the loss of art, music, and drama signaled the death of the basic ethical and moral values that underpinned society and were the necessary soil for democracy to grow and flourish. Without such values that were expressed they believed best in the Western canon which was so firmly associated with Christian religious traditions, the women of Hull-House foresaw a dismal future. The crisis of industrial society was seen in economic and social terms, but the connection between art and labor, articulated by Ellen Starr, was a major factor in the political activism of the Hull-House progressive reformers. Without equity and justice in labor there would be no art.

CHAPTER 6

Democratizing Culture and Mediating Class: The Arts at Hull-House, 1889–1945

Rima Lunin Schultz

1   Introduction

The exploration of cultural programs at Hull-House from the heady days of the arts and crafts movement and other social reform initiatives to bring art to the people during the Progressive Era, to the settlement's engagement with New Deal Cultural Front "people's art" offers a broad, panoramic picture of the usages of culture in American politics for more than fifty years. Historians admit Jane Addams's goal of stimulating her immigrant and working-class neighbors to engage in projects of self-governance was incompletely realized. Her efforts to provide entertainment, and artistic expression through the cultural programs offered at the settlement house could count scores of individual success stories but was the settlement movement a force in shaping the people's culture along directions envisioned by Addams, Eleanor Smith, and other cultural workers? The answer is complicated. Democratizing forces that enabled working people greater access to cultural education were unleashed. Working people and immigrants shared more in common with privileged white Americans than the latter thought, and Addams was keen on making that point to those who doubted the value of immigrants' contributions to the United States or believed that art and music education was an unnecessary extravagance for workers' children. At the same time the reformers, who were deeply disturbed by the class conflict erupting in strikes and violence in American cities, adopted a pedagogy informed both by hegemonic Western Christian cultural values and imbued with a belief in the necessity of mediating class conflicts and curbing new forms of popular expression—movies, jazz, blues—that they perceived as immoral and dangerous. In the process the racism of Western hegemonic culture shaped outcomes by privileging white middle-class domesticity, and capitalist values. Did such cultural programs contribute to the weakness of workers' solidarity and political self-awareness? Did such experiments with the arts, music, and drama breed individualism rather than the cooperative social identity Addams had hoped for? Were the cultural programs encouraging models of "whiteness" thus mediating incipient workers' unity and power economically and politically? The fostering of division along race and ethnic lines that deepened over the decades erupted in urban crises during the 1930s New Deal and the post-World War II white flight from American cities. Even before Jane Addams's death May 21, 1935, Hull-House embraced Popular Front-New Deal politics, but it was in the experimentation with new forms of cultural production that we can see initiatives on issues of class, race, and ethnicity that sought to truly inaugurate a people's culture from the bottom up to replace the top-down efforts of progressive reformers. This chapter closes with an analysis of the post-Jane Addams years that compares cultural production in both political moments. Addams's concern for civic righteousness and her calls for a popular culture with merit and significance to engage the people and develop a social politics for the democracy prefigures the innovations of Cultural Front theater during the New Deal in the 1930s and the differences in Hull-House cultural pedagogy before and after Jane Addams's death provide a critical context to appreciate the innovative qualities and to assess the limitations.

Jane Addams conceived of the arts and cultural events at the settlement house as opportunities for the integration of working people into the social life of the community and into the process of active democratic participation and self-governance. She predicted cosmopolitanism and cooperation when working people shared music, art, and theater. Offering the settlement house as a neutral space for her multitude of nationalities of neighbors, Addams encouraged discussion and education on local issues that she assumed had universal relevance and would forge cooperative approaches to remedy obvious urban ills that plagued the neighborhood. Her problems, however, were many. Since opening the doors of Hull-House in 1889, Addams had found it difficult to reach working people and engage them as political actors on their own behalf. The campaigns to unseat the iconic corrupt politician Alderman Johnny Powers led by Hull-House residents and civic reformers ended in defeat (Davis, 1960, 247–265; Platt, 2000: 194–222). Yet Addams, undaunted ultimately, re-thought her approach and believed that her immigrant neighbors could still assume leading roles, but largely *first* through drama and the arts, by acting in Greek and Shakespeare plays, by listening to what today would be termed "high-brow" music, or by enjoying classical sculpture and paintings in the context of cross-class experiences. We know from Addams's writings and the testimony of sculptor Lorado Taft that affluent Chicagoans sat with working-class immigrants from the neighborhood to view immigrant Greeks perform ancient drama (Taft, 1900: n.p.). Seemingly all classes understood and enjoyed the performance. But for Addams the significance of the production extended far beyond the stage at Hull-House. Addams came to regard the production of a Greek play with immigrant actors as documentation for her advocacy of liberal immigration policy. It was used in her defense of immigrants' cultural contributions. In her view, the play redefined the social role of Greeks with their Italian neighbors and, as well, with the middle-class Americans whose perceptions of immigrants had been altered. Addams believed that Greeks in the Hull-House neighborhood thus were affirmed in the eyes of their neighbors, their own countrymen, and Americans from outside the local environs. At the same time, all participants—actors and audience—were then better able to evolve a social self equipped to participate in the life of the democracy (Addams, 1910: 388–389).

This approach, the introduction of a form of social engineering in the mixing of groups and classes of people, and in the pedagogical strategies of encouraging participation and performance of working class and immigrant neighbors made life at Hull-House different from the atmosphere and cultural exchanges found in the neighborhood saloons, dance halls and vaudeville. It was also different from the *segregated* religious street festes, church or synagogue services, or the communal activities attended *only* by workers in their labor union halls or individual ethnic groups in their fraternal halls. This quality of social integration is apparent in the words, music, and performances of the *Hull-House Songs* by Eleanor Smith that can be distinguished from the labor anthems, folk ballads, or picket-line songs ordinarily associated with American and European working-class and protest culture. Their form is more accurately associated with late-Victorian era respectable bourgeois culture, but their words convey the pathos and plight of workers and demand equal rights, social justice, and humanitarianism. When the National Consumers' League, whose white middle-class and wealthy women members major goal was to buy only products made by union shops and boycott products from sweat shops, invited the Hull-House music school students to perform the "Sweat Shop" song, they found it "stirring and powerful in its moral appeal, as well as interpretative of an experience of the youth of the race" (qtd. in Flood and Bray, 1903: 60). The highbrow European flavor of the songs made sense in the context of the League and other women's organizations of the late nineteenth and early twentieth centuries and, as well, among the immigrants and their children. Lawrence Levine's portrayal of popular culture in the nineteenth century as consisting of elements—symphonies, operas, the plays of Shakespeare—that would by the turn of the twentieth century be considered "highbrow" and generally outside the provenance of commercial and popular culture (Levine, 1988) helps make sense of the naturalness of the *Hull House Songs*. Re-thinking ideas about the introduction of hierarchical categories of culture, the highbrow cultural format of the *Hull-House Songs,* which might sound surprising to twenty-first century ears, would have been familiar to the middle and upper-middle class audiences of clubwomen *and* the working people of Chicago of whom many were immigrants who loved concerts and operas and who had enjoyed the plays of Shakespeare, even adaptations in the language of their homelands. The songs were written at a time when European influences in Chicago, a city of immigrants, were strong. They were also written in this period of cultural transition that Levine considers. Addams's and Smith's pedagogical decisions were made in the context of the emergence of hierarchical categories of culture. The experiences and challenges of life in an immigrant and working-class neighborhood placed the production of culture at Hull-House in the middle of the controversies and anxieties about the commercialization and popularization of culture. These were not minor concerns. Continuing to believe in the salutary and moral results when the *best* art and music was made available to the masses as well as the privileged few, and increasingly anxious about the influence and competitive advantage of movies, cheap amusements, and dance halls, the music, drama, and art pedagogy at Hull-House sought formats that embraced the classical Western tradition—highbrow—but incorporated the narrativity of the neighborhood. This meant translating the factory experiences, the hopes and dreams of children who labored into the classical forms that bespoke of musical literacy and cultural continuities.

Jane Addams's introductory note to the *Hull House Songs* provided some additional explanation:

> We believe that all of the songs in the collection fulfill the highest mission in music, first in giving expression to the type of emotional experience which quickly tends to get beyond words, and second in affording an escape from the unnecessary disorder of actual life into the wider region of the spirit which, under the laws of a great art may be filled with an austere beauty and peace
>
> ADDAMS, "Foreword," 1915: 2

Addams imagined that the young performers were transported from the world of tenement sweatshops to another zone through their musical artistry. At the same time the "Sweat Shop" song, appropriately fashioned in a cultural idiom understood by its middle-class and immigrant audiences, shed light on the horrors of child labor, but did not leave the audiences depressed. On the contrary, the beauty of the songs offered a positive affirmation of the basic goodness and decency of workers and fueled altruistic emotions in the direction of social reform. As Addams put it, it was "perhaps all the more imperative that *socialized emotions should... find musical expression,* if the manifold [reform] movements of our contemporaries are to have the inspiration and solace they so obviously need" ("Songs for the Hull-House Quarter Century," *The Survey*, March 6, 1915: 1, emphasis added).

Twenty-five years into her residency at the Hull-House settlement, which she had co-founded with her college friend Ellen Gates Starr in 1889, Addams delivered a message to Americans to look beyond the immediate chaos and conflict, and the rabble in large industrial districts that were so unfamiliar and difficult to comprehend and see the coming new order. She had written, "We are often told that men under this pressure of life become calloused and cynical, whereas anyone who lives with them knows that they are sentimental and compassionate." She cautioned, "one dares not grow too certain as to the wells of moral healing which is under the surface of the sullen work-driven life which the industrial quarters of the modern city present. They fascinate us by their mere size and diversity, as does the city itself; but certain it is, that these quarters continually confound us by their manifestations of altruism" ("Intro-duction," *Newer Ideals of Peace*, 2003 [1907]: 13). She pointed out the paradox that it is possible "we shall be saved from warfare by the 'fighting rabble' itself, by the 'quarrelsome mob' turned into kindly citizens of the world through the pressure of a cosmopolitan neighborhood" (13). The songs afforded "an escape from the unnecessary disorder of actual life into the wider region of the spirit" providing solace for the workers, and an opportunity for the upper classes to recognize the humanity and goodness of the working people (Addams, "Fore-word," *Hull House Songs*, 1915: 2).

Addams was one of the major intellects influencing the way her generation of middle class reformers, especially organized clubwomen, responded to the important questions of the day. Her writings had a wide readership and her reach through relationships to the networks of progressive reformers was vast. Often Addams used examples from the art work and cultural productions at Hull-House to make important points about social policy, support of working people, and interpretation of immigrants' contribution to the United States. The Hull-House settlement became a salon where cultural activities taught the theory and practice of social democracy far beyond the boundaries of the Near West Side neighborhood. Immigrants had starring roles and were portrayed heroically and sympathetically. In performances of Eleanor Smith's songs, public opinion was marshalled in support of women's, children's, and workers' rights. These were not the labor songs from the Wobblies' *Little Red Song-Book*, that pitted the working class against the capitalist class with their clarion call of "which side are you on?" Far from it. The *Hull House Songs* composed by Eleanor Smith reflected hers and Addams's use of music that had the capacity to socialize emotion and thereby bring about social adjustment between the bourgeoisie and the laboring classes.

This volume of essays approaches the *Hull House Songs* from sociological, musicological, and performance frameworks. As a social historian and biographer, my approach places these songs in Progressive Era reform culture (Filene, 1970: 20–34; Rodgers, 1982: 113–132; Diner, 1998; McGerr, 2003; Flanagan, 2007) examining the reform culture that produced the songs; and about the community of workers, neighbors, and reformers whose relationships to one another were constructed in part through the cultural work of the settlement house. When I listen to the songs I am reminded that the past is, indeed, another country, and while there are continuities with the present, to understand how we have arrived at this moment in American history, it has become more important than ever to appreciate what Addams and her colleagues meant when they talked about "democracy," "working people," and "progress." This exploration, while it focuses on the moral aesthetics of music and art, the interior space, and the performances of art and craft, and drama, seeks to understand and interrogate the political underpinnings of this cultural work. In the case of the arts at Hull-House, there is no hint of disguise: art is used for political reasons.[1]

There is no question that Addams and Smith and their colleagues believed the arts would create spiritual and social unity in a society that was torn by industrial strife. Ideally it would be of enormous historical value to know if the neighbors liked the songs, if they "caught on" and became part of the neighborhood culture, and, perhaps more to the point, whether or not any of the labor unions who had met from time to time at Hull-House adopted some of the songs or somehow made them their own. Writing history from the "bottom up,"[2] the great innovation of the nineteen sixties, is a challenge. No records of any neighborhood reviews of the *Hull House Songs* have surfaced, but there are other sources to search for answers as well as Jane Addams's reflections on

---

1 Here I have been influenced by historian Edward P. Thompson who came to conceive of class as a matter of cultural identity rather than mere economic position, and that this was true for the working class and the middle class as well (Thompson, 1966).

2 Again, I go back to E.P. Thompson. He saw class not as an abstraction, but as a historical process which had in it the tensions of determinism and agency. He looked at all aspects of life in studying working class culture on its own terms. His narrative of the English working class opened up to historians the importance and reality of research that interrogated new sources, statistical, cultural, religious, the oral as well as written, and demanded that historians do history from the nonofficial, non-institutional, i.e., as the English historians termed it, "history from below." Now, Thompson does not use the phrase history from the "bottom up" in his influential *The Making of the English Working Class;* his phrase was history "from below," but American historians, influenced by Thompson, about the same time, began to use the phrase history "from the bottom up" (Heathorn, 1998: 212). See also Sewell's "How Classes are Made" (in Kaye and McCelland, 1990: 50–77).

whether her settlement work had come near to achieving her broader goals of supporting the growth of a viable, vital labor movement and, at the same time, defusing class warfare through cultural understanding.

The publication of *Hull House Songs* in 1915, to commemorate the 25th Anniversary of the Hull-House Settlement came at the cultural and political moment in Hull-House's history when the progressive spirit—the Progressive Era—in the United States was still infused in the discourse of political reform[3] and the connection with a socially engaged cultural agenda was still relevant. Hull-House had been on the cutting edge of social reform movements from the 1890s. The philosopher and educator John Dewey identified Hull-House as a source of personal inspiration and experiential learning critical for his theoretical and practical development as a proponent of educational reform. The settlement's cultural work in bringing art to the people and creating art with social value did not occur in isolation. It was part of larger conversation about the role of education in a democratic society. The role of music, art, theater, and physical culture was hotly debated among school professionals, boards of education, and social activists whose theories of democracy contained the promise of a liberal education as a key for progress in society. Addams never taught school, but she had become one of the authorities who interpreted the immigrant child to the professional educators (Addams, 1897: 104–112; 1912c: 26–30).

Historian Allen F. Davis defined settlement houses—Hull-House being one of the most prominent worldwide—as "spearheads for reform" in the Progressive Era (1967). Men and women participated in settlement houses but in the United States women dominated and established significant innovative roles for themselves. They accomplished this in large part because of the women's political culture that had developed through the struggle for women's rights. Hull-House's cultural work in theory and practice was widely disseminated and became imbedded in the women's political culture of the era and, beyond this, the nation-building project of progressivism which included maternalists, social feminists, socialists and trades unionists (Sklar, 1995; Flanagan, 2002). No aspect of modern industrial life in the United States was untouched by the core ideas held by social reformers like Jane Addams.

---

3 Periodization of the Progressive Movement just as any characterization of it eludes consensus among historians. I am using the dates 1890–1930, but these can be extended in both directions or shortened. There is a vast literature (Filene, 1970). Historians of women's political activism see continuities between the Progressive Era and the New Deal (Ware, 1981). Edith Abbott and the few remaining Hull-House Progressive Era residents saved the federal Children's Bureau in 1946; beyond the New Deal the women in this coalition had lobbied to save the hard-won victories of the maternalist state (June 13, 1946, *The New York Times*: 30).

2   The Progressive Movement (1880–1920) and Jane Addams

Between 1880 and 1920 twenty-three million Europeans came to the United
States (Daniels, 1990). In Chicago, the fastest growing industrial city in the
United States at the turn of the century, more than three quarters of the population were immigrants and their children (Platt, 2005; Holli & Jones, 1995
[1977]; Pacyga. 2009). Catholics made up a large part of the population. Labeled the "New Immigration," their origins in Southern and Eastern Europe,
they were portrayed as racially inferior to the "Old Immigration" from the Anglo-Saxon countries of the North Atlantic (Higham, 2011 [1955]; Cassano, 2015:
96–102; Barrett & Roediger, 1997: 3–44). This racialized discourse on immigration intersected with anxieties about industrial conflicts and class warfare,
and the shock of discovering that American cities had "slums." The "new immigrant" was "the Other"—accused of undermining American workers, targeted
as uncouth and slovenly, and criticized for peasant ways and inferior customs
that could be seen in the way these newcomers crowded in tenements, living
with kin and countrymen, befouling parts of American cities (Zeidel, 2004).
Considered "unchurched" because they did not join Protestant congregations,
and dangerous because foreign neighborhoods were thought to be "infested"
with socialists and anarchists whose international connections to radicals and
revolutionaries jeopardized the safety and stability of the United States, anti-
immigration was fueled by anti-Catholicism and anti-Semitism (Higham, 2011
[1955]).
   The masses had been criminalized for their poverty by politicians, anti-labor
business leaders, laissez-faire economic theorists, and nativist ideologues who
feared the end of the American republic and Anglo-Saxon leadership. In opposition to the credo inscribed on the Statue of Liberty, the country dealt with
poverty with a county poor house system; laws privileged corporations and
prohibited workers' attempts to associate and act collectively as in unions,
boycotts, strikes; critics of unrestricted immigration characterized newcomers as dull witted at the same time that the working classes were demonized
as disciples of radical political theories and efforts were made to shut down
"subversive" newspapers popular in immigrant and workers' neighborhoods.
There was an ambivalence about educating workers and immigrants' children;
an anxiety about extending cultural privileges to the untutored without proper
guidance and interpretation. The background for this ambivalence was the industrial unrest and violence that had become a factor in American life: the
Haymarket police riot (1886), the violent strike at Homestead, Pennsylvania
(1892), and, following George Pullman's wage cuts during the national economic depression, the Pullman Strike (1894) (Smith, 1995). From 1877, the year that

Addams entered Rockford Female Seminary, urban social disorder from conflicts between capital and labor characterized industrial conditions. Dubbed the "Year of Violence," events in 1877 had shocked the industrial and business classes nationwide. The boycott by labor of the railroads across cities in the eastern United States had touched Chicago as well. Only a few blocks from the South Halsted Street site of the future Hull-House settlement, a pitched battle had ensued between workers and the police and memories of this unrest were reignited during the Haymarket police riot (Bruce, 1959).

If you are hearing in this echoes of twenty-first century political rhetoric, you are not mistaken. The political hysteria today harkens back to the turn-of-the-century United States: anxiety-ridden, xenophobic, imperialistic, and aggressively evangelistic in its Protestant crusading mood of nation-building on foreign soil. This was the world in which Jane Addams (1860–1935) and her generation came of age. Hysteria about American Catholic's obedience to papal authority and subservience to authoritarian priests can be compared to anxieties twenty-first century Americans harbor about the Muslim religion and fear of what transpires in mosques.

Among the educated in the late nineteenth-century, there was, as well, doubt caused by the new science of Charles Darwin and the related fields of geology and archeology, combined with discoveries from comparative religious studies and the higher biblical criticism (Carter, 1971). Much has been written about this age of uncertainty; it was also dubbed as an "Age of Progress" and historians have called it "The Age of Empire" because of the advances in science and technology and the expansion of capitalism globally by Western nations (Hobsbawm, 1989). Consider the personality and actions of Theodore Roosevelt, candidate for president of the United States and the standard bearer of the Progressive Party banner, whose nomination for the presidency in 1912 was seconded by Jane Addams (Davis, 1967). Bellicose, imperialist, racist, militarist, Roosevelt also signed on to a political platform written by Addams and the vanguard of social justice reformers and settlement house pioneers. In seconding his nomination, Addams was a woman of the Age of Empire as much as she was one of the founders of the social and cultural movement aimed to tame capitalism and class warfare without guns and class warfare and to spread a new kind of democratic cosmopolitanism that redefined patriotism and nationalism (Addams, 1907, 1912b: 615–619). It would be a *cultural crusade*. It would transform hearts and minds, uplift all social classes, and chart a new ethical path for democracy. The convention that nominated "T.R." exuberantly sang "Onward Christian Soldiers" as the delegates marched. (Davis, 1967: 197).

Addams worked in an imperfect political system to advance goals of social democracy. In backing Roosevelt, she had made compromises in hopes

ILLUSTRATION 6.1   Jane Addams, age fifty-two, 1912
SOURCE: JANE ADDAMS MEMORIAL COLLECTION (JAMC),
SPECIAL COLLECTIONS, DALEY LIBRARY, UNIVERSITY OF
ILLINOIS AT CHICAGO.

of achieving progress along social lines including votes for women and
the prohibition of child labor—two achievements that in 1912 still eluded
movement activists. A lifelong Republican, who supported Progressive Party
candidates including Wisconsin populist Robert La Follette, she supported
Herbert Hoover and was a reluctant convert to Franklin Delano Roosevelt until
she realized the New Deal was putting in place a Progressive agenda (Addams,
1930: 10–48).

Addams had her hand in the major reform causes of the times. She can be defined as a modernist unafraid of machines but dedicated to finding a way to end the dehumanizing effects of industrialism; and an internationalist who was a pacifist during World War I but who had been an ardent supporter (in retrospect) of liberal nationalists like Mazzini and Garibaldi (Addams, 1930: 408–409). Her interest in public health, promotion of Western ideas about women's rights, and her faith in science and technology made her appreciate modernization projects in Egypt carried out by the British imperialist government and, as well, the nation-building work her colleague Julia C. Lathrop contributed in modernizing the schools in U.S.-occupied Philippines (Addams, 2004 [1935]). Having long advocated the expansion of the role of the State, Addams looked forward to global social justice initiatives of international agencies representing national governments willing to cooperate with one another for planetary progress (Addams, 1930: 7–9). She was a social evolutionist who, in a Jim Crow world embraced the anthropologist Franz Boas's universal race theory and was a founding member of the NAACP (Davis, 2000 [1973]: 129). Addams supported liberal immigration policies and advocated extending civil rights and protections to citizens and non-citizens alike (Addams, 1930: 263–303). She realized her generation had not done enough to make certain that the gains of the Civil War, obtained at such a terrible cost, were not only protected but expanded, and Hull-House settlement failed to become an integrated association during her lifetime. Indifference to racism was the "gravest situation in American life," she wrote in 1930 (400–401). She was deeply disturbed by the maldistribution of the fruits of progress, domestically and globally, and horrified by the deplorable social conditions in the industrial districts of cities, and later in her travels, with the conditions she witnessed in non-Western societies. She rejected what she considered were the antiquated eighteenth-century forms of U.S. government, the "poor house" type charity that helped the "worthy" and punished the "unworthy" poor; and she opposed *laissez-faire* economics (Addams, 1964 [1902]: 13–70, 137–177).

Addams also began her young adulthood in the shadow of the Civil War, in the Gilded Age, and at a moment in history when it was possible to be a feminist with Victorian sensibilities—to participate in the moral crusades of the temperance and anti-prostitution movements, to inaugurate movie censorship in Chicago, and to view jazz and the dance crazes of the Roaring Twenties as threats to civilization, *and* to campaign for women's rights and the vote (Addams, 1910: 30; Kenney, 1993; Brown, 2010: 125–158). At the same time her writings and political activities place her in the liberal, pro-labor wing of the Progressive movement in the United States. She wanted the social settlement to be a significant factor in the labor movement as the proponent of the *public interest* in labor relations which was different from the interests of either capital or labor. And as an important corollary, that the settlement house in its promotion and even sponsorship of the movement of workers' associations, had a moral role to cultivate ethical values among workers in opposition to class warfare (Addams, 2007 [1895]: 183–204).

There was a need for a new social ethic to be applied to the labor question. Just as the evolution of the economy from private ownership and craft to corporate ownership and machine labor had changed conditions dramatically, industrial relations needed adjustment. Workers' and employers' interests had to reach beyond the immediate dispute over wages and hours. Addams argued that the labor relationship was an aspect of the economic unity of the whole society. The interests of labor and capital were the concerns of the *whole* community, not just the worker or his family, or the owner and his economic class. When the question was raised, "how do we define the moral man?" Addams had a new answer: "to attain individual morality in an age demanding social morality, to pride one's self on the results of personal effort when the time demands social adjustment is utterly to fail to apprehend the situation" (Addams, 1964 [1902]: 2–3). She reasoned that the settlement could bring "a larger and steadier view" to labor disputes than either the workingman or the capitalist and could keep "the [labor] movement from becoming in any sense a class warfare" while it encouraged the organization of working people (2007 [1895]: 148).

3   Theories of Art, Labor, and Culture and the Butler Art Gallery
       Experiment on Halsted Street (1891–95)

Addams's theories about art and culture were eclectic and drew from the romantic and idealistic novels and essays of the mid-to late-nineteenth century— Carlyle, Emerson, Matthew Arnold, George Eliot, George Sand, William Dean Howells, Walter Besant—and the writings of John Ruskin and William Morris (Joslin, 2004: 38). These ideas, loosely defined as moral aestheticism, "that the *social* ills of poverty could be counteracted not through material charity, but through *one-to-one friendships between the rich and poor, and the dissemination of a bourgeois culture* that the poor had been denied," (Maltz, 2006: 67, emphasis added) were made concrete for Addams in the work of The Rev. Samuel A. Barnett and his wife Henrietta. The Barnetts were leading figures in the British reform movement that pioneered bringing art to the urban working class. They had opened Toynbee Hall in 1884, considered the first social settlement in London. In a lovely, aesthetically appropriate domestic setting amidst the tenements of the working poor of East London, Oxford University students and graduates joined the Barnetts in living among the poor.

Addams was bowled over by what the Barnetts were doing. She wrote her sister, "The most interesting thing that I have done in London was a visit to the Toynbee Hall in the East End. It is a community of University men who live there [and] have their recreating clubs & society all among the poor people yet in the same style they would live in their own circle. It is so free from "professional doing good" so matter of factly sincere and so productive of good results in its classes and libraries that it seems perfectly ideal... I don't know but that the East Side of London is the most interesting side it has" (Addams to Haldeman, June 14, 1888).

Romantic and reformist ideas about music and art were current among a transnational circle of upper-class Americans, British, and Europeans who were eager to find solutions to the problems of slums and poverty (Rodgers, 1998: 64–65). Newspapers and magazines in the United States carried articles about the latest innovations in bringing cultural life to the slums. This idea that music and art had social functions palliative against social disorder and the "maladaptations" in industrial society is at the core of the early cultural production at Hull-House. Addams was not alone in embracing this theory. On April 28, 1889, four months prior to the opening of Hull-House, the Chicago *Inter-Ocean* featured a story about "Music for London's Poor" quoting royalty in their approval of the kinds of theories choral leaders such as choral director and music pedagogue William Tomlins soon would be implementing at Hull-House.[4] Good music was "good" for social order. Reports from London confirmed that classes in choral music were an antidote to the music halls.

The well-known social reformer Lady Campbell, in speaking in favor of music education for the masses in London, quoted Martin Luther: "Music is the fairest and most glorious gift of God. It is a discipline, it is an instructress, it makes people milder and gentler, more moral and more reasonable." Lady Campbell explained: "These words might have been taken as the key-note of the work done by the various societies who set themselves the task of bringing this 'fairest and most glorious gift of God' to the masses of toilers and workers who throng our great city, and to whom the grimy, colorless side of life is so terribly real. And that they have succeeded in carrying out Luther's words *in making the people more moral and more reasonable by the aid of music is proved*

---

4 In a newspaper article about Hull-House comments were made about the morally uplifting qualities of music: "Hull-House is in a ward in which there are 270 saloons and but six churches. a wonderful and interesting feature of Hull-House is the singing of the children under the direction of Professor William L. Tomlins. In 1894 Christine Nillson wrote: 'I recognized at once the careful training the children had gone through. You are now doing a good to the future generation that Chicago and the whole nation ought to be proud of. Mr. Tomlins is singing religion and light and bright thoughts into the lives of the boys and girls of Hull House" (1894, *Chicago Tribune*: 41).

beyond doubt and questions by the altered state of the New Cut and similar met-ropolitan thoroughfares" (Campbell, 1889: n.p.; Walford, 1878: 383–407). (Italics added.) These market districts had their counterparts in American cities.

William Tomlins was one of the first music educators involved with the Hull-House settlement.[5] In Chicago he became known as a great choral con-ductor, "a kind of musical missioner, preacher, prophet, evangelist—dealing with motive forces and inward impulses as awakened by music, and the ethic-psychologic message of art" ("Music as a New Force in Education," *School Music Monthly*, 1906: 34–35).

Teaching music, art, dance, and drama provided pathways for moral train-ing, the promotion of individual discipline, and the cultivation of habits and traits that could be identified with successful middle-class students. Tomlins, a teacher of voice, taught hundreds of children from the Hull-House neighbor-hood. Like so many of his contemporaries who found their way to settlements, he had theories concerning children's voices and he developed methods to teach singing. Tomlins' music loving English family had encouraged his musi-cal tastes. At the age of twenty-two he was one of the board of managers of the London Tonic-Sol-Fa College; at twenty-six he came to New York, and for five years served as organist in various churches. He traveled to Chicago and his ability as a conductor attracted the attention of the Apollo Club, and he was employed as the club's leader (Powell, 1896: 582).

Critical of music training for children as he found it, he discovered that "by breaking down the outer and grosser nature of the boy, that the inner might stand revealed. His first step was to appeal to the higher nature—to ask for 'politeness' in tones as well as manners" (Powell, 1896: 583). Journalist Mary Badollet Powell described how [Tomlins] "draws the children into the warmth of love, and teaches them that real beauty of music, which is love and helpful-ness toward our brothers. Mr. Tomlins claims that in all humanity, at the very heart and soul of the boy, are latent tendencies—for good and for evil—of which the boy himself is ignorant." According to Powell, "Tomlins, likened the boy to a series of circles. His actions were manifested at his circumference. Inside this outer circle is an inner circle which stands for his mentality: what he thinks, calculates, and perhaps, schemes. Inside this inner circle, at the very center, is the smallest circle: what he *is*; what he loves. For what one longs for, that he is already at heart. *'As a man thinketh in his heart, so he is.'* How to reach

---

5   It is worth noting that Tomlins was part of the liberal religious coalition that included Re-form Jews, liberal Protestants, Unitarians, and Ethical Culturists; Addams was a leader in this movement to find a universal religious humanism, and she, as well as Tomlins sought a path of approach through music (April 8, 1894. Liberal Religion Congress. *Chicago Tribune*: 28). See below for further discussion.

these inner tendencies, direct them outward, and harmonize them with his surroundings, is the object of all true education. That it can be helped by music Mr. Tomlins has demonstrated" (584).

Tomlins formed a class at Hull-House in November 1895. At first, he found that no more than ten children had the slightest knowledge of the music; that was remedied quickly, with Tomlin's assistant, Elizabeth Nash, instructing the class. "Only the best is good enough for Mr. Tomlins' classes," Powell claimed. "Handel, Bach, Beethoven, Mozart, Mendelssohn, and all the great composers... are familiar friends to these children. And new songs have been specially written for Mr. Tomlins by eminent poets and composers: of the former, Whittier, Holmes, Julia Ward Howe, Whitman, Gilder, Stedman, Richard H. Stoddard" (Powell, 1896: 588–589). The students did physical exercises to relax their muscles, vocal exercises, and they learned to read music (Ibid). Tomlins believed in "the universality of music and its uplifting, spiritual influences, that music was not only for the leisure class but for the weary, plodding laborer, to lift him from his depths of despondency, out of the commonplace into the rank of brotherhood" (590–591).

In the context of her work with Tomlins in developing music programs at Hull-House, Jane Addams articulated the most direct expression of what she had in mind in the use of music for the working classes. In a flyer announcing a competition for "good songs which shall express the newer sense of fellowship, and being convinced that the labor movement will not attain a full and peaceful development without an orderly and musical expression of its hopes," Addams and a committee consisting of Tomlins and H.N. Higinbotham "invite[d] manuscript copy of original songs in verse form (not to exceed four verses to a song)"(May 1895 newspaper clipping: Scrapbook 3, Hull House Collection). Higinbotham, one of the owners of the Marshall Field Company, was a cultural philanthropist who had been instrumental in securing Chicago as the site of the 1893 Columbian Exposition. There was to be a first prize of one hundred dollars. Jane Addams, Henry D. Lloyd,[6] poet John Vance Cheney and Midwestern writer Hamlin Garland were to make the awards (Ibid). The results of the contest? Addams wrote "The responses to the offer literally filled three large barrels and speaking at least for myself as one of the bewildered judges,

6 Henry Demarest Lloyd (1847–1903), progressive politician and pioneering muckraking journalist known for his exposes of the Standard Oil Company, supported the pro-labor, anti-sweatshop coalition which included Governor John Peter Altgeld, Florence Kelley, and Jane Addams. An early and vocal supporter of Hull-House, he joined Addams, Kelley and other Hull-House residents when they lobbied the State Legislature for factory inspection laws and the 8-hour day (Thomas, 1983).

we were more disheartened by their quality than even by their overwhelming bulk. Apparently the workers of America are not yet ready to sing.... It may be that this plaint explains the lack of labor songs in this period of industrial maladjustment when the worker is overmastered by his very tools" (Addams, 1910, 377). Addams's bourgeois critique of workers' or untrained people's cultural "contributions" and the role of specialists and high culture in the cultural production at Hull-House was expressed in the top-down cultural production at the settlement that characterized and dominated the Addams years. Free concerts were started in 1893. "The audiences were small and the proportion of curiosity-seekers rather large" (*Hull-House Bulletin*, 1896). An article in the *Hull-House Bulletin* (most likely written by Addams who tended to author most of the official publications of the settlement) recalled "It was at the time thought necessary to give very 'popular' music in order to hold the attention of the hearers, as a whole" (Ibid). By 1896, "progress" had been made and the *Bulletin* reported that "The programs have been selected with more and more severity, and the music during the last year has been almost entirely of a very high order. At the same time, the audience has increased in numbers to nearly four hundred and in respectful attention as well. Regular attendants, who come to gratify a love of music, are subjected much less often than formerly to annoyance from conversation" (Ibid).

An important corollary of this top-down approach was the theory that it was crucial to present only the best of paintings and sculpture to the working people, even if reproductions were used. "The first residents... held strongly to the belief that any compromise in the matter of excellence in art was a mistake. They hung their own walls only with such pictures they felt were helpful to the life of mind and soul. Very much of the influence of the House they believe to be due to the harmony and reasonableness of the message of its walls." Addams pointed out "One of the residents has been much interested in pictures in the public schools and hopes to have aroused sufficient interest in the subject to result in providing good sets of pictures for several schools in the poorest localities" (Addams, 1894: 101).

Addams was referring to Ellen Gates Starr, co-founder of Hull-House who initially took charge of the art programs and led in the campaign to distribute works of art throughout the city's schools and other public spaces. This initiative was in accord with the top progressive educators in Chicago at the time and Starr's organization had a list of educators and artists who endorsed the art selections suggested for the public schools. The advisors were John Dewey, professor at the University of Chicago, Col. Francis W. Parker, Principal of the Chicago Normal Training School (Teacher's College), W.M.R. French, Director of the Art Institute of Chicago, sculptor Lorado Taft, and Josephine C.

Locke, Superintendent of Drawing, Chicago Public Schools (Corcoran, 2005).[7] Among the suggestions for display were reproductions of the paintings and sculpture of Augustus St. Gaudens, Daniel C. French, John Singer Sargent, Sir Joshua Reynolds, G.F. Watts, Burne-Jones, J.F. Millet, Corot, Jules Breton, and Puvis De Chavanne. Photographs or engravings of the Acropolis, Parthenon, Temple of Theseus, Temple of Karnak, Pyramids, Temple of Vesta, Forum, Coliseum, Cathedrals of Amiens, Cologne, and Cantebury. Casts of Donatellos, Della Robbias, and photographs of Donatellos, Michaelangelo's head of David, Fra Angelico's Angels, Botticelli's Madonna of the Louvre, Raphael's Sistine Madonna, Madonna della Sedia, and Madonna Gran Duca. Scenes of interests (not from paintings) included the homes of Albrecht Durer, Ann Hathaway, Robert Burns, Sir Walter Scott, Edinburgh Castle, Longfellow, old Spanish missions in California, and Mount Vernon; also, Independence Hall, and photographs from nature including Great Falls of the Yosemite, Grand Canyon, Niagara Falls, Delaware Water Gap. The Society recommended including illustrations of street views and other scenes in beautiful cities "showing that cities have not always been ugly and need not be so" (Chicago Public School Art Society, September 1897. *A List of Pictures and Casts for Use in Schools*: n.p.). The list was an "inventory" of many of the reproductions that had been displayed at Hull-House from the settlement's earliest days.

In her paper, "Art and Labor," Starr pointedly talked about the prospects of an "art of the people" in "our great cities" thus indicating that hers was not a movement of bringing art to the people, it was to engage in actions that would foster an *art of the people* (Starr, 1895a: 165). This goal was greater than the immediate cultural events and classes in art and music that Hull-House would offer. "If we look to any great national art, that of Athens or of Venice or of Florence, we see that it has not been produced by a few, living apart, fed upon conditions different from the common life; but that it has been, in great part, the expression of that common life," Starr argued. "If we are to have a national art at all, it must be art of the people; and art can only come to a free people." She had absorbed these ideas from John Ruskin, who she considered "the great prophet of art in our day" and from his disciple, William Morris. What she saw around her in the industrial district, resulting from "the iron law of wages" producing "squalor, deformity, and irrecoverable loss of health... and Child-labor"

---

7   Deborah A. Corcoran (2005) presents a narrative from the late 1880s to 1910 in Chicago indicating the experimental nature of art education for elementary school children in the Chicago Public Schools and the School of the Art Institute of Chicago. Locke was born in Ireland in 1851, of Irish, Scotch and English parentage. She died in 1919. Locke headed the art department for the elementary schools in the Chicago system from 1890 to 1900.

made art impossible for the workers but, she contended, ultimately impossible for the rich, and for the nation as a whole (Starr, 1895a: 171–172).

Starr was expressing the conviction that society's progress had to be judged on its cultural and artistic productions, which could only come from the just conditions of labor, not on its technology and its production of machine-made goods, which were the products of workers who were slaves to machines. She had asked whether or not it was worthwhile or reasonable—in the recognition of the present dire social and economic conditions of the workers—to have art exhibits and concerts, and to teach children drama, dance, singing. Shouldn't the aim of the settlement house be the amelioration of the workers' conditions and the replacement of the industrial system with one that was just? "A settlement, if it is true to its ideal, must stand equally for both aims" she contended (Starr, 1895a: 178–179).

4   The Short Career of the Butler Art Gallery (1891–1896)

With great fanfare the Butler building, designed by the firm of Irving and Allen Pond, (Pond & Pond), among the group of progressive Chicago architects being influenced by the English Arts & Crafts movement, opened its doors June 20, 1891. The Chicago press anticipated this event the year before. "Art for the Masses" was popular among civic-minded Chicagoans and this attempt to bring fine art to an industrial district a lá the examples of Toynbee Hall and the People's Palace in London's East End slum, was happening as the cultural elite of the city were preparing for the Columbian Exposition and the development of an art institute. In fact, two of the cultural philanthropists who would become prominent trustees of the Art Institute of Chicago were intimately involved with Addams's and Starr's plans for art exhibitions at the settlement house. Charles L. Hutchinson, banker and commodities trader, was also a committed Universalist, a liberal Protestant denomination eventually to merge with the Unitarian movement. The scion of one of the most reckless speculators on the Chicago Board of Trade, Benjamin "The Scalper" Hutchinson, perhaps Charles was pursuing a kind of liberal progressive reformism and cultural philanthropy to redeem himself from his father's sins (Schultz, 1985: 369–371). Charles Hutchinson was a major force in the creation of the Art Institute and he was also a Hull-House trustee. He was willing to loan his paintings to the little gallery on Halsted Street. Edward B. Butler, who contributed the five thousand dollars for the construction of the Butler building, (about $133, 000 in today's value) had settled in Chicago after creating a great retail business in Boston and New York. He was an amateur artist who later settled in California and became one of the *plein air* painters, and an art collector. His collection of George Inness paintings can be seen at the Art Institute of Chicago today; and he was willing to loan some of his Inness paintings to the gallery named for him on Chicago's Near West Side. Unlike developments in the "art for the people" in London or other established cities, the cultural philanthropists in Chicago were undertaking dual projects as they built up the young city's cultural institutions and saw the need to support the Hull-House experiment (Horowitz, 1976: 75–92).

It was quite a feat to place original art works of the caliber of those hung on the walls of Hull-House's first venture into the fine arts. The first exhibit, on view the night of the formal opening, June 20, 1891, had a total of seventeen paintings by George Watts, George Inness, Charles H. Davis, Alice Kellogg, Alberto Pasini, W. Velten, Jean Baptiste Camille Corot, and Jean-Charles Cazin. Many prominent businessmen in the city joined Hutchinson and Butler in loaning their paintings: James W. Ellsworth, Martin Ryerson, Cyrus McCormick, and Bertha Honoré Palmer were among them (Giordano, 2005). The Rev. Samuel A. Barnett and Henrietta Barnett had journeyed from London for the opening of the gallery and to give support to Jane Addams who had become a close personal friend and Barnett's young American disciple. Press coverage was extensive, comparing the Butler Gallery to the People's Palace and to Toynbee Hall. More than four thousand visitors saw the first exhibit in a period of ten days (Addams to Katharine Coman, Dec. 7, 1891).

Addams demonstrated that working people were interested in good paintings. She was pleased that the public library on the first floor of the Butler building was well used. The city supplied English magazines and papers and two librarians who were in charge. There were papers in Italian, German, Bohemian, and French. The number of readers the first month was 1,213, during the fifth month, 2,454 (Addams, 1892: 234; Addams, 1893: 42).

Addams's early ideas of the settlement being a spiritual "cathedral of humanity," surfaced when she began to plan the construction of the Butler building which housed the Butler Art Gallery. She remembered,

> on the exciting day when the new building was promised to us, that I looked up my European notebook which contained the record of my experience in Ulm [Cathedral], hoping that I might find a description of what I then thought "a Cathedral of Humanity" ought to be. The description was "low and widespreading [sic] as to include all men in fellowship and mutual responsibility even as the older pinnacles and spires indicated communion with God." The description did not prove of value as an architectural motive... [but] [a]t the moment when I read this girlish

ILLUSTRATION 6.2   Hull-House settlement: The Butler Building (left, partially obscured by
hay) and Children's Building (right, with open balcony porches), 1895
SOURCE: JANE ADDAMS MEMORIAL COLLECTION (JAMC), SPECIAL
COLLECTIONS, DALEY LIBRARY, UNIVERSITY OF ILLINOIS
AT CHICAGO.

outbreak it gave me much comfort, for in those days in addition to our
other perplexities Hull-House was often called irreligious.

JANE ADDAMS, 1910:151

For Addams Hull-House was a "religious" place although the practice of religion there had been transmuted into an expression of universal ethical values
(Addams, 1910: 151).

In a democracy, Addams contended, there needed to be space in which to experience this "moral" art that was separate from sectarian [church] space. In 1891, this space was the Butler Art Gallery—a modest brick building situated between the old Hull homestead that had become the settlement house and a neighborhood saloon owned by Matthew Murphy. An Irish Catholic immigrant who had lived on Halsted Street since 1880, Murphy and his growing family occupied the second floor of his substantial frame building (U.S. Census [Chicago] 1880: 62).

Addams, who had courageously answered the question of uplift by insisting on giving workers "the best," held onto the power of determining what the "best" was in the arts, and even persisted in interposing the values of the educated bourgeoisie between art and the people. Writing about the art exhibits she explained the need for guidance and selection by the educated and cultivated for the "untrained public":

> An effort has been made in these exhibits to show only pictures which combine, to a considerable degree, an elevated tone with technical excellence, and at no time can a very large assortment of such pictures be obtained. There is an advantage on the side of a small exhibition carefully selected, *especially to an untrained public*. The confusion and fatigue of mind which a person of no trained powers of selection suffers in passing his eyes wearily over the assortment of good, bad and indifferent which the average picture exhibit presents, leaves him nothing with which to assimilate the good when he finds it, and his chances of finding it are small. Frequently recurring exhibitions of a few very choice pictures might do more toward educating the public taste of the locality in which they occur than many times the number less severely chosen and less often seen.
> ADDAMS, 1895b: 616; emphasis added

Addams combined an egalitarian message with a maternalist: everyone had a right to know great art. In a democracy "[w]e ask this not merely because it is the man's right to be thus connected, but because we have become convinced that the social order cannot afford to get along without" such inclusion (Addams, 1964 [1902]: 178). When asked "How Would You Uplift the Masses?" Addams had answered: "In brief my remedy for uplifting the masses is simple: *Give them the best you have*" so convinced was Addams that the masses were capable of acquiring "culture" and that it was their birthright as humans to have the opportunity to benefit from great art. [Italics added.] But the "best" we have would be defined by those, like herself, who had education and cultivation ("Invaded the Sunset Club," *Chicago Times* Feb. 1894).

Despite its ambitious beginnings, the Butler Gallery and its branch of the Chicago Public Library did not last beyond 1896 ("The Hull-House," *West Side Chicago Commercial,* June 8, 1895). As Addams explained, "The loan exhibits were continued until the Chicago Art Institute was opened free to the public on Sunday afternoons and parties were arranged at Hull-House and conducted there by a guide. Even these parties were discontinued as the galleries became better known in all parts of the city and the Art Institute management did much to make pictures popular" (Addams, 1910: 373).

5   Theater as Social Work: Theater for the People or the People's Theater

Theater programs at Hull-House were an important component of both the artistic and social goals of the settlement. Drama clubs were established in accordance with the general approach to providing associations for different age groups and ethnic groups. In the beginning they were open to all regardless of talent but in 1897, when Walter Pietsch (1875–1938),[8] then head of drama at Hull-House, decided to improve the overall quality of Hull-House theater productions. He persuaded Jane Addams that the creation of a special group of Hull-House players who were selected on the basis of talent and artistic standards fit the goals of the settlement. Historian Stuart Hecht, who has written about the Hull-House Theatre and the Hull-House Players, says that this was the first instance of a conflict between artistic standards and the purely social objectives of the settlement (1982: 175).

Pietsch selected a cast from the two hundred young people of both sexes who made up the eight to ten drama clubs that were part of the settlement's diverse drama groups. The selection of the first "all-star cast" was agreed upon by Jane Addams during the summer of 1897; in October a committee of qualified residents evaluated and selected sixteen performers (Hecht, 1982: 175).

At the same time, however, social drama clubs continued to flourish at Hull-House as well. The Hull-House Players, continued to be run by Pietsch until 1900 when Laura Dainty Pelham replaced him and reorganized the dramatics club into an ensemble of fourteen actors who, in time, became a troupe

---

8   Walter Gray Pietsch was a Chicagoan of German descent, who graduated from the Chicago Manual Training School, and then Cornell University in 1896. He was interested in theater, and upon his return to his hometown, where he worked as a journalist and later formed an advertising company, Gale & Pietsch, he began to volunteer at Hull-House. http://faculty. washington.genealogies/1Pietsch.pdf.

recognized nationally and internationally. Pelham directed the Hull-House Players until 1925, when she died. The company continued until 1941 with Maurice J. Cooney as director. The Hull-House Players under Pelham were an important part of the settlement's cultural history; Maurice Browne, innovator of the Little Theatre Movement in the United States, late in life wrote, "Mrs. [Laura Dainty] Pelham, not I, was the founder of the American 'Little Theatre Movement'" (Browne, 1955: 128). The ensemble was composed almost entirely of local Irish Americans who retained their day jobs yet managed to reach professional acting levels under Pelham's tutelage. In 1905–1906 Pelham judged the company ready to attempt George Bernard Shaw's *You Never Can Tell* and staged the American premiere of Henrik Ibsen's *The Pillars of Society*. Pelham directed the group in a series of naturalist works and encouraging their use of what was a new, more lifelike acting style in simple realistic settings.

> This chapter in the company's work culminated in the 1911 American pre-miere of Englishman John Galsworthy's *Justice,* a play already credited with inspiring Winston Churchill to sponsor prison reform in Britain. Theodore Roosevelt, on a visit to Chicago, was impressed with the Hull-House Players' production, and Jane Addams recalled that he had not heard of Galsworthy before seeing *Justice* but was so impressed that he purchased every Galsworthy book he could find to read during his train ride back to New York. When Galsworthy visited Hull-House in 1912, he met with the Players, discussed their work on *Justice*, and invited them to stage the American premiere of his play *The Pigeon.*
>
> STUART J. HECHT with LAUREN BUFFERD, "PELHAM, LAURA DAINTY," 2001: 685

The repertoire included plays by Ibsen, George Bernard Shaw, and Irish play-wrights John Millington Synge, and Lady Augusta Gregory, who became quite friendly with Pelham and the company. Gregory's Abbey Players and the Hull-House Players exchanged visits.

The Hull-House Players' productions became a "tourist" attraction along with the rest of the now-famous settlement house, reminiscent of the attrac-tion that Toynbee Hall held decades earlier. As theatre historian Stuart Hecht has observed, ironically, the more successful and avant-garde the offerings became in the Hull-House theater, the less interest was shown by the neigh-bors. Audiences were filled with affluent Hull-House supporters and interna-tional visitors who had heard about the "little theatre" and journeyed to the immigrant neighborhood to attend the plays (Hecht & Bufferd, 2001: 685). This raises the question of how much of the cultural offerings had ever enjoyed the favor of the neighborhood people.

   Addams crafted meaning and context for the cultural events at the settlement; her voice interpreted the art gallery exhibitions, the music concerts at
the holiday season, the Labor Museum demonstrations, and the Hull-House
Players productions. She arranged for newspaper coverage of these events including the earliest open houses for neighbors, such as the Italian or German
night. It was part of the plan to transform conventional roles and thus redefine
who were the actors and the artists and who would be the audience for cultural production in society. Workers and immigrants were brought inside the
circle ordinarily reserved for the privileged classes. Members of the cultural
elite came to Hull-House and found themselves reconsidering the talents and
capabilities of a whole different set of people. This stimulated a new social
knowledge Addams considered a requirement for democratizing culture and
mediating class conflict in a democracy.

   From the beginning, cultural activities at the settlement were the product
of a visionary approach to education and social improvement of the masses of
workers who, to complicate matters, were overwhelmingly foreign born, representing many different religio-cultural backgrounds. In addition, they had
come to the United States from vastly different political systems, some having endured persecution, others having experienced revolutionary upheavals,
and nationalist uprisings. The cultural project that the Hull-House residents
had before them was complicated also by the stereotypes and prejudices
Americans held about the newcomers. The rapid changes experienced by immigrants in the United States added another layer to the settlement's cultural
work. Addams immediately discovered that it was "much easier to deal with
the first generation of crowded city life than with the second or third, because
it is more natural and cast in a simpler mold" (1910: 231). In this she was referring to intergenerational tensions, the loss of the beauty of Old World customs
and cultural artifacts, and the too rapid absorption by immigrants of the me-
diocre or vulgar popular culture of Americans and of immigrants themselves
who had learned how to get by in the United States from the wrong sort of
guides. In the case of theater, then, Addams was convinced that the production
of high quality, socially relevant drama, with semi-professional level actors as
the Hull-House Players came to be, was one of the strongest antidotes to the
inferior theatricals and five cent movies so available in the city.

   The goal of developing cultural productions or events that connected immigrants more directly with their historical and art heritages continued to
preoccupy Addams and the Hull-House residents who wanted Americans to
see the neighborhood people ennobled by their cultural traditions. The case of
the relationship of the settlement house and the small, but very visible Greek
community demonstrates how the cultural pedagogy used by Addams and her

fellow cultural workers favored high-brow Western European traditions. In 1890, there were only 245 Greeks in all of Chicago. Ten years later that number had increased to 1, 493, still rather small, and by 1920, 15,000 Greeks lived in several different colonies in the city (Nelli, 1970: 76; Kopan, 1989). The "Delta," the triangle formed by Halsted, Harrison, and Blue Island Streets was a "Greektown" in the settlement's backyard. Photographs show Greek men roasting traditional Easter lambs in the open air in the alley just across the street from the settlement house.

Addams was enamored with the Greeks. She imagined them as heirs of great historical traditions and valued them in the context of her memory and respect for Western culture's birthplace. Hull-House cultivated and expressed this attitude through its cultural programs. At the same time, the existence of a self-contained ethnic enclave literally in the shadow of the settlement house, demanded "social work." The authors of the essays about the Italians and the Russian and Polish Jews in *Hull-House Maps and Papers* had been critical of the inwardness and parochial quality of ethnic enclaves, seeing them as divisive in a democracy, and holding back social progress of the group. One of the tensions in Addams's work with ethnic groups was the contradictory impulse to valorize certain ancient cultures yet socialize the immigrants of that group into American life.

"In the midst of American cities there are various colonies of immigrants who represent European life and conditions, and that we who stay at home know so little about them is only because we do not make the adequate effort" (Addams, 1908a: 41). Addams wanted Americans to know how worthwhile these customs and people were but she considered them isolated and deficient unless they were connected to the New World. Hull-House reached out to the Greek community just as she had invited in the Irish, the Italians, the Germans, the Bohemians, and the Jews of Eastern Europe. It would be as complicated a social process as any of the other processes of social integration had been. Greek women, like the Italian women, held back. While Greeks were building their own cultural infrastructure with educational and religious institutions including "afterschool" cultural programs of Greek language and history to supplement Greek student's public school attendance, Addams's vision of constructing opportunities of social integration led her to find ways to address the Greek's "isolation." Conversely, there were Greeks who found the settlement house useful for promoting their agenda and Hull-House could be a good friend for competing visions of Greek organizational life.

The Hull-House residents were dissatisfied with the way most Americans viewed the Greeks. They sympathized with the Greek intellectuals they were meeting who were disturbed by the dismissive attitude of Americans toward their community, characterizing all Greeks as merely fruit dealers, shopkeepers, and laborers. The reformers were willing to romanticize their Greek neighbors by imaginatively recreating the historical culture of Ancient Greece. They had begun to do this even before the first Greek play was produced in the settlement's little theatre. Hull-House resident Edith Abbott told a wonderful story of the imaginative way that Julia Lathrop viewed a young Greek neighbor: "I well remember one very early summer morning, almost dawn, when she [Julia Lathrop] called sleeping residents of Hull-House to a front window in the hall," Abbott recalled. "We looked out to see walking down Halsted Street a young Greek in the white kilted skirt of Hellas, pointed and tasseled slippers, and a tasseled cap, piping very musically on some long reedlike instrument. The lad was evidently on his way home from a national festival of some kind. But Miss Lathrop had been so moved by the wistful figure of the *homesick* young Greek and the flutelike melody that floated through the still morning air that she said: 'When I looked out of the window *I gradually saw the Attic plains stretching out there where last night we saw only the sordidness of Halsted Street.*' She apologized for calling us but she said she knew we would be glad to share in the experience of *the mirage or the vision* or whatever it was that she had seen" (qtd. in Addams, 2004 [1935]: 45–46, emphasis added). Lathrop had imagined the young man was "homesick" of course. Addams elsewhere admitted how subjective such "imaginings" were: "I remember the other evening that a Greek woman was spinning in the museum, and a young Greek was looking wistfully on. I said, "I suppose this reminds you of your mother." He said, "Yes; I don't like to look at a stick spindle; she always beat me with it." So perhaps there is another side to the whole story," Addams noted wryly (1912d: 413–414).

How could Hull-House project this vision of cultural heroism to the non-Greeks? In 1899 Jane Addams contacted a Radcliffe College-trained Classics scholar, Mabel Hay Barrows [Mussey][9] asking her to come to Hull-House and produce a Greek play utilizing Greek immigrants in the neighborhood rather than university students. Addams must have known about Barrows' work on Homeric legends so the idea to produce "The Return of Odysseus" reflected Addams's awareness of the national movement to bring back Greek and Latin in universities and preparatory schools (Hains, 1910: 44–45).

---

9 Mabel Barrows Mussey was part of the revival of Greek and Latin plays in colleges in the United States at the turn of the twentieth century; renewed interest in Greek and Latin as languages to be studied was based on educational ideas that argued such studies strengthened students' abilities in other fields. Mrs. Mussey, when a student at Radcliffe College, managed the "Homeric Pictures" and later arranged the "Return of Odysseus" which was given at Brown University in 1896, at Hull-House in 1898 [sic]; at the Studebaker, Chicago—by a club of Greeks—and at Toronto University in 1899. All performances were in Greek (Hains, 1910: 34–35).

Addams publicized that the actors were drawn from the street vendors and tenement-house population of the neighborhood even as those in charge of the production had been surprised to find that some of these seemingly ignorant people already knew the lines which were assigned to them, having studied the classics as a part of their early education in Greece. "We found that these Greeks knew and had read the stories of Homer, and they were delighted to play before the Americans that they might illustrate and emphasize the fact that they were not barbarians" (qtd. in "Settlement Workers Hold Annual Session." *The New York Times*, March 22, 1903: 8).

Addams wrote Florence Kelley, who was away during the preparations for the play, of the surprising amount of literacy in the Greek community, and that she was amazed to find "at least one [of the actors] was a graduate of the University of Athens" (Addams to Florence Kelley, Nov. 22, 1899). She told Kelley, "The Greek play promises to be one of the most popular undertakings we have ever had, and the greatest interest is being evinced in all the scholastic circles" (Ibid). From the start the performance of a Greek play had been conceived to arouse interest outside the neighborhood. University people would be excited that the classics revival was spreading to a settlement house in an immigrant neighborhood. We have no evidence that the other non-Greek but immigrant neighbors pressed to see the plays. The less than 300-seat theater made it possible to experiment with non-commercial and avant garde material and not worry about ticket sales.

The Hull-House performance was reviewed by sculptor and cultural critic Lorado Taft (Weller, 2014), for the *Chicago Record* of Wednesday, December 13th, 1899. Addams reprinted the review in the *Hull-House Bulletin* the following month. Taft's interpretation of the production makes clear that he understood Addams's goal of social integration and shared the moral aesthetic of the Hull-House residents.

I went over to Hull-House the other evening to see the *Return of Odysseus*, Taft wrote. It was his third and last return. It was well worth the trouble, though the hall was packed too closely for comfort with the most cosmopolitan crowd I have even [sic] seen. Everybody that I know was there or had been on the previous evenings, and there were several hundred present variously from the [upper-class] Lake Shore drive and the 19th Ward whom I did not know. For a couple of hours all distinctions were forgotten—the millennium was here. The primitive little play had brought back primitive conditions; we were all brothers and sisters again.

TAFT, "Hull-House Retrospect," 1900: n.p.

The sense of egalitarian camaraderie was just what Addams had sought. It was, of course, felt by Taft, already committed to beautifying and uplifting American cities through heroic public art and, by other moral aesthetic reformers, who believed in his choices (Garvey, 1988; D'Unger, 1913: 669–675).

"There was more than gayety and good cheer, however, in the eager audience—there was rapt attention, and every now and then a thrill of emotion to which blasé theater-goers are little accustomed," Taft wrote in his retrospective piece for the *Hull-House Bulletin*. He believed the audience were thinking "These are real sons of Hellas chanting the songs of their ancestors enacting the life of thousands of years ago. There is a background for you!" In much the same way that Addams believed such opportunities of cultural exchange could foster social integration, Taft intoned: "How noble it [the play acting] made these fruit merchants for the nonce; what distinction it gave them! They seemed to feel that they had come into their own. They were set right at last in our eyes. The sons of princes, they had known their heritage all the time; it was our ignorance, which had belittled them. And they had waited." Taft was certain that the ~~the~~ people in the audience "will never think of them [the neighborhood Greeks] again in quite the same way as before" (1900, n.p.).

Taft ended his review with a reflection on the social situation rather than on any remark about the stagecraft. "Constantly the thought recurred to me, How [sic] much the people count for; what a chance they have." Addams continued this thought with her own editorial note: "The last sentence quoted from Mr. Taft expresses succinctly the value of the play—it 'gave a chance' which was used with earnestness and patriotism for the best results." Herein was the message: the Greek immigrant community could be American and Greek. In fact, being "Greek" enhanced their becoming American.

Addams recounted the story of one of the Greek men who had a part in the play:

> One man always prayed before rehearsing his part, and I asked him the reason for his prayer. He told me that he prayed for power to properly present the honor and glory of ancient Greece to the ignorant people of America, and he was absolutely sincere. We very freely express our opinion of the immigrants to this country, but we don't always stop to think or to question what they may think of us. The answers would be informative and useful. The social gulf that we used to hear much about is imaginary, but it is deep in the imaginations that are the most shallow. There is good and great work to be done, and the settlements are trying to do it.
>
> "Settlement Workers Hold Annual Session," *THE NEW YORK TIMES*, March 22, 1903: 8

At Smith College years later Addams reiterated her basic message and called attention to the immense influence Hull-House had among the foreigners in its district because it "aimed to reach the better side of the lives of these immigrants by appealing to their natural instincts, by interesting Greeks in the reproduction of the classical play of Greece" which "had done more to make good American citizens of these foreigners than was accomplished by any efforts to Americanize them. It was not the aim of Hull-House," she explained, "to make the people it was trying to assist ashamed of their relations and compatriots, but rather to bring out the best there was in them by creating a feeling of equality and of family and race pride. An over-Americanized spirit in the work of a settlement," she contended, "should be avoided" (qtd. in "Current Happenings." *Massachusetts Ploughman and New England Journal of Agriculture*, April 9, 1904: 63, 29).

In June of 1903 Addams invited Mabel Hay Barrows to return to Hull-House to orchestrate another Greek play production, with the settlement house defraying any costs, and sharing any proceeds from the production. Barrows agreed and was back in Chicago in October to produce Sophocles' *Ajax*. It was so successful that the Chicago cast and Barrows took the play to New York and performed at Clinton Hall, Manhattan, in March 1904 (Addams to Isabel Chapin Barrows, Jan. 23, 1904). "The play was recently at the Hull House, Chicago, by a group of Greeks enlisted by Miss Jane Addams and trained by Miss Barrows," a New York reviewer wrote, "and in both cities the success of the effort has demonstrated the existence among us of men and women who, while they are now engaged in humble pursuits and are getting an economic footing, have within them resources of culture and aptitudes of mind and soul which bode well for the future, once they get established in business or in their professions" ("Pencilings," *Congregationalist and Christian World*, April 2, 1904: 89; 14).

Addams learned that the Greeks were very much surprised when university professors came to Hull-House's theatre and followed the play in the Greek text from books which they brought with them. Addams interpreted this to mean that the Greeks were surprised "because they did not know there were so many people in Chicago who cared for ancient Greece." She explained that the professors "in turn were astonished to know that the modern Greeks were able to give such a charming interpretation of Sophocles."

"It was a mutual revelation on both sides," according to Addams (1908a: 56). This kind of cultural exchange made the immigrants—in this case the Greeks— feel "more nearly a part of America, and on the other side the professors felt that perhaps the traditions had not been so wholly broken in the case of Greece as they had been led to believe" (Ibid). Addams also indicated how much "behind-the-scene" manipulation was required to pull off this sort of cultural exchange. This admission on Addams's part belied her insistence that such events at the settlement were instigated by the neighbors, not the reformers. She acknowledged that "it would have been difficult for the Greeks to have made for themselves all the preliminary arrangements for this play; they needed some people to act as ambassador, as it were," but also held onto the belief that "they themselves possessed this tradition, the historic background, this beauty of classic form, which our American cities so sadly need and which they were able to supply" (Addams, 1908a: 56).

6   [After] Jane Addams: Cultural Production at Hull-House during the
        New Deal Era's Popular and Cultural Fronts (1934–1943)

Addams died on May 21, 1935. Until her death she had been fully engaged in the politics of the New Deal and had testified before the Cook County Commissioners asking for more relief monies for the people only a week or so before she entered the hospital in Chicago. She had spent very little time preparing for a successor or even putting the pieces together of the projects that were on her desk.[10] Addams's generation focused on the dehumanizing effects of industrialism which threatened art and culture by forcing laboring men and women to be divorced from artisanal craft. This movement had a cultural message, a "cultural front" expressed in the language of Matthew Arnold, John Ruskin and William Morris. She was reading Walter Besant who in 1882, published *All Sorts and Conditions of Men*, an early example of slum fiction in the last decades of the Victorian era. The novel, which immediately became very popular and sold 250,000 copies, described the working-class inhabitants of London's East End slums who lived in a cultural void resulting in their almost total social exclusion. His next slum novel, *Children of Gibeon* (1886), recounted the miserable lives of three young girls working in an East End sweatshop. Everyone was reading Matthew Arnold, *Culture and Anarchy* (1869) which had more conservative political implications but aroused a generation to the disintegrating culture as a result of industrialism; John Ruskin wrote *The Stones of Venice* (1851–53) with his views on industrial capitalism in a series of articles which were later published together; *Unto This Last*, first published as a series of articles in 1860,

---

10   Adena Miller Rich, a longtime Hull-House resident with her husband, who was directing
      the Immigrants' Protective League, closely affiliated with the settlement, was appointed
      head resident and served from 1935 to 1937 (Lyons, 2001: 743).

were essays in political economy and culture; William Morris wrote essays, novels, and songs for the working class, as well as his more well-known arts and crafts designs. His lecture "Art and Socialism," delivered before the Secular Society of Leicester, 23 January 1884, argued that art was not an achievable goal under capitalism as presently constituted (Morris, 1915: 192–214).

In the 1930s, world economic collapse and the rise of fascism radicalized the sons and daughters of immigrants in the United States, along with disaffected American middle-class intellectuals and refugees from abroad; they were joined loosely in a social movement of the Left: The Popular Front of the New Deal. It had a cultural component as well: the cultural front used art for social purposes just as Addams and Starr and the artists and writers who had joined them in the 1890s. This new cultural front was different, however. Now the producers and the consumers of art at the cutting edge of political and social change came from a new class. Culture was no longer only the provenance of upper class Bostonians, Ivy-league educated Americans, radicalized Christian ministers, and the daughters and sons of the ruling elites in cities and towns of the Middle West. Carl Sandburg's declaration, "The People, Yes," was an anthem sung by Alexander Saxton, Willard Motley, and William P. Schenk who converged at the Hull-House settlement during the five years of Charlotte E. Carr's tumultuous revival of its activism and cutting-edge cultural innovation. They came not to bring culture to the people but to participate in the people's culture.[11] The neighborhood and the legacy of Jane Addams— as they understood it—beckoned them to write the poetry, novels, and plays

---

11   Charlotte Carr, director of Hull-House, 1937–1942, graduated from Vassar in 1915 and pursued post-graduate studies in economics for three years at Columbia University. She held important positions with the New York State Charities Aid Association, the New York Charity Organization Society and other welfare groups. For six years she was in charge of personnel work in factories. In the New York State Department of Labor Carr worked with Frances Perkins, later Secretary of Labor under Franklin Delano Roosevelt. She was in charge of research work relating to problems of women and children in industry, also problems arising from the administration and extension of the Workmen's Compensation Law. Many of the results of surveys made by Carr were incorporated in the legislative programs of Governor Alfred E. Smith of New York, and President Roosevelt when the latter was Governor of New York. The reputation Carr won by her work caused Gifford Pinchot, while Governor of Pennsylvania, to request Perkins to lend Carr to the Pennsylvania State Department of Labor. While she was serving the State of Pennsylvania Carr's leave was extended several times. She established in the Pennsylvania Labor Department a bureau of women and children similar to the New York bureau, and later became its director. Carr returned to New York City in 1929 to become industrial consultant of the Charity Organization Society, with which she remained until 1930. She also was appointed to the Commission on Unemployment Relief set up by Governor Lehman and just before coming to Chicago she served as assistant director of the Home Relief Division in New York City (20 July 1935, *The New York Times*: 3).

of working-class experience as close to how workers expressed themselves. Michael Denning's encyclopedic work describes the novels, little magazines, and organizations such as the John Reed clubs as a cultural social movement with origins in the advent of the Left's Popular Front, expanded popular cultural medium and the rise of a new class of writers and artists whose roots were authentically in the tenements and the immigrant quarters; while there were notable American middle and upper-class intellectuals who consciously chose, as Addams had done fifty years earlier, to learn about life from real experiences, Mike Gold, Henry Roth, Richard Wright, and Pietro di Donato were working class (Denning, 1998: 230–258).

Ironically, when Addams was reflecting on her generation's "becoming indifferent to the gravest situation in our American life," a new generation of artists, writers, social critics, industrial unionists and radicals, the women and men of the cultural front (Denning, 1997: xiv–xv) were already "stirred" into a new abolitionism. Dismantling Jim Crow and outlawing lynching was their fight and they saw racism used in capitalist exploitation of white and Black workers.

Charlotte Carr told the trustees and residents "that Hull-House ha[d] not been giving adequate service to the Negroes, who [were] comparatively new neighbors, nor [did] the House have the contacts which would enable it to ascertain the type of service needed ("Minutes," Board of Trustees Meeting, Jan. 21, 1938, Hull-House Collection)." Carr was, well-known to Progressives and New Dealers in New York, Washington, and Pennsylvania, and well-liked by Harlem and Washington, D.C. civil rights leaders and CIO union men (Woolf, 1937: 5; Height, 2003: 54; "Friends Give Farewell Fete for New Hull House Head," *Chicago Defender*, 2 October 1937: 7). Instead of ties to the settlement movement, Carr had been a pro-labor government official dealing directly with labor-capital conflicts in industry. Her experience and coming-of-age in the late 1920s and early 1930s gave Carr a different attitude toward working-class culture than the one developed by Addams. Perhaps the greatest difference was her recognition that the working class was now represented by the children of immigrants who felt "American" and whose immersion in 1920s popular culture and 1930s industrial unionism had created a new social and cultural environment for community work (Cohen, 1990: 333–355). It was also the recognition that African Americans had to be front and center of the economic recovery and the political realignment of the New Deal.

There were continuities as well as discontinuities between Addams's and Carr's Hull-House. The two women held similar views on New Deal policies and on the need for an expanded welfare state. "Our most pressing need— one that will do away with much suffering—is the enactment of widespread

measures for insurance against unemployment, old age and other such prevent-
able disasters. There has been a small beginning in this, but it must be carried
out on a large scale to be efficacious," Addams was quoted on the occasion of
her 70th birthday ("Insurance against Unemployment and Old Age: America's
Greatest Need." [interview] Freeport (Ill.) *Journal-Standard*, 1930, Sept. 6: 1).
She had questioned the privileging of private property as a prerequisite for
solving low-income housing needs (qtd. in "Editorial," *The New York Times*,
October 3, 1920: 26) and had made possible the critical cooperation of local
interests in clearing the way for the first public housing project in the United
States which was built in the Hull-House neighborhood (Hunt, 2009: 39). Addams was in the New Deal camp, endorsing Frances Perkins for the position
of secretary of the Department of Labor in Franklin D. Roosevelt's administration. Perkins had been a Hull-House resident in her formative years (Addams,
1933: ix). During the Great Depression Hull-House residents had been leaders
in organizing the non-Communist Workers' Unemployed Councils (Taylor to
Helen Hall, March 10, 1936; McCulloch to Lea Taylor, July 1, 1940).[12] The councils
met at Hull-House. Their politics were pro-New Deal and matched those of
Charlotte Carr's (Binford to Addams, August 19, Sept. 15, 1931; Addams to Rich,
Sept. 21, 1931). In addition, both Addams and Carr had to fight attacks by red-
baiting anti-communists. "Scarlet Carr" and Addams—labeled "the most dangerous woman in the United States" and surveilled by the FBI—supported civil
liberties and left wing political groups publicly as they defended the rights of
labor unions and dissidents (Davis, 2000 [1973]: 251–281).[13] Hull-House in the
1920s had been a haven for pacifists and radicals, and as Robert Morss Lovett
put it, "emphatically the refuge of lost causes (Lovett, 1948: 230)."[14] Hull-House

---

12   Graham Taylor Papers, The Newberry Library.
13   "Asked where she picked up the pseudonym 'Scarlet Carr,' she explained: "'That came out
      of an old trade matter in which Victor Ritter, in charge of the WPA in New York, pointed
      out that I was constantly pointing out the inadequacy of relief. He called me 'Scarlet.' Miss
      Carr readily admitted she is interested in politics and has 'backed many candidates' and
      that she is an active member of the executive board of the Union for Democratic Action,
      which the Dies committee once described as 'the spearhead of creeping totalitarianism.'
      Asked whether the organization is 'red,' Miss Carr retorted: 'That's the wrong color'" (De-
      cember 26, 1942, *American*: n.p., Hull House Collection).
14   Lovett, University of Chicago literature professor, and his wife Ida, who often assisted Ad-
      dams with administrative tasks, lived at Hull-House after World War I thru the 1930s. His
      controversial liberal positions and editorship of *Dial* and the *New Republic*, made him a
      target. Addams defended him. In the mid-twenties at Hull-House, Lovett met once a week
      for the reading and discussion of manuscripts. Any one could come and bring anything he
      had written, poetry or prose, sketches, stories, essays. or sociological studies. "The inter-
      est of the group does not seem to suffer from the fact that some of the work submitted
      is elementary in character and needs correction in use of words and idiom. For the most

residents supported Sacco and Vanzetti, the Scottsboro Boys, and Angelo Herndon; they demanded fairness toward the Soviet Union (Lovett, 1948: 155). Lovett, who "from the onset [...] was in favor of the Russian Revolution," remembered Addams calling it "the greatest social experiment in history." These positions aligned them with the Popular Front.[15] The year before Carr arrived, the International Labor Defense (ILD) had its sixth Illinois state convention at Hull-House in Bowen Hall. ILD decried deportations, lynching and Jim Crowism, and called for building "the most effective united defense of labor and civil rights in behalf of all victims of terror" (April 4, 1936, *Chicago Defender*: 4).

Hull-House's participation in Popular Front politics thus flowed from its earliest pro-labor policies and its openness to left-wing social movements in the 1920s and its advocacy of New Deal programs in the 1930s. It was in the arena of *cultural expression* that Hull-House after Jane Addams more fully separated from the Victorian/arts and crafts aestheticism of its first forty-five years. It also emphatically rejected the social control interpretation of the culturally inferior "Negro." Jazz, long discredited as a dangerous, degenerative form of music, was now a *worthy* art form. For those who knew Jane Addams's opposition to jazz, the Benny Goodman event signaled a new era at Hull-House.

One image stands out as emblematic of this historical cultural shift. It is the photograph of Charlotte Carr introducing jazz clarinetist Benny Goodman to an enthusiastic Hull-House audience. The "King of Swing" had grown up in the neighborhood and studied clarinet from James V. Sylvester, the Hull-House Boys' Band director. Goodman's concert marked one of Hull-House's first performances of Swing, a suspect form of popular culture in the eyes of the Old Guard and Addams, who had called jazz music "the greatest menace to child morality ("Jazz Menaces Child Morality," *The National School Digest*, 1921: 426; Kenney, 1994: 64–65)." Goodman captured the Popular Front sense of jazz when he told the cultural front magazine *Friday*: "Jazz isn't changing; it's just

---

part, improvement comes from practice under the stimulation of the audience, not from application of the blue pencil. The fact that several members have published their work is an added incentive" (*Hull-House Year Book: Forty-Fifth Year*, 1934: 6).

15   Jane Addams sent a telegram: "Those of us long devoted to the Americanization of foreign-born citizens believe that clemency in the Sacco-Vanzetti case would afford a great opportunity for the healing of wounds and for a real reconciliation between the Anglo-Saxon and Latin peoples. I beg you to commute the death sentence because I realize that thousands of our humbler citizens feel as the French felt concerning Dreyfus and ardently long that these men should also have their chance for possible vindication later. Although you yourself are convinced of the justice of the verdict, can you not consider the earnest and conscientious convictions of many of your fellow-countrymen who implore you to refrain from making the situation absolutely irrevocable?" (Aug. 22, 1927, *The New York Times*: 3).

ILLUSTRATION 6.3   Hull-House Director, Charlotte Carr, with jazz clarinetist Benny
                   Goodman on September 15th, 1938
                   SOURCE: JANE ADDAMS MEMORIAL COLLECTION (JAMC),
                   SPECIAL COLLECTIONS, DALEY LIBRARY, UNIVERSITY OF
                   ILLINOIS AT CHICAGO.

being recognized as fine music at last. *It was perfected by all of the 'foreigners' who make up America, particularly the Negroes"* (qtd. in Denning, 2002: 10, emphasis added). Goodman also presciently understood how becoming "white" (American) for immigrants had to do with race identity and Black culture. Popular culture—cinema, music, dance—informed the process of becoming white and American, as sociologist Graham Cassano aptly indicates in the "shadows of blackness" as Black cultural forms were appropriated (Cassano, 2015: 96–98).

Although she conceived of Hull-House as a place where people's culture could flourish, anxiety about the uncontrolled music and dance of the streets, dancehalls and saloons interfered and contradicted Addams's impulse to draw on the historical contributions of Africans in the United States. Reminiscent of the use of high-brow European cultural forms to express working people's experiences—as in Eleanor Smith's labor songs—Addams praised *Porgy and Bess* which showed difficult social conditions in the context of an uplifting message. "It may be significant that the curtain falls on an *advanced* play like 'Porgy' while the Negroes of Catfish Row are singing, 'I'm on my way'" (Addams, 1930: 400). [Italics added.]

ILLUSTRATION 6.4   Benny Goodman performs in Bowen Hall with his integrated
                     ensemble on September 15th, 1938
                     SOURCE: JANE ADDAMS MEMORIAL COLLECTION (JAMC),
                     SPECIAL COLLECTIONS, DALEY LIBRARY, UNIVERSITY OF
                     ILLINOIS AT CHICAGO.

7   The Revitalization of Art and Politics

The chance to do collaborative work that combined the arts and politics with other like-minded people had always attracted bohemians, intellectuals, and artists and writers, and radicals to the settlement. It was the place to be if you wanted to experience social conditions first hand: to find out about poverty, to be part of the trade union movement, to learn about how immigrants lived. There was something exciting about the location of Hull-House that appealed to creative people and drew them in. Addams had capitalized on this, constructing art studios and workshops for crafts, and theaters for drama and music. As much as these facilities were part of the public space for neighbors, the colony of residents, as this chapter has indicated, had a life of its own where they were able to create art and freely enjoy a bohemian existence. There was a connection between the peaks of creativity culturally and the intensity of political engagement. The revitalization of the arts under Charlotte Carr was possible because of the new wave of interest in Hull-House as a center for politics and cultural experimentation. Just as Addams's generation had longed for an entry point to join in the race struggle, and experience the life of workers and immigrants, the young college student Alexander Saxton recalled that in 1939, "For me... Chicago was Mecca. A romantic realist, I had read Carl Sandburg" (Saxton, 2000: 90). The son of middle-class liberals, Saxton grew up in Manhattan; educated at the finest private schools, and then Harvard, he had been radicalized by the Great Depression. Addams had written that she had never been able to rid herself of the memory of East London poverty and "the myriads of hands, empty, pathetic, nerveless and workworn, showing white in the uncertain light of the street, and clutching forward for food which was already unfit to eat" (Addams, 1910: 68).

Saxton remembered the breadline that "looped all the way around the block" that he passed on his way to school:

> New York in winter can be cold, dismal, wet. People waited from before daybreak for a cup of soup and some slices of bread. They had fires smoldering in old drums spaced along the sidewalk, and they took turns crowding up close to warm their hands.
>
> ALEXANDER SAXTON, "Reminiscences of an Octogenarian Radical," 2000: 88

Saxton's first novel, published in 1943, and after his two-year residence at Hull-House, reflected the theme of how "an ethics of individual achievement" had to become "one of moral responsibility for the social order" (91). Addams talked of the need for a new social ethic (Addams. 1964 [1902]). Saxton's decision to leave Harvard and his inherited class position, and choose another life closer to the people, is reminiscent of Addams's rejection of her upper-class existence, and her choice of Chicago's industrial and immigrant neighborhood. Saxton satisfied his father and agreed to finish college at the University of Chicago, but he soon took a series of industrial jobs and began his career as a novelist. In the two-year period (1939–40) he lived at the settlement, first briefly as a single college student, and then with his wife Gertrude (Trudy), Alex met University of Chicago students William Peter Schenk and his wife Beatrice, (Saxton, 2002: 1–4)[16] who was studying social work. They lived at Hull-House and were aspiring writers. African American journalist Willard Motley, who was publishing his short stories and contemplating writing a novel, had moved to the Maxwell Street neighborhood a few blocks from Hull-House. Motley, too, was abandoning his middle-class, interracial family, to seek experiences

---

16   William Paul Schenk (called "Peter" during his Hull-House years), later became the editor of the *Science Digest Magazine*. He met his wife when they were both students at the U. of Chicago; his father was a local department store proprietor in Chelsea, Michigan. Schenk worked for Carl Sandburg briefly as secretary and research assistant.

among working-class ethnic whites in the old Jewish ghetto (Wald, 2012: 253). Schenk and Saxton encouraged "[Motley] to engage in a wide reading of nineteenth-and-twentieth century novelists including John Steinbeck, John Dos Passos, Ernest Hemingway, James Joyce, Leo Tolstoy, Upton Sinclair, Jack London, and Sherwood Anderson. Motley also became familiar with the work of playwrights such as Anton Chekov and Henrick Ibsen and fell under the spell of poet Carl Sandburg. Motley's own production of short fiction now turned more directly toward realist techniques" (Ibid). Chicago's *Hull-House Magazine* was launched in mimeographed form in the autumn of 1939, with Schenk listed as editor and Motley and Saxton as associate editors and represented this new spurt of creative energy linked to the social upheavals and radical movements of the times.[17]

Hull-House Magazine was intentionally experimental fusing nonfiction and fiction in the manner of many similar cultural front publications. Little is known about how it came to be (or why, for that matter, it only produced three issues). The moment was ripe for such a literary collaboration under Charlotte Carr's warm embrace of activism, cultural expression, and interracial exchange. Several themes dominated the three issues of the magazine. One was the identification of the contemporary social struggle as a class struggle, with the writers and editors situating themselves as workers; they felt no contradiction in identifying their struggle for personal recognition as producers of culture with the struggle for transformation of the capitalist system. The group's

---

17   The post-Hull-House careers of these three men are outside the scope of this chapter. There is little known about Schenk, who apparently was the editor of a science magazine and became a collector of Carl Sandburg material. Motley went on to publish a major blockbuster novel: *Knock on Any Door* (1947). It became a film two years later starring Humphrey Bogart. Much of the story and characters can be traced to the Hull-House neighborhood, and the white ethnics, criminality, Catholic institutions & not the race story, a problem that critics—both Black and white—have encountered with Motley's works. Alan Wald, "Willard Motley," op. cit. Alexander Saxton had a double career: first as a novelist and second as an historian. He wrote *Grand Crossing* (1943) drawing on his experiences working in South Chicago steel mills and as railroad freight brakeman and fireman on the New York Central Railroad and on his membership in the American Communist Party. His second novel, *The Great Midland* (1948) was a story about railroading and industrial unionism in the 1930s. He decided to become an historian later in life, received his Ph.D. at age 49; and after teaching at Wayne State for one year, he joined the Department of History at UCLA. He turned to the study of labor and race, publishing *The Indispensable Enemy: Labor and the Anti-Chinese Movement in California* (1971; reissued 1995); his great work is the classic *The Rise and Fall of the White Republic: Class Politics and Mass Culture in Nineteenth-Century America* (1990), a precursor of whiteness studies, and an important analysis of how race-based politics dominated nineteenth-century white American culture (Vitello, Sept. 1, 2012. *The New York Times*: n.p.; Saxton, 2000: 86–102).

politics—expressed through the magazine—advocated ending economic and
social inequality by unleashing the power of democracy itself, which they believed was at risk in the neighborhood and in the world. They were in agree-
ment with Addams that the masses were inherently good, but needed awakening, education, and organization. This process could not be imposed from
on high by professional social workers. This, too, was Addams's position. She
persisted in emphasizing the importance of living in the neighborhood with
the people and she resisted the growing professionalism she saw in the field
that ironically claimed her as founder.

The writers generally supported New Deal programs, trade unions, experiments in the cooperative movement and public housing; they were critical of
the rich, large corporations, politicians who were on the take, and bourgeois
culture. Overall, their faith in "the people" would have appeared hopelessly
simplistic but was saved by the social realism that portrayed the magazine's
major subject matter—the world of the Hull-House neighborhood—with all
its blemishes, inconsistencies, and even its criminal elements.[18]

In its graphics the mimeographed issues had none of the finish and design
motifs of the arts and crafts publications the settlement had produced over
the years. It had an amateurish feel to it, with no attempt at refinement. The
illustrations in black and white were expressionistic woodcuts in keeping with
the turn to social realism.[19] The prose style also departed from the Addams's
era, but not entirely. Use of slang and conversational tone signified the close
relationship writers' chose between fiction and nonfiction as was Addams's
method. Addams had included a modest amount of colloquial dialogue in her
stories about neighborhood people, but she had encased these vignettes in

---

18   Alice E. Treleaven, Don Morris, Harvey O'Connor, Milton S. Mayer, Lawrence Hodges, Bea-
      trice Schenk, John O'Connell, Morris Mitchell signed articles in addition to the three edi-
      tors. Mitchell lived in the neighborhood and gave guided tours at Hull-House; O'Connell
      did not live at Hull-House; he was formerly employed as a receptionist at the Illinois Re-
      search Hospital and, in 1940, was unemployed. Milton S. Mayer was a Hull-House resi-
      dent, a writer, and on the staff of the University of Chicago in the office of the president.
      Don Morris lived at Hull-House and was a publicity writer at the University of Chicago.
      Beatrice Schenk, William's wife, was a social worker. Alice Treleaven lived at Hull-House
      where she taught citizenship and English courses and chaired the United Conference on
      the High Cost of Living. Lawrence Hodges was a Hull-House resident. He had worked in
      co-operative stores and was with the Railroad Retirement Board. Harvey O'Connor was,
      at the time, the most published of the group.

19   Addams had kept up with the times, actually; her *Second Twenty Years at Hull-House*
      (1930), was illustrated with expressionistic, social realist woodcuts of Hull-House artist
      Morris Topchevsky. Of course, as a Hull-House immigrant kid who was one of the "trans-
      figured few," she was inclined to support his work.

ILLUSTRATION 6.5   Alexander Saxton's block print, used as the cover for the *Hull-House*
                     Magazine, December 1939
                     SOURCE: HULL HOUSE COLLECTION, SPECIAL COLLECTIONS,
                     DALEY LIBRARY, UNIVERSITY OF ILLINOIS AT CHICAGO.

her otherwise complex literary style. On the surface, then, *Hull-House Maga-*
zine was a departure from what had preceded it, but in the underlying desire
to connect with the neighborhood and the people, it shared intentions with
Addams.

The subject matter and point of view of the new generation of writers agreed with some of Addams's earlier impressions of working people and the neighborhood. Motley's "Pavement Portraits," connected the local to the global—Jerusalem, Africa, Mexico, Italy, and Greece were in the neighborhood, echoing Addams's cosmopolitanism. He found the people surprisingly intelligent, generous to one another, even though living in poverty and in his story "Handfuls" which portrays working class and poor people's generosity, Motley quotes Jane Addams: "In every neighborhood where poorer people live, because rents are supposed to be cheaper there, is an element which, although uncertain in the individual, in the aggregate can be counted upon" (*Hull-House Magazine*, January 1940: 9, 11).

Alexander Saxton's piece in the first issue argued that democracy was being challenged by the power of big business. In line with Addams's anti-war stances (although his insights were coming less from her writings and more from his own analysis of current events), he questioned England and France's argument that the coming war was necessary to defend democracy. Instead he saw France and England fighting to defend their world dominance as colonial powers. Saxton identified the real enemy facing the United States not in Germany or Russia, but in the domestic troubles of industrial capitalism in the U.S. These economic problems, Saxton feared, would not be solved by the U.S.'s entrance into a world war and, instead, would threaten democracy because of the concomitant consolidation of power that such an undertaking would necessitate. Unlike most of Addams's peace writings, Saxton saw the potential for fascism in "the People." It was possible, he speculated, that the country "may accept government for the people by big business" which would be the end of democracy (*Hull-House Magazine*, November 1939: 1, 5). His reading of history, different from the social evolutionary positivism of Addams's vision, contemplated the bleak, dark, world emerging in Europe and close at hand, in the embrace of Mussolini by some of Hull-House's neighbors. There was historical precedent that confronted with serious challenges, "the people turn[ed] back to answers that were adequate" at an earlier time. "It shuts its eyes to actual conditions, and trusts in ritual phrases—free competition, due process of law, land of the free, always room at the top. It is the people which becomes emotionally attached to old institutions, and which with the highest motives resists all efforts to keep democracy functioning" (*Hull-House Magazine*, November 1939: 1, 5).

One more couple—the O'Connors—fills out the core of the *Hull-House Magazine* group. Harvey O'Connor and his wife Jessie had been invited by Carr to come to Hull-House; they might have been drawn to Hull-House on their own because of its history as a site of unconventional thinking and because it was in a working-class neighborhood. Jessie's connection was deep; her grandparents Henry Demarest and Jessie Bross Lloyd were original supporters of Jane Addams's new project in 1889 (Thomas, 1983: 133–134). O'Connor was, at the time, the most published of the group. He was author of *Mellon's Millions, Steel Dictator, and The Guggenheims: The Making of an American Dynasty*, published yet another critical examination of American wealth, *The Astors*, in 1941. The O'Connors became "representative of Hull-House" (Hodgman, 1943: 31). Their political activities in Popular Front organizations matched the climate at Hull-House. The FBI was surveilling them and had gathered data on Jane Addams before her death (Roediger, 1988: x).

Carr zeroed in on the absence of African American leadership and participation. She opened Hull-House to Blacks in the neighborhood, she said, "not necessarily from the point of view of the racial question, but from the point of view of the lowest wage group" (Trustees' Meeting Minutes, January 21, 1938: 4, Hull-House Collection). The most dramatic changes occurred in the representation of Blacks. Jane Addams had recognized the cultural contributions of African Americans before her death but found it difficult to initiate new strategies for cultural exchange. The new director's efforts changed Hull-House.[20] Carr had friends and associates in New York active in the emerging civil rights movement and the Harlem Renaissance and she brought her intimate knowledge of race issues and interest in the "New Negro" cultural expression to Hull-House.[21]

Carr's appointment of Black journalist Dewey R. Jones as her assistant in charge of social investigation and community education advanced Carr's

---

20   In 1927, the Chicago Woman's Club sponsored a week-long event, "Negro in Art Week." There was a major exhibition at the Art Institute of Chicago of primitive African sculpture and modern paintings and sculpture by African American artists. Jane Addams, Mary Rozet Smith, and Louise Bowen were listed along with other prominent leaders from the white liberal community and Chicago's elite Black leadership. Stimulated by Carter Woodson's efforts to develop an organization to study the history and culture of African Americans in the United States, this was one of the first efforts to seriously consider the achievements and contributions of African Americans and Africa to the arts and the humanities. The exhibit loaned sculpture from the Harlem Museum of African Art that had only a few months before exhibited this collection of African Art from the Blondiau-Theater Arts Collection of the Congo. The introduction to the Art Institute's Catalogue pointed out that "the work of some of our contemporary Negro artists has already begun to show the influence of African art, very much as modernist paintings and sculpture in Europe has also felt and profited by its influence" (1927, *The Negro in Art Week Catalogue*: n.p.).

21   The invited guests included Robert Elzy, founder of the Urban League in Brooklyn, New York; Dr. Channing Tobias, an executive with the YMCA, Bessye Beardon, Harlem civic leader and mother of the artist Romare Beardon; James B. Hubert of the New York Urban League, A. Philip Randolph, and T. Arnold Hill (Oct. 2, 1937, *Chicago Defender*: 7).

agenda on race and labor. The New Deal connection was working. Jones, who had been managing editor of the *Chicago Defender* and a member of the executive committee of the city's NAACP chapter in 1935, had replaced Robert Weaver as Secretary of the Interior Harold L. Ickes' advisor on integrating public housing projects in Chicago. Ickes and Addams were active in the Chicago NAACP and had been planning the first public housing project which was to be located near Hull-House, at the time of Addams's death. The Jane Addams Homes project opened its doors to white and Black families in 1937; situated just a few blocks west of the settlement house, Ickes had hoped to prove that public housing could be integrated. This was Addams's dream as well and derived in part from her theorizing about the lack of race hatred among the neighborhood Italians. It is likely that Charlotte Carr had been encouraged by Ickes to find a position for Jones at Hull-House and to ask the Rosenwald Foundation to offer the journalist a fellowship.[22]

Jones and his wife and their child, Dewey, Jr., a toddler, arrived in 1938, the first Black family to take up residence.[23] Jones, who remained for just short of a year,[24] managed to highlight the settlement's poor record on integration and, at the same time, promoted Carr's efforts to make African Americans in the neighborhood feel welcome. Since his formal education and career as a journalist in the Negro press (*Amsterdam News,* New York, and the *Chicago Defender*) more than qualified him to take on the role of journalist-at-large, even though his primary role was to research the community's low income population, Carr incorporated Jones's talents into the center of settlement life and had him edit the 1939 edition of the *Hull-House Yearbook.*[25] Breaking with the past, the 1939 yearbook was heavily illustrated with current

---

22   Or Carr may have known Dewey through Faith Jefferson Jones, Dewey's wife. Faith, a social worker trained in the graduate program of the School of Social Service Administration at the University of Chicago, had been an assistant supervisor for New York's Home Relief Bureau at the time that Carr was running the Harlem office June 16, 1945, *Chicago Defender*: 10). On the Ickes connection (Hayes, April 11, 1939, *Chicago Daily News*: 6).

23   African American Harriet A. Rice, physician, was a resident (1893–1904) and shared a room with Florence Kelley for a time (Kelley, 1954: 426).

24   Jones died unexpectedly. His wife and child remained at Hull-House, but I'm not sure for how long. Carr did not "replace" Jones, but George McCray and Lillian Summers were resident while she was director.

25   Dewey Jones received his A.B. degree in journalism from the University of Michigan; in 1923, he became a reporter for the *Chicago Defender,* then city editor, and later managing editor of that paper. He had a column, "Lights and Shadows" for many years. With A Rosenwald Fellowship, Jones studied journalism at Columbia University, and obtained a M.S. degree. While in NYC he wrote for the *Amsterdam News* (Hayes, April 11, 1939, *Chicago Daily News*: 6; Kellum, April 15, 1939, Chicago *Defender*: 1).

photographs of people at creative work and play. Addams is absent. The 1933–34 *Hull-House Yearbook*—the last produced during the Addams's era—continued the pattern of publications that had centered on the bourgeois environment of the settlement house itself. This focus on the interior space—pictured in undated photographs reused from early yearbooks—identified one of its major cultural products as the settlement house with its paintings, wall coverings, books and murals, exhibition displays and cultural artifacts. It reflected the preoccupation with a late-nineteenth-century moral aesthetic that stressed the influence of a ethically uplifting physical space appropriately decorated with artifacts of historic and aesthetic significance and its goal of democratizing bourgeois culture by making it accessible to the people. "This Year Book," Addams wrote in 1934, presents not so much the current activities of Hull-House as a slight historical sketch of the foundation and development of each department [and] something concerning the theories underlying these activities" (*Hull-House Year Book*, cover notes). The effect was of timelessness even as Mexicans, the latest to join the neighborhood, were interspersed in the text and images. Only the photograph of the all-Black Hull-House Community Club, showing rows of carefully dressed matrons, shattered the settlement's whiteness and appeared out of place.

Carr and Dewey Jones portrayed Hull-House as an integrating institution in its publications. Carr had made some quick changes when she arrived that immediately reflected her goals of developing an interracial community. She hung a painting of an African American in one of the Hull-House parlors; the Art department curated two exhibits of African American art in the settlement's art gallery (named the Benedict Gallery in honor of Enella Benedict). In retrospect, these changes seemed such obvious ways to construct interracial cultural space. Addams understood this function of art and had, with Ellen Starr, "curated" the Butler Art Gallery. The cultural front aesthetic was replacing the outdated late nineteenth-century aesthetic first brought to the neighborhood by Addams and Starr. Carr had Dewey Jones record this cultural shift in the 1939 *Yearbook* images which, for the first time, included African American cultural production: a photograph of the Benedict Art Gallery's first exhibit of "Negro" art; and an image of one of the Hull-House reception rooms (parlor) that included a portrait hanging on the wall of an African American (*Hull-House Year Book*, 1939). Jones's editorship was noted by the Black press: "Then there is the first [sic] annual *Year Book* of Hull House, in the preface of which Miss Charlotte Carr, headworker, gives complete credit to Dewey Roscoe Jones, former managing editor of the *Chicago Defender*, for editing the book. It is a masterpiece of production and information—and laurels to Miss Carr for knowing her staff talent, using it, and giving credit where credit is due. I know some establishments that would not have given the opportunity; and others, if the opportunity had been given would have hidden the facts. America needs more Charlotte Carrs" (Brascher, April 8, 1939: *Chicago Defender*: 15).

Carr was constructing a vocabulary of Black culture in the settlement house and one of her strategies was encouraging Black artists and writers to join in the settlement community. The Benedict Art Gallery became a venue to intro-duce the works of Black artists. We have little information about the first ex-hibit of "artwork by Chicago Negro Artists" which was held in July 1938; it was probably the first one of its kind at the settlement house.[26] A second exhibit of seventy-two paintings and sculptures at the Benedict in October 1939, received publicity in the Black and white press. Conservative art critic Eleanor Jewett mentioned the event in her *Chicago Tribune* column without critical comment (Jewett, 1939: 4); noted *Chicago Daily News* art critic C.J. Bulliet reviewed the show and deemed it "well-chosen," but found the paintings largely "'deriva-tive,' and about the same caliber of work by white artists of leftist tendencies who over concern themselves with the woes of the downtrodden race" (Bulliet, 1939, n.p.). Bulliet focused on the "race melancholy" he found in most of the paintings and the sculpture and he was disturbed that "the show never gets quite happy," a remark revealing more about the critic than the art on display (Bulliet, 1939, n.p.).

Willard Motley gave the only positive review. He saw real talent and the promise of greatness in the art work of the new generation who were following "the trail blazed" by William E. Scott, Archibald J. Motley, Jr., Charles G. Dawson and William Farrow.[27] He argued that "most of the canvases ha[d] a decisive, finished appearance—disproving the opinion of many white critics who feel that the Negro artist should have something primitive in his soul that should

---

26   In an article describing a Negro Art Exhibit at Howard University, Washington, D.C., there
      is mention that artist Eldzier Cortor had exhibited his work at the Hull-House gallery
      (April 29, 1939, *Chicago Defender*: 5). This may be referring to the Benedict Gallery exhibit
      of July 1938. The second exhibition of Black artists at the Benedict took place in October-
      November 1939.

27   Willard grew up in the extended Motley family household that included his brother, the
      artist Archibald J. Motley, Jr., so his knowledge of the Black art scene was substantial
      (Wald, 1999: 251). Willard and Archibald, Jr.'s actual familial connection is controversial.
      See: Willard Motley's biographer Robert Fleming writes that Archibald Motley, Jr., was
      Willard's brother; Amy M. Mooney more recently claims that Willard and Archibald Mot-
      ley, Jr., were cousins. In the foreword to Mooney's book, Art historian David C. Driskell
      refers to Willard Motley as Archibald Motley, Jr.'s nephew (Fleming, 1978: 15; Mooney
      2004: 83, vi). The artists in the Benedict Gallery show included: sculptors Nate Thomas
      and Olivia Caldwell; and painters Charles White, Eldzier Cortor, Bernard Goss, Charles
      Davis, William Carter, Henry Avery, Ramon Gabriel, Charles Sebree, Earl Walker, and Fred
      Hollingsworth.

find its way to the canvas." Motley chose, instead, to define this new group of Black artists in the cosmopolitanism of the large city in which they lived and painted. He viewed them alongside white artists who were also working with an urban vocabulary (Motley, 1940: 19). This approach distinguished Motley from both white and Black critics and he was often judged to have little connection with the Black community (Wald, 1999: 250–251).

African American art immediately presented transgressive elements and challenged the identity, authority, and legitimacy of the artists and the art. Its presentation was unsettling, disruptive, even provocative. It was the reversal of the ordinary cultural exchange of settlements and their neighbors. Of all the groups in the United States, Blacks were at the bottom of the ladder of cultural prowess. Exhibitions of African American art, literary publications, poetry, drama, and dance performances were an assault on the deep-seated racial mythology held by most white Americans.

Creating Black cultural space at Hull-House was a dramatic departure. In contrast, Addams and Starr's Butler Gallery exhibits in the 1890s, often considered a radical cultural event, were widely acclaimed instantly; support came from Chicago's elite cultural philanthropists whose loans from their own collections hung on the walls of the exhibition rooms. Art critics were uniformly congratulatory; few dared to question the motivations or assumptions of moral uplift in the slums. The daring was in doing the exhibit to begin with—but the art works were conventional, acceptable, unchallenging to the cultural hegemony of the elite and the art's legitimacy made it pedagogically straightforward.

8   The Lilac Ball: Integrating Neighbors

Carr was determined to shake up the club system at the settlement, which she believed kept people separated along ethnic and race lines. She was bold in her direct challenge to this system. As a result of her intervention, Hull-House held its first interracial benefit dance in a downtown Chicago hotel in 1941. It was a big event culturally. The white and the Black press thought so and reported in detail. According to the *Chicago Tribune*, no advocate of integration, the nationality clubs—"the Greek, Negro, Italian, and Mexican Mothers' Clubs"—meeting at the settlement had come together and planned the dance to raise money for their activities (May 4, 1941, *Chicago Tribune*: W5.)

Donna Hodgman, a resident at Hull-House provides an insider's account in her unpublished memoir, "People Live at Hull-House" (1943), of how the event came about as an interracial affair:

"One day a committee from the [Hull-House] Women's Club, [the old-est women's group in the settlement and one composed entirely of white English-speaking women] had a meeting with Miss Carr" Hodg-man wrote. "They told Carr they were thinking about a new way to raise money for the clubs. They proposed renting the ballroom of one of the downtown hotels. Everyone would wear evening clothes and maybe even liquor would be served. Carr thought the plan "ambitious" and wondered if they really meant that everybody would be invited: "I suppose the Mex-icans will be in on it?" she asked. Hodgman wrote that the women replied "Certainly, Miss Carr. We don't have race prejudice, you know." Carr coun-tered, "How about the Negroes?" Hodgman recalled "At that remark the faces of the committee looked surprised and uneasy." Carr suggested to the women that they probably had not thought about that aspect yet; she told them "But you and I know that we have Negroes in this house. They are represented in our Interclub Council." And she went on to say that she could not see how they could give the party without "this important group... left out of the plans." Carr left the decision to them. "Of course, this is your party. You have to work it out yourselves. But I guess you know how I would feel about leaving out the Negroes."

HODGMAN, 1943: 23–26

The committee did not answer Carr right away; several days later, after discus-sions, they told Carr, "We want the Negroes." Once the all-white Hull-House Women's Club had made their decision to integrate the party, the next hurdle was to find a hotel willing to accommodate an interracial group in the segre-gated America of 1941. The committee found two hotels, but the manager of one was not sure his waiters would be polite to the guests. The other hotel, The Stevens, was selected. A politician in the neighborhood told Carr that people in the neighborhood did not like the idea of an integrated party: "Course it may be all right to be in the same room with Negroes," the politician admit-ted, "But I wouldn't sit down at the table and eat with one." Carr told him they were not planning to serve food. But, according to Hodgman, she was quite disturbed. "What if the Italians, who constituted the largest part of our popula-tion, bought tickets [to the event] out of politeness but did not come? A party said to be given by all who used Hull-House but attended only by the Negroes and the Mexicans would be a worse blow to the minority groups than if we had admitted in the first place that the plan would not work" (Hodgman, 1943: 23–26).

The night of the dance, called the Lilac Ball, lilacs were brought from Hull-House settlement's Bowen Country Club Camp, Waukegan, Illinois, to decorate the hotel ballroom. The Hull-House residents dressed in evening clothes and worried about what might happen. Carr was visibly nervous: "I wish to Heaven they were going to sell liquor," she remarked (Hodgman, 1943: 23). This part of the plan had been dropped because some of the Hull-House trustees had objected. Hodgman described the scene at the hotel as the event got underway:

> The Mexicans came, and the Greeks, and the Negroes. A Chinese boy and girl came, and one Armenian and one Japanese. The Italians came and Miss Carr came wearing an orchid. The Mexicans were the fanciest dancers and had their pictures taken for the most newspapers. But the Italians were most at home and specialized in making people comfortable. The Negroes basked in unaccustomed warmth. Pretty soon it was crowded. Pretty soon someone told Miss Carr we had a thousand people.
>
> HODGMAN, 1943, 23–24

Carr had pushed the envelope of interracial activities at Hull-House beyond what other social agencies in Chicago had yet attempted. The *Chicago Defender* acknowledged the event's uniqueness and ran a picture with the caption: "Negroes, Mexicans, Chinese, Italians, Poles, Irish, Greeks, Jews, Protestants, Catholics and almost every other racial and religious group were represented in the hundreds of guests who crowded the ballroom of the world's largest hotel. The spectacle would have pleased the late Jane Addams and given Uncle Sam a good demonstration of real democracy" (7 June 1941, *Chicago Defender*: 11).

9   Conclusion: The Labor Museum at Hull-House Revisited

Charlotte Carr's critique of the Labor Museum, Jane Addams's major attempt to address the contradictions of democratizing culture while at the same time mediating class,[28] takes on greater importance when it is interpreted in the context of broader issues about culture and work. I have argued that the Labor Museum was the center of Addams's cultural program for immigrant workers and their children. It was in the museum that we can see Addams's theory of the usages of art and craft. The museum embodied Addams's ideas about industrial society, immigrant adjustment, and intergenerational social relations. These ideas were based on her theory of evolutionary progress: that

---

28   For a full discussion of Addams's theories and practices in establishing the Labor Museum, see Lunin Schultz, Chapter Five in this volume.

more "primitive" societies were sequentially progressing toward the Western norm and that primitive technology progressed through the identical stages. "Within one room the Syrian, the Greek, the Italian, the Slav, the German and the Celt enable even the most casual observer to see that there is no break in orderly evolution," the *Hull-House Bulletin* explained (1906–07: 10). Addams had faith that the museum's displays, enactments, timeline charts, classes, and cultural performances would equip youth with "the informing mind" able to make sense out of industrial life; would provide solace for the elderly craftsperson; and would generate respect and empathy leading to a reformation of the inequalities and injustices of industrialism in the exchange of cultural expression among different social, economic, religious, and ethnic groups. The effort to aid immigrants in making sense of the new world they now inhabited had conservative and radical potential. Taken in conjunction with the labor activism of Hull-House, part of the "making sense" was the message that worker solidarity bore fruit. The determination that traditional family structures (portrayed as traditional crafts) were valuable in the transition to becoming American had conservative implications. Addams realized these contradictions and in *The Long Road of Woman's Memory* (1916) described working people's daily struggle to maintain the bonds between traditional mothers and their trade unionist daughters. The Labor Museum operated out of these contradictions which were deeply intertwined in Addams's theorizing and in her implementation of programs that both sought to democratize culture and to socialize workers, mediating their frustrations and resentments (Addams, 1916: 43–56).

Returning to the Labor Museum offers a perspective on the cultural and political shifts in American history in the 1930s. There were, of course, the continuities. Carr emphasized work as much or more than Addams. She wanted to provide tools workers needed for advancement and equity, as did Addams. Yet the five-year explosion of culture and politics under Charlotte Carr shines a bright light on the great divide between the Progressive Era and the New Deal. Carr's focus on bottom-up cultural initiatives, and community-based policies for running the settlement house and for re-developing the neighborhood were at the heart of the difference.[29] The upper classes ran settlement houses during the time of Jane Addams. They developed programs for immigrants and workers in poor neighborhoods and built organizations to advocate

---

29 Carr's community development initiatives were a radical departure. They are outside the scope of this chapter, but briefly, she reached out into the community by establishing "annexes" where community people could develop programs on the ground. This was a precursor of the efforts of community organizers at Hull-House after Carr (Lunin Schultz, July 2008).

for better housing, juvenile reform, recreation, and public health. Although a cadre of settlement workers made the decision to live in the neighborhoods, people of wealth and property, and a rising middle class, saw their future in neighborhoods separated from workers and immigrants. New Deal social and cultural activists drawn to workers' neighborhoods identified themselves with the people, not the governing boards of social agencies.

Carr reflected this difference when she organized a Community Relations Department at Hull-House with staff assigned to form community clubs. Unlike the social and ethnic clubs that met at Hull-House, these clubs met in different sections of the community and were formed around local issues of housing. They had the potential of being interracial. They were to act as "outposts for Hull-House in its program of slum eradication" (*Hull-House Yearbook*, 1939). These approaches to rebuilding neighborhoods were possible, Carr argued, when neighbors no longer saw themselves as members of a racial or ethnic group, but as Americans with common problems that could be solved by working together.

Carr's critique of the Labor Museum and its Industrial Shops reflected its outmoded approach. Once again, it was less a criticism of Addams's legacy than a simple appraisal of what had transpired in the almost half-century of settlement house work. In this context, of course the ethnic craft performances were antiquated and had little to do with the realities of working class life. "Why should working people weave rugs in 1938? Let's ship these looms to a mental hospital and send the weavers down to city hall in a nice, orderly committee to tell the mayor what their neighborhood needs," Carr told everyone at Hull-House (qtd. in Mayer, 1938: 199). With federal monies, Carr retooled the old industrial shops and updated technical education (Trustees' Meeting Minutes, December 10, 1937, Hull-House Collection).

The Americans who now dominated the old neighborhood—the sons and daughters (and grandsons and granddaughters) of immigrants—were now held back by the perpetuation of ethnic differences rather than the construction of working-class consciousness and solidarity: "I believe we social workers made a great mistake in the early days in organizing racial groups as such—Bohemian Mothers, Polish Mothers, Italian Mothers and so forth," Carr reflected. "Perhaps it was necessary. They came here friendless and unable to speak English; naturally they turned to others of their own tongue. But the time for all that has passed. The second generation has learned English in the public schools, and it is now most important for all these residents to realize their mutual interdependence as Americans—to learn that Bohemians, Poles, Italians, Mexicans and Negroes must live together as neighbors and partners in the economic struggle" (March 18, 1940, *New York Herald Tribune:* n.p.).

Carr seemed to be making progress in the community when suddenly in a shocking, unexpected move, she announced that she was leaving Hull-House at the end of December 1942. Carr claimed she had been fired; the trustees insisted she had resigned (Jan. 4, 1943, *Chicago Tribune*: 11; Carr, Letter of Resignation, Dec. 17, 1942; Trustees' Special Executive Meeting Minutes, Dec. 21, 1942, Hull-House Collection). There were charges of budget extravagance under Carr's administration, and in a newspaper interview, Louise Bowen, president of the board, admitted that Carr's political activities were a problem (26 December 1942, *American*: n.p.). Another unnamed board member pointed out that the budget at the end of 1942 had been balanced for the first time in six years, with larger contributions than ever before (Harris, 1942: 1, 4) and the record indicates that there was no budget crisis.[30] Bowen did not articulate what arguably was Carr's real sin: successful efforts at organization and empowerment of the neighborhood. This demand alone would have been threatening to the board. Carr believed that the neighborhood people must participate fully in the affairs of the settlement. She saw Hull-House as the community's organization. This effort to curtail the authority of Charlotte Carr marked a turning point in the settlement's role in the neighborhood. "Miss Carr's departure, it was learned today," a newspaper article reported, "was the signal for a long-standing controversy between the Hull-House directorate and the Hull-House customers to come to focus in the form of... demands on the former by the latter" (MacDonald, [December 1942], *Chicago Times*: n.p.). Community leaders were demanding actual representation on Hull-House's board of directors, input from a committee made up of local religious, business, and political leaders, and a "voice in the selection of Miss Carr's successor" (Ibid). None of the demands were met.

Carr's boldness in attempting to bring the residents of the neighborhood into the settlement as partners in determining the direction of Hull-House, political columnist Sydney J. Harris argued, "often antagonized some board members, as did her insistence upon entering political controversies when she felt the welfare of 'the little people was at stake'" (Harris, 1942: 1, 4). Carr believed that she, as director of Hull-House, represented the little people against the special interests.

---

30 Actually, Hull-House had a surplus, but still were faced with essential repairs; endowment was somewhat over $500,000; during 1943, they did not liquidate any endowment securities for current expenses. The increase in the value of the endowment fund came from higher market quotations for their railroad bonds and common stocks not because there were additions to the endowment in 1943 (January 28, 1944, HH Trustees' Annual Meeting, Hull House Collection).

While many people who agreed with her approach liked to say she was carrying out the legacy of Jane Addams, Carr understood the challenges a new generation of working-class Americans presented to the settlement house and its role in the community. She rejected the paternalism of an earlier era, the elitism of Hull-House's governing boards, and the emphasis on preserving Old World cultures. Commenting on the departure of Carr, a member of the West Side Community Committee, who had spent his life in the neighborhood, identified the fundamental issue that prior neighbors had not voiced. He asked rhetorically, "who shall formulate the policies of Hull House? Does Hull-House belong to the people it serves, or to the trustees? Shall it be an 'agency' superimposed from above; or shall it be an instrument of the people themselves? Only by involving the people significantly in the management of Hull-House can it ever become a real part of the attitudes, sentiments and thinking of the people." He continued: "Because Charlotte Carr was thoroughly familiar with conditions as they are and was in complete accord with our aspirations for democracy, we consider her resignation an irreparable loss to our community. And we hope that the trustees will reconsider it" (Harris, 1942: 1, 4).

Carr redefined Workers' Education at Hull-House by bringing in a staff with New Deal experience who shared her objectives. Ironically, she was unable to eliminate the old Labor Museum entirely. The Weaving or Textile Room, a central feature of the Labor Museum, continued to function, although as a small part of the settlement's programming. The the older cultural programs— the elaborate and formal Christmas tableaux, the art and music classes, the children's theater, the ethnic festivals and theater productions—continued for another twenty years (1943–1963) before the coming of the University of Illinois (Rosen, 1980). Sadly, they now reflected stasis rather than growth; familiar programs repeated without the kind of political engagement that had once characterized the place under Jane Addams, and again, briefly, under Charlotte Carr.

CHAPTER 7

Hull-House and 'Jim Crow'

Rima Lunin Schultz

When Charlotte Carr arrived at Hull-House in 1937 she immediately resolved to learn about the settlement's relationship with its Black neighbors. African Americans had lived on the Near West Side in the nineteenth century and their numbers increased following the "Great Migration" from the South during and after World War I. Yet not until 1925 did the settlement officially organize a group for African-American women and their children. Was Hull-House a Jim Crow institution that held the color line like so many other settlements, churches, and private social agencies in the United States? How else to explain the absence of African American artists, craftspeople, and musicians in an institution devoted to cultural production? This essay provides an overview of Jane Addams' ideas about race and her role in the race politics of the Progressive Era and it also re-examines cultural programs at Hull-House from the point of view of whiteness studies (Roediger, 2005).

African American migration from the South posed a greater challenge to Hull-House and to settlement cultural programs in the context of Progressive Era ideas about stages of culture (Schafer, 2000: 72). Here Addams presents us with a paradox. Historians have critiqued the Progressive movement for its failure to deal with race. Settlement houses were initially defined as the social justice/left flank of the Progressive movement: pro-labor, socialistic; but that characterization now must be evaluated with the knowledge that social settlements, including Hull-House, upheld Jim Crow like almost all the private social agencies and churches in the United States (Muhammad, 2010; Roediger, 2005; Lash-Quinn, 1993; Philpott, 1978).

The explanation of why African Americans posed a greater challenge to Addams and Hull-House programs resided in her interpretation of race, evolution, and culture. Historian Khalil Gibran Muhammad explains that sympathetic liberals like Addams "turned to culture rather than biology" to account for the differences in moral and criminal behavior between Blacks and whites that they perceived in their work in cities. Addams saw Blacks as being culturally inferior (Muhammad, 2010: 122). As much as Addams was sympathetic and able to escape many of the stereotypes and myths about immigrants and the more obvious slanders against Blacks, she was also influenced by the social mores that shaped American society. Addams, expanding her idea of social control, juxtaposed the strong family sense of Italians with the lack of restraint among Blacks. Other settlement workers argued that Blacks were unlike immigrants and that the process of assimilation would not work with the migrants from the South who needed self-improvement first. Addams was in the "camp" of progressives who assumed Blacks' present-day cultural inferiority was temporary and that they shared the values and aspirations of white society and were thus redeemable but needed to be exposed to higher forms of culture. This meant "white" culture. Before World War I Addams believed in the emancipatory quality of white high culture. Her idea of progress of the [human] race was based on the acceptance of a common humanity. The social evolutionary and positivist conception of a cathedral of humanity envisioned by Addams, while Eurocentric in its expression, even appealed to W.E.B. Du Bois, who saw in this conception of a *social* construction of culture, the potential for the inclusion of Blacks (Schafer, 2000: 72–73; Aldridge, 2007: 416–446).

Addams described this social construction of race when she explained that Italians learned racial bigotry through the process of becoming American:

> A colored man had been lynched in an Italian neighborhood, about half a mile from Hull-House. I had been in Europe that summer and upon my return I one evening consulted an association of Italian physicians who occasionally held their professional meetings in one of the Hull-House rooms. When I asked them why, in their opinion such a shocking incident was possible in the United States, when the friendly attitude of the South Italian to his African neighbors is well known, the professional men replied with the utmost sincerity: "Of course this would never have happened in Italy; they are becoming Americanized." This was said in an honest effort to interpret a puzzling situation, and perhaps it did interpret it.
>
> ADDAMS, 1930: 283–284

In the context of this explanation, Addams was not surprised that Italians and Greeks—also of the Mediterranean region—were welcoming to Du Bois when he lectured at the settlement in 1909 (Addams, 1910: 255–256). They knew from experience that they were considered inferior to people of Anglo-Saxon lineage by many Americans. One of the functions of Greek plays and exhibitions of different nationalities weaving textiles was to illustrate commonalities across ethnic groups and to restore feelings of self-respect by illustrating *social* evolution. Addams made the connection between American racism and anti-immigrant hatred which, she contended, "would be much minimized in America, if we faced our own race problem with courage and intelligence." Addams looked to "these very Mediterranean immigrants [who] might give us valuable help" (1910: 255).

Since 1889, Hull-House had gained a reputation in large part as an interpreter of the immigrant urban experience. In her writings and speeches, Jane Addams challenged nativist characterizations of the "New Immigrants" as a threat to the American way (Higham, 1955). On the contrary, she feared that in the rush to be assimilated the children of immigrants would lose touch with their parents and with valuable historic traditions. She believed that popular culture, business greed, and politics were the wrong "agents" of Americanization and that they weakened democracy. Addams looked to the virtuous qualities she found in immigrants themselves to do the work of becoming American. Addams recognized this process in the neighborhood as the older and more settled Irish for example, were part of the acculturation of Italian immigrants. Addams expanded upon the natural process at work in the neighborhood in the theater and Labor Museum demonstrations and the social clubs at Hull-House. This was an imperfect model of cosmopolitanism as it allowed self-segregated ethnic groups to cohere in the early stages of acculturation and less frequently led to inter-ethnic mixing and, as this chapter will argue, did little to develop interracial connections.

Jane Addams's cultural initiatives were developed in the historical circumstances of race politics in Chicago and in the context of the racism imbedded in the process of Americanization in a society that privileged whiteness, equating "becoming white" with success, social mobility, and full citizenship. This brings a new and critical dimension to the study of cultural pedagogy at Hull-House. The settlement had gained its reputation in large part as an interpreter of the immigrant urban experience. Addams positive approach to immigrants had a basis in theories of social evolution and historicist critical thinking. Axel Schafer makes a strong argument that among progressives, "ethical-historicist ideas may have spawned a trans-ethnic vision, but certainly not a trans-racial one" (Schafer, 2000: 73). A balanced analysis of cultural pedagogy at Hull-House requires a study of Addams's ideas about race and her role in the race politics of the Progressive Era. Jane Addams used cultural production in the Labor Museum and in the Hull-House theatrical performances to counteract nativist characterizations of the "New Immigrants" as unassimilable and a threat to the American way (Higham, 1955). Addams turned this thinking around and blamed the problems in American society on the homegrown American citizens who themselves needed to live up to democratic principles. Protecting the rights of immigrants and dissidents instead of arresting and deporting them demonstrated the value of the rule of law and the superiority of democratic self-governance. When an immigrant Jew, Lazarus Averbuch, suspected of being an anarchist was killed by Chicago's Chief of Police under unusual circumstances, Addams took up Averbuch's defense. The incident happened during a period of hysteria against anarchism and heightened nativist calls for immigration restriction and deportation of radicals already in the country. Addams's clear call was for more democracy including the protection of the right of freedom of speech for noncitizens as well as citizens (Addams, May 2, 1908b: 155–166). Anti-immigrant hysteria during and after World War I again demanded, from Addams's perspective, upholding the rights of the citizen and non-citizen.

Addams went further than this call for the rule of law. She critiqued the Americanization process long before the debates over cultural pluralism, the "melting pot," assimilation, and Americanization came to dominate intellectual circles after the publication in the *Nation* of Horace Kallen's article, "Democracy versus the Melting Pot" in 1915 (February 18 and 25, 1915: 190–194, 217–220). Kallen argued that the very idea of the melting pot contradicted the core democratic principle: the inalienable right to be different, to follow one's own conscience (Greene, 2006: 179–180). While Addams fought against rapid assimilation as a goal, she was not a cultural pluralist (Lissak, 1989) willing to step back from the process of becoming American. Instead she argued that immigrants, while they were their own best missionaries, *still* needed guidance from the right sort of native-born Americans, i.e., progressive settlement workers and appropriately trained school teachers (November 7, 1898, *Chicago Tribune*: 10). *Twenty Years at Hull-House* is filled with anecdotes that identify how *in the context* of the settlement house, with *guidance from residents*, the more Americanized immigrant neighbors helped newer arrivals adjust to life in the United States. She has the tale of the Hull-House Women's Club's outreach to the Italian men in the neighborhood; the women are of Irish or German descent, living in the neighborhood before the Italians moved in. In the context of a social event at Hull-House one of the clubwomen told Addams, "Do you know I am ashamed of the way I have always talked about 'dagos,' they are quite like other people, only one must take a little more pains with them. I have been nagging my husband to move off M Street because they are moving in, but I am going to try staying awhile and see if I can make a real acquaintance with some of them." Addams then reflects: at that moment "the speaker had passed from the region of the uncultivated person into the possibilities of the cultivated person... the former... bounded by a narrow outlook on life, unable to overcome differences... [with] interests... slowly contracting within a circumscribed area; while the latter constantly tends to be more a citizen of the world because of his growing understanding of all kinds of people with their varying experiences" (1910: 358–359). The neighborhood as imagined by Addams, had the potential of developing a democratic cosmopolitanism with a socialized citizenry whose ethical behavior and sense of interdependence brought about the political transformation that was the goal of progressive reform. Addams was not alone in her thinking about the possibilities of democratic cosmopolitanism. Settlement leader Mary E. McDowell, of the University of Chicago Settlement located in the working-class meat-packing neighborhood called "Back-of-the-Yards," held similar views from her experiences with race and ethnicity.

"We did not have to meet the American prejudice against the Negro, for then there were no colored people in the community. So far as we could see, the foreign born held no feelings towards the darker-skinned people." She qualified her statement with the observation that "The first generation of Irish had a latent sentiment against colored laborers, who interfered with their so-called 'American rights'; and the second generation held a deeper-seated prejudice which showed itself during economic clashes; but among the Slavic peoples any antagonistic feeling against negroes grew very slowly" (qtd. in Hill, 1938:28).

McDowell had started her career as a resident of Hull-House and her lifelong reform politics and peace activism attests to Addams's influence. The two women observed that prejudice and discrimination against Blacks was learned *after* immigrants' arrival. They did not use the language of current scholars who have identified "becoming white" in the acculturation and assimilation processes, but their observations of neighborhood life offer evidence that this phenomenon was real.

This realization of the racializing tendencies of the process of "becoming white" did not deter Addams from her overall confidence in democratic cosmopolitanism, which is evident in *Newer Ideals of Peace* (1907). In this confusingly titled analysis of municipal politics Addams identifies the progress of a more evolved urbanism based on the interactions of *ethnic* groups in cities. In *Newer Ideals* Addams cautioned her readers not to get bogged down in the details but to conceive of the larger patterns of social evolution that were evident all around them in the chaotic industrial cities with diverse populations. Addams saw groups whose rivalries and ancient animosities had caused wars in Europe living side by side in her neighborhood. This powerful idea sustained Addams and propelled her to contemplate the American neighborhood model of democratic cosmopolitanism as having relevance to solving international conflicts.

On the other hand, the race question seemed less susceptible to such theorizing. Addams and others at Hull-House were being challenged by data that contradicted their vision of the dynamics of community. Even before the outbreak of war, Louise Bowen's *Survey* magazine article, "The Colored People of Chicago" (1913), compiled from the information gathered by the Juvenile Protective Association, found that segregation of Blacks interfered with socialization processes Addams saw at work among diverse ethnic whites. The Irish might find commonalities with the Italians, but would either group form productive social relations with Blacks? Addams had a hand in the interpretation of the data and emphasized the deleterious effects on African Americans, whose family structures she argued had been hurt by enslavement. In a letter Addams explained that "Mrs. Bowen and I have just finished an article on the Colored People in Chicago from a lot of stuff collected by the J.P.A. *It is a sad tale as everywhere*" (Addams to Sophonisba P. Breckinridge, 25 August 1913, emphasis added). Her faith was shaken but not dislodged by World War I and the Chicago Race Riot in 1919. More significantly, Addams moved very slowly toward any adjustment of her cultural pedagogical approaches even as she witnessed negative changes in social life and evidence of a growing Jim Crowism at all levels of government.

Locally, segregation isolated Black children and their families from more socialized ethnic groups and this was occurring in the new social institutions conceived and implemented by progressive reformers. Black children were especially vulnerable to inappropriate placement in facilities for delinquents, at least in part because of the limited services for Black dependent children. The Juvenile Protective Association (headed by Bowen) was an organization formed to support the juvenile court through investigations of children at risk; Bowen's studies pointed out in 1913 that one-third of the girls and young women in the Cook County jail were Black (Bowen, Nov. 11, 1913: 117–120).

By 1925 Blacks and Mexicans were moving into the Near West Side where Hull-House was located (*Hull-House Year Book*, 1925: 23). Addams did little to revamp the settlement's program but she began to depart from her earlier narrative of neighborhood transformation where she had envisioned inter-ethnic socialization so optimistically. A "goodly number of old groups were still there," she told a *The New York Times* reporter, "but they were the unsuccessful, the futile, the ineffective, those who could not pull themselves out of the depths of poverty and reach the higher social stratum attained by their former neighbors who were gifted with more push and more ambition" (Feld, March 15, 1925: SM10). How were these old groups, or the "remnants," now presumably the Italians who were in the majority, going to "socialize" the southern American Blacks and the Mexican migrants? Addams had relied on the Irish to work with and live alongside the Italians. It is not clear where Addams placed the Italians who by 1925 had developed significant economic, religious, and educational institutions in the neighborhood and were *not* leaving it in droves (Cipriani, 1933). Sure, there were poor Italians, and criminal activities had spiked in the neighborhood during the prohibition era, but many Italians owned their own homes, commercial enterprises, and even manufacturing firms related to the local food industries supplying products.

On two points Addams had imagined Italians incorrectly: they were by the 1920s probably more *race-conscious* than she thought. At the same time, remaining in the neighborhood did not automatically signify failure or a lack of ambition, talent, or drive. Addams, probably talking about the Italians since they had become the dominant ethnicity, continued to be insistent that "The people around Hull-House are not fiercely race-conscious" (Feld, 1925: SM10). This is curious since Addams had already asserted in her testimony to the Chicago Commission on Race Relations convened after the 1919 Race Riot in the city, that relations between Italians and Blacks had soured (Guglielmo, 2003: 48). Why Addams downplayed the mounting racial tensions between Italians and Blacks in the demographically changing neighborhood is not clear. The earlier tale of the Irish American clubwoman who could leave the neighborhood for a more up-and-coming address, but took the socially evolved position of staying, had been replaced with a new narrative. Now the neighbors are perceived as passive and lacking initiative or innovation presumably when faced with the challenge of integrating African Americans into the fabric of neighborhood life, even though Addams contended that they were "not fiercely race-conscious." And so, it seems, did the settlement house itself have problems. This was made even more apparent when compared to settlement initiatives with the Mexicans. These efforts followed patterns of engagement developed earlier with immigrant groups. Addams had traveled in Mexico after the 1920 revolution as one of "many U.S. intellectuals, artists, and social and political idealists attracted by the cultural work the government was undertaking to elevate Mexico's rural masses" (Lopez, 2004: 91). Morris Topchevsky, one of Hull-House's art school protégés, traveled with her. While in Mexico, himself an immigrant Russian Jew, Topchevsky studied with the muralists and absorbed the cultural pedagogy of the artists and intellectuals involved with educating the masses. Back in Chicago it seemed easier to develop cultural relations with Mexicans than with African Americans. Topchevsky became frustrated with the lack of programs for Blacks at Hull-House; his Left political ideals turned him toward work with American Blacks. He determined that to engage in this cultural pedagogy with Blacks, Mexicans, and whites, he had to leave Hull-House. In 1932, he joined the faculty of the Abraham Lincoln Center in Chicago where he found greater opportunities for interracial cultural work and for radical politics. Topchevsky was a member of the Chicago John Reed

Club where he met the African American writer Richard Wright and the two developed a friendship (Wright, 1998: 317).

The absence at Hull-House of Black artists, musicians, and craftspeople and their cultural work until the late 1920s cannot be explained by the geography and demographics of race in Chicago. Syrian rug makers were represented, as were Navajo weavers and neither group had much of any population in the neighborhoods near Hull-House, so the claim that there were hardly any Blacks in the neighborhood is not a reasonable argument for their *cultural* absence. Addams always made clear that it was not the neighborhood but *neighborliness* that she was promoting; participants in the programs often lived far from the settlement's location and, even when nearby neighbors moved away, Addams noted how often they would return and remain active in Hull-House clubs. In 1921 neighborhood groups meeting at Hull-House included Armenian, Bulgarian, Greek, Italian, Jewish, Lettish, Lithuanian, Portuguese, Mexican and Russian. African Americans were not listed (*Hull-House Year Book*, 1921: 11). They were a small but growing population by this time, but numbers and location had never been the issue. Had they been made to feel unwelcome? Was there a color line policy in place?

Addams had identified the immigrants, especially the Italians, in her neighborhood as being far less race conscious than most Americans. Instead of building on this potential valuable help from immigrants to make Hull-House an interracial community, historian David Roediger says Addams "tragically" took the route of "the typical settlement house practice of accepting Jim Crow and consequently barring African American participation, on the theory that bringing in Black residents would cause immigrants to withdraw" (Roediger, 2005: 93–94).

Is Roediger correct about Hull-House's Jim Crow policy? This is an enormously critical point for a consideration of cultural work at Hull-House. Let's turn first to Jane Addams and her attitude about the role of Blacks in American society. Addams was modeling a domestic cosmopolitanism that rejected Jim Crow in her affiliations and the visitors she welcomed to Hull-House. Neighbors witnessed Addams's hospitality to African American associations—from the NAACP of which Addams was a founding member, to national and local African American women's clubs. These groups were *always* welcome at Hull-House and were visible as respected guests, as lecturers and teachers, and, as friends of Jane Addams. Addams personally engaged in friendships and collegial relations with African Americans and even suffered the scorn and recriminations of the Jim Crow press as a result. W.E.B. Du Bois worried about her traveling in Atlanta and gave her special instructions on getting a reliable cab from the train station to Atlanta University. The Jim Crow world was a dangerous, horrific nightmare

for Blacks. Even Race friends, such as Addams, had to learn to tread carefully in
the uncertain currents of segregated waters. Du Bois wrote:

> I forgot to say in my last letter that we shall of course expect you to stay
> at the University as our guest, and wish to defray your traveling expenses.
> When you reach the depot any colored hackman will bring you to our
> door. Ask him to leave you at South Hall, and be particular to say <u>Atlanta
> University</u>, West Mitchell Street. I wired last Tuesday for a short report
> of your speech for northern papers. This is to circumvent the Associated
> Press which will ignore or misquote us. If you have not time to prepare
> this however let it go and do not worry over it.
>
> W.E.B. DU BOIS to JANE ADDAMS, May 19, 1908

In another letter the next day about her visit, Du Bois was anxious about making sure that Addams is not waylaid or deterred in staying at Atlanta University: "Our experience is when our guests stay with friends in the city this most
extraordinary series of accidents are sure to occur which nearly always mar or
spoil our exercises" (Du Bois to Addams, May 20, 1908).

Addams pressed for full acceptance of African Americans in the country's
political, economic, and social spheres. A review of national positions taken by
Addams illustrates her level of engagement in this struggle. The Black women's
club movement was vigorous and when the Massachusetts group applied for
membership in the white General Federation of Women's Clubs Addams became their advocate. She did so with considerable anxiety knowing full well that
white southern women's clubs in the federation would resist (Addams to Mary
Rozet Smith, April 8, 1902; "Women Rule on Color Problem," *Chicago Tribune*,
May 6, 1902: 7). She lost. In 1903 Mary White Ovington and Addams began discussions that precipitated the formation of the NAACP six years later. Ovington's ardor for a new form of abolitionism probably surpassed Addams's, but
she saw in the Chicago leader a kindred spirit and an influential opinion-maker
(Ovington to Addams, Jan. 19, 1903). Addams fought to seat African American
delegates from the southern states at the National Progressive Party convention
in 1912; her hand was in the writing of the minority resolution and the Black
Progressive caucus, realizing the influence she had with Roosevelt, met at Hull-
House to strategize ("Platform Makers Disagree," *The New York Times*, Aug. 6,
1912: 2; "Negro Question Up Again," *The New York Times*, Aug. 7, 1912: 2; "Important Conference [at Hull-House] on The Negro," *Chicago Defender*, Aug. 17,
1912: 8). When the delegates were not seated and Addams seconded Theodore
Roosevelt's nomination anyway, she was rebuked and praised by Black leaders
and Du Bois, editor of *The Crisis*, the organ of the NAACP, published Addams's

rationale. Addams, then, had no qualms about taking unpopular positions in favor of African American's equality and inclusion and she influenced the discourse on race (Addams, 1912e: 30–31).

Addams did not have a Jim Crow policy for Hull-House residents. Dr. Harriet Alleyne Rice was an African American woman who grew up in Newport, Rhode Island, graduated from Wellesley College, the Woman's Medical College of New York, and after residencies in Boston and Philadelphia, moved to Chicago and Hull-House, perhaps influenced by her mentor, Alice Freeman. Freeman had been president of Wellesley and in 1893 became the dean of women at the University of Chicago and soon was in the network of Hull-House women who were graduate students or faculty. More qualified than most of the Hull-House residents, Rice initially worked in the settlement's medical dispensary and clinic, which served immigrants (Knight, 2001: 740–742). Rice remained at Hull-House until 1904 and had a rocky relationship with Addams who, at one point, complained that Rice didn't have the settlement spirit (Addams to Mary Rozet Smith, Feb. 2, 1895). Blacks made up less than 2% of the city's population when Rice first lived in the settlement, and medical services in hospitals and clinics were segregated. Only Provident Hospital had Black and white physicians and patients. Hull-House's clinic was most likely the only one in the city where a Black female physician could work. Additionally, Rice served as physician for the Hull-House residents and often attended Addams (Ellen Gates Starr to Sarah Alice Addams Haldeman, Sept 10 [1895]). Rice was proud, defiant, and initially chose to affiliate and live in the house, but not be an official resident, but she participated in the meetings of the Hull-House residents, even serving as "Sec. pro tem" ("Residents Meeting Minutes," July 24, 1896, Hull-House Collection). She roomed for a time with Florence Kelley and participated in the residents' meetings nonetheless. There is no record of any other African American resident until 1936 when a young artist from the South on a scholarship to the School of the Art Institute, Lawrence A. Jones ("Va. Painter Scores with Latest Work." *Chicago Defender*, June 1, 1935, 4) lived at the settlement, but it is not clear whether he was considered a "resident"; and when Charlotte Carr arrived there was no one to tell her about Dr. Rice's history with the place. Carr assumed that Blacks had never been in residence; she rushed to remedy this by inviting journalist Dewey R. Jones to become Hull-House's "first African American resident" ("Minutes," Board of Trustees, Jan. 21, 1938, Hull-House Collection).

African American students at the Chicago School of Civics and Philanthropy seemed likely candidates for residency at Hull-House, but none found their way to the settlement even though Civics and Philanthropy was the collaborative work of Graham Taylor and Jane Addams. Hull-House residents included educated immigrants, Jews and Catholics, women and men whose sexual orientation, and religious and political beliefs covered a wide range. However, the Jewish residents were of German Jewish Reform beliefs—assimilated, liberal, and cosmopolitan. One unsuccessful resident, Josefa Humpal Zeman, Bohemian, and editor of a Czech language newspaper for women, was rejected in her bid to be an official resident by a divided vote. Addams had encouraged Humpal Zeman but not a majority of the residents felt she belonged. She had lived at Hull-House and contributed an article on the Bohemian community in Chicago for *Hull-House Maps and Papers* (1895) but the majority of residents felt she was too involved with her own ethnic community ("Residents Special Minutes," May 26, 1896, Hull-House Collection). The few exceptions to the whiteness of the hundreds of residents make the case that Hull-House had constructed a culturally white residency. Dr. Rice's passport photograph shows her to be light complexioned; as one of the "talented tenth" she exuded culture and education that was as Eurocentric as any upper class white woman. Addams's fit of pique with Dr. Rice, in which the ordinarily tolerant leader privately criticized the physician, opens the inner workings of Hull-House and illustrates how race was an unresolved, systemic problem in society that seeped into Hull-House. Rice was fighting layers of personal problems of which Addams was unfamiliar and seemingly at a loss of her normal wellsprings of empathy. The biggest conflict between Rice and Addams had to do with Jim Crow in Chicago. Rice refused to accept the role of physician to Blacks *only*. Although Hull-House was an "oasis" where Rice could practice medicine caring for white patients, to earn her living and assert her hard-won professional status, she needed to find other employment. The solution, in Addams's mind, was for Dr. Rice to work at the "colored" hospital—Provident. But Harriet Rice resisted. "She [Rice] is also desperate about her financial situation," Addams wrote Mary Smith, "she has no practice save the Jane Club & H.H. Sister [Julia] Lathrop has taken her life in her hand and is trying to induce her to go to the colored hospital [Provident]. She [Lathrop]said that I might find her [Rice] in fragments upon my return" (Addams to Mary Rozet Smith, Jan. 15, 1895). Addams already was subsidizing Rice's room and board at Hull-House, a practice not reserved for just this case, since there were other residents who needed "scholarships" or subsidies (Addams to Mary Rozet Smith, Oct. 1, 1894, Aug. 15, 1895). Rice never made the inner circle of Hull-House residents, who seemed to jockey for intimacy with Addams and addressed one another as "Sister" acknowledging a deeper sense of comradeship. Harriet Rice was never referred to as "Sister Rice" in any of the correspondence I have found.

When Blacks first came to Hull-House in any significant numbers, Addams created all-Black groups just as she had learned to do with immigrants.

Journalist Dewey Jones, as one of the first African Americans resident at Hull-House, offers an important perspective when he reported that the all-Black women's group, the Hull-House Community Club, and their children who were also organized into a club, were kept away from settlement life, not integrated into general activities; and he misdated the introduction of African American campers to the settlement's summer camp—they were a small number of Black campers about ten years earlier than he suggests. This report, which was written for the Welfare Council of Metropolitan Chicago, (Jones, March 15, 1939) is one of the few documents that historians reference about race policies at Hull-House. Had historians read the Black press, they would have found a different tone in comments on the Hull-House Community club.

> "The Community Club," the *Chicago Defender* reported, "came into being some time ago as a result of the changing conditions in and around Hull House: a large number of the foreign population moved into other neighborhoods, and their places have been taken by our group; the residents of the famous social settlement are still living up to their ideals of helping the people in the neighborhood to adjust themselves, and our boys and girls are cordially invited to take part in all of the activities of the place. The Community club, Mrs. Adkins president, is sponsored by the Committee of 15, five from each of the following clubs: West Side Woman's Club; New Method Industrial Club; and the Clover Leaf Club. *The club is at Hull-House every Monday evening, and most enjoyable interracial get-together meetings are held monthly; the contact has been not only harmonious and satisfactory, but very helpful.*
>
>   "District Federation in Quarterly Meeting," *Chicago Defender*, Dec. 11, 1926: 5, emphasis added

The details of Jones's report indicate a more complex story. Jones had interviewed one of the club members who complained that in the twelve years she had been attending "they weren't invited to take part in any of the activities that had been set up for the general community. They were not on any mailing list. They had their meetings only. Their children came the same night, and when the Federal Government began to assist in this type of program Hull House ...one of [the WPA] workers was assigned the job of corralling the Negro children and keeping them busy" (qtd. in "Minutes," March 15, 1939, Executive Committee, Division of Education and Recreation, Welfare Council of Metropolitan Chicago Papers.). Jones's report reflected the militancy of "the New Crowd," the labor and civil rights activists more militant and demanding of jobs who were aligned with the National Negro Congress (NNC)

(Hegelson, 2014: 69; Mullen, 1999: 3). Jones, who was president of the Chicago NNC, was judicious in his nuanced understanding of the race situation at the settlement:

> I think [...] the facts have shown that Hull House has not done very much in an inter-racial sense as far as Negroes are concerned. I do not believe that this was because of any policy of the House or any decision on anyone's part but just because of a sort of taking for granted that if an institution was in the heart of the community and had facilities, everyone who needed them would take advantage of them. That didn't happen in the case of the Negro because the experience of Negroes has been that when they assume too quickly that whatever facilities are available, are available to them, they have found they are not intended to participate at all. They are sometimes told in subtle fashion and sometimes in brutal fashion that they are not wanted.
>
> Qtd. in "Minutes," March 15, 1939, EXECUTIVE COMMITTEE, DIVISION OF EDU-
> CATION AND RECREATION, WELFARE COUNCIL OF METROPOLITAN CHICAGO

The membership of the Community Club remained all Black, but there were signs that the changing demographic patterns and violence against Black families crossing "invisible" race boundaries to find better housing, had instigated minor changes in the cultural activities of the settlement. Adeline Titsworth, a weaver who worked at the Labor Museum, began a weaving class for "Mexican and Negro children" in 1934 (*Hull-House Year Book: Forty-Fifth Year:* 14).

More generally, cultural activities began to include "colored" groups. Ida Roppolo, a volunteer at Hull-House, wrote Addams about her experiences as "director" of Sweetie Haygood's Junior Colored Girls' Club. "It is very interesting [,] and we get along fine! As you may know, the entire colored set at Hull House is now doing chorus work under the able leadership of a Mr. Garner... a very fine singer and a well-known one." Ida explained that Garner was "colored and that is the reason he gives so much of his valuable time to the colored folks at Hull-House. His is a fine contribution, indeed." Sweetie Haygood's Junior Colored Girls' Club performed in the Christmas celebration that year (Ida Roppolo to Jane Addams, Chicago, Dec. 1, 1931).

These initiatives took place in the context of the original Eurocentric, Christian cultural milieu and standards and values of the Western bourgeois canon for training, performance, and audience behavior. Hilda Satt Polacheck, one of Addams's favorite Hull-House girls who she encouraged and advised, found out about racism *away* from Hull-House. Hilda read *The Quest of the Silver Fleece* by W.E.B. Du Bois just after it was published, finding it in a bookstore where she had a part-time job (Polacheck, 1989: 93–94). "It aroused my interest in the growth of cotton in the South and the part that the Negro played in the industry," she wrote. Although Hilda had been taught how to demonstrate spinning techniques of Polish peasants and had also learned how to weave in the Navajo Indian tradition—both traditions which she demonstrated in the Labor Museum, she had not been taught the history of cotton and textiles and slavery in the American South. The historical method imbedded in the pedagogical approach of the museum, however, provided Hilda a method of critical thinking (Polacheck, 1989: 64, 94). After reading Du Bois, Hilda "found a copy of *Uncle Tom's Cabin*." She "was deeply moved" and when it was her turn to present a book review to her Hull-House young adult club, she chose Harriet Beecher Stowe's novel. "A great discussion followed" Hilda recalled, and she discovered "most of the club members had no contact with Negroes. We even found that some of the members had never seen a Negro." The club advisor was happy to devote an extra meeting to the topic. Hilda "was thankful that [she] was being cured of this disease of intolerance" (Polacheck, 1989: 94–95).

This could be seen in the cultural milieu created in the Labor Museum and Industrial Shops and in the Music and Art Schools at Hull-House. Teaching neighborhood children had never been an easy road for the art, music, and theater programs when the children were from the "New Immigrant" groups. Interviewed in 1909, when the neighborhood was still composed of families of Irish and German descent and recent immigrants from Southern and Eastern Europe, Eleanor Smith revealed "that the teaching of singing at Hull-House is not that light and easy undertaking which it is sometimes thought to be. What we accomplish is accomplished by bitterly hard work" (Anonymous 1909: 115). The barriers of class and the lack of experience with bourgeois culture and the Western canon had to be overcome as skills and discipline were inculcated. Yet the challenges for the transmission of Western cultural traditions appeared more arduous when the neighborhood children were Mexican and African American (Nesta Smith Oral Interview transcript, January 19, 1982: 10, Hull-House Oral History Collection). Nesta Smith, not related to Eleanor, taught music before and after the Jane Addams years. Her interview reveals the cultural and racial biases at work even in settlement houses committed to working in changing neighborhoods:

> Towards 1950 maybe, along in the '50's, then the Latinos came in by the hundreds, and then the Blacks began to come in. And by that time most of our old reliable European families were moving out. The Italians were going. The Greeks were moving out, although they kept still some of their businesses there. The Jewish people all moved out to Rogers Park and different places like that. So that these new groups that came in were

culturally of a much lower level to work with. You see, they didn't come with the kind of culture back of them that the Italians and the Jewish people and the Greeks did. Besides the Blacks that we got mostly were the southern Blacks that migrated... and, morally and culturally and everything, they didn't have back of them what these other groups did. So it was quite a turn over.

NESTA SMITH Oral Interview transcript, January 19, 1982: 10, HULL-HOUSE Oral History Collection

Many of the immigrant neighbors had not arrived in Chicago or elsewhere with artisan skills. Addams's portrayal of the Italian women's alienation as linked to the failure of their children to appreciate spinning skills assumes that such knowledge of traditional craft was common in the immigrant neighborhoods. I am arguing that Addams's cultivation of a new American identity for immigrants, based on a traditional European-derived craftsman ideal, required middle-class cultural workers to educate immigrants and provide context. A Greek woman, a "Mrs. Konomidis" taught weaving. She was asked, 'You learned in the old country?' 'Oh no, I learned at Hull-House, and Miss [Emily] Edwards helped us to get started over here.' She showed work that she had done herself—beautiful drapes that would grace a Gold Coast home but which actually hung in her own rooms" (O'Connor, 1940: 13).

Addams was *constructing* respect for crafts associated with European ethnic identity. This may have convinced her that she was not bolstering narrow nationalistic ideas but encouraging, instead, a transcultural acceptance of the similarities across these crafts. I have already mentioned how Hilda Satt learned to weave in the Labor Museum, not in her native Poland or in her mother's household in the United States. For Hilda, the museum's pedagogy struck an inner need in her life. She was working in a factory and hated the monotonous work. "As I look back, and this may be wishful thinking, I feel that [Jane Addams] sensed what I needed most at that time" (Polacheck, 1989: 64). After instructions by weaving teacher Mary Hill, Hilda became part of the Saturday evening exhibit: she wore a costume presumably appropriate for a Polish peasant and performed in the museum, even though she was not a Pole but was a Jew whose family had lived in the Pale of Settlement. She loved doing this play acting, however, and learned Navajo rug weaving. Hilda performed this craft, too (Polacheck, 1989: 63–65). I tell this anecdote not to dismiss Hilda's feelings or diminish the good will and cultural exchange experienced, but to critique the pedagogy.

This *constructed craftsmanship* was to happen on the American panoramic stage of public space where people from all lands participated alongside.

Addams's interest in playgrounds field houses, recreation programs and public schools was in large part to build the space where this cosmopolitan cultural exchange could occur. She endorsed celebrating Washington's Birthday with a "large meeting in which all nationalities assemble and mingle their national anthems with patriotic airs of America" (Jane Addams to [Cook County (Illinois) Board of Commissioners, [1912] [ca. Nov. 3]). It appears that African American groups were excluded from these events. The blindness not to see that they were missing, underscores the failure of Progressive reform and the self-complacency of progressives who believed they were advancing democratic cosmopolitanism in breaking away from Anglo-Saxon veneration by embracing southern and eastern European immigrants' cultures.

These public displays may have been efforts by reformers to valorize folk art and craft in an increasingly dehumanizing machine age, but the results could be understood as legitimating only *nationalistic* portrayals of group identity. Not only did they valorize whiteness, but they identified with concepts of patriotism that strengthened tendencies that contradicted Addams's cosmopolitan and international ideals (Sarvasy, 2009: 189). Some Americans began to comprehend the harm caused by the absence of Black cultural representation.

In Chapter Six of this volume I have identified Addams's initiatives to bring African and American Negro culture to the public view in the late 1920s. In 1927, the Chicago Woman's Club sponsored a week-long event, "Negro in Art Week." There was a major exhibition at the Art Institute of Chicago of primitive African sculpture and modern paintings and sculpture by African American artists. Jane Addams, Mary Rozet Smith, and Louise Bowen were listed along with other prominent leaders from the white liberal community and Chicago's elite Black leadership. Stimulated by Carter Woodson's efforts to develop an organization to study the history and culture of African Americans in the United States, this was one of the first efforts to seriously consider the achievements and contributions of African Americans and Africa to the arts and the humanities. The exhibit loaned sculpture from the Harlem Museum of African Art that had only a few months before exhibited this collection of African Art from the Blondiau-Theater Arts Collection of the Congo. The introduction to the Art Institute's *Catalogue* pointed out that "the work of some of our contemporary Negro artists has already begun to show the influence of African art, very much as modernist paintings and sculpture in Europe has also felt and profited by its influence" (November 16–23, 1927). Addams's involvement in this project indicates she had recognized the cultural contributions of African Americans before her death but had found it difficult to initiate new strategies for cultural exchange at Hull-House.

Addams offers a critique of her generation's response to racism:

Because we are no longer stirred as the abolitionists were, to remove fet-
ters, to prevent cruelty, to lead the humblest to the banquet of civilization,
we have allowed ourselves to become indifferent to the gravest situation
in our American life. The abolitionists grappled with an evil intrenched
[sic] since the beginning of recorded history and it seems at moments
that we are not even preserving what was so hardly won.

JANE ADDAMS, 1930: 401

It is an acknowledgement of the lack of progress in civil rights, but we do not
find in her writings any focused reconsideration of her theories of culture and
art and the social evolution of groups. Although Addams identified how immigrants became race-conscious and racist during the process of becoming
acculturated or Americanized, she did not recognize the part played by the
settlement's cultural pedagogy that valorized Western European highbrow culture and the folk traditions and crafts of white ethnics and, as an unintended
consequence contributed to elevating whiteness.

It is safe to say that if you participated in the settlement during its first twenty or thirty years, you would have had very little contact, if at all, with Chicago's
Black population. You were not likely to have been exposed to the politics and
history of race in the United States. I suspect that if questioned the residents
at Hull-House would have denied that they intentionally kept Blacks out. They
would have answered that there were almost no Blacks living in the Hull-
House neighborhood until the end of World War I. What they were unable to
see, of course, was how the high European culture of music, art, and drama at
the settlement implicitly privileged Western Europe and Anglo-Saxon traits.
Immigrants and their children received mixed messages at Hull-House. In the
absence of art, music, craft display, or drama that provided positive images
of African Americans, immigrants learned to identify with whites rather than
with people of color. Addams was rejecting the negative messages about the
so-called inferior immigrant groups with demonstrations of positive but white
cultural constructions.

Addams had introduced an intermediary stage in this process of becoming American. It was the conscious effort to value and preserve European cultural antecedents from Eastern and Southern Europe. These were generally
high culture, requiring discipline, training and skills guided by enlightened
and cultured teachers, overwhelmingly white, upper-middle-class women and
men of the Western European tradition by inheritance and by training and experience. Becoming American, emulating Jane Addams, and becoming white
were relationally complimentary and supportive in the cultural exchanges occurring at Hull-House.

There were clear limits to Jane Addams's cosmopolitanism when it came to race. Jane Addams's own ideas about Negroes shaped cultural production at Hull-House and these ideas share a commonality with the white supremacy of the United States and the privileging of Anglo-Saxon and Northern European culture. Jane Addams was also a founding member of the NAACP and crossed racial lines in her own public life but failed to proactively develop relationships with Black Chicagoans inside her social settlement. After Dr. Harriet Rice there were no other residents of color at Hull-House until the new regime of Charlotte Carr. Addams's protégé Hilda Satt Polacheck discovered the "Race problem" away from Hull-House; another Hull-House graduate of the Art School Morris Topchevsky, who did so much to feature Mexicans at Hull-House, left for the Abraham Lincoln Center where he found greater opportunities for interracial cultural work and for radical politics. Jane Addams and Hull-House had internalized American ideas about race and found, with music teacher Nesta Smith, greater comfort in dealing with "old reliable European families" (Nesta Smith Oral Interview transcript, January 19, 1982: 21, Hull-House Oral History Collection). This internalization of racism must be acknowledged in any explanation of the absence of Black artists, musicians, and craftspeople at Hull-House and for the lack of proactive and innovative approaches to constructing space for Black cultural production during Addams's lifetime. Black leaders saw Addams as a friend who they believed never stood in the way of the Black struggle. Civil rights activist Eugene K. Jones, an advisor on Negro affairs to the United States Department of Commerce commented at her death: "At Hull-House they [Negroes] had no set place but they were eliminated from no place" ("E.K. Jones Pays Tribute to Hull-House Founder." *Chicago Defender*, June 29, 1935: 3). In its measured tone, this may be the best answer to the question of whether Hull-House had a Jim Crow policy. It had no such policy, but its founder acknowledged that not enough had been done to grapple with what she came to understand as the "gravest situation in our American life" (Addams, 1930: 401).

Eleanor Smith's *Hull House Songs*: A Singer's Perspective

Jocelyn Zelasko

1   Introduction

I am drawn to Eleanor Smith's authenticity and the layers of sympathetic and empathetic storytelling embedded throughout her compositions of *Hull House Songs*. Smith tells compelling stories of suffering sweat-shop workers, child laborers, coal miners, and women's rights advocates. The anguish she depicts is personal and her compositions poignantly elicit emotional responses. In setting these harsh realities, Smith announced to the world great strength and compassion. She gave the oppressed a new approach to being heard; she gave them a voice.

I had the great honor of performing the *Hull-House Songs* at the Hull-House in Chicago, Illinois exactly one hundred years after they were published. As part of the lecture recital, we compared Smith's compositional style to German composers Schubert and Mahler. We also compared Smith with one of her female contemporaries, composer Carrie Jacobs-Bond, before performing the five *Hull House Songs* as a complete set.

After the event, I was not expecting to hear that my colleagues were delightedly surprised that I "acted out" the songs. It had not even occurred to me that someone might plainly sing them without performing them! The songs are not from a musical or an opera, but they demand emotional depth and portrayal of characters. They demand the same kind of empathetic embodiment as any other role or character. The following is my response to their surprise.

2   Embodiment of Empathy

> *The arts provide new perspectives on the lived world. As I view and feel them, informed encounters with works of art often lead to a startling, defamiliarization of the ordinary.*
>
> GREENE, 1995: 4–5

Authenticity in writing and performing has a great deal to do with sympathy, empathy, and compassion. Sympathy can be defined as recognizing someone else's feelings; empathy, as seeing someone else's situation from her perspective and sharing in her emotions; while compassion is feeling compelled to help as a result of feeling empathetic.[1] Smith understood the physical, mental, and emotional turmoil of these horrible working conditions. Beyond feeling sympathetic though, she felt compelled to do something about it; and wrote the *Hull House Songs*. Her understanding and compassion are what make these songs so powerful.

While Smith had the compassion to write the songs, she gives the performers the enormous responsibility of empathizing with the characters. The performers are not narrators; they do not share stories from a third person narrative. Each story is told from a first person perspective. The following is found poetry I wrote using all five of the songs within the *Hull House Songs* to depict the first person perspective:

> Why do I pick the threads all day?
> Toiling and toiling,
> Myself, my soul in chaos disappears,
> From that fierce anguish wherein we languish,
> Our inmost soul is defiled.
> Let our purpose be known,
> As we feel the sunshine never.[2]

The performers are not only tasked with the responsibility of empathizing with the characters; but they must also authentically embody their character's unique spirit. It is not enough to simply sing well in grandiose costumes. The performers must become real, living beings on stage in order to provide the audience with the opportunity to emotionally connect with their characters.

---

1 Retrieved from *Psychology Today*, https://www.psychologytoday.com/blog/hide-and-seek/201505/empathy-vs-sympathy July 14, 2017.
2 Line 1 from "Shadow Child."
Line 2 from "Sweat-Shop."
Line 3 from "Sweat-Shop."
Line 4 from "Prayer."
Line 5 from "Land of the Noonday Night."
Line 6 from "Suffrage Song."
Line 7 from "Shadow Child."

We are not satisfied merely with the visual and audible effects. What we hold in highest regard are impressions made on the emotions, which leave a lifelong mark on the spectator and transform actors into real, living beings whom one may include in the roster of one's near and dear friends, whom one may love, feel one's self akin to, whom one goes to the theatre to visit again and again.

STANISLAVSKI, 1936: 320

Each actor has her own process, method, and technique, but we all aim to "put together, to enliven, and to create a sense of life in a whole and fulfilling theatrical experience" (Cohen, 1978: 2). I shape each character's life by piecing together clues given by the lyricist and composer. Using these clues, I try to visualize the character's environment, imagine her circumstances, and respond to her situation intellectually, physically, and emotionally.

I feel I am who I am playing.... You must somehow be that man— not just the part that shows in the role, but the whole of the man, his whole mind.... you have to feel it to do it. If you do it right, you do feel it. The suffering, the passion, the bitterness, you've got to feel them. And it takes something out of you and puts something in, as all emotional experiences do.

OLIVIER qtd. in COHEN, 1978: 17

The best definition of technique I know is this: that means by which the actor can get the best out of himself. It's as simple and as broad as that – and as personal and private.

CRONYN qtd. in COHEN, 1978: 1

Creating a sense of life for each character also fosters the vital connection between the characters and the audience. If I am able to connect the audience with the characters, I may also be able to create a space for potentially transformative experiences. Walter Felsenstein (1975), describes this transformative experience:

This unity [of music and theatre] is achieved when the dramatic action alone determines all vocal statements. In that case, the human truth of the event being portrayed and sung will attain such power of conviction that the spectator will be drawn into the metamorphosis as a co-actor, and will experience a more intense feeling of reality and community than he has known before.

FELSENSTEIN qtd. in COHEN, 1978: 204

The transformative experience must first begin with the singer transforming herself into her character. With imagination, creativity, and my own lived experiences, I created each character's life attempting to capture (and ultimately portray) her unique spirit. Character work is often intertwined with voice work because voices are indicative of emotional states. For many singers, that means the transformation process begins with the voice.

We may choose to slightly modify our voices to fit each role. Some of the factors that contribute to selective vocal changes include time period, style, genre, character's age and emotional state, ensemble configuration, and performance practice. I chose to take the "opera" out of my vocal sound. I believe an operatic vocal approach would have over-complicated the honesty of the text. Additionally, an operatic approach may have created a foreign vocal sound for audience members who are not familiar with opera. The sound I hoped to achieve is closer to my speaking voice. It is equally bright in color and warm in timbre; my vibrato is not as present; the vowels are tall, but not round; and I do not roll or flip my "r's." I believe my delivery of this text setting is cleaner, more audible, and better understandable when sung as an extension of my speaking voice. It was my hope that this voice would add a sense of authenticity, vulnerability, and accessibility to the portrayal of the characters.

The remainder of this chapter details my process of embodiment and portrayal of the characters within Smith's *Hull-House Songs*. For each piece, I created a mental music video. I see the characters' surroundings and emotionally step into those spaces when I perform. Lyrics are always my starting point because they evoke Black and white sketches of the character's surroundings and spirit. The music adds emotional depth and vivid color to each character sketch. In order to properly present my process, I will include the lyrics for each piece as well as additional subtext, related musical analysis, and detailed descriptions of my mental music videos.

3   The Sweat-Shop

The lyrics for "The Sweat-Shop" describe the emotional turmoil of a girl working in poor sweatshop conditions. The song is a setting of a poem written by Yiddish poet, Morris Rosenfeld, translated into English by James Weber Linn. The sweat-shop girl sings of losing herself in the toiling, chaos, and the din of the wheels. I imagine our young sweatshop girl dressed in stained rags that were once a pretty pink dress with her long dark hair pulled-up into a disheveled bun. She sits in an intolerably noisy room full of metal sewing machines frantically fretting over her work. Rosenfeld translated by Linn used harsh words to describe the sounds of the workroom:

> The roaring of the wheels has filled my ears,
> The clashing and the clamor shut me in,
>> SMITH, 1915: 3

He described the sweatshop girl's laborious emotional state:

> Myself, my soul in chaos disappears;
> I cannot think or feel amid the din.
> The clock above me ticks away the day,
> It cannot sleep nor for a moment stay,
> It is a thing like me and does not feel.
> It throbs as though my heart were beating there.
> A heart? My heart? I know not what it means.
> The clock ticks and below I strive and stare,
> And so we lose the hours.
> We are machines!
>> Ibid: 3–6

Rosenfeld even likened the workshop to a battlefield and the sweatshop workers to dead soldiers:

> Noon calls a truce and ending to the sound,
> As if a battle had one moment stayed.
> A bloody field, the dead lie all around,
> Their wounds cry out until I grow afraid.
> It comes, the signal, see the dead men rise,
> They fight again, amid the roar they fight,
> Blindly, and knowing not for whom or why
> They fight, they fight, they fall,
> They sink into the night.
>> Ibid.

Having studied composition in Berlin, Smith set the text in the style of traditional German Lieder (art song). Setting this piece as a Lied adds complexity, depth, and seriousness to the text. Smith sharpens the austere picture described above by providing a repetitive "spinning" figure in the piano accompaniment that is reminiscent of Franz Schubert's (1814) song, *Gretchen am Spinnrade* (Gretchen at the Spinning Wheel). The accompaniment figures in both works represent the physicality of the spinning wheels in addition to the underlying darkness of their respective spinners. Smith used a narrower range than

Schubert to depict the spinning motion. I hear just the sewing needle's movement sharply and rapidly piercing its way through the fabric.

The range of the melody, on the other hand, portrays the magnitude of the character's emotions. It spans a whole-step shy of two octaves. The highest notes of the melody represent peaks of anger and frustration. *Why should the work be done? We are machines! Blindly and knowing not for whom or why...* The height of the emotion also pushes the tempo. There is no con molto (with movement) marking, but it feels necessary to sing these sections with motion due to the fretful emotional distress. The lowest notes of the woeful melody sink to the depth of her despair. *I work until the day and night are one.* She feels a great sense of hopelessness and is unable to see beyond her suffering until the cacophonous sounds of the sewing machines cease at lunchtime.

When *noon calls a truce*, the accompaniment shifts from the constant sixteenth-note toiling movement to sustained half note chords. The soft dynamics, minor harmonies, and slow movement in this new section represent near-death exhaustion, *as if a battle had one moment stayed.* Sweat-shop girls are compared with wounded and nearly dead soldiers fighting to merely survive. After the brief reprieve, the sweat-shop workers go back to blindly following orders and working themselves to death. *They fall. They sink into the night.* After the final note is sung, the left hand on the piano takes over the melody. The spinning ceases only after the melody slowly fades away—just as the spinning only ceases with the deaths of the sweat-shop girls.

Using the song's lyrics and musical setting, I created my own subtext, imagining myself as a sweatshop girl. I wrote:

> This place is deafening
> To my ears... to my soul.
> Everything that makes me uniquely beautiful disappears
> And I become merely a soulless machine.
> Why must I live like this?
> My questions will go unasked,
> Unanswered.
> I must keep workingThe days turn to fleeting years.
> Work faster, work harder!
> My dreams perish.
> I am an empty shell—
> I feel nothing;
> I am nothing.

> Everything ceases.
> We are sick, sore, wounded, bloodied,
> Dead inside.
> Yet, blindly, we follow orders to
> Work to the death.

Working with the lyrics and my new subtext, I now see her horrible surroundings, hear the maddening clattering of the sewing machines, and feel her physical exhaustion and emptiness.

When I perform this piece, I envision these surroundings and feel her distress. Physically, my heart-rate rises; I feel increased tension in my arms, and jaw; and I also feel a heavier weight on my shoulders and in my chest. My head feels full, and my eyes, tired. The frustration and exhaustion are overwhelming, but there is still a story to tell. I must help others to see that this is wrong, show them what it is like to work in my ragged shoes, ask them to empathize with me by sharing my story.

4   The Shadow Child

The second song uses poetry written by American scholar and poet, Harriet Monroe. "The Shadow Child" tells a story of labor and love between a working mother and her child. Like most children, the daughter asks question after question…. Why this? Why that? She asks again and again why she must work, spinning thread, all day long—instead of playing in the sun like the other children:

> Why do the wheels go whirring round, Mother?
> Oh! Mother are they giants bound,
> And will they growl forever?
>   SMITH, 1915: 8

Her mother responds more light-heartedly at first:

> Yes, fiery giants underground,
> Daughter, little daughter,
> Forever turn wheels around,
> And rumble, grumble ever.
>   Ibid: 8–9

The child asks her second series of questions:

> Why do I pick the threads all day, Mother,
> While sunshine children laugh and play,
> And must I work forever?
> > Ibid: 9–10

The more persistent the child becomes, the more heartbreakingly regretful the mother's answers are—understanding that she is forcing her child to work her entire life long:

> Yes, shadow child, The livelong day
> Daughter, little daughter
> Your hands must pick the threads away
> And feel the sunshine never.
> > Ibid: 10

The child clearly picks up on her fate and asks her final questions:

> And is the white thread never spun, Mother?
> And is the white cloth never done,
> for you and me done never?
> > Ibid: 10–11

The mother, full of sadness, regrettably replies:

> Oh! Yes our thread will all be spun
> Daughter little daughter
> When we lie down out in the sun,
> And work no more forever.
> > Ibid: 11

Smith musically depicts a conversation between parent and child in a dialogic exchange that is also characteristic of romantic Lieder, and occurs in Schubert's, *Erlkönig* (Erlking), Mendelssohn's *Winterlied* (Winter Song), and Mahler's, "Das irdische Leben" (The Earthly Life) from *Des Knaben Wunderhorn* (The Boy's Magic Horn), among others. The aforementioned are composed with sinister, agitated piano accompaniments to depict the physical and emotional desperation of the characters' conversation. In contrast, Smith's setting of *The Shadow Child* is quite simple; the simplicity allows the listener to really focus on the conversation.

Being careful not to overshadow the innocence of the child, Smith uses parallel minor sixths and a monotone pulse on the tonic. The tempo marking, *andantino*—a light-hearted moderately slow pace, adds to the daughter's child-like curiosity. The mother's responses are stark in comparison.

There is a musical heaviness accompanying the mother. Every time the mother sings, "Daughter [little daughter]" she sings the dominant (D). The accompaniment alternates between the dominant (D) and downward chromatic movement. The descending line juxtaposed against the dominant (D) reflects laborious work weighing down the daughter's light curious spirit. On her final *adagio*, the mother expresses a moment of rest, "When we lie down out in the sun," But, the potentially hopeful moment of rest is finished with "and work no more forever" declaring that the work will only cease in death.

To portray the child vocally, I create a light, bright vocal sound. I sing with wider vowels, a slightly higher laryngeal position, and a bright placement of sound. I imagine her as an innocent nine-year-old who is desperately hanging on to her childhood. Additionally, I embody a strong sense of curiosity resulting in quizzical facial expressions and body language.

The mother's experience warrants a fuller warmer sound. I utilize a taller more open space in my throat, my normal classical singer laryngeal position, and a deeper more grounded sense of breath to accomplish the mother's sound. I physicalize her with a strong sense of gravitas. I see an aged face and a body worn far beyond its years. A warm smile pierces her lips when she addresses her sweet girl, but her eyes deceive her.

Based on the lyrics and the musical setting, I am able to connect to these characters emotionally and physically. I empathetically feel the curiosity of the child and the agony of the mother while I physicalize their emotions and their experience in my body language and vocal distinctions. I am able to visualize them working side-by-side picking and spinning thread. They have a spot by the window where the girl can see other children gaily laughing and playing in fields. The mother and daughter both long for the girl to be able to play with the other children. But as a child laborer, the carefree playful image is left only to their imaginations.

5   Land of the Noonday Night

The text of "Land of the Noonday Night" by author and American social reformer, Ernest Howard Crosby, paints yet another solemn worker's story through the lens of an anthracite coal miner from the late 1800s. The text conjures up images of coal dust stained brass oil lamps hanging from the pitched black rocky textured walls and miners in stained denim overalls with soot-covered faces and hands.

Eleanor Smith musically paints the bleak darkness of the coal mine in a melancholy B minor and uses slow heavily doubled descending melodic lines to symbolize the miner's descent. I hear the descent and feel the claustrophobic damp darkness surrounding me, the dense musty air in my lungs, the ache in my back and calloused hands from the morning's work, and I feel my tired eyes squint when I emerge from the deep dark hole into the light of the noonday sun.

As a coal miner at a rally, I feel the fear of losing myself in the darkness and I begin pleading with the owners of the mines hoping they will realize that we are people too and that our basic needs are not being met.

> We have eyes to see like you,
> In the heart of the deep, deep mine,
> But there's nothing to mark but the dreadful dark,
> Where the sun can never shine.
> On the banks of clammy coal
> Our lamps cast a flick'ring light,
> At the bottom drear of the moist black hole
> In the land of the noonday night.
> But our home is not like yours;
> 'Tis a bare, unpainted shack,
> Where the raindrops pour on the shaky floor,
> And the coaldust stains it black.
> Not a flow'r or blad of grass
> Can escape the grimy blight,
> For the face of our yard is seared and scarred
> In the land of the noonday night.
> SMITH, 1915: 12–13

Next, I emotionally remind them that our children unnecessarily suffer too. I feel the anger of receiving pittance for pay in exchange for my laborious work and the shame in knowing that my children must give up their education to join me in the hellish pit:

> And we labor with straining arms
> For the pittance they deign to give,
> And our boys must quit the school for the pit
> To drudge that we all may live.

And our teeth feel the grit of the mine
In the very bread we bite,
And our inmost soul is defiled with coal
In the land of the noonday night.
    Ibid.

Desperately, I try my final approach. I feel the bleakness in realizing that this will be my life's work; the humility in understanding my place in the social system; and yet I feel myself maintain a humble pride in knowing that I am good at mining coal. I remind myself that pittance for pay is better than letting my children go hungry. And maybe, just maybe, the mention of God will help them understand the wrongness of their sinful treatment of us:

Who was it that made the coal?
Our Got as well as theirs!
If he gave it fee to you and me,
Then keep us out who dares!
Let the people have their mines
Their own by immortal right,
And the good prevail under hill and dale
In the land of the noonday night.
    Ibid.

I empathetically connect with the coal miners emotionally and physically. I feel their misery and physicalize their pain. I am able to visualize the bleak blackness of their surroundings, their soot filled faces and homes. Physically, I feel the dense musty air in my lungs, the ache in my back, my calloused hands, and tired eyes. I can even almost feel and taste the grit in my mouth. The emotional and physical heaviness of a coal miner are equally painful and exhausting.

6   Prayer

"Prayer" is an impassioned piece, praying for "all strive [to be] reconciled." When I think of a prayer, I imagine a person saying a few words to her God. But the text Smith chose from *Stagirius* by Matthew Arnold does not mention a god at all. I would love to ask Eleanor Smith why she chose a prayer that does not mention a god.

    I, of course, never had the pleasure of meeting her, but I can picture us having this conversation. I imagine her sitting across from me in the Hull-House sipping tea and eating Italian cookies. When I ask, "Why did you choose a prayer that does not mention a god?" I watch as the corners of her mouth turn up and her eyes brighten. She sips her tea once more and replies as her educator self, "Why do *you* think I chose this text?"

I would like to think that she intentionally chose this text—this prayer—because it unites people under any and all gods. Religious affiliation is completely irrelevant. The prayer asks for all of us to be saved from our anguish, tribulations, strife, and pain. Additionally, without the mention of a god, the prayer could be a mantra asking to be saved from the hate, anger, and bitterness between groups of people. Within the context of this set of songs, it is clear the prayer is meant for the oppressed to be saved from their terrible circumstances. I find the poetry and musical setting to be timeless, universal, and relatable to anyone who may be suffering.

I paraphrase the opening strophe, "I pray for you, even if you cannot see beyond yourself":

> Thou, who dost dwell alone
> Thou who dost know thine own
> Thou to whom all are known
> From the cradle to the grave
> Save, oh! Save.
>   SMITH, 1915: 14

Next, we ask to be saved from hunger, the greed of others, and our enduring suffering:

> From the world's temptations,
> From tribulations,
> From that fierce anguish
> Wherein we languish,
> From that torpor deep
> Wherein we lie asleep,
> Heavy as death,
> Cold as the grave,
> Save, oh! Save.
>   Ibid: 14–15

I feel a deep sadness seeing the world through this despairing view. The descriptions make me ache for a better future:

> Where sorrow treads on joy,
> Where sweet things soonest cloy,

Where faiths are built on dust,
Where love is half mistrust,
Hungry and barren and sharp as the sea,
Oh! Set us free,
     Ibid: 15–16

The next section acts like a bridge from giving voice to our suffering to our expressions of hope. We ask for the ability to let go of the materialistic sickness that has its grips on us all:

O let the false dream fly,
Where our sick souls do lie
Tossing continually.
     Ibid: 16

Living in morose conditions, we can only hope for a brighter future. We hope that our next place will be free of doubt, strife, war, and pain:

O where thy voice doth come
Let all doubts be dumb,
Let all words be mild,
All strife reconciled,
All pains beguiled!
     Ibid: 16–17

We hope for a more optimistic life asking for the next chapter to be free of the unkindness and undoing we have endured:

Light bring no blindness,
Love no unkindness,
Knowledge no ruin,
Fear no undoing!
From the cradle to the grave,
Save, oh! Save.
     Ibid: 17

Through Smith's setting of the text, I empathetically feel a deeply sorrowful desperation. I visualize and physicalize a heartbreakingly passionate pleading through prayer. Although there is no mention of a god, the first four chords are reminiscent of a hymn rhythmically and harmonically. Smith conjures a meditative state using a narrow range for the singer and sparse block-chords in the accompaniment for the first two verses. I visualize families on their knees at their bedsides in their fragmented homes. They continually pray for a better tomorrow.

Smith then adds momentum and foreshadowing in the bridge by coupling a rhythmically driving force with chromaticism. This coupling captures the feeling of continually tossing souls. It is almost as if praying needs to be paired with an action. I see men and women pacing like caged animals at the breaking point of faith.

In the final section, Smith beautifully transcends the text. Although the text is hopeful, there is a sense of pleading though sorrowfulness and a flurry of emotions through the end of the piece. Smith builds tension with the use of dissonant harmonies and rhythmic syncopation. I now feel their frustration and am begging to be saved. I desperately cry out on the verge of tears asking for any kind of relief. Humility ensues as I passionately ask one final time for us all to be saved. In the final moments, I send one last personal request for salvation.

7   Suffrage Song

The text for the final piece, "Suffrage Song," was written by American author and nephew of Jane Addams, James Weber Linn. It is hopeful, joyous, and empowering:

> Let us sing as we go,
> Votes for Women!
> Though the way may be hard,
> Tho' the battle be long,
> Yet our triumph is sure
> Put your heart into song:
> Into cheering and song
> Votes for Women!
> For the right shall prevail over wrong!
> See! The banner is bright streaming o'er us,
> And the barred road lies open before us;
> Let the trumpet be blown,
> Let our purpose be known,
> Put your voice and your soul in the chorus!
> There's a voice we have heard,
> And shall hear till we die;

By its word we are stirred
And as one we reply:
It is nigh,
Votes for Women!
For the right shall prevail over wrong!
For the fears of the past lie behind us,
And its fetters no longer can bind us;
Let us march with a will
Till the trumpet be still
In the peace that our struggle shall find us.

SMITH, 1915: 18–20

When I first began learning the *Hull House Songs*, I struggled with my connection to the final piece, "Suffrage Song," because it sounded to me like a stereotypical patriotic march. I was oddly disappointed that Smith chose to set this text as a simple patriotic piece. But the more I reflected on the time period and subject matter, the more I understood her choice.

Marches, protests, and rallies unite people; so does music. Smith's setting evokes visions of people uniting in their cause through music, rather than violently fighting for it. I can picture a peaceful protest rally full of excitement and positivity. As an advocate, I stand tall and feel empowered. I look into the crowd and see so many people raising their voices in support of our cause. Above their heads, I see "Votes for Women" banners and picket signs. The power of music puts a smile on my face as I hear the catchy theme being sung by all in unison: *Votes for Women!* My smile broadens as I recognize the power within each of us, our strength as a unified collective. We will prevail: "For the right shall prevail over wrong!"

8   Conclusion

With imagination, creativity, and my own lived experiences, I create each character's life attempting to capture (and ultimately portray) her unique spirit. Through embodying my empathy for her, I am able to feel her. I feel her suffering, passion, and bitterness. *I get the best out of myself. It takes something out of me and puts something in, as all emotional experiences do.* In doing so, I hope to create a space for the audience to undergo potentially transformative experiences *revising, and now and then renewing, the terms of their lives.* I hope to evoke empathy infused compassion. Perhaps Smith and Addams also believed in creating transformative experiences through moving works of art. Perhaps, it was the impetus of the *Hull House Songs*.

> I connect the arts to discovering cultural diversity, to making community, to becoming wide-awake to the world.... And now and then, when I am in the presence of a work from a place outside the reach of my experience, I am plunged into all kinds of reconceiving and revisualizing. I find myself moving from discovery to discovery; I find myself revising, and now and then renewing, the terms of my life.
>
> GREENE, 1995: 4–5

Libretto for *The Trolls' Holiday* by Harriet Monroe

Printed with permission of the Special Collections Research Center, University of Chicago Library

Source: University of Chicago, Special Collections: Harriet Monroe Papers (Box 14, Folder 9)

Persons of the Play

Granny

Aslog, mother of Meia and Solvy

Peik, a farmer
Olaf, a smith
Svend, a joiner

An aged cobbler

Meia
Ulva
Thea

Solvy
Anders
Tom
Eda
Nora

Other men, women and children of the village.

King
Queen
Graylegs
Bitterkin
Councillors and other Trolls

Ripplewinkel, a noke, or water-sprite

ACT I

SCENE – An open village square in Norway

Peik	Where are you going, Granny?
Granny	Are your five wits snoozing yet, and the sun half-way up the mountain?
	Where am I going, indeed, and the bag on my shoulder? I am going a-milking, I suppose.
Peik	Well, if you're going into the forest to pick up firewood, look out for trolls. They'll carry you off and marry you.
Granny	Good luck to the troll that marries me! He'll have a handsome wife.
Peik	And a wise – and a kind.
Granny	Why don't you marry me then, since you like me so much? I suppose it's for me you're going a-soldiering.
Peik	A-soldiering indeed – with my spade on my shoulder. No, it's harder work than soldiering that I do from sun-up to sun-down.
Granny	And a prettier lass than me you do it for, I warrant. I've seen where your eyes go when you think no one's looking.
Peik	You're jealous, Granny – you're jealous.
Granny	O' course I am, sweetheart.
	(Enter Olaf, a young smith, and an aged cobbler.)
Olaf	Stop gassing in the square, you two, and get to work. You don't have long summer days all the year.
Peik (singing)	Summer days to play in,
	Winter days to sleep.
	Good is the world to be gay in—
	Who would rather weep?
	Get the trolls to work for you—
	So say I!
	Sit on a stile with nothing to do,
	And let the world go by!
Cobbler	Why carry a spade then, good idler?
Peik	It looks well, like your leather apron, good pegger.
	(Enter Svend, a young joiner, also a miller, a mason and three or four women with buckets slung across their shoulders.)
Svend	The sleep gets shorter every day, and the work longer. For one, I'll be glad when St. Hans's Day comes, and the sun gets tired of climbing.

Aslog	It's the women who have to work by dark as well as by daylight, and all the year round and inside out, and mind the babies and scrub and churn, and spin and sew and bake and stew forever! Faith, every man to his trade, but every woman to a dozen!
2nd Woman	And the well and the wood are far away – heavy the burden of water and fire!
Granny	Faith, but it's a weary world this bright morning! Go to work, I say, and be glad of it! Not one o' ye has got so much to do as God – no, nor Saint Peter, nor the jolly St. Hans himself! And yet not a shadow of the blues can creep into Heaven! Do your part, I say. Peik, start us a song!
Voices	You're right, Granny – a song to begin the day with!
Svend	We've got no time to waste.
Cobbler	Tush, man there's no time lost in singing. Look at the birds – no one can say they don't make a living – for all of their singing!
Svend	Well, tune up then, and be quick about it.
Peik (singing)	Look, the sun, my masters –

Each one to his tools.
Idleness and sulking
    Are for lords and fools.
Peg and pound and dig and grind –
Love is but folly and fortune is blind.
    Dawn to dark
    Work! – then hark!
Sleep off the work, for the night is kind.

Svend	But there isn't any night to sleep in nowadays.
Cobbler	I s'pose you'd like to have gloomy winter all the year, with nights twenty hours long. An' you'd like all the children to be grown up and wear long faces!
Peik	Tush, man, he's a good soul, not harder than a hammer nor rougher than a saw. Let him have his grumps – and ours too, say I. For look – here is good cheer enough!

          (Enter a troop of children.)

Chorus of Children

It's summer today –
    Come out in the sun!
Let's play! Let's play!
    Let's dance and run!

The world is all shining
　　For you and for me,
There are flow'rs on the meadow
　　And sparks on the sea.

Let's make us a boat
　　And sail far away,
To the edge of the world!
　　Let's play! Let's play!
Let's play we are soldiers
　　With drum and a gun,
A-marching to battle! Come, come for the fun!

Meia	Oh, mother, mother, may we play out here till the sun chases the elves out of the linden tree?
Aslog	Little children are safer under the eaves. Here the trolls might whisk you away and leave not so much as a hair of you.
Anders	But look! We have brought our drums, and sticks to pound with. When we see them coming we will make a big noise and drive them away.
Meia	They don't like noise. They don't even like beautiful music. And Granny says the bells in our steeple turned a whole troop of trolls to stone. Perhaps if I play my viol –
Granny	Such a wise little maid! – when did Granny teach you so much about trolls? But they have their arts too. Suppose they keep their hats on so you can't see even their coattails; and suppose they come slinking up behind you and chase you, and you find yourselves going you don't know where! And this is one of their holidays too – when they can come down by daylight out of their caves in the hills and cut up all manner of capers. Better for children to be at home, say I.
Aslog	What nonsense! These are good little children, not naughty ones. Is there ever a naughty child here?
	(Solvy sucks his thumb and looks guilty, while the others shout eagerly.)
Children	No! No!
Aslog	Do you all tell the truth and do as you're told?
Children	Yes! Yes!
Aslog	And not one of you has a load on his conscience or any grinning little red devils in his heart?
Children	Oh! No! Never!
	(Solvy starts to speak, coughs and gives it up.)
Aslog	Then let them have their fun, say I. No good child need fear a troll.

Anders	I'm not afraid!
Others	Nor I! Nor I!
Solvy	(weakly) Nor I!
Aslog	Then let us leave these brave little warriors to dance in the sun, while we work hard to get their bread and salt. Come – the sun is climbing.
Svend	Heigh-ho! Let us go.
Granny	Well, I'm no croaker, but child of mine I'd rather leave at home.
Meia	Oh no, Granny, we're tired of home.
Granny	Look out that you don't get punished for that. (Shouldering her bag.) Well, I'm off.
Men & Women	And I. And I. (Exeunt the men and women.)
Meia	Now they're all gone; let's be very still and perhaps the trolls will come.
Anders	Oh pumpernickel and jollykin! Do you dare?
Meia	Course I dare. Ain't you crazy to see one?
Anders	Well, I wouldn't like to be twitched by the ear and carried off to a hole in the ground, where you can't see nothin,' and where they stand over you with a pair of red-hot tongs an' make you dig, dig, dig all day and night.
Solvy	They couldn't make me dig, 'cause I'd just pick up a hammer an' pound a nail right through their stomachs. An' then I guess they'd squeal.
Eda	But s'pose they took away your hammer and nailed you to the wall.
Solvy	They never could, 'cause I'd climb a tree an' throw mud at 'em.
Meia	How could you climb a tree down under the ground, I'd like to know?
Solvy	Pahaw! They're trees everywhere.
Tom	I don't believe there's no such a thing as trolls.
Anders	You don't! Well, just wait till they catch you an' you'll believe.
Tom	Did you ever see one? – I never did.
Anders	No, but my uncle did – when he was a little boy.
Tom	Your uncle!
Eda	Oh, did he? Tell us about it.
Anders	Yes he did. His father was always losing things from his pantry – butter and milk and bacon, and even saucepans. He knew very well it was the troll-folk who lived in the Hill of Fire near by, and one day he took my uncle and they hid down by the brook to watch for the thief. An' bye and bye what do you s'pose they saw? – their tile-stove jumping across on the top of the water.
Nora	As though a troll could lift a tile-stove.
Anders	Oh, but he did – they're awful strong. My uncle laughed and shouted "My, but that's a big jump for a tile-stove!" An' then you should have seen the troll drop the stove at the edge of the water and bob away back to his hill!

Meia	I wish I had. What did he look like?
Anders	Look like – what do they all look like! Ugly little brown fellows, bent almost double – so my uncle said.
Solvy	A troll I saw once had green eyes and horns and a tail.
Meia	Pouf! You're mighty smart. When was that, I'd like to know?
Solvy	When I was a little bit o' boy. I woke up in the dark middle o' the night, and there he was sitting on the corner of the bed grinning at me. An' he carried a little lantern, an' whisked his tail.
Tom	Pahaw! – you were dreaming.
Solvy	No I wasn't – I was dreadfully frightened, and pulled the covers up over my head so's not to see his red eyes.
Anders	Pouf! But you said green eyes!
Meia	A nice troll he saw, an' his sister never heard it till this minute.
Solvy	Well, I guess I know. P'rhaps his eyes were green – how could I tell in the dark? An' anyway, in the morning there was his lantern good as new!
Children	Oh!
Meia	What did you do with it, then?
Solvy	Never mind what I did with it. D'ye s'pose I'd a told you?
Meia	Well, never mind you, say I. Let's play we were fairies – good fairies, bringing good gifts down to the world for little children.
Eda	O, let's – an' I'll be the queen.
Anders	You the queen indeed! You shan't – Meia's the queen, of course. Let's join hands and circle round.
Meia	And sing – let's sing together – while we're floating down to earth on a rainbow.

Chorus of Children

> Come with me!
> Fairies see
> Fine things in this world that be.
> Queens and kings,
> Drums and things,
> Birds that live in the tallest tree.

> Come and listen
> To the flowers,
> Singing as they grow.
> Dance where glisteh
> Sunny bowers
> Then spread your wings and go!

Fly over the housetops and up to the stars,
And watch while the angels peek out through the bars.

In the sky
You and I
Will see babies floating by.
Night and morn,
To be born,
Down they come – I wonder why.
If we kiss them
Then forever
Happy days are theirs.
If we miss them
Joy comes never –
Life is full of cares.

Come, bring now your gifts for girl-babies and boys –
Glory and riches and all the gay toys!

Meia	Don't you feel just like fairies when you're singing it?
Tom	I dunno. I feel hungry.
Meia	Hungry! – that's like a boy. Didn't you just have your bread and milk?
Tom	Well, can't I feel hungry if I want to?
Solvy	I don't feel hungry. I feel's if I had wings, an' was peekin' through a cloud at people.
Eda	An' I feel like I was chasin' butterflies.
Meia	Come, let's join hands and sit down all together. (They join hands.) One – two – three! (They sit down, all but Solvy, who holds aloof.)
Solvy	But I want to see where that rabbit's gone.
Anders	That rabbit – you didn't see a rabbit!
Solvy	Yes, I did – an' he had great white eyes and a long red tail.
Anders	A fine rabbit. Look out or the trolls'll get ye for that rabbit.
Meia	Oh, let him chase his wonderful rabbit. Look, here are lots o' daisies. You take some, an' you, an' you; an' you fasten the leaves on to make wreaths – nice green leaves. An' you –
	(The children pluck and toss daisies to wreathe them.)
Eda	See, I've begun. Let's make a long one that'll go clear round the circle.
Children	Look at this! See here! See mine!
	(Solvy has disappeared. In the background a line of trolls appears, stepping slowly and silently toward the children, their right hands making passes, their left on their lips.)

Meia	I feel sleepy.
Tom	So do I.
Eda	And I.

>   (The children all grow drowsy. Softly the trolls begin to sing; then
>   louder as they approach, while the children fall asleep.)

Trolls, singing

All good children
   Fall asleep –
   Sleep awhile!
All the bad ones
   We will keep –
   Keep while,

Under the world we'll drag 'em down – down,
Where the lights burn low and the days are brown – brown.
   And we'll set 'em to work
   Where they'll dare not shirk.
     He – he! He- ho!
     How good they'll grow –
These bad little children – how good they'll grow!

Sleep, good children
   Never fear!
   Softly – so!
Are there bad ones waitin
   Waiting here?
   They must go,
Down in our caves they'll stow and dig – dig.
If they never come back we care not a fig – fig!
   We'll set 'em to work
   Where they'll dare not shirk.
     He – he! He- ho!
     How good they'll grow –
These bad little children – how good they'll grow!
(Enter Solvy lazily from right.)

Greylegs	(A troll leader) Come with us, bad boy.
Solvy	I ain't bad – I'm good.
Trolls	(Doubling up.) He – ho! He – ho! Ha – ha – ha!

Solvy	I ain't! I ain't! go 'way!
Greylegs	Didn't you put sand in the butter?
Solvy	But that was ever so long ago.
Greylegs	And didn't you steal jam out of the company jar?
Solvy	I dunno.
Greylegs	And didn't you pull feathers out of the chickens' tails? And turn the colt loose? And tell a lie to your mother?
Solvy	How did you find out?
Trolls	He – ho! He – ho! Ha – ha – ha!
Greylegs	Come along with us, and work off all your sins.
Solvy	I don't want to go along with you. Where'd you come from anyway?
Greylegs	(singing)

Seven times a year –
  And this is one –
We dare appear
  And face the sun.

Oh queer it feels
  To kick up our heels
At the burning sun!
  Oh queer it feels!

We like to know
  What's going on,
To see the show
  And share the fun.
Oh queer it feels
  To kick up our heels
At the burning sun!
  Oh queer it feels!
    (The trolls caper and turn somersaults.)

Solvy	That ain't nothin' – look at me!
	(He stands on his head.)
Trolls	He – ho! He – ho! (They seize his heels and bind him.)
Solvy	Lemme go! Lemme go!
Trolls	He – ho! He – ho! –
Solvy	I'll tell my mother on you.
Greylegs	(singing)

Where'll you find her? –
  Under the hill –

	A-turnin' the wheels
	Of our smelter-mill?
	Goodbye to your mother!
	She'll never know
	Where bad little boys
	Like you must go.
	(They strap him to a board and begin to carry him off.)
Solvy	Wake up, you sleepy-heads! They're going to kill me!
	Wake up – Meia! Meia!
Bitterkin	Who's Meia?
Solvy	She's my sister. Just whisper in her ear.
Bitterkin	Meia! Meia! You're as pretty as a ruby. (Meia stirs.)
Solvy	Meia! Meia!
Bitterkin	You shall have my chain with the pearl on it I stole from a mermaid.
	(He puts it around her neck.)
Solvy	(As they carry him off.) Meia! Meia! (Exeunt trolls with Solvy, Bitterkin lingering.)
Meia	(Waking – sees the last of Bitterkin.) Dear me! What dreams! Who's that?
Trolls	(Out of sight.) He – ho! He – ho!
Meia	What do I hear? (She rises – looks about.) What! All asleep?
	Wake up! Wake up! (She runs toward the vanishing Bitterkin.)
	Who are you? Where are you gone?
Anders	Meia! Where'd you get your necklace?
Meia	(Frightened to see it.) Alas! Alas!
Anders	All gold – with a pearl as big as a penny!
Meia	Oh Solvy! Solvy! What have you done?
Anders	Pshaw! Where cud he 'a got it?
Meia	Oh Solvy! Solvy! Where are you?
Tom	He's run away, I guess.
Meia	I saw a little brown man just vanishing into the bushes. Oh Solvy! Solvy!
Anders	They've carried him off! The trolls have got him!
Meia	An' this is a troll-charm – the little brown man tried to pay us for my brother! But I'll go after him – I'll find him! Run and call the people! Quick – run! Run! (The children run out shouting.) There must be some way to find him – down under the hills. An' I'll never be afraid – no, not even if they tweak me in the dark. An' I'll call him – call him – till he can't help hearin' – an –
	(Enter Aslog, followed soon by others.)
Aslog	Oh, woe is me! My son! My boy! How could I leave my children alone on the troll day? Oh Meia, he's gone – he's gone!
Meia	But I'll find him, mother. Don't cry! Don't cry!

Aslog   Who can find him now? Alas! Alas.

(Chorus)

       The brown little troll-folk take him
          Down over and under the hill,
       And then they will pinch him and shake him
          And do him all manner of ill.
Let them mumble and grumble – poor creatures of clay!-
We must bring him back to the light of day!
       Hurry away!
Come – come! He is gone and we may not stay!
       The brown little trolls don't love us
          For they haven't a soul to save.
       The blue sky shines above us –
          They live in a deep black grave.
Though they mutter and sputter and hide him away,
We must win him back to the light of day.
       Hurry away!
Come – come! He is gone and we may not stay.

Cobbler   Just wait a minute, though – we must make a plan – not so fast.
Aslog   Who has wit enough to plan against the hill-folk?
Cobbler   Granny knows how to manage 'em – go find Granny.
Olaf   Look – what a chain they've given her though – the impudent hill-people! We'll put a bell in every house-top and drive them away with noise.
Aslog   But that won't bring back my Solvy.
Cobbler   They won't dare keep him – they'll set him free.
        (Enter Granny)
Granny   What's this – what's this? Just as I said – eh? You'll learn to listen next time when a wise old woman says beware.
Aslog   Oh Granny – save him! Save him!
Granny   It's little that I can do – an ugly old crone like me. But if there's ever a pretty maiden who dares go alone to the dark troll-country –
Meia   That's me, Granny – I'm going!
Voices   Oh!
Granny   That's a brave girl! Why then, if you're going, tune up your viol and sing to them on the way. For the first song they'll lift the rock and open the big iron gate; and once in the troll-country you'll have to use your wits, till bye and bye, if you are clever and keep saying no to their wiles, you can squeeze into the golden council-chamber.

Meia	But how'll I find Solvy?
Granny	Oh, I leave that to you. You much make the trolls do your bidding.
Meia	Oh – oh! How can I do it?
	(Peik comes running in.)
Peik	Meia! Meia! You shan't go after him all alone.
Meia	Shan't I indeed! I will too!
Peik	We'll go together.
Granny	Not so fast, young man. What do the trolls want of you, I'd like to know. Nothing but a pretty maid will do for them.
Aslog	Oh my girl! My girl!
Meia	Now don't you cry. I'll find him and bring him back, I tell you. But as for Peik -
Peik	Oh let me help you!
Meia	Well, he can go to the beginning with me.
Granny	That's all a man's good for anyway.
Aslog	Oh Peik, take care of her!
Peik	If only I could do it all!
Meia	Come, Peik! Good people, give us a song to cheer us on.
Grown People	(Singing)

Her quest will lead her
  Far away –
Under the world
  And under the day.
Ah, brave little lass to take that toilsome way!

Children	Just think! Would you dare?

  She is going down
Where the troll-folk live
  In a world all brown!
Will they keep her there – will she ever come back to town?

Meia	Goodbye – never fear!

  For wherever they hide me
The dear God's here
  To whisper and guide me.
I will seek my brother and find him, whatever betide me!

All	Dark is the way before her

  And the devil may chase and call,
For our troll-folk will adore her –
  Our prettiest girl of all.
May angels walk beside her
  And guide her to the goal,
And may no ill betide her
  To snare her tender soul!

For the good God guardeth his servants wherever they go.
The earth is his and all kingdoms above and below.

Curtain.

ACT II

Meia Oh Peik, we have journeyed a long way into the black earth, and no nearer our goal are we. Never a troll-man –

Peik Patience – patience! They are as coy as moles, and they burrow faster under ground.

Meia And must you leave me when we find them?

Peik Fear not, for they cannot harm you, since you come of your own free will.

Meia But must you leave me?

Peik Don't say the word, Meia – how can I bear to?

   (A grunting sort of chorus is heard in the dark.)

Meia Oh Peik, what noise is that?

Peik Sh!

Trolls (Singing beside a waterfall, whose water runs through their pans.)

   We have dug and dug
    Where the gold-sparks shine.
   Now here we lug
    The glut of the mine.
   Come, Nokken, let your water
    Wash the dirt away! –
   For our king's new royal daughter
    We make a crown today –
   For her who is coming to marry the heir –
   A girl from the sun-world with sun-gold hair.

Meia Oh – oh! Can they mean me?

Peik But you'll never do it – not for all their golden crowns!

Meia Oh Peik – don't leave me!

Peik Will you speak to them?

Meia See their red eyes glare – I am afraid.

Peik But think how brave you were – remember Solvy.

Meia Yes, Solvy – do you think they'll give him up to me?

Peik Would you leave him here?

Meia Oh no – no – never!

Peik Then go forward boldly and ask for him.

Meia Give me something of yours to make me dare.

Peik Something – anything! Here, take the medal they gave me for killing the bear!

Meia	Oh Peik, now I could go anywhere. See! (She walks boldly up to the group of trolls.) Please, kind gentlemen, have you seen my brother Solvy anywhere about?
	(Three or four trolls come up behind Peik, making passes over him. He gradually falls asleep.)
Trolls	He – ho! He – ho!
Meia	But please don't laugh at me! I came out of the sunshine of my own free will to ask you for him.
Trolls	(Singing)
	'Tis she who is coming to marry the heir –
	A girl from the sun-world with sun-gold hair.
Meia	No—no! I don't want to marry anyone—I want my brother.
Graylegs	She wants no sweetheart an' she wants her brother. He – ho!
Meia	(Imploring.) Have pity on me! Have pity on my poor mother, worn out with watching and weeping.
	(The trolls strap Peik to a board and carry him off.)
Graylegs	Weeping for a bad boy – bah!
Meia	(Weeping.) He's our Solvy – we love him.
Graylegs	How much do you love him? Will you stay and marry our king's son and let him go? We'd rather have you than him.
Meia	(Weeping and terrified.) Oh horrible! Peik! Peik!
Graylegs	Call till your voice breaks – he'll never hear. You can't have him and us too. He's far away in the sky-world by this time.
Meia	Oh, he's gone! He's left me! What shall I do!
Graylegs	What do you care for an awkward young fool like him? Just promise to be a troll-queen, and that minute we will be your slaves and give you power over all.
Meia	A queen – I?
Graylegs	You shall have a throne of porphyry and jade, and robes of cloth of gold and pearls. And your jewels shall be finer than a sultana's at her bridal. Come – say the word.
Meia	But I'll have to give up my soul.
Graylegs	What do you want of it? It's a troublesome thing to carry around. We'll bring you the souls of handsome young men to string around your neck like a necklace.
Meia	Like Peik?
Graylegs	Yes, or the Crown Prince, or any mortal. You shall have your choice – a lovely maid like you! – you shall do as you will with them.
Meia	The beautiful Crown Prince!
Graylegs	Yes, look at me! Keep that light in your eyes! Come with us!

(He has fastened his bead-like eyes upon her, and all the trolls stand staring at her and pointing away. She acts as though yielding – under a spell.)

Meia	I think – I will go – if –
Graylegs	Cross your heart three times and swear it!

(Bitterkin suddenly appears as a beautiful young prince, and holds out his arms toward her.)

Bitterkin	Come, ladybird! Come, jewel of light!
Meia	(Moves slowly toward him at first, then throws up her arms with a shriek.)

    Alas, what evil is this! Am I lost?

(She kneels and prays, and during the prayer the trolls, with many gestures
    of disgust and despair, vanish.)

Oh God, the Lord, you live so far above me,
    And I am but a tender little maid.
Ah save me! With your power protect and love me,
    For I am alone and sore afraid!
Save me from evil thoughts that choke and smother –
    Help me to down the foe!
Guide me through danger, give me back my brother,
    Chained to this place of woe!
Grant me, dear Lord,
    A friend or two! –
So little am I
    With so much to do!

(As she sings Ripplewinkel, a noke, or water-spirit, peeps out of the fountain. She rises.)

Rip.	Bravo! That's good singing!
Meia	But who are you?
Rip.	I'm Ripplewinkel, and all this leaping water is mine. So you don't like trolls?
Meia	(Shuddering.) I hope not.
Rip.	Nor do I. They wash their gold clean and give me the dirt. Also, they rob me of pearls. And they dip their ugly faces in my water and make me look back at them. Ugh!
Meia	But I'm not sure that I like you.
Rip.	Oh you will – you will – if I teach you how to conquer them and work off my grudge.
Meia	I think I might like you if you wouldn't look so fierce.
Rip.	How can I help looking fierce when I think of them?

Meia	It's your hair, that stands up like a picket fence – all matted with seaweed. Let me smooth it for you.
Rip.	The very favor I didn't dare ask! Come and comb it out with your soft warm white little fingers, and in return I will tune your viol.
Meia	But I need it to find my brother.
Rip.	I'll tune it, I say. I'll whisper songs to it that would charm your great-grandmother out of her grave.
Meia	No – not that!
Rip.	You have only to sing them to the trolls, and the very king on his throne will have to grant anything you ask. But they're sharp – they won't let you
	begin if you let them get a word in first. Just think how they almost got you that time, and I couldn't say a word to prevent it. But now – shall I teach you?
Meia	Oh yes!
Rip.	Then just keep on with those tangles and don't be afraid of the seaweed; it isn't snakes – it won't bite you.
Meia	It's wet and cold.
Rip.	Of course – spread it out on the rock.
Meia	Oh, it takes me down under the sea.
Rip.	A nice place to be – out of all the storms, with the dark water heavy above you.
Meia	But did you ever see our high green sunny world?
Rip.	Only once a year – it makes me sneeze. And it can't make music like this. Now listen.
	(He strikes Meia's viol and sings.)

> Ripple, ripple –
>   Over and under!
> Come, pretty maid, and take back thy viol from me.

> The drip of its music,
>   More potent than thunder,
> Shall charm the beasts out of the earth and the fish from the sea.
>   And if thou sing to it
>   Thy voice will bring to it
> The paddling of cars that shall carry thee where thou wouldst be –
> The rising and falling of cars to a shore where the heart is free.

Meia	Where is that?
Rip.	It's the land of wishes.
Meia	For Solvy and me? – give me my viol.

Rip.	The music of many waters is in it now – the lapping of little waves, the washing and roaring of tides, the booming of great storms. But beware how you use it!
Meia	Why?
Rip.	Power is for us – not for mortals. It makes them mad. Here – take your viol – and thank you for combing out my hair. Goodbye!
	(Ripplewinkel disappears with a splash.)
Meia	He's gone.
	(She looks in amazement at the waterfall, then fearfully at the viol. She strikes a few chords and the rabbits and moles come out and listen to her. Then Bitterkin, dressed once more like the others, crawls from under a rock and lies down before her.)
	Who are you?
Bitterkin	I'm Bitterkin.
Meia	Where is my brother? Show me my brother.
Bitterkin	How should I know? It's you I want. I'd travel up to the sun any day to see you.
Meia	(Striking the viol.) Take me to my brother.
Bitterkin	(Squirming at her feet.) He – yo! Well, come on then! It's this way.
	(He leads her out, while she holds the viol threateningly over him.)

SCENE II

Another part of the grotto – very splendid. Trolls discovered in council, with a king and queen nicely dressed and throned on finely wrought thrones. Solvy is there, bound to a column.

King	What shall we do with this baggage? –that's the question.
Graylegs	Set him to digging peanuts.
2nd C.	He's no good at digging, nor yet at pounding.
3rd C.	Feed him to the moles – he'll kill 'em off.
Queen	I say give him a needle and thread and set him to stitching
Solvy	(Beginning to cry.) No – kill me first! – that's girl's work.
Queen	Hold your tongue! If your sister won't set you free, you'll get your deserts.
Solvy	How could she set me free! – she's a girl!
King	If she'll marry my only son, and queen it here –
Queen	Queen it here indeed!
Solvy	She shan't! She shan't!
King	But you can go skylarking home then, with gold enough to make you rich for life.

Solvy	My sister marry your son, indeed! I'll kill the whole pack of you first.
Graylegs	Go ahead!
Solvy	I'd rather dig here a thousand years! My sister, indeed.
King	Hold your tongue! Nobody asked your consent. She came mighty near – we'll get her yet!
Solvy	Oh Meia – she didn't! Never – never! If I could only get at you!
King	Take him away! Set him to grubbing for gold till he's ready to listen! (Enter Bitterkin and Meia, unseen, while the trolls are dragging Solvy away.)
Bitterkin	Well, there he is – now don't you tell on me!
Meia	Oh look at them – they are dragging him away! How can I ever reach him?
Bitterkin	I leave that to you. When next you see me –
Meia	Are you going?
Bitterkin	Then I shall be very grand. Perhaps you'd like to stay with me then. You'll be proud to know me.
Meia	You, very grand!
Bitterkin	Well – you just wait! (He vanishes.)
Meia	What will they do, I wonder!
King	It's very troublesome – this getting an earth-maiden to marry the heir every hundred years!
Graylegs	But you know the penalty if we don't.
King	We'll dry up into withered leaves.
Graylegs	Yes, we need some of their good red blood to keep us going.
Meia	(Aside.) Oh Christ in heaven, save me!
King	Often they come gladly – do you remember my grandmother?
Trolls	Oh! Sh! Don't we! Who would forget her!

(Chorus of trolls or solo by troll-king)

> A hundred years ago
>   With joy she came.
> This dark was all aglow
>   With her eyes of flame.
> Her hair from the skies had won
>   The long bright rays of sun.
>
> She loved our world below,
>   And then afar
> She loved among men to go

> Like a wandering star.
> And never a man could see
> But straight her slave was he.

> Three kings to melt her heart
> Fought wars in vain,
> The while on a hill apart
> She snatched at the slain,
> And wove with her song a spell
> That hurried their souls to hell.

> She held two worlds at bay
> With her royal skill.
> She was queen of the night and the day
> And she had her will.
> For glory and splendor and power
> We give to our queen for her dower.

An Aged Councilor	She was beautiful – our queen of long ago. Once she smiled at me till I gave her a key of gold that would unlock my heart.
King	But this Meia is as beautiful as she. Her hair is as bright – and her eyes –
Meia	Oh – am I?
King	She will do for my son – call him here.
Trolls	Bitterkin!
Meia	Alas – I am afraid!
	(Enter Bitterkin as the fine young prince. He sits in state beside his father.)
King	Will she do, Bitterkin?
Bitterkin	Yes, she's a spark of new fire. But that soul of hers holds off. And she has a magic.
King	That's what we want.
Bitterkin	Catch it quick then! It rubs three strings on a lute, and you forget to command and begin to obey.
King	Where is she? We'll break the strings and bring gifts no woman can refuse.
Graylegs	Look at this!
Meia	A crown!
2nd C.	And this!
Meia	Robes of gold! Jewels in heap! Little bleeding hearts! Oh, let me not look! Let me hear no more. Quickly – quickly, my viol – thou shalt save us both. (She strikes it.)

Bitterkin	Do ye hear?
King	Come – put out the noise! Seize her!
	(They come running down, with many cries, but try in vain to touch her while she sings to them.)
Meia	(Singing to the music of her viol.)

From out of the day,
   From the hills and the flowers,
I come to find thee, my brother.
   Ah, heavy the way,
And the long dark hours,
   And the chains that bind thee, my brother!

Be true, be free,
   And the bonds must fall –
No slave is he
   Who on God will call.
Haste, or darkness will blind thee, my brother!

They would give me a throne
   In this darksome glade –
If I yield they will free thee, my brother.
   I am cold and alone,
And my soul is afraid,
   Yet I wait here to see thee, my brother.
I come to save –
   Ah, save thou me!
Be bold and brave –
   We shall both be free!
Come, and evil shall flee thee, my brother.
   (Solvy comes running in.)

Solvy	Oh Meia! Meia!
Meia	Solvy! – thank the good saints!
Solvy	Meia – go back! You shan't marry a troll!
Meia	My own brother! Come with me – they can't harm us.
	(Meia, in embracing Solvy, has dropped her viol, and Graylegs starts to pick it up, when Solvy rescues it.)
Solvy	Here – isn't this yours?

Meia	Oh the cunning of these underground creatures! Without that we should be
	In their power. Come away! Come quickly!
Bitterkin	But don't you know I love you? What is a brother's love compared to mine? He shall have gold in bagfuls, and –
Solvy	Hush up! I can get all the gold I want.
Bitterkin	Let him just try without our help! How can he find where it lies? And you shall have a kingdom – two or three if you like! You shall have a palace in every country, and sail the sea with your men-servants and maidens, and wear silken gowns every day, and necklaces of rubies and emeralds. And if you don't like me you may take a few other husbands. I don't care – you'll come back to me.
Solvy	You groveling base-minded earthworm! Get out of our way!
Meia	Oh Solvy – isn't he wicked?
	(The trolls have surrounded the two, joining hands to stop them.)
King	Stop them – the silly children, who don't know which side their bread is buttered on. Keep them here till we pound some sense into their noodles!
	Bind her – take that devil's music – quick!
	(Graylegs snatches for the viol, and the trolls try to seize the children. But Meia strikes a chord.)
Meia	(Singing.)
	Stand back! Stand back!
	You have no power to harm us!
Trolls	Alas! Alack!
	With magic she will charm us.
Meia	We love the open day.
	The straight and honest way.
Trolls	She loves the foolish day.
	The hard and toilsome way.
Meia	Oh keep your riches – keep your power and glory –
	Yes, all the kingdoms of the earth below!
	I'm for the sun – ours be a sweeter story!
	Back with our loved ones in the gay green world we know!
Trolls	She scorns our riches, all our power and glory –
	These wondrous kingdoms of the earth below.
	Away she goes to tell her silly story –
	Back to her loved ones in the soft green world they know.
	(Exeunt Meia and Solvy. Tableau.)

Curtain.

ACT III

SCENE – Same as Act I – the village square; arranged for the Johannesnacht festival with bonfires and colored lights. A crowd of gaily-dressed young peasants and children are whirling around in a merry rough dance, to the music of a piper or fiddler.

A Girl	Ho – yay! You can't catch me!
A Man	Can't I, though? I can catch you and hug you. There – there!
Crowd	Ha –ha! He's got her! Ho –ho! Punish her well!
Girl	Help! Help! Oh! Take him away!
	(The man lifts her to his shoulder, whirls her about a little, and
	then lets her down in the middle. The others form a circle around them.)
3rd Man	Keep her now you've got her!
Girl	Not while my legs will wag!
	(She darts back and forth in the closed circle, till another youth
	breaks it, seizes her and dances off, saying –)
2nd Man	He's no match for you – try a turn with me!
Girl	I could dance up to the hilltop and out into the air!
2nd Man	With me?
Girl	If you make me!
2nd Man	Come on then!
1st Man	Run away – there are plenty of girls! Here, you Hedda, what are you
	moping for out in the dark?
Hedda	You leave me here alone!
1st Man	One – two- three! Come and dance with me!
3rd Man	Here, Thea my sweetheart, let's whirl till your heart is mine!
Thea	Sweetheart, indeed!
3rd Man	You've given me such a turn – give me another!
Thea	Catch me! Catch me!
1st Man	Come – come now! All join hands! A health to Saint Hanoe!
	(They join hands and circle swiftly, singing.)

Praise to Saint Hanoe –
   He's a jolly fellow!
He likes a dance
   And a drink that's mellow.
His day is the longest,
   His legs are the strongest.
He dares not sleep
   While we watch him keep.

Sing to Saint Hanoe –
  While the slow sun's sinking!
While bonfires dance
  And the stars are winking!

His day's never over,
His night is a rover.
  Come sing! Come dance! –
With the good Saint Hanoe!
  (Enter Peik, sadly.)

Peik	For shame! Here you are merrymaking, with Meia and Solvy still among the trolls.
1st Man	Well – would you have us wear long faces on Saint Hanoe's day? We've been glum for a week, and still the trolls don't give them up. Now we'll try the rattle of our heels on the ground above them.
Peik	You ought to be fasting and praying! Think of the mother's sorrow!
1st Girl	And of Peik's! Poor Peik – the trolls have stolen his sweetheart.
Peik	She went for all of us – she took our task upon her. Beautiful Meia – she went bravely, alone, into the dark.
Thea	He is right – we have no business to be dancing. Shame to all of us!
3rd Man	So say I!
Others	And I! And I!
Thea	You see, we all love Meia and Solvy just the same, only it's so hard to be Mournful on Saint Hanoe's day.
	(Enter Aslog, Meia's mother.)
Aslog	I've been wandering out on the hills – I've peered down into the shadows. And not a trace of them can I find, not even a little footprint in the soft earth!
	(Enter other people, including the cobbler, the joiner, and Granny.)
	These three nights I have not slept, these three days I have roamed the hills – and not a sign, not a sign. My children! My children! Oh, my heart will break!
Granny	Now don't you grieve! The troll country is big – it takes a deal of time to find one's way through it. I've known people to stay there for weeks, and still come out safe at last.
Cobbler	But they lose their memory, or their wits.
Granny	That's only when they go there for an evil purpose, with greed or malice in their hearts. Meia went bravely, nobly, to find her brother. She will withstand all temptation and bring him back.

Peik	And isn't it on Saint Hanoe's night that the hills open, and one may see the red-pillared palaces, and the trolls carousing within?
Granny	Even so, if you can catch the exact instant, and don't wink when it flashes in your eyes.
Peik	She'll see it then, and run out fast between the columns.
Aslog	Oh Peik, how could you leave her!
Peik	Leave her, do you say! I tell you it was magic.
	(He sings.)

Down in the underworld,
    here never a chink to the sun is,
I saw them cramped and curled,
    Washing their filthy moneys.

Oh Meia, – sweetheart beautiful and brave,
    Flee from them – flee!
Haste from that darkness deeper than the grave –
    Come back to me!

They shut mine eyes with sleep,
    They bore me away unknowing;
Lo, I woke on the hillside steep,
    And the sun in my face was glowing.

Oh Meia, weak, alone, I left thee there –
    Flee from them – flee!
Wanton are they, and thou art wondrous fair.
    Come back to me!

Anders	I see a shadow away off under the bonfire. It's moving – look!
Girl	A rabbit, maybe.
Anders	No, it's bigger than a rabbit, an' blacker. There's a two of them.
Aslog	Hush! It's only a flicker of the flame.
Girl	Now it's disappeared.
A Man	Where is it? I don't see it.
Peik	Look there! Look there!
Aslog	Oh, if it could be my children!
A Man	I see it now – it grows bigger – it comes nearer!
Peik	Along the hillside – I must run and see!

Aslog	Oh Peik, if it should be my girl, wave a torch from the fire!
Peik	Yes, let me go!
	(Exit Peik)
Thea	If it should be Meia, what stories she will have to tell!
2nd Man	Three days she has spent in the hills!
Ulva	Sometimes, they say, a girl is wooed by the troll-men.
Thea	Oh horrible! I should think she would fall dead with fear.
Ulva	I don't know. She would have gold by the bagful – and rubies and pearls. And then she would have magic and make people do her will. That wouldn't be bad.
Granny	Look out, child – the trolls may take you at your word.
Ulva	And after all, what is there for us poor girls but to work hard from morning till night, and wither before we bloom?
Granny	Beware! Did you ever hear of my great-aunt?
Many	No – oh tell us! Tell us!
Granny	She was very fair to look upon, and very proud. She wanted riches and beautiful jewels, she wanted to see the great world. And one dark night she disappeared.
Many	Oh!
Granny	After that my grandmother used to hear her mocking laugh now and then, but she never could turn quick enough to see her – except once, when she caught a flash of white teeth and blue eyes and a jeweled crown above them – all leaning over her baby's cradle. You may be sure she made the sign of the cross and prayed her away.
Ulva	I would have clutched her and made her talk to me.
Granny	After that my grandfather went forth to battle for the king. And one night, on the eve of a great victory, he saw his beautiful lost sister carousing with the princes. He was only a common soldier at the door of the tent, but he saw her as plain as the king – all at the king's right hand, in her dress of satin and lace, with the jeweled crown on her head, more splendid than a queen's. She laughed and lifted her glass and fixed him with her basilisk eye; and then he fell down in a swoon, and saw no more.
Ulva	Ah, but that was life!
Granny	Beware! Beware!
Mother	Look – the torch! The torch! It waves – once – twice – they are found!
Many	Glory to Saint Hanoe! They are found – they are found!
1st Man	Come – let's run and meet them!
	(Many of the young people run out. Mysterious voices are heard singing.)

Woe! Woe! Dole and woe!
   She has left us – she would not stay!
What will become of us? Heigh – ho!
   We shall blow on the winds away.
   The rivers are rumbling,
   The forests are tumbling,
   The tempests are grumbling,
      Ho – hay!

Hear! Hear! She is near!
   If we chase her, 'tis all in vain!
Free is she, for she knew no fear –
   And she laughs at our love and pain.
   The wind is our sighing,
   The storms are our crying –
   For soon we'll be dying
      Again!

Ulva	Do you hear the music?
Granny	It's troll music – it sounds from underground. Beware!
Ulva	I like it. I'd like to run away forever like your great-aunt, and wear fine robes and a crown, and revel with princes!
	(Song repeating.)

A queen for our sighing!
Give heed to our crying,
Or soon we'll be dying
Again!

1st Girl	I want to go! I want to go!
Granny	Look out, I tell you! Shake off the spell, or it will hold you. Are you possessed? Look where Meia is coming! (Some of those who went out come running in.)
Voices	She is here! She is safe!
Granny	Thank God!
Voices	And Solvy too – she has brought Solvy! (A youth runs in with Solvy on his shoulder.)
Voices	Hurrah! Hurrah!
Ulva	What did you see, Solvy? Tell me! Tell me!
Solvy	See! 'Twas too dark to see, I tell ye – 'cept when –
Ulva	Well?

Solvy	'Cept when their little eyes burned –
	(Enter others, and finally Peik and Meia, and Aslog.)
Aslog	Glory to God and Saint Hanoe! My darlings! My darlings!
Peik	Light the red fire! Beat the drums! Shout the good news!
	Meia is here – she is safe – they could not cajole nor frighten her!
Meia	Oh Peik, are you glad to see me?
Peik	I am yours, Meia, and no one else's – for as long as you'll have me.
Meia	I like you better than Bitterkin.
Peik	Bitterkin! Who's Bitterkin?
Meia	He wanted to marry me and make me a queen! And he was kind – he said
	I might have plenty of other husbands.
Peik	The burrowing blackguard!
Ulva	And she wouldn't do it!
Meia	And handsome too – and rich! Such jewels! – A crown all emeralds and
	sapphires!
Peik	And a nice little prison-palace under the earth where you could never see
	daylight!
Meia	Ah, but I should be free – free to come and go through all the palaces
	under the sun. That's more than you will do for me!
Ulva	Free!
Peik	Well, go back to your base-minded little prince then! Run away!
Meia	Tomorrow, Peik.
Peik	I haven't a single jewel –
Meia	Beads and shells!
Peik	Nor ever a palace, -
Meia	The forest, the sky, and a cot to be warm in!
Peik	And I shan't share you with any other man!
Meia	What others are there for me?
Peik	Nor let you go roaming over the world.
Meia	Away from you!
Peik	Just an everyday common lot ours will be, and you an everyday hard-
	working woman –
Meia	But with a song in the work!
	(Meia puts down her viol, and sings with Peik a rollicking duet.
	Two or three trolls peek out at the viol, and try to reach it.)
Meia	With a cot and a garden
	And a chicken or two –
Peik	And a girl like a rose on my heart –
Meia	With a cow and a dairy
	And plenty to do –
Peik	And a man to do his part –

Meia	But what need of a man?
Peik	Oh what need of a wife?
Both	I shall live in content
	The most rapturous life!
	We shall live all alone
	Oh the merriest life!
Meia	And never a troll shall find us
	In the sun – on the height!
	And never a woe remind us
	Of our plight that night!
	(The children surround Meia with joyous cries.)
Cries	Meia! Our Meia! Solvy! – How far did you go? Tell us about it!
Solvy	They was green, and red, and some o' them had horns!
Children	Oh!
Solvy	An' they chained me to a pillar, but I wouldn' give in.
Anders	What did they want o' ye?
Solvy	Dunno. Meia only sang to 'em, an' they had to let go.
Eda	Oh Meia, sing to us – tell us about it.
Meia	Where's my viol?
Peik	Where did you put it?
Meia	Oh my viol! My viol! There's a magic in it! If the trolls get it – find it, quick!
	(A troll, who, unseen, has been dragging the viol away, flees in terror, leaving the viol half hidden.)
Peik	(Finding it.) Here it is, Meia. Give us a tune.
Meia	There's a magic in it – would you all obey my will?
Peik	I've known worse luck.
	(She strikes her viol and sings, and the people gather entranced. Others enter, all stand spellbound.)

Far into the dark I wandered
  With never a star to bless,
And the world hung black around me,
  And I staggered with dizziness.
Voices and shadows crept and cried,
  And all my courage died –
When twinkle, twinkle, Ripplewinkel –
  My very good fried was he!
For out of the fountain – tinkle! Tinkle!
  He sang to my viol and me.

Chorus:

Twinkle, twinkle, Ripplewinkel –
   Her very good fried was he,
For out of the fountain – tinkle! Tinkle!
   He sang to her viol – see!

Meia:

Down in their council-chamber
   They tricked out a prince to woo,
And a royal crown they offered,
   And my will in the world to do.
Devils of greed stood by my side,
   And all of my courage died –
When twinkle, twinkle, Ripplewinkel –
   I sang to my viol – no! -
And they had to obey me – tinkle, tinkle,
   Whether they would or no!

Chorus:

Tinkle, tinkle, Ripplewinkel –
   She sang to her viol – so! -
And they had to obey her – tinkle, tinkle!
   Whether they would or no.

Solvy	An' then we just prayed a prayer an' ran an' ran, an' bimeby there was a chink, an' we squeezed out on the hill –
Peik	And then we saw them coming far away –
Meia	And then Peik came with a torch, and all the world –
Aslog	And then they were in my arms again – thank God!
Meia	And here we are.
1st Man	Cakes and wine – cakes and wine for all. And come, children, dance the festal dance! Let us be merry, for Saint Hanoe has brought us luck in bringing back our wanderers. (Cakes and wine are passed.)
Ulva	Here's enough and to spare – let us eat and be gay.
Peik	For it's Saint Hanoe's day, the longest of all in the year. The sun scarcely winks all night, and it's for us to be as merry as he.

(All now sit on the ground in a circle eating and drinking, while the children dance. As they finish their dance, troll-voices are heard in their wailing song.)

Woe! Woe! Dole and woe!
   She has left us – she would not stay!
What will become of us? Heigh – ho!
   We shall turn into stone today!
       (The trolls now appear from behind the rocks, taking off
       their hats as they become visible.)

Have pity, sweet maids –
   Is there never a one
Who is weary of working
   And eager for fun?
Come – come! She shall queen it –
   Geld and power
And glory we give her!
   'Tis the hour!

Ulva	I want to go – I want to go!
Meia	Come quickly, my viol. Oh, Ulva, beware! (She sings to her viol.)
	Be still! Be still!
	And trouble not the sun –
	Sprites of the dark!
Trolls	Ah dole and woe
	Ah dole and woe!
Meia	And thou, whose will
	In evil ways would run,
	Hark to me – hark!
Trolls	She will not go!
Ulva	I must not go.
Meia	Desire but holy things!
	Let the earth take back her own!
	Oh cease your wanderings –
	Brothers of clod and stone!
Trolls	(Faintly)
	We cannot move –
	We are stiff and cold!
	Our hearts are stone
	And our flesh is mold.

All   They cannot move –
       They are stiff and cold!
     Their hearts are stone
       And their flesh is mold.
     They are gone – into earth they have vanished!
       Let's be happy the livelong day!
     For the sun shines bright through the merry night,
       And sorrow shall pass away.
     For the world is a world of gladness,
       Where all the dreams come true!
     For the summer is here – it's the green o' the year,
       And the midnight skies are blue.

THE END

Bibliography

Archival

Jane Addams Papers (Microfilm Compilation).
Chicago History Museum: Welfare Council of Metropolitan Chicago Papers.
Chicago Public Library: Marion Young Collection.
Mount Carmel Archives, Sisters of Charity of the Blessed Virgin Mary: Sister Sariel Redding File.
Newberry Library: Modern Manuscript Collection; Graham Taylor Papers.
Smith College: Ellen Gates Starr Papers, Sophia Smith Collection.
University of Illinois–Chicago: Art Resources in Teaching Records; Eleanor Smith Papers; Hull-House Collection; Hull-House Oral History Collection; Mary Hill Swope Papers; Near West Side Community Committee Records; Wallace Kirkland Papers; Donna Hodgman Mss.
University of Chicago: Harriet Monroe Papers.

Newspapers, Periodicals, and Digital Archives

Jane Addams Digital Edition.
The American.
Brooklyn Daily Eagle.
Charities.
The Chautauquan.
Chicago Daily News.
Chicago Defender.
Chicago Evening Post: Friday Literary Review.
Chicago Times.
Chicago Tribune.
The Etude.
Hull-House Bulletins and Yearbooks.
Newberry Library: The Chicago Foreign Press Survey Database.
The New York Times.
New York Herald Tribune.
The Sun (Baltimore).

Works Cited

Addams, Jane. 2007 [1895]. The Settlement as a Factor in the Labor Movement, pp. 138–149 in Rima Lunin Schultz (ed.), *Hull-House Maps and Papers: A Presentation of Nationalities and Wages in a Congested District of Chicago, Together with Comments and Essays on Problems Growing Out of the Social Conditions*. Urbana: University of Illinois Press.

Addams, Jane. 2004 [1935]. *My Friend, Julia Lathrop*. Urbana: University of Illinois Press.

Addams, Jane. 2003 [1907]. Introduction, pp. 7–20 in Marilyn Fischer and Judy D. Whipps (eds.) *Jane Addams's Writings On Peace*, Vol. 1. Bristol, England: Thoemmes Press.

Addams, Jane. 1990 [1910]. *Twenty Years at Hull-House*. Urbana: University of Illinois Press.

Addams, Jane. 1972a [1909]. *The Spirit of Youth and The City Streets*. Urbana: University of Illinois Press.

Addams, Jane. 1972b [1932]. *The Excellent Becomes the Permanent*. New York: Books for Libraries Press.

Addams, Jane. 1964 [1902]. *Democracy and Social Ethics*. Scott, Anne Firor (ed). Cambridge: The Belknap Press of Harvard University Press.

Addams, Jane. 1933. Letter to the Editor. *Forum and Century* 89(2): ix.

Addams, Jane. 1930. *The Second Twenty Years at Hull-House*. New York: Macmillan.

Addams, Jane. 1916. *The Long Road of Woman's Memory*. New York: The Macmillan Company.

Addams, Jane. 1915. Foreword. *Hull House Songs*. Chicago: Clayton F. Summy.

Addams, Jane. 1912a. *A New Conscience and An Ancient Evil*. New York: The Macmillan Company.

Addams, Jane. 1912b. Recreation as A Public Function in Urban Communities. *American Journal of Sociology* 17: 615–619.

Addams, Jane. 1912c. The Child at the Point of Greatest Pressure. *National Conference of Charities and Correction Proceedings*: 26–30.

Addams, Jane. 1912d. The Hull-House Labor Museum, pp. 410–414 in Sophonisba Breckinridge (ed.), *The Child in the City: A Series of Papers Presented at the Conferences Held During the Chicago Child Welfare Exhibit*. Chicago: Chicago School of Civics and Philanthropy, The Department of Social Investigation, The Hollister Press.

Addams, Jane. 1912e. The Progressive Party and the Negro. *Crisis* 5: 30–31.

Addams, Jane. 1910. *Twenty Years at Hull-House with Autobiographical Notes*. New York: Macmillan.

Addams, Jane. 1908a. Woman's Conscience and Social Amelioration, pp. 39–60 in *The Social Application of Religion, The Merrick Lectures for 1907–8*. Cincinnati: Jennings and Graham.

Addams, Jane. 1908b. The Chicago Settlements and Social Unrest. *Charities and The Commons* 20: 155–166.

Addams, Jane. 1907. *Newer Ideals of Peace*. New York: Macmillan.

Addams, Jane. 1902. *Democracy and Social Ethics*. New York: Macmillan.

Addams, Jane. 1901–02. *First Report of the Labor Museum*. Chicago: Hull-House.

Addams, Jane. 1900. Labor Museum at Hull House. *Current Literature* 29(4) American Periodicals Series Online: 423.

Addams, Jane. 1899a. Trade Unions and Public Duty. *The American Journal of Sociology* 4(4): 448–462.

Addams, Jane. 1899b. A Function of the Social Settlement. *American Academy of Political and Social Science Annals* 13: 33–55 [orig. numbering 323–345].

Addams, Jane. 1899c. Traits of the City Poor. *Friends' Intelligencer*: American Periodicals Series Online.

Addams, Jane. 1898a. Ethical Survivals in Municipal Corruption. *International Journal of Ethics* 8: 273–291.

Addams, Jane. 1898b. Why the Ward Boss Rules. *Outlook* 58(14): 879–882.

Addams, Jane. 1897. Foreign-Born Children in the Primary Grades. *National Educational Association, Journal of Proceedings and Addresses* 36: 104–112.

Addams, Jane. 1895a (ed). *Hull-House Maps and Papers: A Presentation of Nationalities and Wages in a Congested District of Chicago, Together with Comments and Essays on Problems Growing Out of the Social Conditions*. New York: Thomas Y. Crowell & Company.

Addams, Jane. 1895b. The Art-Work Done by Hull-House, Chicago. *Forum* 19: 614–617.

Addams, Jane. 1894. Hull House as A Type of College Settlement. *Annual State Conference of Charities and Corrections*. Madison, Wisconsin: Democratic Printing Company.

Addams, Jane. 1893. The Subjective Necessity for Social Settlements, and The Objective Value of a Social Settlement, pp. 1–56 in *Philanthropy and Social Progress: Seven Essays by Jane Addams, Robert A. Woods, Father J.O.S. Huntington, Professor Franklin H. Giddings and Bernard Bosanquet*. New York: Thomas Y. Crowell & Company.

Addams, Jane. 1892. Hull House, Chicago: An Effort Toward Social Democracy. *Forum* 14: 226–241.

Adorno, Theodor and Max Horkheimer. 2002. *Dialectic of Enlightenment*. Trans. Edmund Jephcott. Stanford: Stanford University Press.

Adorno, Theodor. 1996. *Mahler: A Musical Physiognomy*. Trans. Edmund Jephcott. Chicago: University of Chicago Press.

Agnew, Elizabeth. 2017. A Will to Peace: Jane Addams, World War I, and "Pacifism in Practice." *Peace & Change* 42(1): 5–31.

Allott, Kenneth. 1958. Matthew Arnold's "Stagirius" and Saint-Marc Girardin. *The Review of English Studies* 9(35): 286–292.

Alper, Clifford D. 1980. The Early Childhood Song Books of Eleanor Smith: Their Affinity with the Philosophy of Friedrich Froebel. *Journal of Research in Music Education* 28(2): 111–118.

Alter, Sharon Z. 2001. Bowen, Louise deKoven, pp. 101–106 in Rima Lunin Schultz and Adele Hast (eds.), *Women Building Chicago 1790–1990: A Biographical Dictionary*. Bloomington: Indiana University Press.

Ammer, Christine. 2001. *Unsung: A History of Women in American Music*. Portland: Amadeus Press.

Anonymous. 1921. Jazz Menaces Child Morality. *The National School Digest*: 426.

Anonymous. 1915. Songs for the Hull-House Quarter Century. *The Survey* 33(23): 597.

Anonymous. 1909. An Interview with Eleanor Smith. *The Journal of School Music* 1(4): 112–116.

Anonymous. 1906. Music as a New Force in Education. *School Music Monthly*: 34–35.

Anonymous. 1904a: Current Happenings. *Massachusetts Ploughman and New England Journal of Agriculture* 29: 63.

Anonymous. 1904b. Pencilings. *Congregationalist and Christian World* 89: 14.

Anonymous. 1902. The Third Monthly Conference. *Charities* 8(13): 284.

Anonymous. 1895. The Hull House. *West Side Chicago Commercial*: n.p.

Arnold, Matthew. 1922 [1853]. *The Forsaken Merman*. Leeds: The Swan Press.

Arnold, Matthew. 1903. *The Works of Matthew Arnold in Fifteen Volumes: Literature and Dogma,* Volume 7. London: Macmillan.

Art Institute of Chicago. November 16–23, 1927. *The Negro in Art Week Catalogue*. Chicago: Art Institute.

Art Institute of Chicago. 1904. *Third Annual Exhibition of Original Designs for Decorations and Examples of Art Crafts having Distinct Artistic Merit*. Chicago: Art Institute.

Auerbach, Nina and U.C. Knoepflmacher 1992. *Forbidden Journeys: Fairy Tales and Fantasies by Victorian Women Writers*. Chicago: The University of Chicago Press.

Barnett, The Very Rev. Samuel A. 1899. The Mission of Music. *International Journal of Ethics* 9(4): 494–504.

Barrett, James R. 1992. Americanization From the Bottom Up: Immigration and the Remaking of the Working Class in the United States, 1880–1930. *The Journal of American History* 79(3): 996–1020.

Barrett, James R. and David Roediger. 1997. In Between Peoples: Race, Nationality, and the "New Immigrant" Working Class. *Journal of American Ethnic History* 16: 3–44.

Barzilai, Shuli. 2008. Ritchie, Anne Thackeray, p. 810 in Donald Haase, *The Greenwood Encyclopedia of Folktales and Fairy Tales*. Westport, CT: Greenwood Press.

Bisno, Abraham. 1967. *Abraham Bisno, Union Pioneer*. Madison: The University of Wisconsin Press.

Blair, Karen J. 1994. *The Torchbearers: Women and Their Amateur Arts Associations in America, 1890–1930*. Bloomington: University of Indiana Press.

Blair, Karen J. 1980. *The Clubwoman as Feminist: True Womanhood Redefined, 1868–1914*. New York: Holmes & Meier.

Blood, Melanie N. 1996. Theatre in Settlement Houses: Hull-House Players, Neighborhood Playhouse, and Karamu Theatre. *Theatre History Studies* 16: 45–69.

Boris, Eileen. 1986. *Art and Labor: Ruskin, Morris, and the Craftsman Ideal in America.* Philadelphia: Temple University Press.

Bosch, Jennifer L. 2001. Starr, Ellen Gates, pp. 838–842 in Rima Lunin Schultz and Adele Hast (eds.), *Women Building Chicago 1790–1990: A Biographical Dictionary*. Bloomington: Indiana University Press.

Bosch, Jennifer L. 1993. Ellen Gates Starr: Hull House Labor Activist, pp. 77–88 in Ronald C. Kent, Sara Markham, David R. Roediger, and Herbert Shapiro (eds.), *Culture, Gender, Race, and U.S. Labor History* Westport, CT: Greenwood Press.

Bowen, Louise de Koven. 1926. *Growing Up with A City*. New York: Macmillan.

Bowen, Louise de Koven. 1914. *Safeguards for City Youth at Work and Play*. New York: Macmillan.

Bowen, Louise de Koven. 11 November 1913. The Colored People of Chicago. *The Survey* 31: 117–120.

Bowie, Joanne W. 2001. Kellogg Tyler, Alice DeWolf, pp. 468–470 in Rima Lunin Schultz and Adele Hast (eds.), *Women Building Chicago 1790–1990: A Biographical Dictionary*. Bloomington: Indiana University Press.

Brascher, Nathum Daniel. 1939. A Little Light Along the Way. Random Thoughts. *Chicago Defender,* April 8: 15.

Brandes, Roslyn Leigh. 2016. *"Let Us Sing as We Go": The Role of Music in the United States Suffrage Movement.* (Master's Thesis, University of Maryland at College Park.

Brazier, Richard. 2007. The Story of the IWW's 'Little Red Songbook', pp. 375–390 in Archie Green, David Roediger, Franklin Rosemont, and Salvatore Salerno (eds.), *The Big Red Songbook*. Chicago: Charles K. Kerr Publishing Company.

Bremer, Sidney H. 1992. *Urban Intersections: Meetings of Life and Literature in United States Cities*. Urbana: University of Illinois Press.

Bremer, Sidney H. 1989. Introduction, pp. i–xxii in Elia Wilkinson Peattie, *The Precipice*. Urbana: University of Illinois Press.

Bremer, Sidney H. 1981. Lost Continuities: Alternative Urban Visions in Chicago Novels, 18901915. *Soundings: An Interdisciplinary Journal* 64(1): 29–51.

Brown, Victoria Bissell. 2010. Sex and the City: Jane Addams Confronts Prostitution, pp. 125–158 in Maurice Hamington (ed.), *Feminist Interpretations of Jane Addams*. University Park, PA: The Pennsylvania State University Press.

Brown, Victoria Bissell. 2004. *The Education of Jane Addams*. Philadelphia: University of Pennsylvania Press.

Brown, Victoria Bissell. ed. 1999. Introduction in *Twenty Years at Hull-House with Auto-biographical Notes by Jane Addams*. New York: Bedford/St. Martin's.

Browne, Maurice. 1955. *Too Late to Lament: An Autobiography*. New York: Victor Gollancz.

Bruce, Robert V. 1959. *1877: Year of Violence*. New York: Bobbs-Merrill Company.

Bryan, Mary Lynn McCree (ed). 1996. *The Jane Addams Papers: A Comprehensive Guide*. Bloomington: Indiana University Press.

Bryan, Mary Lynn McCree, and Allen F. Davis (eds.). 1990. *100 Years at Hull-House*. Bloomington: Indiana University Press.

Bryson, Gladys. 1936. English Positivists and the Religion of Humanity. *American Sociological Review* 1(3): 343–362.

Buhle, Mari Jo. 1983. *Women and American Socialism, 1870–1920*. Urbana: University of Illinois Press.

Burke, Kenneth. 1984. *Permanence and Change: An Anatomy of Purpose* (Third Edition). Berkeley: University of California Press.

Bzowski, Frances Diodato. 1992. *American Women Playwrights, 1900–30*. Westport, CT: Greenwood Press.

Carrell, Elizabeth. 1981. *Reflections in a Mirror: The Progressive Woman and the Settlement Experience*. (Doctoral Dissertation, The University of Texas at Austin).

Carter, Paul A. 1971. *The Spiritual Crisis of the Gilded Age*. De Kalb: Northern Illinois University Press.

Cassano, Graham. 2015. *A New Kind of Public. Community, Solidarity and Political Economy in New Deal Cinema, 1935–1948*. Chicago: Haymarket Books.

Cipriani, Lisi. 1933. *Italians in Chicago; the Selected Directory of the Italians in Chicago listing 4,500 firms, stores and professional men*. Chicago: Lisi Cipriani.

Clague, Mark. 2002. *Chicago Counterpoint: The Auditorium Theater Building and the Civic Imagination*. (Doctoral Dissertation, University of Chicago).

Cohen, Lizabeth. 1990. *Making A New Deal. Industrial Workers in Chicago, 1919–1939*. Cambridge: Cambridge University Press.

Cohen, Robert 1978. *Acting Power*. Palo Alto: Mayfield.

Comment, Kristin M. 2009. "When it ceases to be silly it becomes actually wrong": The Cultural Contexts of Female Homoerotic Desire in Rose Terry Cooke's "My Visitation." *Legacy* 26(1): 26–47.

Conway, Jill K. 1998. *When Memory Speaks: Reflections on Autobiography*. New York: Alfred A. Knopf.

Conway, Jill K. 1987. *The First Generation of American Women Graduates*. New York: Garland.

Cooley, Charles Horton. 1902. *Human Nature and the Social Order*. New York: Charles Scribner & Sons.

Corcoran, Deborah A. 2005. *A Study of Josephine Locke, Her Influence on Elementary Art education in the Chicago Public Schools and Her Work at the Art Institute of Chicago.* (Doctoral dissertation, Northern Illinois University).

Corcoran, Theresa. 1982. *Vida Scudder.* New York & Boston: Twayne's United States Authors Series.

Cords, Nicholas John. 1970. *Music in Social Settlement and Community Music Schools, 1893–1939: A Democratic-esthetic Approach to Music Culture.* (Doctoral Dissertation, University of Minnesota).

Cremin, Lawrence A. 1964. T*he Transformation of the School: Progressivism in American Education, 1876–1957.* New York: Vintage.

Crosby, Ernest Howard. 1905. The Land of the Noonday Night, pp. 29–31 in *Broad-cast.* New York: Funk and Wagnalls Company.

Crosby, Ernest Howard. 1902. The Land of the Noonday Night. *The International Socialist Review: A Monthly Journal of International Socialist Thought* 3(3): 133–134.

Curti, Merle. 1959. *The Social Ideas of American Educators.* Totowa, N.J.: Littlefield, Adams & Co.

Daniels, Roger. 1990. *Coming to America: A History of Immigration and Ethnicity in American Life.* New York: Harper Collins.

Davis, Allen F. 2000 [1973]. *American Heroine: The Life and Times of Jane Addams.* Chicago: Ivan R. Dee.

Davis, Allen F. 1967. *Spearheads for Reform. The Social Settlements and the Progressive Movement.* New York: Oxford University Press.

Davis, Allen F. 1964. The Social Workers and the Progressive Party, 1912–1916. *American Historical Review* 69(3): 671–688.

Davis, Allen F. 1960. Jane Addams vs. The Ward Boss. *Journal of the Illinois State Historical Society* 53(3): 247–265.

Deegan, Mary Jo and Ana-Maria Wahl. (eds.), 2003. *Ellen Gates Starr: On Art, Labor, and Religion.* New Brunswick and London: Transaction Publishers.

Deegan, Mary Jo. 2002. *Race, Hull-House, and the University of Chicago: A New Conscience Against Ancient Evils.* Westport, CT & London: Praeger.

Deegan, Mary Jo. 1988. *Jane Addams and the Men of the Chicago School, 1892–1918.* New Brunswick: Transaction Publishers.

Denning, Michael. 2002. The Laboring of American Culture, Keynote Address at Conference on *Hull-House Magazine* and the Cultural Front (12 April), Jane Addams Hull-House Museum, University of Illinois at Chicago.

Denning, Michael. 1997. *The Cultural Front.* London & New York: Verso.

Diggs, Marylynne. 1995. 'Romantic Friends or a Different Race of Creatures?' The Representation of Lesbian Pathology in Nineteenth-Century America. *Feminist Studies* 21: 317–340.

Di Grazia, Donna M. (ed.). 2013. *Nineteenth-century Choral Music.* New York: Routledge.

Diner, Steven J. 1998. *A Very Different Age: Americans of the Progressive Era.* New York: Hill and Wang.

D' Unger, Giselle. 1913. A Sculptor's Dream of the Chicago Beautiful. *Fine Arts Journal* 29(5): 669–675.

DuBois, W.E.B. 1996 [1899]. *The Philadelphia Negro: A Social Study.* Philadelphia: University of Pennsylvania Press.

Durst, Anne. 2010. *Women Educators in the Progressive Era: The Women Behind Dewey's Laboratory School.* London: Palgrave Macmillan.

Ebner, Michael. 1989. *Creating Chicago's North Shore: A Suburban History.* Chicago: The University of Chicago Press.

Eddy, Beth. 2010. The Struggle of Mutual Aid: Jane Addams, Petr Kropotkin, and the Progressive Encounter with Social Darwinism. *The Pluralist* 5(1): 21–43.

Edwards, Emily. 1932. *The Frescoes of Diego Rivera in Cuernavaca.* Cuernavaca, Mexico: Editorial "Cultura."

Elbert, Monica M. 2002. Striking a Historical Pose: Antebellum Tableaux Vivants. *Godey's* Illustrations, and Margaret Fuller's Heroines. *The New England Quarterly* 75: 235–275.

Elrod, Pamela. 2001a. *Vocal Music at Hull-House, 1889–1942: An Overview of Choral and Singing Class Events and a Study of the Life and Works of Eleanor Smith, Founder of the Hull-House Music School.* (Doctor of Musical Arts Thesis, University of Illinois).

Elrod, Pamela. 2001b. Smith, Eleanor Sophia, pp. 810–812 in Rima Lunin Schultz and Adele Hast (eds.), *Women Building Chicago 1790–1990: A Biographical Dictionary.* Bloomington: Indiana University Press.

Elshtain, Jean Bethke. (ed.). 2002. *The Jane Addams reader.* New York: Basic Books.

Epstein, Dena J. Polacheck. 2001. Polacheck, Hilda Satt, pp. 703–705 in Rima Lunin Schultz and Adele Hast (eds.), *Women Building Chicago 1790–1990: A Biographical Dictionary.* Bloomington: Indiana University Press.

Faderman, Lillian. 2005. Love Between Women in 1928: Why Progressivism is not Always Progress. *Lodestar Quarterly* 13: 1–19. http://Lodestarquarterly.com/work/281/.

Falcone, Joan Stevenson. 1992. *The Bonds of Sisterhood in Chicago Women Writers: The Voice of Elia Wilkinson Peattie.* (Doctoral dissertation, Illinois State University).

Fantasia, Rick. 1988. *Cultures of Solidarity: Consciousness, Action, and Contemporary American Workers.* Berkeley: University of California Press.

Feffer, Andrew. 1993. *The Chicago Pragmatists and American Progressivism.* Ithaca: Cornell University Press.

Feld, Rose C. March 15, 1925. An Early Morning Call At Hull House. *The New York Times:* SM10.

Ffrench, Florence. 1899. *Music and Musicians in Chicago.* Chicago: Ffrench.

Filene, Peter G. 1970. An Obituary for 'The Progressive Movement. *American Quarterly* 22(1): 20–34.

Fitzpatrick, Ellen. 1994. *Endless Crusade: Women Social Scientists and Progressive Reform*. New York: Oxford University Press.

Flanagan, Maureen. 2007. *America Reformed: Progressives and Progressivisms, 1890s-1920s*. New York: Oxford University Press.

Flanagan, Maureen. 2002. *Seeing with Their Hearts: Chicago Women and the Vision of the Good City, 1871–1933*. Princeton: Princeton University Press.

Fleming, Robert E. 1978. *Willard Motley*. Boston: Twayne Publishers.

Flood, Theodore L. and Frank Chapin Bray (eds.). 1903. *The Chautauquan*, Vol. 38: 60.

Flower, B.O. 1901. A Civic Leader of the New Time. *The Arena* 24(4): 386–400.

Fones-Wolf, Elizabeth. 1983. The Politics of Vocationalism: Coalitions and Industrial Education in the Progressive Era. *The Historian* 46(1): 39–55.

Frank, Henriette Greenebaum and Amalie Hofer Jerome. 1916. *Annals of the Chicago Woman's Club for the First Forty Years of Its Organization*. Chicago: Chicago Woman's Club.

Ganz, Cheryl R. 2001. Benedict, Enella, pp. 75–77 in Rima Lunin Schultz and Adele Hast (eds). *Women Building Chicago 1790–1990: A Biographical Dictionary*. Bloomington: Indiana University Press.

Ganz, Cheryl R. and Margaret Strobel. (eds.). 2004. *Pots of Promise: Mexican Pottery at Hull- House, 1920–1940*. Urbana: University of Illinois Press.

Garvey, Timothy. 1988. *Public Sculptor: Lorado Taft and the Beautification of Chicago*. Urbana: University of Illinois Press.

Gioia, Ted. 2011. *The History of Jazz*. Second Edition. New York: Oxford University Press.

Giordano, Stephanie. 2005. In the Butler Building. *Urban Experience in Chicago: Hull-House and Its Neighborhoods, 1889–1963*, http://www.uic.edu/jaddams/hull/urbanexp.

Glauert, Amanda. "Hänsel und Gretel," in *Oxford Music Online* (accessed 9 July 2016).

Glowacki, Peggy. 2004. The Practice of Art at Hull-House, pp. 5–30 in Cheryl Ganz and Margaret Strobel (eds.), *Pots of Promise: Mexicans and Pottery at Hull-House, 1920–40*. Urbana: University of Illinois Press.

Glowacki, Peggy. 2001. Culver, Helen, pp. 202–205 in Rima Lunin Schultz and Adele Hast (eds.), *Women Building Chicago 1790–1990: A Biographical Dictionary*. Bloomington: Indiana University Press.

Gordon, Linda. 1994. *Pitied but Not Entitled: Single Mothers and the History of Welfare, 1890–1935*. New York: The Free Press.

Green, Nancy E. (ed.). 2004a. *Byrdcliffe: An American Arts and Crafts Colony*. Ithaca: Cornell University Press.

Green, Nancy E. 2004b. Byrdcliffe and the 'Dream of Somewhere'. *Journal of the Decorative Arts Society, 1850 to the Present* 28: 56–81.

Green, Shannon. 1998. *'Art for Life's Sake': Music Schools and Activities in U.S. Social Settlement Houses, 1892–1942*. (Doctoral Dissertation, University of Wisconsin).

Greene, Daniel. 2006. A Chosen People in a Pluralist Nation: Horace Kallen and the Jewish-American Experience. *Religion and American Culture: A Journal of Interpretation* 16(2): 161–194.

Greene, Maxine. 1995. *Releasing the Imagination: Essays on Education, the Arts, and Social Change.* San Francisco: Jossey-Bass.

Gutman, Herbert. 1987. Class Composition and the Development of the American Working Class, 1840–1890, pp. 380–394 in Ira Berlin (ed.) *Power & Culture: Essays on the American Working Class.* New York: The New Press.

Hains, Dickey D. 1910. Greek Plays in America. *The Classical Journal* 6(1): 34–35.

Hamilton, Alice. 1995. *Exploring the Dangerous Trades: The Autobiography of Alice Hamilton, M.D.* Beverly, MA: OEM Press.

Hamington, Maurice. (ed.). 2010. *Feminist Interpretations of Jane Addams.* University Park: The Pennsylvania State University Press.

Hayden, Dolores. 1995. *The Grand Domestic Revolution.* Cambridge: MIT Press.

Hayes, Frank L. 1939. Dewey R. Jones Dies; Assistant at Hull-House. *Chicago Daily News,* April 11: 6.

Heathorn, Stephen J. 1998. E.P. Thompson, Methodism, and the 'Culturalist' Approach to the Historical Study of Religion. *Method & Theory in the Study of Religion* 10(2): 210–224.

Hecht, Stuart J. with Lauren Bufferd. 2001. Pelham, Laura Dainty, pp. 684–686 in Rima Lunin Schultz and Adele Hast (eds.), *Women Building Chicago 1790- 1990: A Biographical Dictionary.* Bloomington: Indiana University Press.

Hecht, Stuart J. with Lauren Bufferd., 1982. Social and Artistic Integration: The Emergence of Hull-House Theater. *Theatre Journal* 34(2): 172–182.

Height, Dorothy. 2003. *Open Wide the Freedom Gates.* New York: Public Affairs Books.

Helgeson, Jeffrey. 2014. *Crucibles of Black Empowerment: Chicago's Neighborhood Politics from the New Deal to Harold Washington.* Chicago: University of Chicago Press.

Higham, John. 1955. *Strangers in the Land: Patterns of Nativism, 1860–1925.* New Brunswick: Rutgers University Press.

Hill, Caroline. 1938. *Mary McDowell and Municipal Housekeeping: A Symposium.* Chicago: Millar Publishing Company.

Hinderliter, Alison. 2008. *Inventory of the Frederic Grant Gleason Papers Finding Aid.* Chicago, IL: Newberry Library Online. https://mms.newberry.org/xml/xml:files/Gleason.xml.

Hobsbawm, Eric J. 1989. *The Age of Empire, 1875–1914.* New York: Vintage Books.

Holli, Melvin G. and Peter d'A Jones. (eds.). 1995. *Ethnic Chicago: A Multicultural Portrait.* Grand Rapids, Michigan: Eerdmans Publishing Company.

Hooker, George E. 1895. Tom Mann, the English Labor Agitator, at Home. *New Outlook* 52: 382–383.

Horowitz, Helen Lefkowitz. 1976. *Culture & The City: Cultural Philanthropists in Chicago from the 1880s to 1917*. Lexington: The University Press of Kentucky.

Howe, Sondra Wieland. 2014. *Women Music Educators in the United States*. Lanham: Scarecrow.

Howe, Sondra Wieland. 2009. A Historical View of Women in Music Education Careers. *Philosophy of Music Education Review* 17(2): 162–183.

Hoy, Suellen. 2010. *Ellen Gates Starr. Her Later Years*. Chicago: Chicago History Museum.

Hunt, D. Bradford. 2009. *Blueprint for Disaster: The Unraveling of Chicago Public Housing*. Chicago: University of Chicago Press.

Jacobs, Glenn. 2006. *Charles Horton Cooley: Imagining Social Reality*. Boston: University of Massachusetts Press.

Jacobson, J.Z. 1933. *Art of Today: Chicago 1933*. Chicago: L.M. Stein, 1933.

Jackson, Shannon. 2001. Nancrede, Edith de, pp. 618–620 in Rima Lunin Schultz and Adele Hast (eds.), *Women Building Chicago 1790–1990: A Biographical Dictionary*. Bloomington: Indiana University Press.

Jackson, Shannon. 2000. *Lines of Activity: Performance, Historiography, Hull-House Domesticity*. Ann Arbor: University of Michigan Press.

James, Barbara and Walter Mossmann. (eds.). 1983. *Glasbruch 1848: Flugblätterlieder und Dokumente einer zerbrochenen Revolution*. Darmstadt: Luchterhand.

James, Cathy L. 1998. Not Merely for the Sake of an Evening's Entertainment: The Educational Uses of Theater in Toronto's Settlement Houses, 1910–1930. *History of Education Quarterly* 38(3): 287–311.

James, William. 1987. *Writings: 1902–1910*. New York: Library Classics.

Jewett, Eleanor. June 16. 1929. Students' Work Shown at Institute. News of Exhibits. *Chicago Tribune*: 17.

Jewett, Eleanor, May 4, 1935. Tense Realism Key of Equity Art Exhibition. *Chicago Tribune:* 17.

Johnson, Stanley C. 2010. *The Joyful Stoic: A Study of the Poetry and the Prose of Matthew Arnold*. (Doctoral dissertation, University of Nebraska).

Joslin, Katherine. 2004. *Jane Addams, A Writer's Life*. Urbana: University of Illinois Press.

Kallen, Horace M. 1915. Democracy Versus the Melting Pot. *Nation* 100: 190–194, 217–220.

Kaye, Harvey J. and Keith McClelland (eds.). 1990. *E.P. Thompson: Critical Perspectives*. Philadelphia: Temple University Press.

Keil, Hartmut and John B. Jentz (eds.). 1988. *German Workers in Chicago: A Documentary History of Working-Class Culture*. Urbana: University of Illinois Press.

Kelley, Florence. 1898. Hull-House. *New England Magazine* 18(5): 550–566.

Kelley, Nicholas. 1954. Early Days at Hull House. *Social Service Review* 28(4): 426.

Kellum, David W. April 15, 1939. Death Claims Dewey R. Jones; Journalist is Buried After Simple Rites; Loses Fight with Death After Illness of Nine Days. *Chicago Defender:* 1.

Kennedy, Albert J. 1929. The Merman's Bride. *Neighborhood: A Settlement Quarterly* 2(2): 84–96.

Kenney, William Howland. 1993. *Chicago Jazz: A Cultural History*. New York: Oxford University Press.

Knight, Louise W. 2010a. *Jane Addams: Spirit in Action*. New York: W.W. Norton.

Knight, Louise W. 2010b. Love on Halsted Street: A Contemplation on Jane Addams, pp. 181–197 in Maurice Hamington (ed.), *Feminist Interpretations of Jane Addams*. University Park, PA: The Pennsylvania State University Press.

Knight, Louise W. 2005. *Citizen: Jane Addams and the Struggle for Democracy*. Chicago: University of Chicago Press.

Knight, Louise W. 2001. Rice, Harriet Alleyne, pp. 740–724 in Rima Lunin Schultz and Adele Hast (eds.), *Women Building Chicago 1790–1990: A Biographical Dictionary*. Bloomington: Indiana University Press.

Kolb, Fabian. 2004. Moszkowski, Moritz in *Die Musik in Geschichte und Gegenwart Online* (accessed 25 April 2017).

Kopan, Andrew T. 1989. *The Greeks in Chicago*. Urbana: University of Illinois Press.

Lasch-Quinn, Elisabeth. 1993. *Black Neighbors: Race and the Limits of Reform in the American Settlement House Movement, 1890–1945*. Chapel Hill: The University of North Carolina Press.

Lear, T.K. Jackson. 1981. *No Place of Grace: Antimodernism and the Transformation of American Culture, 1880–1920*. Chicago: University of Chicago Press.

Levine, Lawrence W. 1988. *Highbrow/Lowbrow: The Emergence of Cultural Hierarchy in America*. Cambridge: Harvard University Press.

Liebergen, Patrick M. 1981. The Cecilian Movement in The Nineteenth Century Summary of the Movement. *The Choral Journal* 21(9): 13–16.

Lieberman, Marcia. 1972. Some Day My Prince Will Come: Female Acculturation through the Fairy Tale. *College English* 34(3): 383–395.

Lindow, John. 2014. *Trolls: An Unnatural History*. London: Reaktion.

Linn, James Weber. 1935. *Jane Addams: A Biography*. New York: D. Appleton-Century Company.

Lissak, Rivka Shpak. 1989. *Pluralism & Progressives: Hull-House and the New Immigrants, 1890–1919*. Chicago: University of Chicago Press.

Lopez, Rick A. 2004. Forging a Mexican National Identity in Chicago: Mexican Migrants and Hull-House, pp. 89–110 in Cheryl Ganz and Margaret Strobel, (eds.), *Pots of Promise: Mexican Pottery at Hull-House, 1920–1940*. Urbana: University of Illinois Press.

Lovett, Robert Morss. 1948. *All Our Years*. New York: The Viking Press.

Luther, Jessie. 1902. The Labor Museum at Hull-House. *Commons* 7(70): 7–8.

Lyons, John F. 2001. Rich, Adena Miller, pp. 742–744 in Rima Lunin Schultz and Adele Hast (eds.), *Women Building Chicago 1790–1990: A Biographical Dictionary*. Bloomington: Indiana University Press.

Marx, Karl and Friederick Engels. 1988. *The German Ideology*. New York: International Publishers.

Massa, Ann. 1986. "The Columbian Ode" and *Poetry, A Magazine of Verse*: Harriet Monroe's Entrepreneurial Triumphs. *Journal of American Studies* 20(1): 51–69.

Matz, Diana. 2006. *British Aestheticism and the Urban Working Classes, 1870–1900. Beauty for the People*. New York: Palgrave Macmillan.

Mayer, Milton. 1938. Charlotte Carr—Settlement Lady. *Atlantic Monthly* 162(6): 741–748.

McCarthy, Kathleen. 1982. *Noblesse Oblige: Charity and Cultural Philanthropy in Chicago, 1849–1929*. Chicago: University of Chicago Press.

McCarthy, Malachy R. 2002. *Which Christ Came to Chicago: Catholic and Protestant Programs to Evangelize, Socialize and Americanize the Mexican Immigrant, 1900–1940*. (Doctoral Dissertation, Loyola University Chicago).

McCreesh, Carolyn Daniel. 1985. *Women in the Campaign to Organize Garment Workers, 1880–1917*. New York: Garland Publishing.

McGerr, Michael E. 2003. *A Fierce Discontent: The Rise and Fall of the Progressive Movement in America*. New York: Free Press.

McLoughlin, William G. 1978. *Revivals, Awakenings, and Reform*. Chicago: The University of Chicago Press.

Michael, Vincent L. 2005. Recovering the Layout of the Hull House Complex in *Urban Experience in Chicago: Touring the Buildings: Inside the Complex*. http://www.uic.edu/jaddams/hull/urbanexp.

Miller, Edith Wylie. 1991. *Harriet Monroe: The Formative Years*. (Master's thesis, Stephen F. Austin State University).

Miller, Elisabeth. 1918. Fairy operetta at Hull-House. *Social Progress* 2: 317–318.

Miller, Marc. 2007. *Representing the Immigrant Experience: Morris Rosenfeld and the Representation of Immigrant Experience in America*. Syracuse: Syracuse University Press.

Mink, Gwendolyn. 1996. *The Wages of Motherhood: Inequality in the Welfare State, 1917–1942*. Ithaca: Cornell University Press.

Monroe, Harriet. 1938. *A Poet's Life*. New York: Macmillan.

Monroe, Harriet. 1918. Editor's Note, *Poetry* 13(1): 37–41.

Monroe, Harriet. 1914. The Shadow Child, pp. 84–87 in *You and I*. New York: Macmillan, 1914.

Monroe, Harriet and Alice Corbin Henderson. 1918. *The New Poetry: An Anthology*. New York: Macmillan.

Mooney, Amy M. 2004. *Archibald J. Motley Jr*. San Francisco: Pomegranate.

Morgan, Anna. 1918. *My Chicago*. Chicago: Ralph Fletcher Seymour.

Morris, William. 1915. Art and Socialism, pp. 192–214 in May Morris (ed.), *The Works of William Morris, Vol. 23*. London: Longmans, Green and Company.

Motley, Willard. 1940. Negro Art in Chicago. *Opportunity: Journal of Negro Life* 18(1): 19–22; 28.

Muhammad, Khalil Gibran. 2010. *The Condemnation of Blackness: Race, Crime, and the Making of Modern Urban America.* Cambridge: Harvard University Press.

Mullen, Bill V. 1999. *Popular Fronts: Chicago and African-American Cultural Politics, 1935–46.* Urbana: University of Illinois Press.

Muncy, Robyn. 1994. *Creating a Female Dominion in American Reform, 1890–1935.* New York: Oxford University Press.

Nancrede, Edith de. 1928. Dramatic Work at Hull-House. *Neighborhood: A Settlement Quarterly* 1(1): 23–28.

Nelli, Humbert S. 1970. John Powers and the Italians: Politics in A Chicago Ward, 1896–1921. *The Journal of American History* 57(1): 67–84.

Nillson, Christine. Dec. 12, 1894. Chicago: The Culmination of the Religious Movement of the Nineteenth Century. *Chicago Tribune*: 41.

Nugent, Walter T.K. 2009. *Habits of Empire.* New York: Vintage.

O'Connor, Harvey. 1940. Mansion On Earth. *Hull-House Magazine* 1 (3): 13.

Orsi, Robert A. 1988. *The Madonna of 115th Street.* New Haven: Yale University Press.

Otis, Philo Adams. 1924. *The Chicago Symphony Orchestra: Its Organization, Growth, and Development, 1891–1924.* Chicago: Clayton F. Summy Company.

Otis, Philo Adams. 1913. *The First Presbyterian Church, 1833–1913.* Chicago: F.H. Revell Company.

Pacyga, Dominic. 2009. *Chicago, A Biography.* Chicago: University of Chicago Press.

Pagano, Mary Jo. 1996. *The History of the Third Street Music School Settlement, 1894–1984.* (Doctor of Musical Arts Thesis, Manhattan School of Music).

Palmieri, Patricia Ann. 1995. Symmetrical Womanhood: The Educational Ideology of Activism at Wellesley. *Academe* 81(4): 16–20.

Paris, Bernard J. Dec. 1962. George Eliot's Religion of Humanity. *English Literary History* 29(4): 418–443.

Payne, Elizabeth. 1988. *Reform, Labor, and Feminism: Margaret Dreier Robins and the Women's Trade Union League.* Urbana: University of Illinois Press.

Peiss, Kathy. 1986. *Cheap Amusements: Working Women and Leisure in Turn-of-the-Century New York.* Philadelphia: Temple University Press.

Philpott, Thomas Lee. 1978. *The Slum and the Ghetto: Neighborhood Deterioration and Middle-Class Reform, Chicago, 1880–1930.* New York: Oxford University Press.

Pinkerton, Jan and Randolph Hudson. 2004. *Encyclopedia of the Chicago Literary Renaissance.* New York, NY: Facts on File.

Platt, Harold L. 2005. *Shock Cities.* Chicago: University of Chicago Press.

Platt, Harold L. 2000. Jane Addams and the Ward Boss Revisited: Class, Politics, and Public Health in Chicago, 1890–1930. *Environmental History* 5(2): 194–222.

Polacheck, Hilda Satt. 1989. *I Came A Stranger: The Story of a Hull-House Girl*. Dena J. Polacheck Epstein (ed.). Urbana: University of Illinois Press.

Polanyi, Karl. 2001. *The Great Transformation*. Second Edition. Boston: Beacon Press.

Powell, Mary Badollet. 1896. The Story of a Child Trainer. *The Cosmopolitan* 21(6): 582–591.

Prieto, Laura R. 2001. *At Home in the Studio: The Professionalization of Women Artists in America*. Cambridge: Harvard University Press.

Prindiville, Kate Gertrude. 1903. Italy in Chicago. *Catholic World* 77(460): 452–461.

Provenzo Jr., Eugene F. 2009. Laboratory School, University of Chicago in *Encyclopedia of the Social and Cultural Foundations of Education*. Thousand Oaks, CA: Sage.

Raleigh, John Henry. 1961. *Matthew Arnold and American Culture*. Berkeley: University of California Press.

Ramsey, Martha and Duane Ramsey. 1933. The Settlement Music School. *Music Supervisors' Journal* 19(5): 21–23, 34.

Rawick, George. 1972. *From Sundown to Sunup: The Making of the Black Community*. Westport, CT: Greenwood Press.

Rehm, Maggie Amelia. 2011. *The Art of Citizenship: Suffrage Literature as Social Pedagogy*. (Doctoral dissertation, University of Pittsburgh).

Reinecke, Carl. 1884. *Glückskind und Pechvogel*, Op. 177, trans. William Grist, London: Augener.

Reyland, Nicholas W. 2014. Narrative, pp. 203–223 in Stephen Downes (ed.), *Aesthetics of Music: Musicological Perspectives*. New York: Routledge.

Rodden, John. 1999. *Lionel Trilling and the Critics: Opposing Selves*. Lincoln: University of Nebraska Press.

Rodgers, Daniel T. 1998. *Atlantic Crossings: Social Politics in a Progressive Age*. Cambridge: Harvard University Press.

Roediger, David R. 2005. *Working Toward Whiteness: How America's Immigrants Became White*. New York: Basic Books.

Roediger, David R. 1988. Foreword in O'Connor, Jessie Lloyd and O'Connor, Harvey, *Harvey and Jessie. A Couple of Radicals*. Philadelphia: Temple University Press.

Roscigno, Vincent J. and William F. Danaher 2004. *The Voice of Southern Labor: Radio, Music, and Textile Strikes, 1929–1934*. Minneapolis: University of Minnesota Press.

Rosen, George. 1980. *Decision-Making Chicago Style: The Genesis of a University of Illinois Campus*. Urbana: University of Illinois Press.

Rosenzweig, Roy. 1983. *Eight Hours For What We Will: Workers & Leisure in An Industrial City, 1870–1920*. London and New York: Cambridge University Press.

Ross, Dorothy. 1998. Gendered Social Knowledge: Domestic Discourse, Jane Addams, and the Possibilities of Social Science, pp. 235–264 in Helene Sliverberg (ed.), *Gender and American Social Science. The Formative Years*. Princeton, N.J.: Princeton University Press.

Rupp, Leila J. 1999. *A Desired Past. A Short History of Same-Sex Love in America*. Chicago: University of Chicago Press.

Sarvasy, Wendy. 2009. A Global 'Common Table,' Jane Addams's Theory of Democratic Cosmopolitanism and World Social Citizenship, pp. 183–202 in Marilyn Fischer, Carol Nackenoff, and Wendy Chmielewski (eds.), *Jane Addams and the Practice of Democracy*. Urbana: University of Illinois Press.

Saxton, Alexander. 2002. Presentation given at Hull-House Third Annual Conference (12 April). Hull-House Oral History Collection, Spec. Coll., Daley Library, UIC.

Saxton, Alexander. 2000. *The Indispensable Enemy* and Ideological Construction: Reminiscences of an Octogenarian Radical. *Amerasia Journal* 26(1): 86–102.

Scambray, Kenneth. 1976. From Etruria to Naples: Italy in the Works of Henry Blake Fuller. *Italian Americana* 3(1): 156–171.

Schafer, Axel R. 2000. *American Progressives and German Social Reform 1875–1920*. Stuttgart, Germany: Franz Steiner Verlag.

Schenck, Janet D. 1926. *Music, youth and opportunity: A survey of settlement and community music schools*. Boston, MA: National Federation of Settlements.

Schiltz, Mary Pieroni and Suzanne M. Sinke 2001. DeBey, Cornelia, pp. 214–216 in Rima Lunin Schultz and Adele Hast (eds.), *Women Building Chicago 1790–1990: A Biographical Dictionary*. Bloomington: Indiana University Press.

Schubert, Franz. 1814. *Gretchen am spinnrade*, op. 2. Leipzig: Breitkopf and Härtel.

Schultz, Rima Lunin. 2017. Public School 'Secularists' vs. Women Religious: Competing Visions for Educating Catholic Immigrants in Jane Addams's Progressive Era Chicago, 1890–1925, pp. 338–379 in Kyle Roberts and Steven Schloesser (eds.), *Crossings and Dwellings: Restored Jesuits, Women Religious, American Experience, 1814–2014*. Leiden and Boston: Brill.

Schultz, Rima Lunin. 2015. Jane Addams, Apotheosis of Social Christianity. *Church History* 84(1): 207–219.

Schultz, Rima Lunin. 2008. The Challenge of Community-Based Planning for Urban Renewal: The Case of Hull-House and the American Reform Tradition, 1930–1963. International Planning History Society, 13ᵗʰ Biennial Conference (July 10).

Schultz, Rima Lunin. 2005. Garnering Support for Hull-House from the Clergy. *Urban Experience in Chicago: Hull-House and Its Neighborhoods, 1889–1963*. http:// hullhouse.uic.edu/hull/urbanexp/main.cgi?file=new/subsub_index.ptt&chap=7.

Schultz, Rima Lunin. 2001. Introduction, pp. xix–lx and Smith, Mary Rozet, pp. 817–819 in Rima Lunin Schultz and Adele Hast (eds.), *Women Building Chicago 1790–1990: A Biographical Dictionary*. Bloomington: Indiana University Press.

Schultz, Rima Lunin. 1992. Woman's Work and Woman's Calling in the Episcopal Church: Chicago, 18801989, pp. 19–71 in Catherine Prelinger (ed.), *Episcopal Women: Gender, Spirituality, and Commitment in an American Mainline Protestant Denomination*. New York: Oxford University Press.

Schultz, Rima Lunin. 1985. *The Businessman's Role in Western Settlement: The Entrepreneurial Frontier, Chicago 1822–1872.* (Doctoral dissertation, Boston University).

Schwendener, Susan R. 2001. Gyles, Rose Marie, pp. 335–337 in Rima Lunin Schultz and Adele Hast (eds.), *Women Building Chicago 1790–1990: A Biographical Dictionary.* Bloomington: Indiana University Press.

Scruton, Roger. 2016. *The Ring of Truth: The Wisdom of Wagner's Ring of the Nibelung.* London: Allen Lane.

Scudder, Vida D. 1931. *The Franciscan Adventure.* New York: Dutton.

Seigfried, Charlene Haddock. 1999. Socializing Democracy: Jane Addams and John Dewey. *Philosophy of the Social Sciences* 29(2): 207–230.

Sewell, Jr., William H. 1990. How Classes are Made; Critical Reflections on E.P. Thompson's Theory of Working-Class Formation, pp. 50–77 in Harvey J. Kaye and Keith Mc-Clelland (eds.), *E.P. Thompson: Critical Perspectives.* Philadelphia: Temple University Press.

Sicherman, Barbara. 1984. *Alice Hamilton: A Life in Letters.* Cambridge: Harvard University Press.

Skerrett, Ellen. 2000. The Irish of Chicago's Hull-House Neighborhood, pp. 189–222 in Charles Fanning (ed.), *New Perspectives on the Irish Diaspora.* Carbondale: Southern Illinois University Press.

Sklar, Kathryn Kish. 1997. *Florence Kelley and the Nation's Work: The Rise of Women's Political Culture, 1830–1900.* New Haven: Yale University Press.

Sklar, Kathryn Kish. 1990. Who Funded Hull House? pp. 94–115 in Kathleen D. McCarthy (ed.), *Lady Bountiful Revisited: Women, Philanthropy, and Power.* New Brunswick: Rutgers University Press.

Sklar, Kathryn Kish. 1985. Hull House in the 1890s: A Community of Women Reformers. *Signs* 10(4): 658–677.

Sklar, Kathryn and Beverly Wilson Palmer (eds.). 2009. *The Selected Letters of Florence Kelley, 1869–1931.* Urbana: University of Illinois Press.

Sklar, Kathryn, Anja Schuler and Susan Strasser (eds). 1998. *Social Justice Feminists In the United States and Germany: A Dialogue in Documents, 1885–1933.* Ithaca: Cornell University Press, 1998.

Smith, Carl. 1995. *Urban Disorder and the Shape of Belief: The Great Chicago Fire, The Haymarket Bomb, and the Model Town of Pullman.* Chicago: The University of Chicago Press.

Smith, Adam. 1976. *The Theory of Moral Sentiments.* Indianapolis: Liberty Classics.

Smith, Eleanor. 1918. *The Children's Hymnal.* New York: American Book Company.

Smith, Eleanor. 1916. The Music of School Entertainments. *Music Supervisors' Journal* 2(3): 7–9.

Smith, Eleanor. 1915. *Hull House Songs.* Chicago: Clayton F. Summy.

Smith, Eleanor. 1912. The Making of a Musician. *Proceedings of the Fifteenth Meeting of the National Education Association*: 1014–1017.

Smith, Eleanor. 1909. *The Eleanor Smith Music Course: Manual*. New York: American Books.

Smith, Eleanor. 1908. *The Eleanor Smith Music Course: Book One*. New York: American Books.

Smith, Eleanor. 1892. Music for Young Girls. *Christian Union* 46(11): 454–455.

Smith, Eleanor. 1885. *Five songs, opus 7*. Cincinnati and Chicago: W.H. Willis and Company.

Sokol, David. 2013. *The Art of Leon and Sadie Garland Exhibition Catalogue*. Chicago: Koehnline Museum of Art.

Spain, Daphne. 2001. *How Women Saved the City*. Minneapolis: University of Minnesota Press.

Stansell, Christine. 1987. *City of Women: Sex and Class in New York City, 1789–1860*. Urbana: University of Illinois Press.

Stanislavski, Constantin. 1936. *Building a Character*. Trans. Elizabeth Reynolds Hapgood. New York: Routledge.

Starr, Ellen Gates. 2003. *On art, labor, and religion*. Mary Jo Deegan and Ana-Maria Wahl (eds.). New Brunswick, NJ: Transaction.

Starr, Ellen Gates. 1924. A Bypath into the Great Roadway. *Catholic World* 119: 167–200.

Starr, Ellen Gates. 1895a. Art and Labor, *Hull-House Maps and Papers: A Presentation of Nationalities and Wages in a Congested District of Chicago, Together with Comments and Essays on Problems Growing Out of the Social Conditions*. New York: Thomas V. Crowell.

Starr, Ellen Gates. 1895b. Chicago's Hull House. Report on Address by Ellen Starr, *Hull House Scrapbook III*, JAMC, Spec. Col., Daley Library, UIC.

Starr, Ellen Gates. 1895c. *College Settlement Work: Hull-House*. Byfield, Mass.: Society of the Companions of the Holy Cross.

Stebner, Eleanor J. 2010. The Theology of Jane Addams. Religion "Seeking Its Own Adjustment," pp. 201–222 in Maurice Hamington (ed.), *Feminist Interpretations of Jane Addams*. University Park, PA: The Pennsylvania State University Press.

Stebner, Eleanor J. 1997. *The Women of Hull House. A Study of Spirituality, Vocation, and Friendship*. Albany: State University of New York Press.

Stevenson, Andrew. 1907. *Chicago: Pre-eminently a Presbyterian City*. Chicago: Winona Publishing Company.

Stilson, Jan. 2006. *Art and Beauty in the Heartland: The Story of the Eagle's Nest Camp at Oregon, Illinois*. Bloomington: AuthorHouse.

Sunderland, Eliza. 1893. Hull House, Chicago: Its Work and Workers. *The Unitarian* 8(9): 400–402.

Taft, Lorado. 1900. Hull-House Retrospect. *Hull-House Bulletin*: n.p.

Tax, Meredith. 2001. *The Rising of the Women. Feminist Solidarity and Class Conflict, 1880–1917.* Urbana: University of Illinois Press.

Thomas, John L. 1983. *Alternative America: Henry George, Edward Bellamy, Henry Demarest Lloyd and the Adversary Tradition.* Cambridge: Harvard University Press.

Thompson, E.P. 1966. *The Making of the English Working Class.* New York: Vintage Books.

Tingley, Donald F. 1987. Ellen Van Volkenburg, Maurice Browne, and the Chicago Little Theatre. *Illinois State Historical Society* 80: 130–146.

Tomko, Linda J. 1999. *Dancing Class: Gender, Ethnicity, and Social Divides in American Dance, 1890–1920.* Bloomington: Indiana University Press.

Tunbridge, Laura. 2010. *The Song Cycle.* Cambridge: Cambridge University Press.

U.S. Census [Chicago] 1880: 62.

Vaillant, Derek. 2003. *Sounds of Reform: Progressivism and Music in Chicago, 1873–1935.* Chapel Hill: University of North Carolina Press.

Vitello, Paul. Sept. 1, 2012. Alexander Saxton, Historian and Novelist, Dies at 93. *The New York Times:* n.d.

Von Glahn, Denise. 2013. *Music and the Skillful Listener: American Women Compose the Natural World.* Bloomington: University of Indiana Press.

Wald, Alan M. 2011. Motley, Willard, pp. 250–273 in Steven C. Tracy (ed.), *Writers of the Black Chicago Renaissance.* Urbana: University of Illinois Press.

Walford, Edward. 1878. Lambeth: Introduction and the Transpontine Theatres, pp. 383–407 in *Old and New London*: Volume 6. *British History Online* http://www.british -history.ac.uk/old-new-london/vol6/pp383-407 (accessed 15 July 2016).

Ware, Susan. 1981. *Beyond Suffrage: Women in the New Deal.* Cambridge: Harvard University Press.

Warnke, Nina. 1996. Immigrant Popular Culture as Contested Sphere: Yiddish Music Halls, the Yiddish Press, and the Processes of Americanization, 1900–1910. *Theater Journal* 48(3): 321–335.

Washburne, Marion Foster. 1904. A Labor Museum. *The Craftsman* 6(6): 572–573.

Weiner, Lynn. 1989. Introduction, pp. xi–xx in Dena J. Epstein Polacheck (ed.), *I Came a Stranger: The Story of a Hull-House Girl.* Urbana: University of Illinois Press.

Weller, Allen Stuart. 2014. *Lorado Taft: The Chicago Years.* Urbana: University of Illinois Press.

Whitfield, Rachel. 1937. *A History of Chicago Little Theater From 1912–1917.* (M.A.Thesis, Northwestern University).

Wiggins, Ella Mae. 2014. Mill Mother's Lament, pp. 99–100 in John Cohen, Mike Seeger, and Hally Wood (eds.). *Old Time String Band Songbook.* London: Oak Publications.

Williams, Ellen. 1977. *Harriet Monroe and the Poetry Renaissance: The First Ten Years of Poetry*. Chicago: University of Illinois Press.

Williams, Joyce E. and Vicky M. MacLean 2016. *Settlement Sociology in the Progressive Years: Faith, Science, and Reform*. Chicago: Haymarket.

Wood, Elizabeth. 1995. Performing Rights: A Sonography of Women's Suffrage. *The Musical Quarterly* 79(4): 606–643.

Woods, Robert A. 1891. Mr. and Mrs. Barnett and Their Work in London. *The Christian Union* 44(3): 150.

Woolf, S.J. August 8, 1937. Miss Carr Takes a Social Ideal to Hull House. *The New York Times Magazine*: 5.

Wright, Richard. 1998 [1945]. *Black Boy (American Hunger) A Record of Childhood and Youth*. New York: Perennial Classics.

Wrightson, Herbert J. 1915. Reviews. *The Musical Monitor* 4(8): 284.

Zeidel, Robert F. 2004. *Immigrants, Progressives, and Exclusion Politics: The Dillingham Commission, 1900–1927*. De Kalb: Northern Illinois University Press.

Zipes, Jack. 1997. *Happily Ever After: Fairy Tales, Children, and the Culture Industry*. New York: Routledge.

Zipes, Jack. 1995. Breaking the Disney Spell, pp. 21–42 in Elizabeth Bell, Lynda Haas, and Laura Sells (eds.), *From Mouse to Mermaid: The Politics of Film, Gender, and Culture*. Bloomington: Indiana University Press.

Index

www.ingramcontent.com/pod-product-compliance
Lightning Source LLC
Chambersburg PA
CBHW070902030426
42336CB00014BA/2291